Music,
Modernity,
*and the*
Global Imagination

# Music,
# Modernity,
# *and the*
# Global Imagination

*South Africa and the West*

VEIT ERLMANN

New York      Oxford

Oxford University Press

1999

Oxford University Press

Oxford   New York   Athens   Auckland   Bangkok   Bogotá   Buenos Aires   Calcutta
Cape Town   Chennai   Dar es Salaam   Delhi   Florence   Hong Kong   Istanbul
Karachi   Kuala Lumpur   Madrid   Melbourne   Mexico City   Mumbai
Nairobi   Paris   São Paulo   Singapore   Taipei   Tokyo   Toronto   Warsaw

and associated companies in
Berlin   Ibadan

Permission to reprint excerpts from the following is gratefully acknowledged:
*The Song of Zulu*, text copyright © 1993 by Tug Yourgrau, song lyrics copyright © by Tug Yourgrau
and Ladysmith Black Mambazo, photographs copyright © by Jack Mitchell.
Published by Arcade Publishing, New York, New York.

Library of Congress Cataloging-in-Publication Data
Erlmann, Veit.
Music, modernity, and the global imagination :
South Africa and the West / Veit Erlmann.
p.   cm.
Includes index.
ISBN 0-19-512367-0
1. Music—South Africa—Western influences.   2. Music—African influences.
3. Intercultural communication.   4. Ethnicity.   5. South African Choir.   6. Zulu Choir.
7. Ladysmith Black Mambazo (Musical group)   I. Title.
ML3760 .E75   1999
780'.968—ddc21        98-7806

1 3 5 7 9 8 6 4 2

Printed in the United States of America
on acid-free paper

# Acknowledgments

Parts of this book were previously presented at conferences and seminars at the University of Chicago, York University, the Graduate Center of the City University of New York (CUNY), the Advanced Studies Institute of the University of Michigan, Washington University, the University of Cologne, and the Centre National de Recherche Scientifique in Paris. I would like to thank Carolyne Johnson, Beverley Diamond, Stephen Blum, David Cohen, Nicholas Dirks, Dick Fox, Heike Behrend, and Bernard Lortat-Jacob for hosting these events.

In addition to these occasions, I benefited enormously from the interaction with my colleagues at the University of Texas at Austin, most notably Gérard Béhague, Stuart Goosman, and Steve Slawek. Drafts of various chapters have also been read by Peter Wicke and Stuart Goosman. Thomas Turino read the entire manuscript and provided invaluable comments and criticism. Tom Gruning prepared the index, and Ian Eagleson read the page proofs.

Thank you all.

# Contents

Introduction    3

*Part I  "Heartless Swindle":*
   *The African Choir and the Zulu Choir in England and America*    11

1. Archaic Images, Utopian Dreams:
   Forms of Nineteenth-Century Historical Consciousness    15

2. "Style Is Just the Man Himself":
   (Auto)Biography, Self-Identity, and Fictions of Global Order    32

3. Inventing the Metropolis:
   Josiah Semouse's Travel Diary and the Dilemmas of Representation    59

4. "Spectatorial Lust":
   Spectacle and the Crisis of Imperial Knowledge    86

5. Symbols of Inclusion and Exclusion:
   Nationalism, Colonial Consciousness, and the "Great Hymn"    111

6. Variations upon a Theme:
   The Zulu Choir in London, 1892–93    133

7. "God's Own Country":
   Black America, South Africa, and the Spirituals    144

8. Interlude    165

Part II "Days of Miracle and Wonder":
   Graceland and the Continuities of the Postcolonial World    167

9. Figuring Culture:
   The Crisis of Modernity and Twentieth-Century
   Historical Consciousness    173

10. Hero on the Pop Chart:
    Paul Simon and the Aesthetics of World Music    179

11. Fantasies of Home:
    The Antinomies of Modernity and the Music of
    Ladysmith Black Mambazo    199

12. Dream Journeys:
    Techniques of the Self and the Biographical Imagination of
    Bhekizizwe J. Shabalala    214

13. Songs of Truth and Healing:
    Searching for a New South Africa    234

14. Communities of Style:
    Musical Figures of Black Diasporic Identity    246

15. Dances with Power:
    Michael Jackson, Ladysmith Black Mambazo, and
    the Ambiguities of Race    268

16. Epilogue:
    The Art of the Impossible    281

Notes    283

Index    308

Music,
Modernity,
*and the*
Global Imagination

# Introduction

It has become a truism that the world in the global age has become a smaller place and that, hence, everything that happens in one place always and in some unpredictable and disordered way conditions what happens in other places. And it has become commonplace to point to a number of wide-ranging developments in domains such as the mass media, travel, and "world music" to explain this turn toward the global, the eccentric, and the chaotic. The main argument of this book derives from this basic idea of a rampant global culture, but it also departs from it in several respects.

First, *Music, Modernity, and the Global Imagination* advances the notion that the new global reality marks a critical moment in the history of the world's cultures that engages Westerners and non-Westerners in complex, multiply mirrored ways. At the same time, although the West seeks to retain a major stake in the attempts at stabilizing this crisis, the fictions, aesthetic regimes, and epistemological orders that are involved in this project do not emerge from strictly Western premises alone. Rather, these global fictions—of modern statehood, national identity, history, subjectivity, art, music, writing, and so on—result from the fact that the making of modern subjectivities in Africa and the West was not determined by mutually opposite positions: of conqueror and conquered, of master and servant. Rather, it was determined by an articulation of interests, languages, styles, and images. It is this articulation that I call the *global imagination*.

Second, the notion of an imagination that takes as its field the world does not indicate an order of magnitude. Nor is it an attempt to intervene in the name of a notion of modernity as a monolithic, homogeneous order. The order of knowledge and regimes of *aisthesis* which came to dominate nineteenth- and twentieth-century politics and culture were not a unitary phenomenon, an "iron cage," as Max Weber famously called it. Rather, the term "global imagination" denotes the means by which people shift the contexts of their knowledge and endow phenomena with significance beyond their immediate realm of personal experience.[1] As a result of this, one of the central features of this book is that it does not concern itself with the effect imperialism and postcolonial power structures have had and continue to have on the various players involved. Nor do I believe that imperialism and its legacies in the postcolonial world can in any sense be described as uncontested and unambiguous historical moments. Rather, what my analysis seeks to uncover is the extent to which the constitutive categories of the global imagination of the past 100 years—categories that revolve around differences of race, class, and gender—derive from an epistemological symbiosis between African and Western modernities.

Finally, I deviate from more common readings of what has come to be termed global culture by arguing that the global age—a period which in my view began in the 1890s—differs from earlier periods by special kinds of fictions and that the imagery—and here especially musical forms of the global imagination—takes on a completely new role by virtue of a series of fundamental shifts in the relationship among the subject, knowledge, and the real. More specifically, the line of reasoning that I pursue in this book proceeds from the hypothesis that this global reality, like all socially constituted realms of practice and meaning taken for worlds, is an imagined totality—a totality united not so much by things such as international trade, multilateral agreements, or the institutions of modern society as by a regime of signs and texts. The study of some of these forms and narratives—some of them literary, but most of them musical, motivated by music, or about music—is the goal of this book.

To avoid a possible misunderstanding that might arise from this notion of global culture as a totality of texts, let me hasten to say that these new global narratives are not fictitious in the sense that, as some have suggested, *il n'y pas un dehors du texte*. My interest is not to demonstrate that outside the text there is only a further text and that the modern world and social life are nothing but a hermetically self-referential web of signs and simulations devoid of any meaningful connection with human action. Nor do I believe that these imaginings are, as Niklas Luhmann somewhere has defined culture, mere "islands of understanding" amid a sea of restlessly self-generating systems and subsystems. If the true shock of modernity, as Jean-François Lyotard has shrewdly remarked, is the recognition that so little about reality is real, we nevertheless do not all live in illusory worlds.[2] (Nor does, of course, attention to the fictional character of colonial and postcolonial identities render the analysis of global imbalances of power obsolete.) Rather, what has changed is the measure of the real and of what is taken for truth. Hence the aim of an ethnography of the global imagination must be to examine why and in what way people's measures of the real, truthful, and authentic change and through which discursive and expressive genres and by which technological means they create a sense of certainty about the world they live in. Or, put differently, knowledge never exists beyond the contexts in which it is used and, hence, to paraphrase Nicholas Thomas, the task of a study such as this is not to separate fact from fiction, true knowledge of the Orient from Orientalism, but to examine the kinds of truths that are produced in colonial and postcolonial contexts.[3]

To be sure, most of these changes have to do with empire and globalization. It is no coincidence that modern technologies of simulation and an aesthetics of the surface begin to make progress at precisely the moment when nineteenth-century imperialist expansion opens up a global horizon for Western inspection. Nicholas B. Dirks is certainly right in suggesting that colonialism was "good to think," in the sense that it marked a historical moment when "new encounters with the world facilitated the formation of categories of metropolis and colony in the first place."[4] But where late-nineteenth-century colonialism (and possibly even late-twentieth-century postcolonialism) differs from earlier moments even in the nineteenth century (and, by analogy, in the twentieth century before World War II) is in the specific media and technologies of representation and simulation used to mediate these encounters with the world. In other words, unlike earlier forms of colonial power, the late-nineteenth-century order of empire and the late-twentieth-century postcolonial order are at heart societies of the spectacle. But the narratives arising from these new technologies— and here I am thinking primarily of key forms and genres of late-nineteenth-century popular culture such as colonial shows, adventure literature, and the like—are more than mere "dramatic falsification," as one of the earliest critics of imperialist expansion, John A. Hobson, called the discourse and ideology of imperialism.[5] The "spectatorial lust" of the imperialist mind does not so much mask colonial conquest and the triumphant capitalist world market as it makes evident how empire and unreality constitute each other in ways rooted in the deepest layers of modern consciousness.

In this sense, speaking of the unreal in fictions of global order, of their absoluteness, totality, and even peremptoriness, suggests that something else, something more fundamental, is at issue here, too. The opening of the world as a site for the modeling of bourgeois identities and its simultaneous self-enclosure in panoramic superficies go hand in hand. From the beginning of the nineteenth century, the emerging modern world system and the systematic conquest of the universe by the bourgeois gaze have been continually rehearsed and glorified in forms of what Walter Benjamin called "hundred per cent image-space"[6]: the panorama first, then film, and finally cyberspace.

But although the panorama—like the film much later—prided itself on an unprecedented degree of realism, ironically, what characterized the panorama and diorama of the nineteenth century was not so much the realism of the individual scenes depicted as the smoothly revolving canvas, the "sliding closure," the transition without catastrophe from image to image, as Dolf Sternberger called it.[7] The panorama thus simulated, for the first time in history, a total space. It was the first mass medium to set up a perfect enclosure, a proto-cyberspace that enabled the viewer to become an inhabitant of image-spaces, someone who enters an image rather than someone who contemplates it from outside. The phantasmagoric panorama, then, does not primarily reflect a reality located in a space beyond the canvas. Rather, the act of viewing itself *is* the reality, the three-dimensional experience of vision within the circular structure. Panoramic apperception, as Paul Virilio calls the experience of total image-space, breaks up the framed specter. The panoptical viewer turns around his own ocular axis and cannot see that all he sees is what he sees. As the earliest form of mass media the panorama thus prepares the ground for a monadic consciousness that mirrors the world in the bourgeois interior and keeps it there as true and real. In short, modern worlds, be they local, regional, or global, are always image worlds taken for real.

*Music, Modernity, and the Global Imagination* is not a book about "world music." A number of theoretically sophisticated and ethnographically rich studies on the world's musics at the end of the twentieth century have appeared in recent years, books that concern themselves, in the broadest sense, with the politics and aesthetics of musical production in global mass culture.[8] Many of these works devote a great deal of attention to such issues as the operations of multinational media, the role of music in national politics and antihegemonic movements, and so on—topics, of course, that no serious analysis of the new global musics can ignore and that remain crucial in coming to terms with a forbiddingly complex picture. Yet my reason for emphasizing the role of music in the global imagination of Europeans, African-Americans, and Africans is a slightly different one. If, following Anthony Giddens,[9] the "lifting out" of social relations and individual experience from local worlds and their recombination across a variety of time-spaces is one of the distinguishing features of modernity, music is not only affected by these processes but is also itself one of the most prominent means of bracketing new time–space relationships. Unlike any other aspect of mass culture, music organizes social interaction in ways that are no longer determined by the primacy of locally situated practice and collectively maintained memory. This new role of music in global culture concerns the fact that music no longer signifies something outside of itself, a reality, the truth. Instead, music becomes a medium that mediates, as it were, mediation. In other words, music in global culture, by dint of a number of significant shifts in the production, circulation, and consumption of musical sounds, functions as an interactive social context, a conduit for other forms of interaction, other socially mediated forms of appropriation of the world.

Much of this mediation, to be sure, still occurs by way of some type of meaningful narrative, via some intact idiom still available. Regardless of their semantic content, however, I would argue that the most prominent of such narratives of the modern age—the mythologies, tonalities, and rhythms of nation, race, and ethnicity—are, in fact, tales of forgetfulness, memories of a time that never was. And so with the beginning of empire various forms of global music—but most notably, perhaps, the world music of the 1980s and 1990s—became the expressions and principal conduits of an aesthetics of amnesia, an a-semantic syn-chronicity.

One final cautionary note: This is not a book about history. A gap of something like 100 years separates the chapters in part I and part II—years in which the world became a very different place and a century in which some of the texts and narratives examined in this book changed enormously. This emphasis on the *longue durée,* in spite of all the differences highlighted, seeks to draw attention to two crucial aspects of modern global culture. In the first instance, my view of late-nineteenth-century and twentieth-century Euro-African cultural ecumenes as a relatively contiguous stretch of world history attempts to come to terms with the perturbingly tenacious longevity of a global cultural order that rests, quite deceptively, on the central position of the West. In other words, this book is not about the world as it may have developed between 1890 and 1994—a world that clearly is no longer Eurocentric in any sense—but about the amazing durability of a number of fantasies about the order of things in two periods of world history in which the very idea of universal history was being called into question. In this sense, then, historical ethnographies of colonialism can never be just histories of the past; they are always, to borrow a phrase from Michel Foucault's *Discipline and Punish: The Birth of the Prison,* histories of the present.[10]

The second reason for taking what might be called a more systemic approach to world cultural and historical dynamics also comes out of a certain sense of frustration with the current debates on postmodernity and postcolonialism. Although I do engage with postmodernist claims that for every truth that is supposedly global—including the one that the world has become more unified and similar—there are other truths elsewhere that contest such claims, I am not concerned with the legitimacy of either position. Although there are substantial reasons for us today to desist from vast system building—reasons so well known that I need not reiterate them here—and to acknowledge the multiplicity of powers and histories that undermine Western claims to some supreme organon of universal knowledge, my interest is in the social and cultural dynamics of such arguments. I want to show how such critical differences conceal and enhance each other through a series of long and sustained entanglements, and I ask what such processes tell us about the moment we live in and where we might go from here. I would like to investigate what alternative fictions of global order may be usefully created—fictions that recognize the irrevocable internationalization of the world and the overwhelming presence of technologies of simulation, but that also complicate simplistic notions of social identity by probing some of the more diasporic, hybrid, and heteroglossic forms of the global imagination.

As these remarks suggest, this book also rehearses a different approach to ethnography. In large part, although not always in explicit ways, it is an interrogation of what one might call anthropological reason and its tense relationship with modernity. It aims at an ethnography of a different kind—a historical ethnography or, perhaps better still, a topography of global culture. Instead of portraying *a* culture as being in *a* place, I seek to offer a picture of cultures in a constant state of movement and displacement. Instead of describing cultures in contact, as the phrase went in most of postwar anthropology, I wish to provide a sense of cultures that to a substantial degree derive their multiple and fluctuating identities from those of others. And finally, rather than concentrating on one set of symbols and one core expressive genre, my account cuts across the boundaries between numerous such sets and genres. In short, I aspire to a historical and ethnographic treatment of the global process itself; a preliminary and partial account of how and why particular actors in certain parts of the world by creating specific sets of texts and discourses participated in a more general process of global imagination.[11]

Ultimately, this position rests less on the desire to know "them" and their cultural practices than on an effort to find out how we made them and they made us. Unlike the majority of studies concerned with global culture, in this book I try to move beyond an examination of the effects of modernity and global capitalist expansion on the colonial and postcolonial world. Instead of figuring, then, the "colonial" as an external object of study, I attempt to shift the emphasis more toward the cross-cultural trafficking of a whole range of fictions—fantasies of world, place, and time—and the role of these symbolic transactions in the mutual creation of collective identities across vastly disconnected social spaces and geographical terrains, between the metropolis and the colony, among different diasporic communities. If it is undeniable, I argue, that Africans and Europeans have represented each other for centuries, if not millennia, through a variety of media and objects, imagining common spaces and narratives, it follows that no "local" identity can ever be construed from grounds circumscribed purely by a bounded, defined place. The formation of modern identities always already occurs in the crucible of intensely spatially interconnected worlds. In this sense, then, this book is just as much about the invention of Europe as it is about the African gnosis in Europe. Like other work in colonial studies it seeks to challenge, as Ann L. Stoler has written, "the bracketed domains of European history and what counts as Europe itself."[12]

Moving thus beyond Orientalism as well as Occidentalism, I am making a parallel argument for the realm of music. Just as colonialism and its "informal continuities" with the postmodern world create colonized and colonizers alike, they also provide the stage for the emergence and transformation of certain musical givens, of things such as European music, music history, primitive music, non-Western music, and so on. Thus one of the conclusions one might draw from a book such as mine is that musicology, as a mode of knowledge about an object called European music, in fact could have only emerged in relation to colonial encounters.

The choice of texts and geographical areas, in spite of the global scope of some of my theoretical claims, is hopelessly limited and thus reflects my research interests as they developed over the past few years. I confine my inquiry to England, the United States, and South Africa, three regions whose links with one another, for various reasons, have been particularly deep and engaging. This is not to suggest, of course, that other ethnographies of the making of transnational and cross-cultural macroworlds—of, say, France, francophone West Africa, and the Caribbean or of Brazil, Portugal, and the West African coast—would be less urgent and less stimulating. But the three countries I have selected here lend themselves particularly well to the sort of project that I pursue in this book, because no one who has followed the popular struggles of the past four or five decades would want to deny that the opposition to racial discrimination in England was impossible without the struggle for democracy in South Africa, just as the long march to freedom in South Africa has energized the dreams of black people in the United States. Moreover, the connections that had developed among these three countries helped to undermine unilateral, one-way relationships of imperialist domination or postcolonial hegemony. And, most important of all, these transatlantic linkages entailed experiences and specifically black constructions of modernity in which music was to become the privileged signifier for what Paul Gilroy has called an "obstinate and consistent commitment to the idea of a better future."[13]

In discussing these musical peregrinations I limit myself to a rather small set of examples, all of which form part of a powerful body of Nguni "traditional" choral music. Yet these examples, in spite of their having deep roots in the southern African past, are far from being mere mirror reflections of a timeless tradition. They represent, each in its own way, concrete means by which worlds have been actively made and are constantly being remade. In fact, it is through such musical fictions that worlds become historical worlds in the first place— fantasies of temporal order, I repeat, that become culturally salient and consistent not through some innate objective quality but through an intense entanglement with other historical worlds, equally fictional. Modernity and tradition, as I have indicated earlier, are not only the two most significant historical fictions here but also the tropes whose role in the Western discourse about itself and the others is reflected and configured in the very grammar of musical performance itself. And, as the musical examples examined in this book also show, similar notions of tradition and modernity also intervene in African discourses— musical and verbal—about the West.

As will also become clear in my account, the two musical traditions examined in part cross-index each other as a result of a series of concrete geographical and historical conjunctions. Thus, far from being mere manifestations of tightly knit local worlds, most of these interregional and intertextual correlations are mediated through complex and often truly global entanglements. Although, then, the musics originated in South Africa, the examples—and the various transformations, versions, and interpretations they engendered—are also inextricably tied up with places and events far beyond South Africa. In fact, it is in the light of these far-reaching linkages that a future South African musical history might conceivably have to be written as a chronicle of much larger spatial dimensions. But that is a story for another time and another book.

Here then, finally, is what the two parts of my book, far more modestly, strive to describe. The first genre and series of texts, which I shall examine in part I, are set during the 1890s, at the height of the "scramble for Africa." The story—the historical text, as it were—with which these texts are interwoven is of the extraordinary world tours of two groups of young South African singers, respectively called the African Choir and the Zulu Choir. The cause of great controversy and prelude to an intense and sustained entanglement of South African performers with the outside world, these tours were part and parcel of a late Victorian order of knowledge that persistently sought to incorporate the colonized on terms which, albeit frequently contested, ultimately met with their approval. The cultural and historical premise for such approval, I argue, rested not on the imposition of a Western social model and epistemology but on the coauthoring of global identities at home and on the periphery. In other words, the African faith in Western fictions of modernity and progress was worked out through Western assumptions about Africans as they were, in turn, enabled by African stagings of something taken for an African past.

At the center of the second set of fictions, explored in part II, stands one of the key texts of world music of our era: Paul Simon's Grammy Award–winning album *Graceland* of 1986. Like the other examples discussed in this book, the making of the album and a series of subsequent world tours involved a substantial number of well-known South African performers, most notably the male a cappella group Ladysmith Black Mambazo. And, even more significantly, *Graceland* helped to reactivate and widen the dialogue between black performers on both sides of the Atlantic in ways that challenge tidy conceptions of race, nation, and ethnicity while at the same time opening up new avenues for exploring diasporic modes of thinking and being. At the center of my efforts to account for these black polyphonies stands a critical reading of the collaborative efforts of Ladysmith Black Mambazo, African-American author Ntozake Shange and filmmaker Spike Lee, the Anglo-African a cappella group Mint Juleps, and, finally, Michael Jackson.

If my emphasis on this limited, but as I like to believe fairly representative, set of examples is meant to address a series of broader theoretical issues related to the study of culture in the postcolonial world, these issues cannot be understood unless we gain a better sense of the making of this late modern world of global interdependencies and its roots in the nineteenth century. It is this era—the Victorian age and the world of Universal Exhibitions, mission converts, and scientific racism—that will preoccupy us in the next seven chapters.

# PART I

## "HEARTLESS SWINDLE"

### The African Choir
### and the Zulu Choir in
### England and America

Poster for a concert of the African Choir in South Shields, November 1891 (South Shields Public Library).

In September 1891, a young black South African woman named Charlotte Manye made the following statement in a London monthly:

Let us be in Africa even as we are in England. Here we are treated as men and women. Yonder we are but as cattle. But in Africa, as in England, we are human. Can you not make your people at the Cape as kind and just as your people here? That is the first thing and the greatest. But there are still three other things that I would ask. Help us to found the schools for which we pray, where our people could learn to labour, to build, to acquire your skill with their hands. Then could we be sufficient unto ourselves. Our young men would build us houses and lay out our farms, and our tribes would develop independently of the civilisation and industries which you have given us. Thirdly, give our children free education. Fourthly, shut up the canteens, and take away the drink. These four things we ask from the English. Do not say us nay.[1]

Charlotte's statement appeared in the *Review of Reviews*, a liberal monthly launched the year before by William T. Stead, a former editor of the *Pall Mall Gazette* and a leading figure of Britain's New Journalism. Thus, her statement has to be placed within the larger context of British politics, jingoist imperialism, and the emergence of black nationalism in South Africa. Above all, however, it must be seen against the backdrop of a rather special train of events: the tours of a group of young South African singers called the African Choir to England and the United States between 1890 and 1894. The story of these tours, briefly, is this.

The idea to send a group of students on a tour to raise funds for an industrial school dated back to the world tours in the 1870s of the celebrated Fisk Jubilee Singers from Tennessee and was given new momentum in 1890 by the South African tour of another African-American group called the Virginia Jubilee Singers. Although an infinitely more commercial enterprise, the latter choir, under its redoubtable director, Orpheus McAdoo, with unprecedented ardor and clarity had set the minds of black South Africans ablaze by evoking visions of freedom and development and, more important still, by connecting these with the experiences of black people elsewhere in the world, just risen from centuries of racial oppression themselves. Roused by the experience, a small group of young people from Kimberley's Fingo location got together in the fall of 1890 and decided to try their hands at a similar venture.

In January 1891, under the direction of the two white professional performers Walter Letty and John Balmer, the African Choir set out on a tour of the Cape Colony. Here, after a hurried series of performances in the eastern Cape, the group was enlarged by Johanna Jonkers and Sannie Koopman and, during a flying visit to Lovedale College, by a number of erstwhile students including Paul Xiniwe; his wife, Eleanor; son John; and nephew Albert Jonas, as well as Frances Gqoba, John Mbongwe, George McLellan, Samuel Konongo, and Neli Mabandla.

Finally, the promoters, back in Kimberley to finalize the deal and to enlist high government patronage, persuaded Josiah Semouse and the white pianist Lilian Clark to join the group and with their 15-piece ensemble left Kimberley again on April 15, 1891, this time for one of the most extraordinary episodes in the early history of black South Africa's encounter with the wider world.

The venture failed dismally—or, at any rate, the first tour did. By 1893, after a two-year tour of the British Isles, losses of more than £1,000 had been incurred, and with most of the musicians having fallen ill or been abandoned by their white agents in London, the whole enterprise ended in a fiasco: a "sorry business," as a colonial paper wrote in denouncing Charlotte's "appeal to Englishmen against colonists"; a "heartless swindle," as Lovedale's principal, James Stewart, castigated the tour, "perpetrated at the black man's expense."[2]

If the European tour reinforced and to a certain extent even exposed the delusive character of late-nineteenth-century culture and consciousness, a second tour to North America, in 1894, was to open up alternative models for interpreting and interrogating modernity—models that reverberated with specifically black experiences both in the diaspora and in Africa. And even though the North American tour eventually suffered the same fate as its predecessor—the singers were once again abandoned by their white managers—it initiated another string of events, no less spectacular than the tour itself. Ministers of the African Methodist Episcopal (AME) Church in Cleveland, Ohio, offered hospitality to the stranded performers, and before long half a dozen of them, including Charlotte Manye, were enrolled at Wilberforce University, to embark on distinguished careers as missionaries and political leaders.

But the tours not only marked a dramatic juncture in the culture and consciousness of a handful of South Africans. They also set in motion and, in turn, were propelled by a whole series of Occidentalisms and Africanisms. In fact, the tours initiated a drama of truly global dimensions, one whose acts were set in places as far apart as London, Kimberley, and Cleveland, Ohio, and whose dramatis personae included individuals as varied as Queen Victoria, South African black leader John Tengo Jabavu, a Glasgow shipbuilder, the principal of one of the leading black South African colleges, and American bishops of the AME Church. Likewise, the scripts by which this drama was acted out consisted of texts as diverse as American minstrel tunes and Negro spirituals, Sesotho press reviews, the earliest known forms of Christian hymns sung in Xhosa, English concert reviews, and Sesotho travel accounts.

The chapters in part I trace these remarkable transatlantic episodes (as well as the parallel tours from 1892 to 1893 of a group called the Zulu Choir, which I examine in chapter 6) and discuss a broad range of issues that arise from the intertwined histories, experiences, and narratives of people on both sides of the Atlantic. But before taking a closer look at the extraordinary series of events and the remarkable set of actors and scripts that make up this panorama of the late nineteenth century, we need to sketch, in a few quick strokes, some of the cultural dynamics of this era.

# Archaic Images, Utopian Dreams

*Forms of Nineteenth-Century Historical Consciousness*

The nineteenth century was an era in which, on the face of it, everything was new: new physiognomies of people and goods, new modes of transport, new markets, and new sensations. Yet of all the new forms, objects, and practices, probably the newest was the changed spatial contours of the world themselves. Not only was the world in the nineteenth century coming to be united by a net of steel, telegraph wires, and ideologies of progress, but also, and perhaps more significant, for the first time in history growing numbers of people in societies around the world—societies that differed greatly in structure, cultural practice, and historical experience—were coming to the realization that their daily experience and the structural conditions of that experience were ever more rapidly drifting apart. It was in the nineteenth century that for the first time self and society were beginning to be interrelated in a global milieu, that both Cockney and Polynesian islander, say, found themselves in a situation in which their understanding of themselves and sense of the social world no longer coincided with the place in which it took place.[1] Never before the nineteenth century had it been the case that an average individual's experience of London or Tahiti—in fact, his or her almost entire everyday thinking and practice—was so closely bound up with and dependent on the experience of people living elsewhere in the imperial order. In fact, the changes in the everyday perception of time, place, and identity that had occurred during the nineteenth century, and particularly during the second half of the century, were so sweeping that the sociologist Roland Robertson is able to speak of the period between 1870 and the mid-1920s as a "take-off phase" of globalization in which the "globalizing tendencies" of earlier ages gave way to "a single, inexorable form."[2]

It is obvious that this perspective, with its echoes of the Weberian iron cage, is itself a function of globalization. The emergence of a singular conception of something called humankind and the rise of ideologies and scientific theories of an increasingly interconnected world are unthinkable without the growing functional complexity of supralocal communities and the expanding scope of long-distance communications. On the ground, however, this new reality was beyond the conceptual grasp of any one individual living under its sway. In the imagination of the man in the streets of London and on the Polynesian island this "global" system took a wide range of forms and symbolic meanings—forms whose main stimulus still came from a rich and largely intact body of local knowledge and practice but whose "content" could no longer be identified as the exclusive property of only one place, only one tradition. This situation is one of the principal reasons for the emergence of what I consider to be one of the main features of the late-nineteenth-century global imagination: a "play of figuration" through which an enormous and new totality, although essentially unrepresentable, expresses itself. Here I am borrowing the terms of Fredric Jameson, for whom a new "play of absence and presence" is the hallmark of the rising colonial system—a new form of sociospatial imagination that inscribes itself in the very syntax of poetic language itself.[3]

Throughout this book we shall see how indeed this play of figuration became ever more pertinent as performers and audiences in the twentieth century were grappling with the growing internationalization of the world. But as I shall also argue, during the late nineteenth century, and possibly even toward the end of the twentieth century, this play of figuration even extended to forms and practices rooted far deeper in everyday life than the artistic sensibilities of high modernism. The culture of high imperialism, I believe, rested fundamentally on a form of consciousness that had permeated even the most mundane aspects of life in the metropolis and on the periphery. But although nineteenth-century cultures and forms of consciousness *everywhere* were formed within an increasingly interconnected world, significant differences existed in the manner in which the play of absences and presences shaped the discourses, performances, and texts in the center of the empire and on its margins. Before I embark, then, on a detailed examination of how this play of figuration was enacted by the tours of the African Choir, it is necessary to consider these differences in greater detail. We will have to examine, from a somewhat comparative perspective, the broader processes at work in the making of nineteenth-century culture and consciousness.

## The Time of Hell

Let me begin my inquiry into nineteenth-century consciousness in the West. Here, especially in the heart of the old continent, the beginning of the new century was quite patently perceived, as the historian Eric Hobsbawm puts it in rather prosaic terms, as an "age of revolution."[4] It is difficult to disagree with him and to dispute the notion that in the period between 1789 and 1848 a revolution was under way in Europe and North America which not only transformed all known relations and means of production but also had a thorough-going impact on virtually every aspect of the political order, social structure, and cultural life of Western Europe and the United States. And thus, for the majority of Westerners, as the title of Charles Dickens's celebrated novel so inimitably suggests, the nineteenth century was first and foremost a time of "great expectations," a time when people of all classes were kept enthralled by utopian dreams of a Golden Age in which industry and technology, despite all social antagonisms, would almost mythically bring about a world of peace and prosperity, a Heaven on earth. The rapid upsurge of industrial production and the sciences, as the young John Stuart Mill surmised, was to usher in a whole new world, "farther advanced in the road to perfection; happier, nobler, wiser."[5]

To more skeptical minds, however, the age gave far less ground for messianic excitement. As the century drew to a close, the optimistic mood, the confidence in the boundlessness of human knowledge, and the blind faith in technological progress were beginning to dwindle. Despite all the truly momentous transformations and wondrous innovations, critics at the turn of the century found that nineteenth-century society represented but the zenith of a long process that had begun since at least the fifteenth century. Theirs was a view of the modern era that did not conceive of the nineteenth century as a radical break with previous times or as the mere beginning of an endless ascent to Olympian heights of ever-greater freedom and material abundance. In other words, modernity represented a profoundly paradoxical historical experience, one in which, as Marx famously put it, "everything seems to be pregnant with its contrary." Or, as Nietzsche registered with an even sharper sense for jarring paradox, the nineteenth century was an era in which there was a "fateful simultaneity of spring and autumn" and in which, in fact, man himself was "a kind of chaos."[6]

As to the forms and fictions by which Westerners represented to themselves the contradictory structure of nineteenth-century society, they were determined by what Ernst Bloch has called a "historical dream appearance"—a peculiar form of consciousness that resulted from the contradiction between a massively socialized mode of production and a private mode of appropriation. Acting according to bourgeois principles as it did, bourgeois society masked this fact and could not find a form for it.[7] Thus the examples of this "narcotic historicism" and "craving for masks"[8] range from Nietzsche's philosophy of the eternal return to an architecture in which the rational constructions of steel and glass are concealed behind a massive facade of stone ornaments. In short, the late-nineteenth-century European societies, utterly infatuated with the idea of progress and at the same time nostalgically looking backward, were caught up in a circular, self-referential structure of feeling.

Of all the critics of the past century, nobody understood better perhaps than Walter Benjamin the mirages of the modern and the archaic, the constant vacillation in nineteenth-century bourgeois consciousness between a concept of history as natural evolution and the mythical idea of occurrence as recurrence. In his monumental but unfinished *Passagen-Werk*—a study of nineteenth-century Paris, its arcades, gamblers, prostitutes, and flaneurs—Benjamin provides a biting critique of both notions and what must be one of the most incisive analyses of nineteenth-century Western consciousness. By deciphering the ruins of the material world of the nineteenth century—in the early shopping arcades of Paris and their commodities—Benjamin hoped to discover how the archaic and the modern mirrored each other.[9] At the same time, he worked toward a somewhat more dialectical notion of modernity that differed sharply from other, uncritical views of the past century. Thus on the one hand he rejected the notion of progress as "one of the strongest narcotics of the nineteenth century," while, on the other hand, he found the idea of eternal recurrence simply "ur-historical, mythical thinking" that had emerged at precisely the moment when the bourgeoisie no longer dared to face the impending results of the mode of production it had set in motion.[10] And it is against these twin "dream forms of the occurrence" in nineteenth-century bourgeois consciousness—the relentless drive for the most modern and the eternal return of the same—that Benjamin sets one of the most terse images of the nineteenth century, a direct counterimage to the bourgeois "thirst for the past" and reveries of a coming fairyland: "[t]he 'modern,' the time of Hell."

The image of modernity as an inferno registers, of course, the rise of fascism and the profound estrangement Western intellectuals had experienced between the two world wars. But, as Benjamin explains further, this image of modernity as the time of Hell

> does not deal with the fact that "always the same thing" happens, let alone that the question here is about eternal recurrence.
>
> Rather, the point is that the face of the earth never changes in precisely what is newest and that this "newest" in all its pieces keeps remaining the same. This is what constitutes the eternity of Hell. To determine the totality of features in which the "modern" expresses itself, is to represent Hell.[11]

Thus, for Benjamin, the nineteenth century was a deeply ambiguous period of human history—modern and archaic at the same time. Modernity is a "world of strict discontinuity" in which "the ever-new is not something old that remains, nor is it a has-been that returns. Rather, it is the one and same that is crossed by innumerable intermittences."[12] But this ambiguity, as Benjamin makes clear, was, in fact, one that stood at the very heart of the historical dynamic of nineteenth-century European societies. The deadly repetitiveness of time, the fact that, as French surrealist poet Jean Vaudal put it, "monotony is nourished by the new,"[13] was an *objective* feature of capitalist society that was most clearly revealed in forms such as machine work and gambling and, above all, in this society's commodities. In other words, the image of nineteenth-century commodity society as Hell, as an endless cycle of repetition and innovation, depicts what is truly novel about this society.

Powerful though the image of the nineteenth century as Hell certainly was, its author was himself a product of the nineteenth century: torn, like most nineteenth-century intellectuals, between a thrilled enthusiasm and an unyielding aversion toward modern life. Although it was Benjamin's intention to unravel in the archaic elements of modernity the destructive ever-sameness of evil, he also romantically sought to find in them a primordial potential to be directed against the destructive effects of modernity. Yet this original moment to him was not merely a question of retrogressive ideologies. It was contained in the new technologies of the machine age and, above all, in the commodities that were produced by them. Inscribed into the mass-produced commodities, Benjamin held, are wish-images, archaic images that imbue the new means of production with the potential to bring about the transition to a socialist society. Yet prevented by the private ownership of these technological means from fully developing their hidden potential, the commodities of necessity take a phantasmagoric form, masking themselves as archaic symbols that express the persistent human desire for Utopia. But these masks, Benjamin contends, even as they conceal the new and represent it only in dream form, are necessary and temporary preconditions for a collective reawakening. Commodities, therefore, through the wish-images contained in them were what Benjamin called dialectical images: the source of the old-in-the-new, the substance of Western society as Hell and, at one and the same time, the means for the redemption of mass culture.

Benjamin's almost romantic, if not plain *lebens*-philosophical stance, so fashionable at the present time, could but provoke the criticism of Theodor W. Adorno, perhaps his earliest and sharpest critic. For Adorno as well as Benjamin, the unity in the disunity of modernity resided in the commodity form and only the historical analysis of the industrial commodity form as one sharply distinguished from earlier forms would deliver the "primal history" and "ontology" of the nineteenth century. However, Adorno took a radically different position from Benjamin with regard to the redemption of mass society, insisting that there could be no recourse to some archaic moment that might put in the wrong modernity, of which it was, after all, according to Benjamin, a dialectical part. The archaic, to Adorno, was in its entirety historically produced. Thus, far from being prehistorical, the archaic was the locus of what history had locked into silence. There could be no primordial, authentic moment of truth hidden by modernity that was not itself owed to the regressive elements of modernity. What appeared as archaic and spontaneous was, in fact, pure masquerade and hence cast a false spell. In short, the "category under which the archaic was bound up with modernity was not so much the Golden Age but catastrophe."[14]

Ultimately, of course, Adorno's critique of what he took to be a dangerous nostalgia in Benjamin's thought for nature aimed at a notion of the commodity form far more dialectical than Benjamin's. To understand the commodity as a dialectical image, Adorno wrote, meant to grasp the commodity "also as the motif of its own ruin and 'negation' [*Aufhebung*] instead only of the mere regression to the older." It is because of this position that Adorno resisted both a simplistic vilification of exchange value, on the one hand, and a glorification of use value, on the other. The commodity was in itself not only an element of alienation through which use value is gradually lost but also, at the same time, something that had survived the immediate by virtue of its having become alien. Because, as Adorno argued, this constituted the moment of truth in the commodity form, commodity fetishism cannot be criticized by merely dissolving it in the act of consumption and the appropriation of use value.[15]

If Benjamin's thought was as much indebted to romantic mysticism as it was to Marxist political economy, he was a product of the nineteenth century in another sense as well. For in many ways what the dialectic of the archaic and the modern implied was in no way different from the nineteenth-century grand narratives such as those that underlie universal history. Both fold difference back into some sort of homogeneous scheme. Both fail to recognize the fact that not only was nineteenth-century Europe far from being a unified space subsumed under one overarching political economy, but also the differences of historical experience, cultural practice, and worldview in various parts of Europe cannot be temporalized in terms of historical stages.

Despite these shortcomings, this rather long detour on Walter Benjamin's posthumous work and Theodor Adorno's critique of it was necessary because the categories and theoretical rigor both authors developed in the course of their debate have far-reaching implications—apart from the *prima philosophia* that Adorno had envisioned—not only for the analysis of the nineteenth century but also for the global imagination of Africans and Europeans in general. The dialectic of the archaic and the modern, as well as its foundation in the commodity form, is the central feature of twentieth-century global culture. In due course we shall return to the Benjamin- Adorno debate (see chapter 7), but first it is necessary to consider some of the "dream forms" and aesthetic forms generated by nineteenth-century European mass culture. To do this, I shall shift the focus to a discussion of a specific expression of nineteenth-century Western consciousness: the panorama.

## Panorama

The magic and almost claustrophobic circularity of nineteenth-century social life was not Benjamin's concern alone, but also figures prominently in the work of Dolf Sternberger, a contemporary of Benjamin. Sternberger's book *Panorama of the Nineteenth Century* is a momentous and ambitious attempt to grasp, in one sweeping gesture, an entire age by subsuming it under the idea of one of the main forms of nineteenth-century public spectacle: the diorama or panorama.[16] Unlike few other works written during or immediately after the phase of high imperialism, *Panorama* locates the very essence of the nineteenth-century bourgeois social order and consciousness in the panoramic gaze it cast on itself and the world. *Panorama* is a book about an era that, like the peculiar form of mass entertainment it had invented, arranged its own history into an imposing circular and yet illusive spectacle. The cause of considerable controversy during its appearance in 1938, *Panorama* is an exceptionally rich work in that the author, does not present us with a systematic analysis as such, with a synopsis of key events, imperial powers, or economic facts. Rather, Sternberger is interested in the physiognomy of the period, in the phenomena, thoughts, figures, gestures, and sentiments. His is a historical topography, a method that is informed by the intense queries to which he subjects even the most innocuous detail of everyday life, the seemingly peripheral object of everyday use, and the forgotten texts. It is this attention to the contingent (a method he shares with Walter Benjamin) that is said to preserve the element of chance which characterizes history itself.

Examples of this physiognomy of the nineteenth century are to be found in a stupendously broad range of artifacts, practices, texts, and ideologies. For instance, from a startling reading of *Uncle Tom's Cabin* Sternberger proceeds to a description of the embittered debates around vivisection that preoccupied the European public during much of the mid–nineteenth century. In yet other parts of the book he looks at manifestations of nineteenth-century society and culture as varied as colonial expansion, Oriental painting, travel, and the bourgeois interior, all the while constantly returning to the profound changes that occurred during this period in the uses and perceptions of light and color, time and space. What Sternberger thus makes available to critical scrutiny is not simply an inventory of abstract worldviews or the "spirit" of an age. Rather, he takes us on an intellectual journey through a series of what he calls "historical spaces": places that themselves have been the object of observation and reflection from the time of their coming into being.

One such historical topos is the genre. More than just a literary form and the arrested moment depicted in the panopticon, the genre is the predominant structure of perception and, indeed, of human relationships and life in the nineteenth century in general. As such, the genre has little in common with the allegories of former times, such as, for instance, the Baroque allegories of beauty, good, and evil. Unlike these, the figures and scenes in the nineteenth-century genre, arrested in midmotion as they appear, entreat the beholder so he may complete them for himself. And thus the *tableaux vivants* into which everything human had disintegrated in the late nineteenth century are not allegories but human actors playing allegories. Hence, Sternberger writes, no experience, no notion of good, evil, innocence, or brutality, was possible that was not in one form or another affixed to an arranged scene. And as in art, it was up to the onlooker to rebuild, through his emotions, the ruins of the human order.[17]

Another object of Sternberger's historical topography is Social Darwinism. In by far the most substantial chapter of his book, Sternberger puts forth a devastating critique of Darwin's theory, arguing that in it history, conceived of as a "panorama of evolution," is depicted as a "natural progression." In the same manner as the spectator's gaze scans the pictures on the revolving canvas "un-hindered, up and down, back and forth, across the pictures as they themselves 'evolve,'"[18] so the ideology of "evolution" and "progress" arranges everything into a strict sequential regime. Nothing remains that might be alien to this tightly ordered whole and its autonomous succession and sliding closure. The ultimate means of bringing organic nature into the "panorama of evolution"— the canvas, as it were, on which the drama of life unfolds—is, of course, time, with the gradual passage of the enormous unmeasured phases of evolution as such. It is this time that allays all differences, conveys all limits, and fills all gaps with countless transitions.[19]

The effects of Social Darwinism—especially on the practices and ideologies of those very settlers in South Africa who, as we have seen, regarded black peo-ple like the choristers as "cattle"—are of course well known and need not be re-counted here. Nor do I have to remind the reader of what Sternberger calls the "back view" of Darwin's theory: the paradox, namely, that "civilization" and "improvement" keep busying themselves with extinction and extermination, as if indeed civilization were not itself. As the "civilised races have gained the upper hand," Sternberger concludes, "they are really for this reason more savage than the savages."[20]

In the final analysis, however, the real panorama of the nineteenth century consists in the notion of the very act of seeing as one of idealization. The eye, Sternberger observes, in much of nineteenth-century thinking becomes the passive organ of an imagination that aspires to the "Higher" and that "beauti-fies" everything that comes within its reach. At once instrument, electrician, and costume designer, the eye remains a static apparatus that completes the fragmentary and the merely real as something higher, ideal, and whole. Yet the ideal itself, far from being named, reveals itself only in the act of idealization, of "upliftment," and of dressing up the model.[21]

The idealizing collective imagination of the nineteenth century not only produced hypocritical forms of social life and a hollow aesthetics but also found a correlate in the peculiar inwardness that characterized the prevailing ideas of the time about subjectivity and domesticity and their relationship with society and the world at large. A sense of this may be gained from a somewhat cryptic note in Walter Benjamin's *Passagen-Werk*, in which the author discusses the re-lationship between universalism and the panorama. The universalism of the nineteenth century, Benjamin writes, has its monument in the panopticon: "[N]ot only that one sees everything; one sees it in every way.[22] What Benjamin alludes to here is, in the first instance, the fact that in the early panoramas the central platform enabled the viewer to glance at the surrounding scene from any possible angle. Furthermore, in the composite image that results from the panoramic inspection the "inhabitant of the city attempts to bring the country into the city," while, conversely, "the city expands to a landscape."[23] The world and the home thus blend perfectly into each other. Even so, despite all these en-larged vistas and intermeshed perspectives on an immeasurably widened but closed and finite horizon, the position of the spectator remains pivotal. It was the spectator's consciousness and sensitivity that made sense of the spectacle around him or her and thereby ensured that panoramic inspection remained the principal form in which the subject asserted its authority.

Ultimately, of course, this authority is tied up with a sense of place that is squarely planted in the bourgeois domestic sphere. In one of the vignettes in his collection of childhood memories of Berlin, Benjamin provides a fascinating illustration for this relationship between the panoptic gaze and nineteenth-century domestic sensibilities. In a short text titled "Kaiserpanorama" he describes the "imperial panorama" in Berlin. Opened in 1883, this panorama offered a dazzling range of scenes and vistas which, oddly enough, to the young Benjamin did not always seem strange. For the desire which these revolving images of distant places evoked in him was not always one drawing him into the unknown. Rather, this longing was at times like the yearning for the home. Perhaps as a result of the soft gas light inside the panorama, the light that fell on Norwegian fjords and coconut trees to Benjamin seemed the same as the light that lit his desk at home.[24]

I have dwelt rather extensively on Sternberger's book (and, in passing, on Benjamin's notes on the panorama) in order to prepare the ground for two crucial points of the argument I make in this chapter and, indeed, throughout this book. The first point is that one of the main forms of the panoramic consciousness and one of the main images in which the nineteenth-century bourgeois collective dreamed itself was that of empire. I want to propose the notion that of all the manifestations of this cavernous, circular structure of feeling, especially during the second half of the century, imperialist power was by far the most pervasive. Where imperialist doctrine, Social Darwinism, and Eurocentrism claimed to have excised mythical consciousness from Europe's midst and banished it to foreign lands, myth in fact resided in the very material structure and psychosocial constitution of the European colonial powers.

But this hypothesis, although it may seem self-evident, is far from being commonly accepted. For until recently only scant attention has been given to the fact that the making of modern European self-consciousness was directly tied to the imagination of a world beyond the borders of Europe—a process so all-encompassing that by the end of the nineteenth-century empire had become an all-consuming concern. True, the nineteenth century, in more than one study, has been justly, if rather broadly, called the age of empire and the structural coordinates of this process are by now sufficiently known. Sharp class divisions within the metropolitan societies, for example, not only formed the social fluidum necessary for the rise of industrial capitalism but also provided the backdrop to the ascent to global dominance of, say, Britain—a framework so inevitable in its presence and consequences for daily life that it is difficult not to accept Victor G. Kiernan's assertion that the ultimate causes of modern imperialism are "to be found less in tangible material wants than in the uneasy tensions of societies distorted by class division, with their reflection in distorted ideas in men's minds."[25]

What appears to be less clear is precisely what these distorted ideas were, how they came to be produced, and how they came to be so widely accepted throughout European society. In other words, analyses of the colonial encounter have as yet to shed light on the practices, social position, and everyday consciousness of colonial agents within metropolitan society. The overwhelming bulk of the literature that deals with the past century—from the major works of European historiography to much of recent literary criticism—by and large has ignored the reality of empire. In fact, the oversight has been such that, as Edward Said has recently suggested, critical scrutiny of nineteenth-century European society, economy, and culture by ignoring or otherwise discounting the overlapping experiences of Westerners and Orientals puts itself in danger of missing what is essential about the world in the past century.[26]

In contrast, Said's own interrogation of the culture of imperialism is concerned with the way in which "processes of imperialism occurred beyond the level of economic laws and political decisions"—"by predisposition, by the authority of recognizable cultural formations, by continuing consolidation within education, literature, and the visual and musical arts."[27] The striking thing about the complete centrality of the West to him is thus not its economic and military power and the sheer force deployed to subdue virtually all of Africa, Asia, and Oceania. What is so extraordinary about empire is "how totalizing is its form, how all-enveloping its attitudes and gestures, how much it shuts out even as it includes, compresses, and consolidates."[28] In short, imperialism has "monopolized the entire system of representation."[29]

One of the consequences of this monopolization of representation is an aesthetics, an epistemology, of empire that produces a mentally unassailable "circularity," a "perfect closure"—a panorama—in nearly all manifestations of social and cultural life.[30] Conrad's *Heart of Darkness* is the key text of this epistemology of empire. The colonial setting and Conrad's overt sympathies for the colonial adventure set aside, it was texts such as *Heart of Darkness* that played a crucial role in consolidating colonial consciousness by simple virtue of their structure. In telling the story of his African journey in search of Kurtz, Marlow repeats and confirms Kurtz's action. By narrating its strangeness, Marlow restores Africa to European hegemony and places it under the overarching temporality of narratable history.[31] Moreover, even where colonialism as such is not explicitly referred to, its structure of feeling remains a central feature of much of nineteenth-century European art and literature. Thus, as Said points out, writers such as Conrad and Flaubert created characters who, like "guardians of a magic totality," withdraw into a strange kind of solitary imperiousness and whose "capacity for isolating and surrounding themselves in structures they create takes the same form as the colonizer at the center of an empire he rules."[32]

Said is, of course, far too astute a critic to think of this relationship between culture and imperialism only in terms of crude analogies. It is "too simple and reductive to argue that everything in European or American culture . . . prepares for or consolidates the grand idea of empire." But, he goes on to state, it is also "historically inaccurate to ignore those tendencies . . . that enabled, encouraged, and otherwise assured the West's readiness to assume and enjoy the experience of empire." European culture often, if not always, characterized itself in such a way as to validate its own preferences—such as ideas of home, nation, language, proper order, and moral values—while at the same time advocating those preferences in conjunction with imperial rule.[33]

Said's intervention is an important reminder of just how much empire by the end of the past century had become part of Europe's entire habitus, how, in fact, as Hobsbawm puts it, "colonialism was merely one aspect of a more general change in world affairs."[34] Yet at the same time I would argue that colonial consciousness was based on feelings running far deeper than those instilled by bourgeois high culture. In the colonial structure of feeling we are dealing with more than just analogies between political hegemony and aesthetic form. As Sternberger's discussion of the panoptic gaze of the nineteenth century illustrates, another, a deeper, significance comes into play here. The panorama is more than a metaphor for a world whose last remaining frontier by the turn of the century had become outer space. In the panorama of nineteenth-century society it is consciousness itself that is being reconfigured. Under the conditions of high imperialism, it is no longer possible to break up the delusionary tableau of people, objects, and vistas that eliminates the sharp and contradictory distinctions of reality. Quite to the contrary: the panoptic gaze gives itself up completely to the pleasant sensation of being its own mellow sphere, its own cavern into which enter few of the bright distinctions of the exterior world and where they melt into a subdued, radiant glow.

It is in light of this, Sternberger argues, that the cultural significance of a scientific theory such as Hermann von Helmholtz's *Sinnesphysiologie* has to be seen. The relevance of Helmholtz's theory for nineteenth-century consciousness did not consist only of his assertion that the harmonization of dispersed fragments through illumination was a physical necessity. The question that preoccupied the collective imagination of the era was this: If, according to Helmholtz's theory, it was in the nature of human perception to adjust the sharp contrasts of light, how could art—in fact, culture in general—possibly escape from such a law of nature? The answer, according to Helmholtz and many of his contemporaries, was that art had to create and even better the pleasant and positive feelings that were innate in human perception as such. And thus there resulted from this ideology a certain sedate middleness, a sepia-colored indulgence that permeated every aspect of nineteenth-century life and that offered ready glorification—mostly of itself and of the collective it held enthralled.[35]

I hardly need to belabor the point. It is clear that the emergence of capitalist society and, within it, the rise to global hegemony of the leading European powers and the United States were based on a mode of apprehending the world of which Eurocentrism and the imperialist imagination were but a facet. It may well be, as Said suggests, that "at the heart of European culture during the many decades of imperial expansion lay an undeterred and unrelenting Eurocentrism."[36] And clearly, as Said insists, the moving to the historical center of the bourgeois subject and the Eurocentrism that had gone with it from early on in the modern era did not occur solely at the level of economic and political processes. Infinitely more deep-rooted than these century-old mechanisms of commodification, subjugation, and exoticism were a whole range of changes in everyday practice and consciousness that bore only an indirect relationship to imperial expansion and Eurocentrism. And it is precisely here, at the almost subliminal level of nineteenth-century bourgeois society, in the figures and orders Sternberger charts so compellingly, that these transformations of the Western mind are to be traced. Thus the fact that, as Benjamin put it, "one sees it in every way" was not a consequence of but one of the fundamental preconditions for imperial domination.

These, then, are the outlines of the cultural and historical topography of the age during which our story took place. But my examination of the nineteenth century would be incomplete without paying equal attention to the intertwined manifestations of panoramic consciousness among the colonized. And so I now shift the focus from Europe and Britain to South Africa, the place from which, as we have seen, originated the other set of actors in our global drama.

### Mythical Time: Narrating Colonial Conquest in South Africa

In South Africa, as in Europe, a series of dramatic events had restructured the social fabric and consciousness of a great number of polities. Over the course of two centuries, the area up to the Orange River had been consolidated into a fairly unified colonial society that was slowly widening its boundaries and drawing ever-larger numbers of Africans into its realm of jurisdiction and productive relations. Whereas prior to 1870 the majority of Africans had lived in independent chiefdoms and retained control over their land and labor power, by the 1890s few were able to fully escape from the growing impact of industrial capital, merchant activities, settler rapacity, and missionary indoctrination. In fact, as Shula Marks sums it up rather laconically,

> by the end of the nineteenth century the "peculiarity" of South Africa consisted in the dominance of a highly advanced form of monopoly capital on the gold and diamond fields, with the most sophisticated capital structure and technology, based on a mass of unskilled migrant labour, still dependent on pre-capitalist social formations for its reproduction and controlled by a series of coercive devices such as the compound and pass laws.[37]

The sweeping picture Marks so deftly sketches here is one of a modern society in the making in which any peculiarities of African culture and consciousness appear to be completely submerged under or, better still, functional to an overarching system of capitalist relations of production and power. While there is much in this picture that outlines rather succinctly the convulsive and abrupt nature of South Africa's entry into the world economy, what it captures perhaps less cogently are the cultural implications of this process for those who lived under its sway. For clearly, the rise of a modern industrial society at the end of the nineteenth century for the overwhelming majority of South Africans was not a matter of a whole new world of goods, ideologies, and practices descending upon them. Likewise, as John and Jean Comaroff have stated, the "colonizing process itself is rarely a simple dialectic of domination and resistance."[38] Finally, colonial conquest did not just affect the bodies of colonial subjects. At the heart of the colonial relationship, as Terence Ranger asserted as early as 1975, stood the "manipulation and control of symbols."[39] And, as much recent scholarship has shown, it is primarily through these symbols and a wide range of strategies of adaptation, resistance, and eager appropriation that the subjects of the imperial order became implicated in its making. Furthermore, if Western supremacy was rooted in a vastly restructured epistemology, Britain's hegemony over the very imaginations of the dominated was due primarily to the fact that Britain had saturated, as Bernard M. Magubane has written, South African colonial society with its values "to the extent that they would become common sense for the people under its sway."[40]

Regrettably, current historical scholarship does not permit us to ascertain how deeply Western hegemony affected nineteenth-century African culture and consciousness. To be sure, a fair number of studies are available that chart African engagements with modernity in domains as diverse as royal praises, the role of ethnicity among early labor migrants, and performance.[41] The picture that emerges from these works is primarily one of a clash between two worlds — one Western, industrial, and modern, the other one African, rural, and traditional. The social practices and cultural forms that emerge from this encounter are often viewed as flowing almost naturally from the respective antagonistic positions taken by the colonizers and the colonized. Likewise, the role Africans played in this meeting of two worlds, is said to be overwhelmingly determined by the ideologies and practices of the rural economy and, hence, constitutes little more than the "early" stage of a process putatively leading toward a full-fledged working-class consciousness. In this manner, then, and notwithstanding numerous assurances to the contrary, essentially hybrid and composite ritual, linguistic, and political forms are posited as following given trajectories in a global scheme of modernization, urban adaptation, and capitalist development. Much less often are these forms and practices seen as being driven by the conflicts and turmoil that grew from the colonial encounter itself and that thus transcended the taken-for-granted spatial, social, and symbolic worlds of the actors on either side.

Clearly, then, as useful as much of the literature on nineteenth-century South African culture and consciousness undoubtedly is on several levels, what appears to be lacking are three things. First, we need more work that probes in imaginative ways the making of such historical worlds through the interplay between structure and agency, fragment and totality. What is required are ethnographies that, as John and Jean Comaroff have stated in their call for an anthropology of the historical imagination, capture the "simultaneous unity and diversity of social processes, the incessant convergence and divergence of prevailing forms of power and meaning."[42] Second, there is a pressing demand for a new kind of critical reading of the historical record—one that brings anthropology into a dialogue with some of the more recent critical work developed by scholars of Western mass culture. Among the first tasks to be tackled by such an *ethnographic theory of modernity* would be grasping the specific cultural logic of the colonial world by unraveling the tangle of fetishisms and twisted subject–object relationships embedded in the goods and commodities that circulated through a wide range of social worlds. In short, what we need are studies that examine how the "time of Hell" is configured in specifically colonial "dream forms," how the imagination of the colonizers and the colonized and the mirror images they have created of each other are intertwined and constructed through the circulation and consumption of imported and indigenous commodities, symbols, and narratives.[43]

While there is an increasing number of stimulating texts that explore these and other issues, within the South African context useful examples, among others, are Keletso Atkins's work on the origins of an African work ethic and concepts of labor time among Zulu workers in nineteenth-century Natal and Isabel Hofmeyr's insightful study of historical narrative in the northern Transvaal.[44] While both of these studies explore in fascinating detail some of the discursive and practical strategies Africans developed in the latter half of the nineteenth century to grapple with the radically altered sense of time introduced by colonial rule, a more immediate sense emerges from Hofmeyr's account of the twisted and mythical modernities that ensue from these entangled concepts. The focus of her discussion is one of the innumerable little episodes in the drawn-out history of nineteenth-century colonial conquest: the siege of the caves of Gwaša or Makapansgat in the northern Transvaal by Boer commandos in 1854.[45] Here, in the area of Potgietersrus, relations between the resident Ndebele polities and invading Boers were becoming increasingly strained as certain Boers attempted to reconstitute the slave society they had left behind and began to raid some of the local chiefdoms. The Ndebele rulers, for their part, retaliated to these raids by severely mutilating Boer subjects and cattle and eventually killing a party of 28 Boers. This series of events in turn provoked further Boer reprisals in the course of which several thousand followers of chief Mokopane, after having been besieged in the caves of Gwaša for two weeks, either perished or ended up as indentured laborers on Boer farms. Encounters such as this continued to trouble the area until well into the late nineteenth century, and it was not until the 1890s that the Boers could claim anything like decisive authority over the Ndebele communities in the region.[46]

Of course, the series of events that surrounded the Gwaša siege is embedded in a drama of much larger dimensions, one that saw African autonomous power coming under the steadily rising pressure over several decades of Boer military conquest in combination with land dispossession, indenture, and labor migrancy. And it is within this larger context that present-day and, somewhat more sparsely recorded, nineteenth-century attempts at narrating these events have to be seen. Most retellings of the Gwaša episode, as Hofmeyr's careful analysis reveals, are concerned not so much with establishing a chronology of facts as with resolving the tensions that pulled at the fabric of the Ndebele world. These tensions are resolved primarily, Hofmeyr argues, by constructing a "panorama of happenings" that is centered on a view of meaningful social existence based on chieftaincy. Oral performances of the Gwaša story subtly concatenate a number of variable narrative fragments into a continuous plot through which the force of chiefship flows strongly, shaping and controlling the destiny of the characters while subordinating them to its larger designs.[47]

For instance, labor migration had been a major component of the Ndebele economy since at least the 1860s and, more significant perhaps, a source of recurrent tension between the customary rulers and returning migrants eager to shield their earnings from chiefly control. Yet in direct opposition to the historical evidence, Hofmeyr has found in several of the tellings of the Gwaša incident a proclivity for depicting migrants as the vassals of the Ndebele chiefs and as the ones who extend the sinews of chieftaincy into the wider world.[48] Thus through historical fiction and the structural properties of storytelling South Africans have retrospectively closed up to a coherent panorama of nineteenth-century Ndebele life two vastly distinct levels of time and experience—ancient chiefly history and the modern process of labor migration. In the resultant cluster of images, Hofmeyr concludes, "the social tensions around migrancy are muted and then projected back into a past which is simultaneously glossed with the trappings and detail of the present."[49]

Overall, then, what all these stories around the Gwaša case illustrate are the mechanisms by which the memory of a chiefly class is encoded. And it is in this sense that these stories clearly represent what Hofmeyr calls a "historical record replete with symbolic truths."[50] Beyond this, an alternative way to read these stories might consist in viewing them as another variant of the sort of fictions of global order that are the subject of this book. By upholding the idea of chiefly power as a metaphor of the ideal social order against modernity—its contrarieties and, as Nietzsche caustically phrased it, "virgin-forest-like," "tropical tempo" of destruction and self-destruction[51]—the accounts of the siege of the Gwaša caves, though invested with local meanings, reverberate with all the unsettling rhythms of the encroaching global order. At the same time, the poetic structure of these tales, the rendition of a series of cataclysmic events as the unfolding of the ideal of chiefly power, adumbrates and glosses the incursion of the forces of modernity into Ndebele rural life as mythical occurrence and a moment in the "natural history" of indigenous power relations. In a sense, as Hofmeyr suggests, it may even be said that a taciturn symbiosis—evident in numerous borrowings across ethnic and cultural divides and a certain fervid preoccupation with leadership—links these stories to some of the mythologies Afrikaner nationalists have woven around the Gwaša happenings in an attempt to legitimize and heroize Boer rapacity.[52]

Be this as it may, in examining Ndebele historical consciousness in the northern Transvaal I do not mean to suggest that the panoramas of time that are constructed through these fictional genres belong to the same order as those prevalent in nineteenth-century Europe, much less that they are mere translations into the vernacular of a neutral modern code, "folk" restatements of an exogenous epistemology. Nor do I think that these panoramas are only about resisting an alien order. Rather, it seems plausible to suggest that these discourses and constructions, like the coexistent European expressions of the aesthetic of the genre, are attempts to recast radically altered domains of personal experience and action by shifting and adjusting the contexts for making sense of these changing worlds. That is to say, strategies such as storytelling and negotiating an African work ethic, while they may seek to turn back the estranging West, contain within them the new global reality as the template against which local phenomena are endowed with meaning. Like their European counterparts, these strategies are "dream forms of the occurrence." As such they mask the jarring strangeness of white hegemony and the Protestant work ethic behind the conventions of indigenous literary forms and temporal cycles.

My synopsis of the making of nineteenth-century European and South African social worlds, as the reader will have noticed, was itself somewhat panoramic in structure. It could hardly have been otherwise. But to place the story that concerns us here within this global matrix a change of analytic mode is now required. For as much as Europe's modern mythologies may have been embedded in the unitary logic of commodity fetishism, Europe was by no means the sort of homogeneous terrain that this notion suggests. Rather, because it was so riven with conflict—albeit not just class conflict, as Kiernan suggests—there was a need for some unitary vision. Colonialism was "good to think," because it offered one of the key structures that allowed colonizers and colonized to deal with and ultimately to deny this hybridity.

The following chapters will explore a range of such fictions of identity and examine in detail the formal means they offered. Turning to a more ethnographically grounded perspective, then, we will have to examine how the nineteenth-century panoramic consciousness expressed itself in certain symbolic forms and signifying practices. We will examine how the global imagination of Europeans, African-Americans, and black South Africans functioned as both the outcome and medium, product and process, of social agency, reflecting and organizing specific historical actors' practices and sense of a world whose social, spatial, and symbolic contours were becoming subject to dramatic displacements and vital reformulations—shifts that are reflected as much in the discourses and performances of the South African singers as in their biographies. It is to the latter that we must turn first.

## 2

# "Style Is Just the Man Himself"

## *(Auto)Biography, Self-Identity, and Fictions of Global Order*

Biographies, one might argue, are a good way of beginning a story. To know how a story began, the reader must have an idea of the principal dramatis personae. He or she will approach a story on the assumption that not only do the protagonists have something to do with the plot in which they figure, but it is also they who keep the narrative thread running, that somehow a connection exists between the main actors' lives or aspects of their lives and the story itself. In fact, as I have shown in the previous chapter, it was this sort of reasoning that characterized the sciences, arts, and historical consciousness of the nineteenth century—their obsession with progress and, as an immediate corollary of this, the fascination with identity, origins, and the primordial. But, as we shall now see, it is this kind of thinking about "improvement," the self-reflexive person, and narrative that also stands at the outset of our story.

### *Allegories of Identity: Individual and Empire in Nineteenth-Century Biography*

After a shakedown tour of the Cape and the arrival of the African Choir in England in July 1891, there appeared in the *Illustrated London News* an article of several columns titled "The African Native Choir." It contained the life stories—compiled from "notes written by themselves"—of Paul Xiniwe, Eleanor Xiniwe, Charlotte Manye, Josiah Semouse, and Johanna Jonkers, all of whom, with the exception of Johanna and Charlotte, who had been trained by Xiniwe in Port Elizabeth, were alumni of Lovedale College. With their rich local tint and together with five fine etchings of these performers, these autobiographies in

Figure 2.1. Paul Xiniwe (T. D. Mweli Skota, *The African Yearly Register*, Johannesburg, 1932).

miniature became the basis of most subsequent press coverage in Britain. The following, for instance, is the vignette of Paul Xiniwe (fig. 2.1), the senior member of the choir and, apart from Charlotte Manye, whose appeal to the British public opened chapter 1, perhaps also the most vocal of the choristers:

> I was born in November 1857, of Christian parents. I attended school from my youth, and contributed in some measure to the cost of my education by doing some domestic work for an English family before and after school-hours. This materially assisted my mother in paying the school fees and for my clothing. At fifteen years of age I left school and entered the service of the Telegraph Department as lineman, having to look after the poles and wires, and to repair breakages, by climbing the poles in monkey-like fashion.
>
> Being transferred to the Graaff Reinet Office, 130 miles from home, I had

to go there alone, without any knowledge of the road, or of any person there; but I got there in three days, travelling on horseback. The officer in charge at Graaff Reinet found my handwriting better than that of the European clerks, and, in consequence, gave me his books to keep, with additional pay, and any amount of liberty in and about the office. This was a privilege which I highly valued and turned to the best advantage by studying the code-books, taking them home to pore over them at night, and coming to the office about two hours before opening time, as I kept the keys, to learn, privately, the art of telegraphy. I surprised the master and the clerks one day by telling them that I could work the instrument, and, to dispel their serious doubts went through the feat to their great astonishment, but, happily, also, to the pleasure of my master. After three years' service I left the post of lineman, quitted Graaff Reinet, and was employed on the railway construction as telegraph clerk, timekeeper, and storekeeper: a highly respectable and responsible post for a native to hold. When I left school and home I only had a little knowledge of the "three R's"; but I was assiduous in improving my learning and seeking to qualify myself for a higher position. I had now earned a good sum of money on the railway, as well as a good name, as the testimonials I hold from there could show. Still desirous of greater improvement, I went to Lovedale, and held the office of telegraphist also in that institution, which helped me to pay my college fees. I stayed there two years, and passed the Government teachers' examination, being one of only two who passed from the institution out of twenty-two candidates presented. I then took charge of a school at Port Elizabeth, which I kept for four years, and which I gave up to carry on business at King William's Town, until the period of my joining the "African Choir."

What is one to make of a text such as this? What is it that is being narrated here? Of course, it takes little to realize that Xiniwe's narrative fuses a number of familiar elements of late-nineteenth-century colonial discourse, elements such as the founding role of Christianity and education, the benevolent intentions of the colonial state, the "progressive" function of technology, and several others that I shall examine in more detail later in this chapter. And, to wit, Xiniwe's account bore out the editors' confidence that the "simple and truthful statements, in very fair English," would "gain substantial aid for wise efforts to improve the general condition of their race." But there is also something deeper in Xiniwe's text that I would like to briefly dwell on in opening this chapter— something that speaks perhaps not so much through the text itself but through the operation that preceded it or, better still, through what appears to be the text's true symbolic dimension: writing. For, as Michel de Certeau has observed, not only did the nineteenth-century fixation with the past give history the central locus and the totalizing function it had in its role of stating sense and meaning,[1] but also, as writing—that is, as historiography—such history had a ritual and a symbolic function. On the one hand, it was a burial rite in that it "exorcises death by inserting it into discourse." On the other hand, it "allows a society to situate itself by giving itself a past through language," thus opening to the present a space of its own.[2] Ultimately, de Certeau concludes, citing Jacques Lacan, that it is this ambivalence of historiography ("it is the condition of a process and the denial of an absence") that makes historical discourse, instead of an "objective science," the favored representation of a "science of the subject."[3]

The purpose of this chapter is to introduce the members of the African Choir through an examination of a series of texts that were written by and about some choir members both during and after the tours: press interviews and biographical works as well as encyclopedia articles and autobiographical vignettes such as the one of Paul Xiniwe quoted earlier. But this prologomenous effort is equally embedded in a more general discussion of the biography and the autobiography as key formats of a "science of the subject" in an emerging global context. As quintessential nineteenth-century fictional genres for the imagination of self-identity, biography and autobiography require a special mode of interrogation that arises from the very processes of globalization I seek to elucidate in this book. They call for a type of analysis that quite literally considers the making of subjects in a global milieu as a process of authoring—a process built on the capacity, as Anthony Giddens puts it, "to keep a particular narrative going."[4] Within this analytic framework, I am going to concentrate on the close links constructed by the South African performers among biography, literacy, and the fashioning of subjective identities—links that were themselves predicated upon a variety of images and discourses pulled together from a wide range of sources but most notably from Christianity, a tradition of mid–nineteenth century political ideology known as Cape liberalism, and emergent African nationalism and Pan-Africanism.

There is another reason for beginning this book with a chapter on biography and autobiography, one that appears to be of fundamental importance for an ethnography of the global imagination. For if consciousness, however much it is part of individual agency, is equally determined by the unsaid forms, subconscious codes, and tacit conventions that have accumulated in the historical process, it follows that the effort to illuminate the emerging global imagination of colonizers and colonized at the end of the nineteenth century must be embedded less in the analysis of the overall power structures, economic strategies, and political discourses of the colonial world than in the interpretation of its rituals, routines, and representations. In other words, what is needed is a revision of the scholarly procedures and models by which the colonial encounter is commonly accounted for. The making of colonial Africa, for instance, may well have been the outcome of the rivalry among the major imperial powers or the inevitable result of the structural crisis of monopoly capitalism. And, to be sure, the partition of this vast and underpopulated continent into a series of insufficiently controlled extensions of European national economies may be profitably described (as, for instance, it was in a recent authoritative account of sub-Saharan Africa) as the transformation of predominantly agrarian societies into specialized producers for the world market.[5] While there is nothing inherently objectionable in such an approach, in this and all subsequent chapters I am joining the attempts of Frederick Cooper, Ann L. Stoler, Edward Said, and other students of colonial consciousness to cast the colonial encounter in slightly different terms. Like these scholars, I see the power of imperial conquest and colonial hegemony residing as much in the forms, discourses, and commodities it created to colonize other people's minds as in the violence with which it subjected their bodies.

Among the many facets and forms of colonial culture in need of critical scrutiny, one in particular seems to require substantial rethinking: the nature of the person and Western literary representations of the self. The notion inherited from classic liberalism of the bourgeois subject as a radically individualized human being that is placed under a transcendental goal and endowed with an innate capacity to construct itself and the world has been deconstructed in much recent critical writing as one of the chief myths of modernity. Although this is not the place for an exhaustive discussion of the discourses on the self that run through the history of modern philosophical thought, one of the more auspicious outcomes of the much-debated entropy of the *grands récits* and of postmodern criticism is a certain uneasiness with biography, arguably one of modernity's most salient literary genres and forms of mythologizing the individual.

But not only does biographical fiction count, as I have indicated, among the principal forms of nineteenth-century historicism, for a writer such as Pierre Bourdieu, biography is marked by a more fundamental fallacy. It is, quite simply, a form of "illusion," a kind of fiction that sees individuality where there are fragments and that seeks logical sequence in actions by bringing actions into sequence.[6] Michel de Certeau, for his part, sees biographies as discourses of power, playing "a role of distance and a margin proportioned to global constructions." Like most nineteenth-century Western orders of knowledge, he maintains, biographies create their objects by keeping a relationship with supposed totalities, with social systems, historical logic, and the like.[7] Beyond this, I would add, biographies resemble the genre, the panorama, and other nineteenth-century aesthetic forms in that they set up a cause–effect relationship between individual and society, seeking individual causes in historical events and social causes in individual action.

Interrogating the biography in this manner has two implications for the sort of inquiry into the production of African biographical accounts that I attempt in this chapter. First, biographical narrative (and the analysis of such narratives) centrally turns on the problems the individual encounters in seeking to come to terms with what I take to be one of the fundamental contradictions of the modern self. The construction of a modern self-identity, I believe, has essentially been viewed in much of Western modern thinking as a tug-of-war between the conflicting forces of monadic self-enclosure and an opening out onto an ever more complex and hybrid social world. And it is this conflicted field that accounts of individual lives, whether in the historical or in the anthropological mode, grapple with. As occasions for doing identity work they wrestle with the danger that Nietzsche saw of being displaced onto the individual, onto the nearest and dearest, onto the street, into one's own innermost secret recess of wish and will.[8] At the same time, as myths of modern lives, such accounts gloss over the fact that modern life is itself not of one piece, that biographical events, to quote Bourdieu once more, cannot be described other than as mere "positions and shifts in social space."[9]

Second, by the end of the nineteenth century the social space that Bourdieu talks about and that provides the context for the events we call life had irrevocably turned into a global space. Hence what makes stories such as the ones examined here so intriguing is not some intrinsic documentary value but the fact that they take place in precisely such a global space. And, ironically, it is this aspect that seems to have been largely neglected in the debate on the crisis of the modern subject—the fact, namely, that the idea of the self-reflexive individual, the hero, and the civilizing mission were all tied up with one another in an osmosis of practice and discourse. What Emile Durkheim and Max Weber, the foremost turn-of-the-century theoreticians of individualism, and subsequent neo-Marxist and poststructuralist critics of the philosophy of the Enlightenment overlooked is that individualism and universalism not only constitute each other as key tenets of nineteenth-century liberalism but are also mediated and produced by the imperial project. Not only were universal history and the panopticon—the key configurations of nineteenth-century dream consciousness—to record the accomplishments of autonomous, right-bearing individuals; they were also the framework within which modern imperialism was to be enacted.[10]

A good way to gain a sense of all this may be to take a quick look at the substantial body of biographical fiction concerned with empire. Take, for instance, the following brief passage from a text published in 1908 about James Stewart, next to David Livingstone probably Africa's most renowned missionary and, as I have mentioned earlier, principal of Lovedale College at the time of our musical tours. "Africa had cast its spell upon James Stewart," the author James Wells opens his account of Stewart in the imagery of magic and mystery typically at hand for the description of all manner of military and missionary projects. Or, as Wells goes on to assert:

> Perhaps it should be said, that he felt Africa to be the sphere of action for which he was fitted, that from Africa came the call for such powers as he was conscious of—powers of hardihood and endurance, with stern joy in committing himself to the toils and hazards needed there for humanity's sake."[11]

The tightly knit universe of Promethean power, Protestant work ethic, Christian salvation, and charity that we see present here in one man renders in a nutshell the ideological hodgepodge that shaped the Western global imagination, just as it neatly conveys the charitable tone this ideology assumed within the evangelical enterprise. But the passage quoted is interesting in another respect as well. It illustrates to what extent the making of the quintessential atom of bourgeois society—the individual—and its apotheosis in empire were quite literally matters of writing, of style. For the paragraph on James Stewart, as the reader may have surmised, is taken from a copious biography of the missionary and thus represents *in nuce* the dominant stylistic template in the West for narrating the individual. It sets the scene for a truly modern, global form of epic— an epos in which Africa becomes a mere "sphere of action"—action that is directed not at Africa itself but at the salvation of humanity. And, at the same time, the excerpt makes the "hero" of the story appear in a somewhat ambiguous light. Western individual action, held in Victorian liberalism to be the source of all wealth and civility, is mythologized as if occurring, almost passively, under a spell.

The Orientalist image of the European explorer stirred into action by Africa's "call" was of course a rhetorical device that, as we shall see in more detail in the following chapter, from early on in the nineteenth century had been consolidated in a deluge of popular travel and exploration writings. It was an established trope in Western constructions of a romantic Africa whose ideological mission consisted in masking the regnant power relations—relations in which Africa had been anything but eagerly awaiting the arrival of the European colonizer. Moreover, by the late nineteenth century the picture of benign colonization painted in the opening sections of Wells's Stewart biography had also come to betray a certain ambiguity, one that only superficially seemed to contradict the more heroic tone that usually pervades such genres. For in reality, this was an ambiguity that lay at the very heart of the crisis of modernity: the crisis of the subject. And thus the ambivalence in Stewart, despite (or, better still, together with) all the commitment and hardy perseverance, was not only one about the hazardous terrain to be opened up to Christianity and civilization but also, fundamentally, one about the narrator's own self. And it is in this sense that works such as Wells's biography of Stewart and many other autobiographical narratives could be seen indeed as "highly self-conscious texts," as the Comaroffs have observed of missionary accounts.[12] But these texts were self-conscious, I would argue, not so much because they positioned the European travelers on the moral and colonial margins, framing the journey into "darkest Africa" as an "odyssey of sacred incorporation,"[13] but because through them the nineteenth-century Western ego, acutely confronted on the colonial frontier with its own fragility, stylized itself as a unified personality, anchored in something like an ethical center and a sense of personal coherence. In fact, one is tempted to view these imperial fictions of self, as James Clifford has noted about the novels of Conrad and the anthropology of Malinowski, as strategies of "ethnographic self-fashioning." What makes these fictions essays in ethnographic comprehension, in Clifford's view, is the fact that they enact the process of self-fashioning in "relative systems of culture and language." They are ethnographic because in them "wholes of a self and of a culture seem to be mutually reinforcing allegories of identity."[14]

Clearly, then, biographies and autobiographies were more than realist, factual accounts of the lives of great men (and, more seldom, of women and other ordinary folk). They were the essential discursive media of the Western global imagination of the nineteenth and early twentieth centuries—media that depended for their affective and ideological power on the dichotomies they set up between the self and the larger world around it. By the same token, it is these dualisms that were to gain the genres validity beyond Europe's borders. And it is for the same reason that the rapid spread of these forms to the margins and interstices of empire cannot simply be ascribed to imperialist indoctrination alone. As allegories of identity these wholes of a self became the template for most African biography and autobiography, because embedded in them was a discursive structure that reached into deeper layers of African modernizing consciousness. Hinted at in these allegories were both African aspirations of incorporation and the possibility of reversing the colonial order of representation—the prospect of establishing modern African selves by using Europe as its exotic Other. And, finally, there seemed to be intrinsic to these discursive genres an anticipation of authority that answered a concern, fundamental with modernizing Africans, with writing, identity, and, above all, "opening to the present a space of its own."

All this was possible, I argue, because to be a person in black South African society in the 1890s meant to imagine oneself as being connected with places and events far beyond one's immediate grasp and experience and to have at one's disposal a greatly widened range of myths and models in which to think through these vastly extended coordinates. Conversely, these altered time–space relationships also entailed a new definition of what it meant to live a life. Beginning in the 1890s, there emerged among mission-educated black South Africans the belief that something like a meaning or an order only accrues to a person's existence to the extent that it assumes the form of a "life," that it is crafted like a work of art, arranged into some form of novel-like narrative sequence, to be written down and ultimately circulated across a wide spatial terrain by means of the printing press. In sum, for black South Africans at the end of the nineteenth century the notion of identity, literacy, the self-reflexive stylization of life, and the biography all increasingly came to constitute one another. Or, as one reader of the black newspaper *Imvo Zabantsundu* suggestively put it: "Style is just the man himself." [15]

*Metaphors of the Self: Heroic Poetry and Personal*
*Identity in Precolonial Southern Africa*

The shifts growing numbers of individuals in Europe and Africa experienced from at least the beginning of the nineteenth century entailed dislocations and discontinuities of a new kind—ruptures of established social norms and the disintegration of moral canons more radical and more disturbing than anything experienced before. Yet however sharply these discontinuities may have been felt, they were not total. Similarly, even if it is through novel techniques and genres of inscription such as the biography that modern bourgeois notions of personhood and individual identity eventually came to saturate the popular discourses of the time, this was not an uncontested process. Elsewhere, at the margins of the imperial order, people had different memories as well as varying notions of self and ways of describing them.[16] Even in Europe, there was still present for large sectors of the nineteenth-century public what Marshall Berman calls an "inner dichotomy," a sense of living simultaneously in worlds at once modern and not modern at all.[17] And thus the new spatial consciousness that was emerging in Europe and beyond did not simply efface older sensibilities but also coexisted with them in new and interesting ways, turning biography, autobiography, diaries, and other forms of autopoesis into fundamental means for framing a new sense of identity and for ordering the bewildering simultaneity of the old and the new. In essence, the question that these genres grappled with was which memory was to be kept alive, what narrative should be kept going, and which notions of temporal order were to prevail: those of earlier generations or the ones that the missionaries, merchants, and colonial administrators were promulgating in their evangelical texts and train schedules. Was the model for a new identity to be sought in the tellings and performances of the ancient past with their characteristic images, cycles, and cadences and/or in the panoramic chronological flow produced by modern time machines like the printing press and the telegraph?

Questions such as these were embedded, as John and Jean Comaroff have nicely demonstrated for the Tswana of southern Africa, in a tense and drawn-out dispute over two opposite linguistic worlds and practices of inscription. Yet although it would follow from much of the available evidence that the Christianized elite, from at least the late nineteenth century, had increasingly opted in their vernacular oratory and praise poetry for biblical imagery and English styles of preaching, not all black intellectuals had uniformly "internalized the lessons of linguistic colonialism."[18] As we shall see later, even in the most threadbare narrative produced according to missionary taste there existed numerous openings for an alternate politics of language and poetic imagination. Nor did all forms of autopoetic fiction deny Berman's inner dichotomy in quite the same way as did speech-based types of narrative. As we shall also see in part II, other types of media and other modes of performance, such as music and dance offered far more malleable symbolic spaces for constructing ambiguous self-identities.

Still, the overall dilemma that expressed itself in these conflicting attitudes toward time, narrative, and identity amounted to more than a dispute over lexicons, historical narratives, and Utopia. In essence, this was a clash between two radically different epistemologies, two fundamentally opposed ways of thinking about reality, communication, and experience.[19] To better grasp this antagonism between Western and African politics of memory and social poetics, it may be useful to briefly review here some of the performance genres used in indigenous, precolonial practice for the construction of self-identity. By examining these poetic traditions I hope to bring into sharper relief the considerable epistemological break that occurred in the 1890s and that the tours, to a significant extent, helped to bring about. In this context, it will also be necessary to consider the contrasts between African notions of speech and late-nineteenth-century European ideas about language and verbal communication as well as the role of the Christian missions in reshaping South Africa's linguistic landscape.

The quintessential traditional South African genre for the definition of personal identity, without any doubt, is praise poetry. As an extremely varied and complex body of styles, performance contexts, and meanings, such genres of eulogy as the Zulu and Xhosa *izibongo* and the Sotho *lithoko* or *lifela* are ineluctably concerned with the building of personal identity. The power and social significance of poetry composed in performance, both in chiefly and in commoners' praises, lie in the idea that through the use of metaphor a person builds up his or her name—a densely charged, compact image of a person's heroic deeds and valor. It is for this reason that Daniel P. Kunene wisely, in my view, abandoned the term "praises" in favor of the more general "heroic poetry," a term that conveys the idea of Basotho verbal arts as figuratively transforming the activities of ordinary human beings "to a level of extra-ordinariness." Heroic poetry, according to Kunene, is the medium through which men in "pursuit of honour" record their commitment to a "spirit of heroism."[20]

Kunene's concept of heroic poetry is interesting in another respect as well. For in stressing the transformative power of such verbal arts he points to an essential distinction between the bourgeois individual with his aspiration toward unity, determination, and self-control and the hero in Basotho society. Put another way, and in the terms proposed by classical Weberian and Simmelian sociology, such a notion of heroism contrasts markedly with bourgeois individualism.[21] Whereas the latter entails the concept of the individual as ultimately defining itself in distinction to society through the continuous display of extraordinary powers of self-assertion and what Weber called "hero ethics," the hero in the preindustrial societies of southern Africa is essentially a social creation. Rather than rebelling against the alienation and mundaneness of everyday social routine, the hero in these societies effectively seeks to live up to a role. Unlike Western bourgeois liberalism, and within it, the missionaries' disdain for pomp and ostentation, the hero, in African thinking, is a kind of social summation that excels in the overtly extravagant performance of a given social role.

At the same time, African notions of personhood rest on a view of body and mind as two conjoined realms of human existence. A person is not a mind that inhabits a body. Corporeality, spirituality, and intellectuality are not, as in modern Western thought, assigned to different hierarchical positions in the order of being; they are different aspects of a richly interwoven field of matter, meaning, and movement. In a similar fashion, the hero was not someone who elevated himself above other bodies and made himself independent of social approval by virtue of recurrent demonstrations of his charismatic qualities. Rather, he was himself the materialization of a blurred social terrain, a person whose position and identity were intricately enmeshed with those of his dependents, clients, and subordinates in ways that symbolized the unity and diversity of social processes and the ever-changing distribution of wealth and power.

A good sense of these notions of personhood and heroism may be gained from the following example of self-praise in Basotho poetry. Here the poet sings of Basotho king Masopha, one of the Basotho king Moshoeshoe's sons:

Seodi sa mmannete 'a koma,
Se sa keng se hopolwa ka mahopolo,
Se ereng ha ngwana a se hopola kwana Maseteding,
Mo-na-ngwana a mo hlathe ka lenala,
Ntat'ae a mo hlabe ka leswai,
Ba re: "O re hopotsa moloi wa motona,
Ya kileng a diha ntho ya tona, moraparapa!"

---

A Seodi warrior true and undisputed,
Who is never contemplated in people's minds,
That when a child speaks of him there among the Masetedi,
Then the mother of the child digs her nails into him,
And his father strikes him with a stick,
And they say: "You remind us of a great sorcerer,
Who once brought down a great big thing, a huge monster that lay on the ground!"[22]

Similar notions and styles of autopoesis are also found in more recent Basotho poetic genres, such as the *lifela* recitations by migrant miners. Having emerged in the hostile environment of South Africa's mines and labor compounds, these socially resonant autobiographies are concerned with the assertion of migrant workers' identity as men and individuals. In the following example, recorded by the Basotho scholar R. I. M. Moletsane, the poet imagines himself, in deliberate inversion of the dominant images of chiefly power, as a trickster, an uncanny and unruly cannibal:

Lelimo le bua le lona, litsamaea-naha.
Joale lelimo ho puruma, la habo Mosenyehi;
Joale ke ena e puruma, nong-thoboro,
Lena ke lehipi, ngoana Makoloane. . . .

---

The cannibal speaks to you, travelers.
Now the cannibal roars, the one of Mosenyehi's;
Now it's this one roaring, the black vulture,
This one, the "hippie," child of Makoloane. . . .[23]

As these examples illustrate, the notion of the hero and the person as an accretion of social bonds (or, conversely, as in modern Basotho migrants' poetry, as the personification of the antisocial creature) mirrored a wide-reaching concern with the foundations of social order. And, as far as the arts were concerned, it generated a whole ethos of eloquence along with complex grammars of poetic recital, political oratory, and ritual incantation. Yet implicit in all this were also concepts of language, communication, and even modes of appropriating the world that differed sharply from those operating in the West. Words did not have an existence separate from those who uttered them, nor was speech thought to be a disconnected representation of a third realm, such as an object reality. Words were essentially endowed with an illocutionary force that had the capacity to act on their referents, a property that Victorian scholars mistook for magic or "animism." Objects, in turn, were known to impinge on words, enhancing their power and that of the interlocutor.

Early missionaries such as the Morija pioneer Eugene Casalis had a clear sense of this mimetic play of parallelisms, semblances, and differences. Writing of his own efforts to learn Sesotho, he noted in 1861 that the language "is admirably adapted to the sententious style, and the element of metaphor has entered so abundantly into its composition, that one can hardly speak it without unconsciously acquiring the habit of expressing one's thoughts in a figurative manner."[24] But aesthetic admiration aside, churchmen like Casalis also viewed this intricate web of social practice, language, and cosmology with considerable misgiving. Being products of Western nineteenth-century empiricism and having introduced literacy to South Africa's societies, the missionaries not only brought with them a new body of knowledge and a new mnemotechnical device but also spread an altogether new concept of inscription as an almost accidental form, a neutral mold into which an idea or a meaning could be cast. Like some of the early Orientalists such as Max Müller and Michel Bréal, the churchmen believed language to be a neutral medium, indifferent to the social context in which it is used. Words were thought to be semantically transparent, outer shells through which two distinct realms, the physical and the metaphysical, could be conjoined in some sort of meaningful way. Consequently, semantic content was something that could be managed, transferred, and even translated into different languages by simply maintaining proper channels of communication. Meaning was to be found outside the words, in a structure that the communication between speaking subjects aimed at eliciting. By the same token, this view of language presupposed a subject that stands apart from both the words it uses and the world in which it lives.

As all this illustrates, there could hardly have been a starker contrast than that between the view of language as code and form and African notions of the richly interwoven realms of the subject, the word, and the object. It was thus perhaps not a coincidence that it was telegraphy, one of the core technologies of the late Victorian age, that was to mark most strikingly the transition from hero ethics and poetry to what Stephen Kern has called the "culture of time and space."[25] From 1880, in what was described as the "Lovedale experiment," some

Lovedale students had been trained to fill various positions in the civil service of the colony, most notably as telegraph messengers in the Kimberley Post Office. Not only were both Paul Xiniwe's and Josiah Semouse's early careers the direct result of this "experiment," but also telegraphy was the most important component of their experience of the imperial order. But if telegraphy was important, perhaps more so than literacy, musical literacy, too, in its specific form as tonic sol-fa notation, was no less indicative of the emerging global consciousness of the South African performers. Most of them were fully conversant with Curwen's method of notating pitches (such as do, re, mi, sol, fa, etc.) and duration in a relatively basic system of letters that referred to a fixed tonic (hence tonic sol-fa). Xiniwe even went to the trouble of taking additional tonic sol-fa classes in England and, no doubt inspired by the example of the Fisk Jubilee Singers, produced his own tonic sol-fa score, *Izingoma zaseAfrican Jubilee singers* (The songs of the African Jubilee Singers).

Be this as it may, the technological advance and the linguistic colonization I have just discussed entailed a whole series of far-reaching innovations, several of which I shall return to in this and following chapters. Most fundamental among the transformations it produced, however, was a change in the mode of representation as such or, better still, a change from presentation to representation. In the precolonial forms of inscription, as we have seen, the world was made through the power of the word.[26] The project of the missionaries, by contrast, consisted in devising a code by which the world could be contracted into telegraphlike signals and phonetic transparencies that conveyed a set of clearly circumscribed meanings.

The result of this shift was the same dilemma that Fredric Jameson faced in accounting for personal experience in a global space and that he identified as one of the founding moments of modernism: the dilemma, namely, of how to capture an authentic experience of personal identity that is at the same time a truthful reflection of the vast colonial network that increasingly came to determine individual lives. The dilemma which Xiniwe, Manye, and Semouse were facing was therefore primarily one located at the level of representation. The question most mission-educated African intellectuals were addressing at the time was how to construct in the code of the colonizer plausible accounts of heroic "lives" that could be considered as modern and yet authentic representations of an African identity, how to solve the problem of being truthful to the inchoateness of individual experience while still recognizing through it the validity of universal "truths"—of things like God, the individual, and, of course, the idea of objective truth itself. As we shall see in a moment, most of the singers in their autobiographies tried to resolve this dilemma by flatly subjecting their own notions of self to some of these universal truths, inserting themselves into a narrative of cultural wholeness and a mythology of universal reason. At the same time, although few traces remained in these texts of the traditional metaphors of the heroic self, there became visible through some of the biographical texts that followed them the signs of a different kind of "sci-

ence of the subject," one that allowed for the intervention of multiple and culturally variable determinants in a person's life choices. In order to push the
analysis further in the direction of these hybrid linkages of the local and the
global, tradition and modernity, self and society, let me continue my inquiry
into the life trajectories of the South African singers by returning to the remaining autobiographical sketches in the *Illustrated London News* and taking a
closer look at how these late-nineteenth-century self-constructions opened up
a complex discursive field of black South African biographical writing, elite oppositional politics, and Pan-Africanist thinking.

## Relative Systems of Culture and Language

At the beginning of this chapter we saw how Paul Xiniwe in his vignette took
great pains to depict himself as the self-made man whose life story unfolds and
validates the grand imperial scheme, as he aspires to ever higher levels of perfection. As we shall see, the singers in the remaining three autobiographies in
"The African Native Choir" adopted much the same self-reflexive pose. For the
most part, they reiterated the same well-worn points about the role of heroic
self-determination, Christianity, and British civil rule in shaping their careers.
The short vignette on Makhomo Manye, for instance, opens with the observation that Charlotte (fig. 2.2) is "the best linguist in the choir, speaking and writing five languages—namely, English, Boer Dutch, High Dutch, Amaxosa Kaffir,
and Basuto, her own language." After further stating that Charlotte was born on
April 7, 1871, at Blinkwater, in the district of Fort Beaufort, the article then continues with her own story as follows:

> My father is a Basuto of the Transvaal, and my mother an Umbo, the peo-
> ple commonly known as Fingos. Both are Christians of the Independent
> Church; my father is a local preacher at that church. I was brought up at
> Uitenhage and at Port Elizabeth, where I got my schooling under efficient
> teachers, who passed me through the Government requirements of mission
> schools. My parents being unable to send me to one of the girls' high schools,
> I therefore had to stay and work under mistresses. We left Port Elizabeth and
> came to Kimberley, where, after two years or a little more, I was engaged as
> an assistant teacher and sewing mistress in a Wesleyan Government-aided
> school; there I served for a year. During my stay there, a Government inspec-
> tor visited our school, and gave a favourable report of its condition; he spoke
> in high terms of the lower section, which was under my supervision. During
> my time of service in the above school, we had local concerts, in which I was
> the conductor's assistant and leading voice. I resigned, through unavoidable
> circumstances, and joined the African Choir.

In somewhat modified form, the themes of Christian upbringing and the redeeming role of education foregrounded in Manye's account recur in a third
text, written by another female member of the choir, named Johanna Jonkers.

Figure 2.2. Charlotte Manye (*Illustrated London News*, Aug. 22, 1891).

But in addition to this motif, her portrait included another trope that rang powerfully in the minds of the British public and modernizing Africans. For it appears that Johanna Jonkers was of *inboekseling* (Africans pressed into semiservitude on Boer farms) origin. She was the daughter of Zulu-speaking parents who, as the singer opens her statement, "were taken captives by the Dutch when they were about twelve years of age." And, as her brief note continues, deftly weaving bits of anti-Boer rhetoric into the fresco of personal betterment and Protestant ethic:

> They were badly treated by the Dutch, till it happened that some good friends pitied my mother, and advised her to go to the town, where she might hear everything about the law. So she did go to Burghersdorp, but was afraid to go into the town, and she was waiting outside when she met a gentleman who passed her three times that day. At last he spoke to her, and bade her to come to his house. She went with him, and told him, as she reached the house, that she came from a farm-house where the Dutch people were very hard and cruel to her. The new friends who now received her, being very sorry to hear her sad story, took good care of her, and she stayed with them

till she got married, and had a happy life. I was born there, at Burghersdorp; my parents were Christians.

It is, of course, possible to view these two texts as polite (and perhaps also rather bland) transcripts of colonialist ideology and metropolitan liberalism. And, in a certain sense, this is an interpretation that would appear to have some credibility to it because of the context in which these statements were made. But it would also be a mistake, I think, to see these tales about freedom, individual property, and legal equality as the mere outcome of metropolitan discourse implanted in the minds of South Africa's fledgling black elite. The liberal tradition that is being evoked here by Xiniwe, Manye, and Jonkers and that had materialized in South Africa in a political dispensation often mythologized as Cape liberalism was equally the product of an intense and drawn-out process of negotiation in which imperial control was made possible through selective incorporation and consensus from below. Thus although on paper the chief provisions contained in the idea of Cape liberalism—such as a color-blind, qualified franchise for all colonial subjects—may have looked like privileges that had been bestowed by agents of the imperial state on the colonial population, in reality they were far more than humanitarian-minded concessions. As the pioneering work of Colin Bundy, Stanley Trapido, and others has shown, Cape liberalism was based on a delicate web of mutual dependencies that had developed in the eastern Cape among merchants, colonial administrators, missionaries, and black peasants. Wrought out in ever-changing, everyday social relationships, Cape liberalism was thus more than a "catalogue of rhetoric" that served specific projects and economic interests.[27] It was ideology in practice or, to use Giddens's felicitous phrase, practical consciousness, a type of political fiction through which social practices, institutions, and symbolic worlds mutually determined one another. In short, liberalism in the Cape was a universal narrative about the place of the individual in modern society, but it was also a discourse that acquired local salience as a relative system of culture primarily through the agency of local actors and the social relationships in which they were implicated.

The vicissitudes of Cape liberalism as a fictional framework for imagining modern African selves are further complicated by another current of the African global imagination that was taking shape in the Cape toward the end of the nineteenth century—often alongside liberalism but also increasingly working against it—and that faintly announces itself in some of our autobiographies. Thus even where most of these texts portray Christianity as the founding moment of a new type of personhood that disentangles the individual from the oppressive sociomoral universe of the tribe, this notion also merges with an almost taciturn ambivalence about this plan of universal salvation. Thus one might observe in Xiniwe's tale of self-improvement and thirst for knowledge a certain sense of frustration, a barely discernible, but carefully calculated, annoyance at the limits imposed on his aspiration by white obstinacy. Similarly, one senses in Charlotte's story the crippling effect it must have had on her to have to "work under mistresses." The strongest expression, however, of this anti-European resentment is found perhaps in the fourth and last account from the *Illustrated London News* I shall examine here. It is the life story written by Josiah Semouse (fig. 2.3), a choir member who enjoyed the privileged attention of the British press mainly, it appears, because of his involvement in the Gun War against Britain in 1880–81 and as a result of the queen's special request to see him shortly after the choir's arrival in England. I reproduce here the main section of his account, which deals with his life up to the departure of the African Choir for England:

> I was born in 1860, at Mkoothing, in what is now known as one of the conquered territories (Basutoland). My parents being Christian people, I was naturally so brought up; I first attended school at a small village called Korokoro, where my father was appointed local preacher, and there I learnt to read and write my own language. Then I went to the Morija training institution, about thirty-six miles from my home. I heard from a native teacher that there is a school in Cape Colony, called Lovedale, which is famous for the practical knowledge that it imparts to its pupils. But, a few months after, war broke out between Basutoland and the Cape Colony about the order of disarmament. I took part against the British during this war, but I was not happy, because I did not know the English language then. When this war was over, which was decided in our favour, I left Basutoland for Lovedale, travelling day and night; I slept for a few hours till the moon came out, and then pursued my course, till I reached my destination in eleven days, the whole distance being about 600 miles. At Lovedale, I received both education and civilisation, then one day, in March 1886, the principal of the college received a telegram from Kimberley to say that there was a vacancy in the office there for an honest, educated young man. I was sent to fill up the vacancy, and I remained there till the end of March 1891, when I received an esteemed offer from the manager of the African Choir to join the choir for England.

The historical background against which this statement must be read and that Semouse alludes to differs, of course, from that of the Cape Colony in one crucial respect. Basutoland, as the kingdom of Lesotho was then known, through a number of costly wars such as the Gun War of 1880–81, and under considerable duress, had managed to retain a certain measure of political autonomy. Although economically increasingly dependent on the Cape Colony, the country enjoyed the ambiguous status of a protectorate of the British Crown, and it is this feature of Semouse's background that explains the surprisingly unambiguous political tone of his remarks. Conversion and conquest—considered in imperialist ideology as largely coterminous aspects of colonial reality—in Semouse's thinking almost appear as contradicting each other. Basutoland is "one of the conquered territories," and the Gun War against Britain "was decided in our favour."

One way of looking at these early expressions of African nationalism is to see in them the rather timid beginnings of a counterdiscourse to the prevailing Eurocentric models of progress and development. But whatever the pitch of these anticolonial statements, in the final analysis one might concur with Partha

MR. JOSIAH SEMOUSE.

Figure 2.3. Josiah Semouse (*Illustrated London News*, Aug. 22, 1891).

Chatterjee's contention that nationalist thought, even where it challenges and deals the death blow to the civilizing mission of the West, ultimately leaves untouched the ideology of progress, science, and technology as the founding elements of what he calls the marriage between universal reason and capital. And one might agree with his conclusion that it is through nationalist thought that the national state eventually justifies its project of finding for the nation—and by implication the citizen of the nation-state—a place in the global order of capital.[28]

I am, of course, anticipating here the succession of historical events and, since this is not an event history, perhaps quite deliberately so. I want to advance the discussion of these texts by probing those elements of black South African autobiographical writing and anticolonial discourse that reveal not so much their place in literary and political history than some of their byways and dead ends. I want to unravel some of the obstacles and tensions young Africans

like Josiah Semouse and Charlotte Manye encountered as they (as later generations would do) attempted to write themselves in (and into) a world that offered increasingly scantier grounds for rooting individual identity in global narratives of redemption and reason. Finally, by looking ahead to some of the
succeeding expressions of this literary and political legacy in the 1930s I seek to
understand the role of nationalist constructions of the self in the overall making of the African global imagination and, through this, to see more clearly the
structures of subordination and control that resulted from these constructions
and that constituted the most important aspect of their impenetrably panoramic
self-enclosure.

In other words, if the meaning of autobiographies such as the four stories
from the *Illustrated London News* that I have reprinted here was not as individual
life histories but rather as demonstrations of a concern with writing and narrativity as formative elements in a process of self-fashioning called modern life,
we must ask ourselves what limits, if any, Christianity, Cape liberalism, and especially African nationalism imposed on the expression of this concern. As we
also have to inquire, of course, how much such fictions of collective life offered to the fragmented individual him- or herself stable and especially gendered allegories of identity and precisely what constituted their role as mutually enforcing wholes of a culture. And, finally, we need to determine whether
any counternarratives at all could be developed from these models of self-
fashioning.

The first argument that I would venture to put forward in this regard is that
what made the nation such a powerful allegory of identity in South Africa and
elsewhere is the extent to which nationalist discourse continually works around
certain metonymies of gender. The nation encloses its women just as women
stand for the whole. The second hypothesis I would like to propose is that the
new forms of biographical narrative that were emerging in South Africa were
not uniformly, qua narrative, repeating and extending what Edward Said has
called "imperialism's appropriative and dominative attributes."[29] Although they
were types of autopoesis that still operated within the same overall essentialist
logic of selves fashioned in contrast to wholes of a culture, these narratives of
the self, because they ran counter to the dominant representations of power
and because they imagined more crossbred and hybridly disseminated black
communities, had the potential of opening up alternative systems of culture
and new ways of social ordering. Both these contentions are neatly exemplified
in two further texts that deal with two of the singers, written some forty years
after the tours by people closely connected with the individuals they describe.

The first text I would like to consider is a biography of Charlotte Manye published sometime in the 1930s by Dr. Alfred Xuma, at one time a president of
the African National Congress (ANC) and, like Charlotte Manye, a graduate
from a black American college and active member of the AME Church. Titled
*Charlotte Manye (Mrs. Maxeke): What an Educated African Girl Can Do* and with a
foreword by W. E. B. Du Bois, Charlotte's onetime teacher at Wilberforce (and

as such "next only to God"), the 27-page pamphlet begins with a strangely paradoxical statement in which Xuma in one breath both demonstrates his intimate familiarity with the genre of the biography and distances himself from it. Whereas biographers create "hero and heroine rather than relate true history and activity," Xuma intends to use Charlotte "only as an argument for higher education of our African women." Charlotte Manye's career, he writes, not only served as an example for "education translated into service for humanity" and "better race relations in South Africa" but also was an inspiration for the reader "to work spiritually and materially for the redemption of the African—body, mind, and soul." And it is in this vein that Xuma then begins his "biography" on a note of truly global design:

> Now known, appreciated, and admired in three continents by different racial groups, "Charlotte" Manye was born at Fort Beaufort, Cape Province, South Africa. A Basuto woman by nationality but born among the Xosa tribes. Through her mother, a Xosa woman, she had already acquired a strong blood bond with those people.[30]

But this cosmopolitan background, Xuma goes on to say, did not come about by chance. Although "there is often nothing strange or extraordinary about one's birth or birth place," it is of great importance to note that Charlotte's father, Jan, a Basotho from the Transvaal, had come to the Cape Colony for the sole purpose of buying guns "with which to fight the Boers." (This was a plan devised by the Basotho king Moshoeshoe and which eventually led to the Gun War of 1880–81 in which Josiah Semouse also participated.) Yet instead of acquiring weapons, Charlotte's father came into contact with the missionaries who since the early nineteenth century had been working successfully with the Mfengu people uprooted and dislocated by Shaka's expansionist policy. And it was thus, Xuma writes, that "he [Jan] was himself shot down by the 'Big Gun,' the Word of God." In fact, he "had been born again."

What we see here in the opening paragraphs of Xuma's text is a biographer gradually building up the allegorical thrust of his overall narrative by depicting, in a rather conventional manner, African history and its more personal manifestation in the story of the Manye family as the result of a rather violent and pelemele of tribes, blood ties, and territorial expansion. Yet Xuma does not waste much time in providing the reader with a realistic representation of this past, and, it seems, he does so for a good reason. For the point that Xuma seems to be making is that this past and, within it, the genealogy of the Manyes have no value in themselves. There is nothing "extraordinary" about them. The past is narrated only, it seems, in order to be interred and then to be disinterred again for a teleology to be brought into the course of events that led up to Jan Manye's conversion and rebirth—an order whose worldly shape was as much due to the activities of the Cape evangelists as it was ultimately predestined by Providence.

After the dramatic turning point of Jan's redemption, Xuma then takes the reader back to Charlotte and the now-familiar heroic tale of light, enterprise, and self-redemption. For this "change of mission, of outlook," Xuma goes on to relate, "was going to have a tremendous influence over the new family life":

> The children had to be led through the paths of peace into light and full-ness of life. Charlotte, with her sister, then entered the mission school of the Congregational Church at Uitenhage. Later the family moved to Port Eliza-beth where she continued her education. It was here that she began to show some buds of vocal musical talents.
>
> Later she went to Kimberley to teach in a Wesleyan School. It was there that these buds of musical talent attracted the attention of music lovers among both races. Some enterprising white people, with artistic tempera-ment, who had come to Kimberley in search of diamonds, now discovered a new and undreamed of diamond—Africa's own riches in the beautiful con-tralto voice of Charlotte Manye. Her voice was successfully trained by a competent artist. The bud of musical talent that appeared at Port Elizabeth had now, under the care of an expert florist, blossomed into a beautiful flower with its aroma. It was as though one of those large, blue, precious stones from the sands of Kimberley has been washed, cut, and polished by an ex-pert diamond cutter until its radiance made the darkest night brighter than the light of the moon and all the stars in a cloudless wintry night. Charlotte had now become the idol of music lovers in the Town Hall at Kimberley. It was her talent that inspired J. H. Balmer, R.A.M., Blackpool, England, to or-ganize and train a group of young men and women for a two years' concert tour in British Isles. So successful were their performances that they had the unique experience of singing before the late Queen Victoria and other mem-bers of the Royal Family, who enjoyed their rendering of English songs and still more particularly of the native compositions set to more or less tradi-tional tunes.

At this point Xuma goes on to relate Charlotte's studies in North America, the marriage to Marshall Maxeke, and her subsequent career as a social worker and teacher in South Africa. Xuma accentuates each of these stages by quoting from carefully chosen white endorsements of Charlotte's achievements and, in the same sweeping gesture, by extolling the virtues of black patriotism and leadership. The whole hagiography then ends, in a rather unexpected move, on a note of domestic harmony and African tradition that brings the entire narra-tive full circle. "Leadership, public service, and even the exercise of the new freedom by women receive our applause," Xuma sums up his account in a rubric titled "In Her Home." But, he goes on to state, "it is the woman as wife and mother that we admire most":

> Nothing was more pleasing and inspiring to me than to see Charlotte with her husband. Theirs was a partnership and companionship characteristic only of the newly weds. In our Native custom and tradition a wife never calls her husband by his name, but under a custom known as *ukuhlonipa* (to have def-erence for), she called him "Yise ha Clarke" (father of Clarke)—their son—and he called her "Nina ka Clarke" (mother of Clarke).

This passage is twice revealing. First, it showed that Charlotte had never completely abandoned her own distinctive blend of cosmopolitan modernism and Africanism in evidence already in her statement to the *Review of Reviews* quoted at the beginning of chapter 1. Like many women of her generation, she took a rather conciliatory stance toward customary marriage, wondering whether it was better suited than its Western counterpart to ensuring female chastity and parental authority.[31] Second, Xuma's concluding remark about *ukuhlonipa* refers to one of the most contested aspects of black middle-class culture and consciousness after World War I: the "new freedom" of women. It points to a debate in which women became one of the main targets of liberal education reform, and also the subservient position of women as wives and mothers of men served as an allegory for the welfare and progress of the black nation as a whole. Indeed, Xuma closes his work: "Africa thanks God for Charlotte!"

There exists a formidable literature about the underpinnings of gender in colonial culture and nationalist discourse that I cannot go into here. But in the South African context, as the work of Shula Marks, Deborah Gaitskell, and others has shown, the concern with growing female autonomy, sexual morals, and traditional African forms of etiquette was part of a broader politics of patriotism, patriarchy, and purity that had been formulated by the state, mining capital, and the "traditional authorities" in response to the massive social transformations in black society in the 1930s.[32] Control of women was central to this politics, Shula Marks points out, because the state and capital up until the mid-1930s had an economic interest in keeping women on the land and subject to the control of the homestead head, because the agricultural labor of women would subsidize the reproduction costs of the male migrant workforce and because through their continued control over women chiefs would also control the return of the young men to the reserves and white farms.[33] The extent to which African women had a stake in this project and effectively shared the views of their conservative menfolk is beside the point I am making here. What I want to argue instead is that in metonymically associating national liberation with female docility black biographers such as Alfred Xuma did more than simply propagate the inferior social position designated for women by the ideological alliance of state, capital, and black patriarchs. He basically reproduced one of the root symbolic operations of the Victorian global imagination: the construction of the private female world of home and family on the one hand and of the public male world of the state and the nation on the other hand, as mutually determining frames of social order.

My reading of Xuma's text may have been somewhat unrelenting in its critique of the author's patriarchal perspective and thus might have underrated the genuinely antiessentialist and radically anticolonial thrust in Xuma's account as a whole. But rather than overwork the exegesis of this piece of writing, I would like to now move on to the second text, a biographical effort that raises all these and similar questions in a much more comprehensive and compelling way. The work I refer to is T. D. Mweli Skota's *The African Yearly Register*, one of the most striking documents of black South African history and biography.[34] First published in 1931 and subtitled, in true Du Boisian style, *Being an Illustrated Biographical Dictionary (Who's Who) of Black Folk in Africa*, Skota's manual is, in the words of James T. Campbell, "the centerpiece of a lifelong effort to lend the black elite historical depth and a consciousness of its own reality and role."[35] Beyond this, with its more than 370 entries, *The African Yearly Register* is a prime document of the style, imagery, and, indeed, whole symbolic universe of a class of Africans intensely and consciously entwined with the expanding and conflicting forces of modernity and globality. One of these entries which I would like to quote here in its entirety is about Paul Xiniwe:

> Mr. Paul Xiniwe went to Lovedale in 1881 as an advanced student on the recommendation of Rev. Edward Solomon, of Bedford, from whence he came. He had worked previously on the railway as timekeeper and later as telegraph operator. At Lovedale he entered the students' classes in January, 1881. In the second year he obtained the seventy-fourth certificate of competency at the Elementary Teachers' Examination. He became teacher in the Edwards Memorial School, Port Elizabeth. His school was said to stand high in the classification of schools of the district in efficiency. After some years he tired of the teaching profession, and having saved some money, resigned in order to become a business man. He bought property at East London, Port Elizabeth and Kingwilliamstown, and opened stores as merchant and hotel proprietor. At Kingwilliamstown his property was conspicuous, being a double story building and known as the Temperance Hotel. In a very short time the Temperance Hotel was known through the Cape Province. Paul Xiniwe took a very keen interest in the welfare of his people. An upright man, honest gentleman, and a thorough Christian and a staunch temperance apostle. He married a Miss Ndwanya, sister of Mr. Ndwanya, a law agent who was respected by Europeans and natives at Middledrift. Mr. Xiniwe was the father of five children. The eldest son, Mr. B. B. Xiniwe, was a law agent at Stutterheim for a number of years; the second son is in Johannesburg; the third, a daughter, Frances Mabel Maud, is the wife of the editor of this book; the fourth, another daughter, Mercy, is the wife of Mr. Ben. Tyamzashe, a schoolmaster and an author; and the youngest son, Mr. G. Xiniwe, is a clerk in a solicitor's office, Kingwilliamstown. Mr. Paul Xiniwe died at an early age leaving a widow and five children to look after themselves. Mrs. Xiniwe who, with her husband, had been to Europe as a member of a native choir, was a lady of experience, tact, character and business acumen. Difficult though it was, she maintained her late husband's property, and carried on the business and educated her children. This lady indeed commanded the respect of all who knew her, white and black. Paul Xiniwe was a man of his word. He swore he would never touch liquor. When he became very ill his doctor advised him to take a little brandy, but he made up his mind that he would not do so, although it was said brandy was the only thing that would save his life.[36]

As we can see, it is no coincidence that Skota's book devotes such a detailed entry to Paul Xiniwe. But beyond these ties of consanguinity and apart from the rich detail, earnest diction, and modernist thrust in this and other articles,

Skota's inventory is intriguing for two further reasons. First, like Xuma's pamphlet, *The African Yearly Register* is the work of an African biographer, and as such it documents the ongoing concern—prefigured to a certain degree, as we have seen, in Josiah Semouse's, Charlotte Manye's, and Paul Xiniwe's own writing—of generations of black South Africans with personal narrative as a key strategy for the construction of a modern elite identity. Second, it reveals an enduring preoccupation of more than 40 years with the crafting of autonomous, self-reflexive selves, an obsession with individual achievement and self-control that was to reach new heights of black literary achievement at precisely the moment when the corrosion of liberal ideology had become all but irrevocable.

Skota's own biography, carefully reconstructed by Campbell, is perhaps the best illustration of this entanglement of private, local worlds with an eminently public, national, and global space, and as such it is worth being briefly considered here. Like many of the choristers, T. D. Mweli Skota came from an eastern Cape family, but—strange irony of history—he was born in 1890 in Kimberley, at precisely the same time and location that saw the formation of the African Choir. And it is to the eastern Cape and Kimberley—and in a certain sense, as mentioned in the entry on Xiniwe, to the African Choir as well—that Skota owed the most personal foundations of his life, for in the 1920s he married Francis Xiniwe, one of Paul and Eleanor Xiniwe's five children. With elaborate and, as we have seen, loving biographical vignettes and photographs of Paul and Eleanor and short entries (and sometimes photographs) on virtually all of their children and in-laws, the register duly reflects this shift in Skota's life and his initiation into one of the oldest middle-class presegregation families of the eastern Cape. But Skota was not only well placed to write the biographies of his immediate kith and kin. Like Alfred Xuma, Skota was also an influential figure in the ANC himself. As general secretary of the organization throughout much of the 1920s and 1930s and as an editor of the ANC weekly *Abantu-Batho*, he not only came into close contact with many of the people listed in his book but was also influential in shaping the cultural and intellectual milieu that was developing in and around the ANC.

It was especially two conflicting notions of personhood and self—and, by implication, society—that reflected the ANC's and Skota's ideas of modernity and its representation in narrative. On the one hand, the individual life trajectories of individuals such as Charlotte Manye and Paul Xiniwe are construed—perhaps inevitably so in a work of this nature—as quintessential manifestations of such key tenets of Victorian ideology as improvement and education, values that make the individual stand apart from the masses. On the other hand, Skota's subjects are depicted as driven and kept on track by a course of much greater events: the history of the nation. The putative royal genealogies of many of his subjects illustrate this quite clearly, as do recurrent phrases such as "has an interest in the welfare of his people" and "takes a keen interest in the affairs of his people." In other words, modern biographies such as those assembled in Skota's work narrate the self by narrating, in the same frame, the nation.

At the same time, a certain tension arose out of this precarious relationship between, on one side, the self-made leader and, on the other side, the individual wrapped up in the equation of the people and the nation-state he or she was striving toward. This was an ambiguity that was not easily resolved given the broader context in which it had emerged. And it was one that reflected a deeper-seated predicament. Wedged between a highly repressive hegemonic order and rapidly radicalizing masses perceived as untutored and caught up in tribal ways, black intellectuals such as Skota had to cobble together oddly contrasting tropes of historical event and social structure to mold their own distinct identity. In order to confront the growing disparity between the universal, liberating promise of modernity and its more repressive, specifically South African manifestations, members of the black elite such as Skota literally renarrated and rewrote themselves in a range of modern fictions made available by the very conjuncture of the local and the global.

One such type of fiction—widespread, as we have seen, throughout metropolitan and colonial society—rested on a linear and panoramic conception of history as a steady ascent of humanity to ever-higher levels of perfection and rationality. Another type of fiction, often implicit in the former, was a view of history as a process of redemption. And it is this latter notion that Skota and many other South African intellectuals came to reinterpret in a specifically local, African sense. As Campbell observes, Skota's conception of African history (a conception that he took from Marcus Garvey) argued for a need to return to some putatively wholesome and noble past. His compendium shares with Xuma's text a certain Africanist orientation. Both works express a regained black pride in the African past and a new confidence in the prospects for distinctly black elaborations of modernity.

At the same time, Xuma and Skota recognized and celebrated the redeeming impact of Christianity on a barbaric history. Only in this way, they believed, was it going to be possible to rescue the African past from colonialist condescension and to revitalize it as a point of identification for anticolonial action under adverse conditions. Consequently the register—and this is perhaps its most striking feature—reconciles the legacies of Christianity and Cape liberalism to what its author took to be an inalienable African tradition.[37] Skota not only established, as I have noted, the chiefly lineages of many of the individuals featured but also offered revised interpretations of major figures of the precolonial past. The Zulu monarch Shaka, for instance, is portrayed as "philosopher, a poet and a musician," while one of the main concerns of the great Basotho monarch Moshoeshoe is said to have been the "evangelisation of his people" and the need to "present Christ in an African way."[38] Here the precolonial past, then, was not written out of history and into some mystical realm "before time," as in more conservative and especially white interpretations of the making of modern South Africa; it was the sine qua non of a modern black South African identity.

By far the most important aspect, however, of this Africanist turn in black South African biography was the way in which Skota sought to connect the elite's reawakened historical consciousness with the experiences and struggles of people of color in other parts of Africa and in the diaspora. Thus the register contains the biographical data of a great number of West African chiefs and educators, the Egyptian cabinet, Haile Selassie of Ethiopia (whose photograph appears as frontispiece), Bishop Samuel Adjayi Crowther, the Sultan of Morocco, and the Zanzibari "Conqueror-Explorer" Tippu Tip. To these articles Skota added a section on the AME Church in which he offered a summary of its history—Skota ascribes the origin of the South African branch to the "dictatorship of some of the European missionaries and superintendents over their African brother-ministers"—and provided basic information about the church's leading African-American figures, such as Bishop Turner.

Overall, however, and despite his intimate knowledge of the writings of Marcus Garvey, Skota's identification with the black diaspora was rather hesitant, especially when compared to the sweeping impact the Harlem Renaissance and Garveyism had on black artistic life and nationalist politics in South Africa from the 1920s.[39] One reason for Skota's prudence might be that it reflected the formidable pressures such attempts at forging transatlantic countercultures were facing from the black elite and their white liberal allies. But it would be equally plausible to attribute Skota's rather laconic handling of African-Americans to the frustration that had been building up through the years within the AME Church over unmet American promises—a disenchantment which the register readily accentuated by reserving an unusual seven pages for the discussion of J. M. Dwane's Order of Ethiopia, an early South African breakaway group from the main body of the AME Church. Although one of the initiators of the amalgamation in the mid-1890s of the South African independent church movement and the AME Church, Dwane was also to become one of the first black critics of what he saw as black America's infatuation with "Western ideals and aspirations." Black Americans, he even boldly asserted in a strange inversion of African-American constructions of modernity, were ill-suited for the task of African redemption because of the culture and "civilization" that they had acquired in the "hard school" of slavery.[40]

I have closed this chapter on autobiography and biography with a discussion of Mweli Skota's life and work not only because his *African Yearly Register* is a fundamental source for the biographies of some of the South African performers but also because, read in conjunction with the autobiographical sketches presented earlier in this chapter, the entries in Skota's work show how much of his stylistic and intellectual armory drew on and broadened much older currents of African political thought. Skota had his undertaking in common with several generations of black intellectuals who had spent much time and energy reinventing precolonial history and appropriating African-American culture.[41] His own role in this project consisted more in canonizing and extending to an entire class a number of narrative models that had been tentatively explored in several well-known earlier examples of South African black biographical writing, works such as Thomas Mofolo's novel *Shaka* and various hagiographies of the man generally considered the first Xhosa Christian, Ntsikana, by B. Ntsikana and J. K. Bokwe, and, last but not least, in the self-representations, performances, interviews, and public speeches of the African Choir itself.[42]

Another aspect of Skota's and Xuma's constructions of Charlotte Manye's life is that they reveal the considerable ideological stumbling blocks that prevented early black nationalists from experimenting more audaciously with that part of the historical imagination that seeks, in the words of de Certeau, to open to the present a space of its own and that is a condition of a process. The two biographies throw in sharp relief what in the texts from the 1890s was but a dimly perceived predicament of the black discursive entanglement with modernity and its discontents: the problematic relationship among narrative, writing, personal identity, and Western global power. Biographies such as these illustrate that it was people like Charlotte Manye and Paul Xiniwe who were among the first black South Africans whose lives were not simply lived at the margins of a distant imperial power, but whose self-identity was directly shaped by the personal experience of the clash between the West's universal claims and local realities, both Western and South African. And these biographies show that even where these newly fashioned selves never challenged the fundamental allegorical nature of modernity's *grands récits*, they may at least have begun to disturb the cast of characters in the global play of allegories of the self, the nation, Africa, and the empire.

# 3

## Inventing the Metropolis

### *Josiah Semouse's Travel Diary and the Dilemmas of Representation*

On the face of it, modern travel writing is the direct expression of a new relationship between time and space in which individual identity and experience are no longer determined by the primacy of locally situated social interaction. At one level, the production of space through travel, exploration, and conquest creates places that are inscribed with meaning. It is through such processes of inscription that both travel and travel writing become crucial sites for the construction of modern selfhood. Yet at another level, travel accounts are not only textual representations of social relations but also the means for the mediation of such relations. They mediate between spatially dispersed social actors and thereby create a fictitious dialogue between two absent interlocutors. At the same time, and perhaps more important, travel accounts set up an ambiguous kind of relationship between two distinct types of work. For in traversing a territory, a terrain, the traveler works at ordering space by grafting on it a semantic grid, a system of meaning by which it may be known. And as the work of traveling makes available to the experience countless fragments of space, travel writing reworks these fragments into a text that exhibits the work that went into its production and, at the same time, conceals the social relations that underlie this work. It is this double nature that characterizes both European accounts of Africa and African writings about Europe. To gain a better idea of this process I shall briefly summarize some of the main characteristics of nineteenth-century European literary inventions of Africa and then move on to a detailed examination of African travel writing as it emerged out of the tour of the African Choir.

European travel writing and adventure fiction, as is now widely recognized and as Mary Louise Pratt has brilliantly shown in her book *Imperial Eyes: Travel*

*Writing and Transculturation*, were quite patently part of the ideological apparatus of empire. By using a variety of literary tropes, images, and narrative devices, Pratt argues, such literature helped to produce "the rest of the world" for a European readership.[1] At the same time, these genres of the imperial literary imagination were contingent on (and apologetic of) a massive project of global resemanticizing that sought to inscribe—not always in obvious ways—difference into the very syntax of all manner of metropolitan discourse. Put crudely, such discourses aimed at obliterating local forms of practice and knowledge with supposedly universal forms of knowledge—forms that were in reality associated with European relations of power. It is through this process that people with different notions of productivity and value became labeled as lazy, that African systems of economic and symbolic value and of seeing the world differently from Western epistemologies were decried as primitive, and so on. The list of stereotypes is long, well documented, and, it seems, indelible.[2]

What has received far less attention is how such fantasies of European global power constructed not so much images of Africa as a sense of their authors' self. It is in analyzing this more subliminal level of Western self-fashioning that a book such as Pratt's proves to be of particular value. Thus, as Pratt demonstrates, in the late eighteenth and early nineteenth century the European invention of Africa often masked itself behind an innocent posture of what she calls "anti-conquest." In works such as *Travels into the Interior of Southern Africa* by John Barrow (1801)—which Pratt discusses at length—European global authority asserts itself through the detached gaze of the naturalist who scans the landscape in search of traits and specimens to be inserted into a classification and a descriptive discourse.

Parallels between this type of colonial discourse and the emerging forms of mass entertainment such as the panorama and the panopticon are, of course, hard to overlook. For much of the plot and drama of early-nineteenth-century travel writing in the natural history vein, as Pratt deftly remarks, was produced not by history or the agency of the travelers themselves but by "the changing face of the country as it presents itself to the invisible European seers."[3] Mountains and valleys "show themselves," the country "opens up" before the visitors, and so on.

Tropes such as these were to endure throughout the nineteenth century and even the twentieth century, during which the scanning gaze turned into the panning movie camera. But the same obliteration of the social premises of the European inspection of Africa can also be found in other genres of ethnographic writing of the incipient imperial era. As Pratt points out, in such immensely popular works as Mungo Park's *Travels in the Interior of Africa* (1799) the authority of the Western observer lies not in the scientific accuracy of his descriptions but in the authenticity of his felt experience.[4] It is Park's hopes and fears that constitute the narratable events and through the staging of his own sensibility that Africa becomes available for his and the reader's scrutiny.

Of course, the divergence between Park's sentimental mode and the objectivist naturalist gaze could hardly be more pronounced. But, as Pratt observes, the whole point about modern European inventions of Africa lies precisely in the fact that such widely differing discourses are defined in terms of each other. They complement each other, because they stake out two parameters of bourgeois global hegemony: the land-scanning producer of data, associated with the panoptic apparatus of the bureaucratic state, and the sentimental explorer, associated with the domestic sphere. Both the state and the individual, although largely conceived in nineteenth-century European thinking as antithetical, converge here in a picture of the European economic and social order as a reciprocal one. In much the same way as Park and the sponsoring African Association fancied themselves entrepreneurs engaged in mutually beneficial and civilizing trade, Park narrates his itinerary through Africa as though it were a negotiated trajectory. But it is precisely this image of reciprocity that serves as one of capitalism's most potent fictions in enshrouding the decidedly asymmetrical relationships on which it rests. And thus it is, Pratt concludes her reading of Park's *Travels*, that "Park acts out the values that underwrote the greatest non-reciprocal non-exchange of all time: the Civilizing Mission."[5]

The travel and adventure books of the late nineteenth century retain all of these tropes, even though the general tone that pervades this literature reflects more of the chauvinist arrogance, absurd frenzy, and blatant brutality of the "scramble for Africa" that by then was already well under way. In addition, as Mary Louise Pratt illustrates, travel came to be employed as an allegory for progress as such. In much of late Victorian writing on Africa, travel and exploration are heroized through a number of rhetorical devices whose ultimate function is to assert relationships of dominance and mastery. For instance, by permeating the landscape with semantic and aesthetic density late Victorian travel writers constitute the colonies as objects of desire while, at the same time, through idealizing the scenery, these writers fix the seen in a static relationship to the seer.[6]

As is to be expected, these features of the nineteenth-century global imagination were not confined to travel writing alone. They were symptomatic of a whole aesthetic, and especially of that particular figure of modern consciousness which Dolf Sternberger has called the genre. For Sternberger, recall, the late-nineteenth-century social order had disintegrated into a series of vacuous tableaux vivants that appealed to the beholder to fill them, through his or her emotions, with life. The imperial order was no exception to this. As colonial conquest and the expansion of the railway had completed the whole world as a circular sphere available to inspection from a metropolitan center, the beauty and "ardor" of color and light in the Orient—once the sign of the Western search for a more passionate expression of freedom—turned into a mere technicality at the disposal of painters, writers, and ethnographers. Instead of freedom blasting forth colorfully from the depth, in the panorama of imperial power light and color are squeezed into the Orient. And that is where they shall remain, as the abstract seal of an Orient that was brought back and made available.[7] (At the same time as the Orient was opened up to Western scrutiny and exploitation, the very same desire of which the Orient was supposed to be the embodiment began to be tied up with the craving for opulence of a spectator ever more imprisoned by a system of utilitarianism and abstinence.)

As all this suggests, by the time our choristers set out to "discover" England, Africa had already been figuratively produced for a metropolitan readership through a massive body of travel and adventure literature. A certain imagination of African spaces physical and social had solidly implanted itself in the European mind that combined all of these tropes, poses, and gazes and that, by its very structure and intent, mystified the social processes—relations of global inequity and subordination, for the most part—that created these spaces in the first place. We do not know whether any of the South African performers were acquainted with this sort of literature of exploration and conquest. But that is beside the point. What matters is that the aesthetic of genre did not express the epistemology only of the metropolis and its ruling classes. Rather, as I have said, genre was the basis of a process of meaning making and self-fashioning that enveloped colonizers and colonized alike. It was a truly global episteme that governed nineteenth-century African writing about Europe no less than it sustained European fantasies about Africa.[8]

In much the same way as European inscriptions of Africa bore but the most superficial resemblance to Africa, African travel writing about Europe, then, had very little to do with Europe and every bit to do with the fashioning of African subjectivities. But not only did travel, as the short biographies examined in the previous chapter illustrate, constitute an integral part of Xiniwe's, Manye's, and Semouse's encounter with modern South Africa, but early travel writing by Africans dramatized the search for an elite modern identity in opening up the world for its own interpretive powers. This is not to suggest that such writing from the perspective of the dominated constituted merely an inauthentic assimilation of Western narrative models. Nor did, conversely, such work mount a critique of empire from a purely authentic position. Rather, I agree with Mary Louise Pratt that all travel accounts have a heteroglossic dimension. In the colonial mirror dance non-European knowledges infiltrate European ones just as non-European discourses of identity, selfhood, and social relations grapple with European notions of race and evolution.[9] (However, as we shall see in chapter 11, the entanglement of South African local worlds with the world market also produced other forms of travel "writing," other ways of imagining spaces and places through a poetics of displacement that, while by no means "tribal" or authentically "African," nevertheless do not revert to bourgeois notions of travel.)

In order to better situate this intermingling of perspectives and global trafficking of tropes in concrete events it may be useful to briefly review here the trajectory of the tour itself. As the reader will recall, no sooner had McAdoo and his Jubilee Singers left Kimberley and promoters Letty and Balmer taken the African Choir on a whirlwind tour of the eastern Cape that the new, restructured company set out for a second venture, this time to Beaufort West,

Worcester, Wellington, Stellenbosch, Paarl, and, last but not least, Cape Town. From there, their hopes raised and in high spirits, the troupe sailed for England, where, shortly after their arrival on June 13, 1891, the venture received a spectacular boost by a private performance in front of Queen Victoria. The momentum was to last for several months—months filled with acclaimed performances in some of England's most prestigious venues and receptions in the highest aristocratic circles. But then, sometime in September 1891, things took a turn for the worse, with the whole enterprise becoming engulfed by a whirl of financial troubles, internal disputes, lawsuits, and negative press. While the details of this will occupy us in the following two chapters, I am going to shift the focus here from event history and travel as a series of events joined to form a story line to a consideration of travel narrative as a mode of self-fashioning.

By the beginning of the nineteenth century, I argue, certain forms of travel writing came to be used as pivotal forms of the global imagination whose emergence at the colonial periphery coincides with the consolidation of bourgeois forms of subjectivity and power. In analyzing these processes I have found it useful to pursue a writing strategy similar to that in the previous chapter. But instead of using texts (biographies) to look at what they describe (lives), I propose to use places (locations, cities) as prisms for looking at ways of narrating the making of mobile subjective identities (travel accounts). In particular, I am going to discuss three places—and, by the same token, three types of social space—that seem to have been of particular importance in shaping the global imagination and consciousness of the metropolitan public and those of the South African singers, three places through which Europeans came to experience Africa and through which Africans in turn imagined Europe. The first of these places is Lovedale, the college that many of the choristers had attended before embarking on the European tour and that, by virtue of a host of fictions, tied the performers to a very different symbolic order and political vision. The second place is Kimberley, the diamond city where the whole enterprise of the African Choir had its beginning but, in many ways, also one of the most disputed symbols at the southern African periphery of the imperial order. The third place, finally, is London, imperial center of the late nineteenth century par excellence.

## *"Home Sweet Home": Lovedale, South Africa*

Lovedale mission station had been founded by Scottish missionaries in 1824 in an area of the eastern Cape situated around Alice and Kingwilliamstown. As one of the earliest institutions of its kind in South Africa, Lovedale was not only a profoundly rural place but also, like all mission stations on the colonial periphery, the "irreducible atom of Christian society," the model for a human order to be re-created in the image of the Kingdom of God.[10] Most important, however, Lovedale was, ipso facto, an eminently political place. For in preparing heathens for the Empire of God this mission also had a hand in paving the way for an empire of a more secular kind. After all, it was early British missionaries such as John Philip of the London Missionary Society, who had predicted in 1828 that by locating Africans "on a particular place, getting them to build houses, enclose gardens, cultivate corn land, accumulate property, and by increasing their artificial wants, you increase their dependency on the colony, and multiply the bonds of union and the number of securities for the preservation of peace."[11]

Such was, of course, also the credo at Lovedale for much of the nineteenth century. In fact, the very existence of Lovedale itself served as a constant reminder of these "bonds of union" and "securities." And of the special place designed within them for Africans, as the following statement by Lovedale's principal, James Stewart, made in 1884 in front of recalcitrant students, illustrates:

> Starting but as yesterday in the race of nations, do you soberly believe that in the two generations of the very imperfect civilisation you have enjoyed and partially accepted, you can have overtaken those other nations who began that race two thousand years ago, and have been running hard at it for a thousand years at least?[12]

Clearly, there was no essential contradiction here between the role of the missionaries as envoys of God and their views of themselves as representatives of a civilization and agents of political empire. In fact, as Valerie Y. Mudimbe has stated, "All of them implied the same purpose: the conversion of African minds and space."[13]

The specific form this conversion took in the eastern Cape was the creation of a stratified society based upon a capitalist market economy and governed by a set of civil institutions and social practices closely modeled on the metropolis. The backbone, however, of this order and one of its most formidable economic forces was an independent African peasantry, as it had risen from very modest beginnings and as a result of the complex interplay of colonial conquest, internal migration, and missionization. In fact, by the mid–nineteenth century this class had already become so prosperous that in the area of Lovedale alone the number of plows had tripled in eight years and Mfengu peasants had sufficient cash to put £1,660 toward a church building.[14]

But if there was no essential contradiction between missionization and modernization, there was no necessary connection between them either. Although the mission was instrumental in prompting and spreading agricultural technology and peasant production, Colin Bundy is correct in suggesting that the rise of the black peasantry in the eastern Cape and elsewhere in South Africa was not the one-sided process mission and other sources make it out to be. What was hailed in the ecclesiastical press of the day as "missionary successes," in retrospect might be more properly described as African successes, in that the initial decision to invite the missionaries was based on conscious and deliberate choices by traditional African leaders attempting to channel Western education along selected lines.[15] In addition to these factors, the Cape

Colony from the mid–nineteenth century had begun implementing a political dispensation the center of which was the franchise for all its property-holding male citizens and that was ideologically enshrined in a set of local beliefs that, as I have mentioned previously, in time came to be known as Cape liberalism. In terms of this alliance, significant sectors of the white settler population were economically dependent on the prosperous black farmers and hence perceived any attack on the rights of the latter as a threat to their position.[16] Conversely, the black farmers were prepared to accept white liberal tutelage against the demands of African chiefs and increasing pressure of white farmers.

Such, then, were the bonds, real and imagined, that made this world of plows and piety and that tied the colonizers and the colonized—or at least certain sections of the master class and their servants—to one another. But there is more to this. For the symbiosis of commerce, conscience, and civility reached into even deeper layers of consciousness, less easily discernible in the more openly political discourses of the time. Perhaps nothing illustrates better this whole fabric of dependencies and its crystallization in a place like Lovedale than a little episode in the life of the Reverend John Knox Bokwe, a major figure in Lovedale's intellectual history during much of the late nineteenth and early twentieth century. As one of the first ordained black ministers in the area, head of the telegraph department at Lovedale, a composer of considerable stature, and music teacher for some of the choristers, Bokwe was "no mere tribal figure" indeed and thus will occupy us in more detail later.[17] For now let us listen to him recall one of his childhood experiences, the first encounter in 1867 between himself and James Stewart's newly arrived young bride, Mina:

> As a lad of eleven or twelve years old, the writer, along with three companions from the native village, heard of the arrival at Lovedale of a new missionary accompanied by two ladies. Heavy rains had fallen during the week, and these little boys felt some pleasure in puddling the muddy pools of the main street that passed the house where the new arrivals lived. We were anxious to get a sight of them, and be the first bearers of news to our parents of what they looked like. A thick pomegranate hedge partly hid the front view of the mission-house, and it was not easy from the street to gain the object of our visit unless by entering a narrow gateway which led into the house. Halting there, the quick ear of one of the little fellows was arrested by sounds which he thought never to have heard before. He stood still to listen, while his mates continued their puddling excursions. At the gate the listener stood entranced at the music strains coming from within. Peeping in to explore, he saw a young lady seated before a musical instrument. The lower sash window was open. The temptation to the dusky, mud-bespattered lad to enter the gate, even at the risk of rudeness, was too strong for him. The lady observed his slow, frightened approach and quickly wiped off something trickling down her flushed cheek. The music was "Home sweet Home." No wonder the tears. Recovering herself, with a winsome smile she encouraged the intruder to come nearer.[18]

By the time this little episode took place, Lovedale had been firmly wed for several decades to the colonizing process and, as I have said, in many ways the Lovedale missionaries had even been playing a leading role in it. And although by the mid-1870s this process was in no way complete—resistance against colonial rule and armed attacks on the mission station continued until well into the 1880s—the narrator, John K. Bokwe, clearly speaks of himself here as a Christian and self-assured member of colonial society. In fact, the self-confident air exuded by Bokwe's stylish prose did not come out of a vacuum. It had deep roots in the history of the black farming communities in the area. Bokwe's family belonged to the oldest stock of these communities, his grandparents having been among the first people converted in the 1820s by the "prophet" Ntsikana. And thus by the 1860s the "native village" Bokwe mentions—like, in fact, most rural mission stations among Nguni-speaking peoples on the southeastern coast—in reality resembled more a modern farming settlement constituted along the lines of missionary fantasies about the ideal social order than any recognizable "native" form of habitat. Consequently, the excursion from the "native village" to the mission house was not a crossing of two radically opposed worlds but rather a passage between two facets of the same social space. And so, even though the little journey no longer traces out the difference between what early missionaries took to be incompatible and utterly irreconcilable "heathen" architectural designs and enlightened Western layouts, it does reveal some of the more subtle hierarchies and ambiguities at play within the Victorian bourgeois order that held sway over both missionary and congregation.[19]

Note, for instance, that the missionary here is not a man but his wife. The point is crucial in several respects. Although the scene is refracted through the lens of an adult man remembering his adolescence, this narrative gesture is part of the very relationship it seeks to mystify. For in placing the symbiotic relationship of colonizers and colonized under the spell and time of adolescent experience, colonial power structures are downplayed, even feminized. The idyllic scene depicts relations of inequity and subordination as though they were borne by nurturing and trust. Moreover, like Mungo Park, the young missionary bride is made to appear as though she is a victim to whom things happen and who, through her beckoning gesture and "winsome smile," makes the reader forget that it is her class that is the "intruder" and not that of the boy.[20]

And so, as individual agency appears to be written out of this vignette—thus demonstrating perfectly Bokwe's familiarity with the nineteenth-century aesthetic of genre—the scene seems to be governed by objects. Exemplifying core bourgeois assumptions about dwellings, commodities, and clothing literally making people (rather than, as in African thinking, people being producers of people), Bokwe freezes social relations into static designs whose order derives from the fixed position in them of the icons and instruments of property, domesticity, and individuality.

At the center of this pastiche stands, of course, the mission house, the epitome of this whole imagined world. Held up to the converted as the public image par excellence of civilization, the mission house here is also carefully screened from public view by a hedge and a narrow gateway. It is thus that this glimpse of Lovedale, *in nuce*, reveals one of the fundamental principles of modern space–time relationships: the separation of the inside from the outside, the private from the public. At the same time, in Bokwe's piece this rigid grid is shot through with ambiguity. Not only is the mission house the counterimage of disorder, but it is also somewhat of a liminal space, infused with unsettling moments of emotion and marked by uncertain thresholds and places of transit. There is, for example, the window—a highly ambiguous boundary and itself the site of a conflicted aesthetic in nineteenth-century Europe. On the one hand, as Jean and John Comaroff have written, nineteenth-century Protestant missionaries considered windows the preeminent symbol of Western empiricism and transparency. Like glass generally, windows were the medium per se of enlightenment, the aperture of civilization letting in the light to illuminate the dark interiors of Africa.[21] Furthermore, windows were to mark the functional separation of public and private spheres, between exterior, and interior as the cornerstones of the bourgeois order. On the other hand, as the Victorian age drew to a close and its ruling classes withdrew more and more from the world they had created, it happened that windows and glass, once the sign of progress, came to be regarded as standing in the way of the true individual introspectively locked into a windowless world.

The window in Bokwe's story serves neither of these purposes. It is open and thus, instead of demarcating a line of separation, lets the music being played inside flow out into the open. But the window is not the inward-directed passageway of reason either. Rather than allowing the light to shine on and ennoble women's domestic work and thereby constituting the interior, female realm of a rationally construed and functionally differentiated social world, the window reveals—even if most probably rather inadvertently—one woman's emotional turmoil at having lost one home and not being quite at home yet in another. In short, the open window grants a view of women's ambiguous position in colonial society and thereby quite literally sheds light on the shaky ideological grounds on which rested the image of the home as the microcosmic representation of modernity on the colonial frontier.

Then there is the music itself. The surprising fact here is not that the young Mrs. Stewart was playing Henry Bishop's "Home Sweet Home" on what appears to have been a piano, nor that Bokwe invokes the image of the musicking woman as a metaphor of benign domestication, both colonial and sexual. What is paradoxical are two things. First, although "he thought never to have heard before" such "strains," Bokwe immediately recognized the semantic and affective link between the song and the musician's tears. Although the urge to enter came from something strange and unfamiliar, the music was at the same time pleasurable ("the listener stood entranced"). It is as if the music prepared the uncertain and liminal ground on which boy and bride, colonized and colonizer, stand. Second, in this symbiotic bond the gender roles are reversed. The boy is feminized, while the bride by wiping off her tears in turn resumes a more masculine pose.

Such, then, are the twists and turns of colonial consciousness. Bokwe's vignette evokes the key emblems of the Victorian moral landscape and, by the same token that it conceals them, reproduces the dualisms and oppositions of the late-nineteenth-century global imagination: polarities constructed around images of home, civilization, nature, and art. And it was such polarities that were to determine the imagination and worldview of a whole class. It was through this prism that people like Bokwe and the musicians of the African Choir were to perceive and make sense of the world opening up around them—a world that was to engage them deeper and deeper in an ever-widening play of absence and presence, as it in turn was superseded by an even more complex world of industrial production, social divisions, and cultural forms. Kimberley or, as Africans bluntly dubbed it, Daemaneng, the place of diamonds, was far and wide the most palpable symbol of this world.

## Catching Civilization by the Tail: Kimberley in the 1890s

If the foundations for the modernizing identity and consciousness of a whole class of Africans were being laid in Lovedale, it was Kimberley that set in motion the process that led to this class's destruction. Founded in 1870, in the wake of the discovery of large diamond deposits, Kimberley in the 1890s was not only a rapidly expanding city but also, above all, a city of a hitherto-unknown type. It was the first and for quite some time only industrial city on the subcontinent. (The rise of Johannesburg to its present dominant role did not really occur before the 1890s, while Durban and Cape Town were little more than administrative centers with some port facilities.) Yet as such not only was the city the premier site for the incorporation of southern Africa into the world economy, but it also symbolized the dramatic shifts that had occurred in the imperial order itself from the mid-Victorian era of free trade and liberalism to the late-nineteenth-century period of monopoly capitalism and jingoist imperialism.

If there was an aspect of Kimberley's existence that best illustrated this shift, it was the sharp divisions that governed its social relations. At the apex of the social pyramid stood a single company, De Beers Consolidated Mines Limited, embodied in the figure of its owner and director, Cecil Rhodes. Nothing of importance that affected the city or, in fact, almost the entire colony happened without De Beers's consent, and although the importance of Kimberley was soon to be eclipsed by the gold mines on the Witwatersrand, the city in 1890 still bore out Rhodes's optimism expressed in 1880 that it was "the richest community in the world for its size."[22] The basis of all this wealth was, of course, African labor. Although cheap labor had not always been in abundant supply, mining capital over the years and through introducing a series of coercive measures such as the closed compound and an embryonic form of the pass system had managed to create a sizable class of low-paid and tightly supervised black miners—the nucleus of an emerging black South African proletariat. Finally, sandwiched more or less comfortably between these two worlds was a small intermediary class of black and white company employees, government officials, professionals, and small-business people whose social life and cultural activities were probably the single most important factor in lending Kimberley its character as a distinct and self-conscious symbol of empire.

Kimberley and the British Empire: it is this osmosis that was to make the most sense for the city's population—aside, of course, from the more covert and still somewhat underresearched forms of everyday consciousness of the city's black mine workers. Not only were Kimberley's private homes, institutions, and public spaces thought to be replicas of the motherland, but also the city's very social relations were said to correspond to those in the metropolis. "The native labourer," a reporter for the liberal *Daily Independent* wrote in 1880, "is to us what the Irish labourer is at home—the hewer of wood and drawer of water."[23] In short, as Brian Willan sums it up in what is probably the most succinct portrayal of the city and its class relations at the end of the nineteenth century, the "supremacy of British culture and institutions was one of those self-evident facts quite inseparable from Kimberley's existence."[24]

As plain as this picture of the city's social fabric may have appeared to Kimberley's intermediary strata, from the late 1880s fissures began to come to the surface. As control over the destiny of the town had passed into the hands of a few magnates and considerable parts of the market for unskilled labor formerly in the hands of white workers were being taken over by cheaper black laborers, a more skeptical tone was added to the self-congratulatory rhetoric of earlier years. No lesser a figure than veteran Cape politician and Prime Minister John X. Merriman, for instance, expressed his abhorrence at the "appalling crime and the utter hollowness of our civilization which tolerates such things." "I verily believe," he wrote in 1886, "that never was there a labouring population so utterly debased or treated with such complete disregard of their moral and physical welfare."[25]

Merriman's sentiments were not his alone. They were shared by many mission-educated Africans for whom Kimberley was both a dream place and a place of horrors. As a group of residents that never numbered more than several hundred people, these Africans—some of whom even had vested interests in mining and the diamond trade—were particularly alert to any infringements of their social position and political rights by the encroaching antiliberal forces represented by the likes of Cecil Rhodes. They knew, as Josiah Semouse's friend Patrick Lenkoane put it in a humorously double-edged speech to the South Africans Improvement Society, "that the natives of this country have caught hold of civilisation by the tail, and not by the head, and it is therefore dangerous to them."[26] More often than not, however, these dangers were perceived as equally coming from below, from a "labouring population" that threatened to disprove the very aptitude for civilization that Lenkoane and his friends were so eager to demonstrate. And so, one of the typical forms of early antiimperial critique was the lament over the "poor heathens" falling victim to a civilization they were not equipped to handle, a lament embodied best perhaps in a short piece titled "Life at the Diamond Fields," published in 1874 in the Lovedale newspaper *Kaffir Express-Isigidimi Sama-Xosa*. Written by Gwayi Tyamzashe, one of the first ordained black ministers and also one of the last independent black claim holders at Kimberley, the article begins by deploring the fact "that there seemed to be no room left for the great work for which we had come." It ends on a strikingly disparaging note that illustrates all the ambiguity of Kimberley's black elite: "The very low opinion that Europeans have of the natives of this country is not altogether groundless."[27]

It is was through this Kimberley, then, rather than Cecil Rhodes's "richest community in the world," that many of the singers were initiated into yet another set of contradictions that marked the new global reality. Ironically, it was again telegraphy that brought this ambiguity into even sharper relief. Paving as they had for many of the choristers the trajectory from the world of "native villages," agriculture, and crafts into that of industrial production and labor coercion, such positions as telegraph messengers in the Kimberley Post Office were rare and, as Paul Xiniwe's autobiography examined in chapter 2 suggests, highly prized among Kimberley's black elite. Yet by the time that people like Josiah Semouse and Paul Xiniwe eventually came to occupy these posts it had become increasingly clear that Western technological innovation not only was a vehicle for their own class's social advance but also the harbinger of its destruction. For, as Brian Willan has observed, the massive reworking of Kimberley's social fabric in the late 1880s and early 1890s—due in large part to improved mining technology and reduced wage levels for black miners—had also resulted in increased unemployment among a constituency of whites who viewed with utmost distrust any economic and social progress made by the black middle class.[28] The Kimberley Post Office, then, as one of the focal points of African identification in the city of diamonds serves as a further reminder of the vulnerable social position of the choristers.

But this instability not only compelled the African Choir to invoke imperial succor in the face of mounting settler demands and rising Afrikaner nationalism, to accept, in fact, as Shula Marks has written, the imperial state as the "lesser of two evils."[29] It also inscribed itself in the very poetics of place and social space that sustained this class. Although Marks is correct in saying that the Kimberley black petty bourgeoisie was not a "doomed and naive group playing at being European while sitting on a time-bomb,"[30] I would argue that it was primarily through Victorian models of textuality that the members of this class entangled themselves with a highly volatile and increasingly global web of social relations. In appropriating the aesthetic precepts of nineteenth-century genre, middle-class Africans such as Semouse and Xiniwe not only represented their local world to themselves but also simultaneously validated the entire epistemology of empire. It was through certain kinds of fictions that people such as the singers of the African Choir gained a sense of security within this

society, but the same fictions equally served to cloak in mystery the social relations at work on the periphery of the global economy.

One of the best illustrations of this—and possibly one of the earliest known
texts written in an African language about Kimberley—is a newspaper article
titled "Leeto la go ea Daemaneng" (A journey to the diamond fields). It was
published in January 1887 and is one of the first pieces choir member Josiah Semouse wrote in his capacity as a correspondent for the Morija mission paper
*Leselinyana*. It is impossible, of course, to do full justice to a piece of writing such
as this without a detailed linguistic analysis of the original, a task that, for want
of expertise, will have to await a future publication. Suffice it to note here that
Semouse's account is in a form of Sesotho that, on account of its unadorned narrative structure and basic vocabulary, reflects the effects of half a century of missionary linguistic policy such as I have discussed in the previous chapter. (When
I showed the text to Radio Lesotho broadcaster Dira Bereng, he bemusedly took
it to be similar to Setswana and—no doubt because of its missionary associations—rather old-fashioned.) From early in the nineteenth century, as we have
seen, and in keeping with the ideology of rationalist empiricism, missionaries
had been working to turn a number of cognate South African languages of what
is now called the Sotho-Tswana group into what they took to be simple, unvarnished language. Mission stations such as the Morija Training Institute were in
the forefront of this linguistic colonization and by means of restless publication
activities and shrewd political maneuvering eventually came to consolidate elements of the Sekoena, Sefokeng, and Sethlaping languages into a "national"
idiom called Sesotho.[31] Be this as it may, for the purposes of the following
analysis I shall have to rely on the translation provided for me by Naphtali
Morie, himself a teacher at Morija and thus well versed in handling material of
this nature.

"Leeto," as I shall call Semouse's article for short, opens with a description of
the author's feelings upon leaving Lovedale and a brief stopover at Healdtown,
where the quality of choir singing was high and the table manners low. Next Semouse recounts his journey through Adelaide and Fort Beaufort and across the
Orange River until he reaches Kimberley on April 1. And it is here that we join
him in his narrative:

> As it was my way when entering a town, I searched around like a head of
> cattle when entering a field of maize or millet stocks. I found a city without
> beautiful buildings, unlike Cape Town and Port Elizabeth and the surround-
> ing towns of the Colony with their beautiful and lovely buildings.
> As for work, there is no town like Kimberley in the whole of South Africa.
> They work day and night. Many nights pass sleepless because of the noise
> and smoke all night long.
> Sunday (Sondaga) is little recognized. Diamond diggers and Civil Servants
> alike work all day, without rest. I have traveled all over the Cape Colony, I saw
> towns and cities, but I have never seen a city as bad as Kimberley. And its laws
> are also bad.

Black people are pushed around like animals. They are being chased around the city like locusts and put into jail when they have no pass. Because if they have no means to get a pass, they are not given a pass. I have never seen such a calamity. The diamond diggers work naked, their bodies exposed to the sun. After work you are searched, searched thoroughly, turned upside down in a disgraceful manner, the argument being that you are hiding diamonds.

Last year, when I visited the Cape, I saw many kinds of people, but since I have come to Kimberley, I saw many kinds, not only colors. The other kind is known as Indians who are said to be smelling badly and not well liked.

There were also many different kinds of diseased people in Kimberley. One had no feet, only the body, and jumped around like a frog. One day, when he was jumping through the streets, he saw horses approaching him. I thought that they would stop in front of him. But he just looked up and at precisely that moment he made a giant leap forward so that his forehead, nose and mouth touched the ground. I realized that he could really outrun me, even with my two feet.

As for the life of this place, I have no evidence, because I was a newcomer at the diamond fields. I have not exactly realized how the seasons change here. . . .

To summarize about this town, I can say that it is all very bad, except the money earned by some in a disgraceful manner.[32]

Such critiques of the early manifestations of industrialization, as I have indicated, were staple items in the missionary discourse about modernity both in the metropolis and in the "mission field." But beyond this, several other things emerge from Semouse's account. First of all, these texts register an acute sense of rupture, even loss. Semouse very aptly sets up a stark contrast between the rest of the Cape Colony and Kimberley by stressing his experience as a traveler. In fact, here, as in the brief autobiographical sketch quoted earlier from the *Illustrated London News*, the Cape Colony exemplifies the pastoral, as J. M. Coetzee has called one of the dream topographies of South Africa.[33] The colony is depicted as an eminently "travellable" space, a realm of civil order crisscrossed by innumerable roads and railway tracks and dotted with "beautiful and lovely buildings." Although the traveler's anguish increases the farther he moves from Lovedale, finding one's way around presents no problem. It is only upon approaching Kimberley that the author's sense of orientation is suddenly upset and, as if to underline this moment of intense disruption, Semouse for the first time in his narrative invokes an image from the old, rural world. He needs to reorient himself like an ox in a field of corn. But then one indictment follows another: long hours, pollution, harassment, and racism characterize Kimberley life.

Second, "Leeto" is noteworthy for the high visibility and strong moral stance of its author. As Daniel P. Kunene has suggested in a critical review of modern African-language writing in South Africa, the single most important factor in shaping early Sotho or Zulu prose fiction was "the author's moralistic intent."[34]

But this feature, in Kunene's opinion, is something that results not so much from the imposition of Christian doctrine as from the fusion of precolonial verbal arts and Western literature. By using a series of highly developed techniques and genres of oral literature such as eulogy, allegory, and dysphemy and by blending these with the high Christian ethos of Bunyan's *Pilgrim's Progress*—one of the most widely translated works of Western fiction in Africa, available in a Sesotho translation as early as 1876—early African-language writers advanced a richly, poly-idiomatically encoded critique of modernity. They created a hermetically closed triad comprising author, characters, and readers—a courtroom in which modern society itself is on trial.[35]

Contemporary readers may be struck by the relative ease with which precolonial performance genres and nineteenth-century Western "art" literature (or, for that matter, Kunene's interpretations of these) merge in Semouse's account and other better known works such as Thomas Mofolo's *Moeti Oa Bochabela* (Traveler to the East) (1907) and R. R. R. Dhlomo's *Indlela Yababi* (The way of the wicked) (1946). And yet it is this stylistic procedure together with the stark moral dichotomies that makes for much of the stifling effect of such early literature, and thus it may ultimately be attributed to missionary linguistic and pedagogical doctrine. Yet as crucial as the Christian ideological impact may have been, the reader might equally recognize in this literature something that ties this kind of narrative self-fashioning to much deeper layers of global, modernizing forms of consciousness. Take, for instance, the curious episode of the legless man. Although the vignette describes what seems to be a well-known Kimberley original—and not some generic diamond digger or civil servant—it is not the portrayal of a "whole" human being. Sandwiched between highly moralizing statements, the story is an allegory of the quite literally truncated existence of the African masses under a lawless and inhuman system. Or rather, in keeping with the aesthetic norms of genre, the episode contains the portrait of a man playing an allegory. And so this scene, like all nineteenth-century allegories, appeals to the reader to rebuild through his or her compassionate response the ruins of the social order that produced this "calamity." Instead of uncovering the power relations at work in a place like Kimberley and laying bare the hidden forces that make diggers and civil servants work without rest, Semouse conceals these structures by virtue of the very allegorical gaze of the newcomer that is supposed to reveal them. More significantly perhaps, what we see being played out in a piece of fiction like "Leeto" is how the critique of the modern social order—represented here by Kimberley—is inextricably and through the same literary discourse bound up with the mystification of that very order.

But there is also a tragicomic element in the figure of the legless man. While most late Victorian popular fiction and, even more so, missionary and reformist representations of urban poverty would have contained—along with fear and repugnance—a strong sentimental, merciful element,[36] Semouse's figure is something of a trickster. In the end, although he lands on his nose, it is the frog-man who retains the upper hand: he is faster and more dexterous at playing the system than the newcomer from the countryside.

Such, then, are the dilemmas of an elite whose members, because they were part of neither the colonial bourgeoisie nor the masses of the laboring poor, had perhaps few alternative fictional means at their disposal to express their modernizing aspirations. In a moment we shall see how the delusion of invoking mid-Victorian ideology at a time when its material base in merchant capital and in a prosperous black peasantry had become a thing of the past increasingly found itself pushing against the limits of nineteenth-century literary realism as Semouse set out to account for the experience of his journey to England and, eventually, London, the imperial center itself.

### "The African Singers": Josiah Semouse's Travel Diary

After his Kimberley years, Josiah Semouse not only continued as a newspaper correspondent to *Leselinyana* but, in what is perhaps one of the most fascinating aspects of the story of the African Choir, also kept an extensive diary of the tour that he published in eight parts under the title *Libini tsa Africa* (African singers) (fig 3.1). Although reports such as Semouse's were not an entirely novel phenomenon in the South African press (already by 1858 the *Natal Journal* had published the English translation of a conversation between a group of Zulu elders and a young member of the troupe of "Kaffirs" that had been put on display in London in the summer of 1853[37]) *Libini tsa Africa* is likely to be the first account ever written by a black South African about the metropolis *in an African language*. This remarkable feature of Semouse's writing implies two things. First, for a colonial subject to lay claim to the metropolis by literary means implied a bold reversal of colonial asymmetries, in which, as Mary Louise Pratt has written, it is always the metropolis that represents the colony to itself and calls upon the colony to represent itself to the metropolis.[38] Second, although the publication of Semouse's column was designed to give vernacular expression to a specific ideological project within the broadly anticolonial politics of representation, representing the metropolis to a black elite readership, given the specific constraints of South African settler society, called for a reversal of a particular kind. It made it necessary for authors such as Semouse to adopt a special strategy: a poetics of the tightrope that quite visibly inscribes itself in the very structure and imagery of his work.

The reasons for this narrative strategy rested in the very structure or, if you will, the meaning of the journey itself. Conceived, as I have said, as a pilgrimage into the heart of empire, the tours of the African Choir initiated a period of black elite politics that was characterized by decades of futile petitioning of imperial authority to remain true to its mid-Victorian liberal premises and to intervene against settler racism. The form such petitioning invariably took was that of a delegation going on a pilgrimage in search of deliverance. Conse-

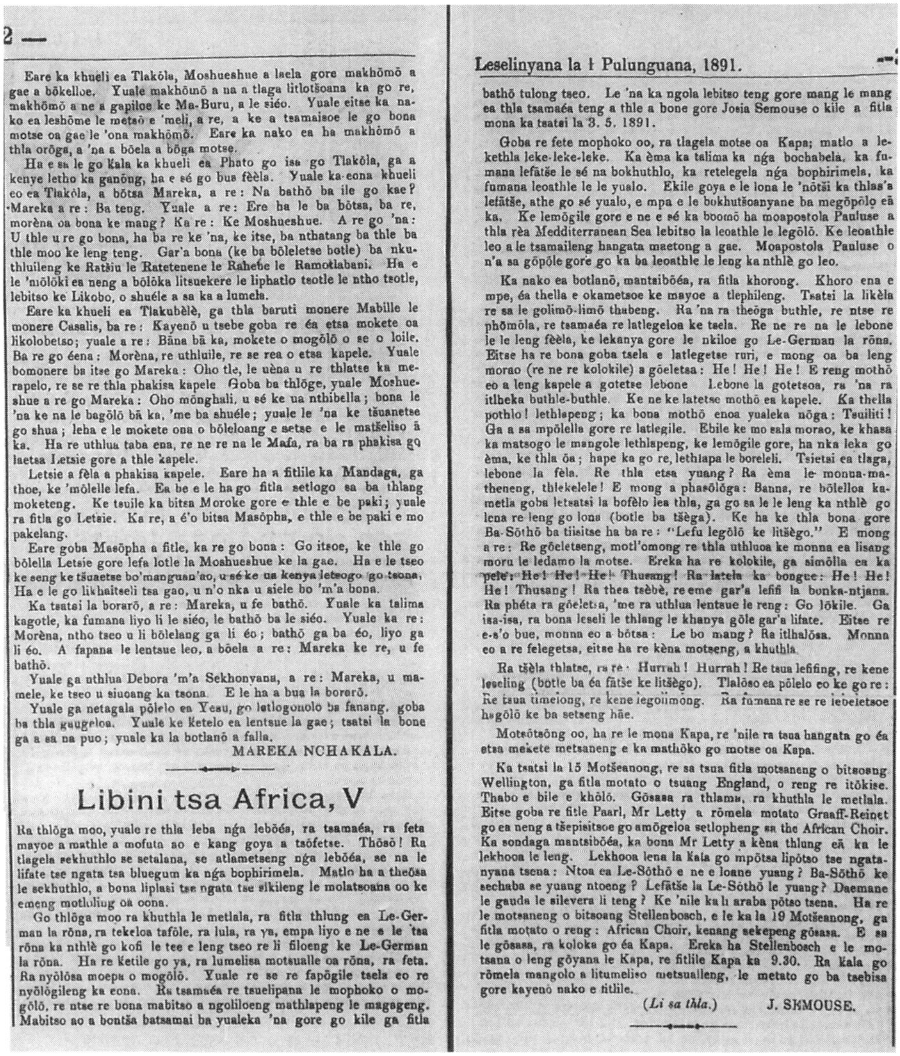

2 —

Eare ka khueli ea Tlakôla, Moshueshue a laela gore makhōmō a gae a bōkelloe. Yuale makhōmō a na a tlaga litlotšoana ka go re, makhōmō a ne a gapiloe ke Ma-Buru, a le siéo. Yuale eitse ka nako ea leshōme le metsō e 'meli, a re, a ke a tsamaisoe le go bona motse oa gae le 'ona makhōmō. Eare ka nako ea ha makhōmō a thla orōga, a 'na a bōela a bōga motse.

Ha e sa le go kala ka khueli ea Phato go isa go Tlakôla, ga a kenye letho ka ganōng, ha e sé go bua fèèla. Yuale ka eona khueli eo ea Tlakôla, a bōtsa Mareka, a re: Na bathō ba ile go kae? Mareka a re: Ba teng. Yuale a re: Ere ha le ba bōtsa, ba re, morèna oa bona ke mang? Ka re: Ke Moshueshue. A re go 'na: U thle u re go bona, ha ba re ke 'na, ke itse, ba nthatang ba thle ba thle moo ke leng teng. Gar'a bona (ke ba bōleletse botle) ba nkuthluileng ke Ratšiu le Ratetenene le Rahebe le Ramotlabani. Ha e le 'mōlōki ea neng a bōlōka litsuekere le liphatlo tsotle le ntho tsotle, lebitso ke Likobo, o shuéle a sa ka a lumela.

Eare ka khueli ea Tlakubèlè, ga thla baruti monere Mabille le monere Casalis, ba re: Kayenō u tsebe goba re éa etsa mokete oa likolobetso; yuale a re: Bāna bā ka, mokete o mogōlō o se o loile. Ba re go éena: Morèna, re uthluile, re se rea o etsa kapele. Yuale bomonere ba itse go Mareka: Oho tle, le uèna u re thlatse ka merapelo, re se re thla phakisa kapele Goba ba thlōge, yuale Moshueshue a re go Mareka: Oho mōnghali, u sé ke ua nthibella; bona le 'na ke na le bagōlō bā ka, 'me ba shuéle; yuale le 'na ke tšuanetse go shua; leha e le mokete ona o bōleloang e setse e le matšeliso ā ka. Ha re uthlua taba ena, re ne re na le Mafa, ra ba ra phakisa go laetsa Letsie gore a thle kapele.

Letsie a fèla a phakisa kapele. Eare ha a fitlile ka Mandaga, ga thoe, ke 'mōlelle lefa. Ea be e le ha go fitla setlogo sa ba thlang moketeng. Ke tsuile ka bitsa Moroke gore e thle e be paki; yuale ra fitla go Letsie. Ka re, a é'o bitsa Masōpha, e thle e be paki e mo pakelang.

Eare goba Masōpha a fitle, ka re go bona: Go itsoe, ke thle go bōlella Letsie gore lefa lotle la Moshueshue ke la gae. Ha e le tseo ke seng ke tšuaetse bo'manguan'ao, u sé ke ua kenya letsogo go tsona, Ha e le go likhaitseli tsa gao, u n'o nka u siele bo 'm'a bona.

Ka tsatsi la borarō, a re: Mareka, u fe bathō. Yuale ka talima kagotle, ka fumana liyo li le siéo, le bathō ba le siéo. Yuale ka re: Morèna, ntho tseo u li bōlelang ga li éo; bathō ga ba éo, liyo ga li éo. A fapana le lentsue leo, a bōela a re: Mareka ke re, u fe bathō.

Yuale ga uthlua Debora 'm'a Sekhonyana, a re: Mareka, u mamele, ke tseo u siuoang ka tsona. E le ha a bua la borarō.

Yuale ga netagala pōlelo ea Yesu, go letlogonolo ba fanang, goba ba thla gaugeloa. Yuale ke ketelo ea lentsue la gae; tsatsi la bone ga a sa na puo; yuale ka la botlanō a falla.

MAREKA NCHAKALA.

## Libini tsa Africa, V

Ra thlōga moo, yuale re thla leba nģa lebōéa, ra tsamaéa, ra feta mayoe a mathle a mofuta ao e kang goya a tsōfetse. Thōsō! Ra tlagela sekhuthlo se setalana, se atlametseng nģa lebōéa, se na le lifate tse ngata tsa bluegum ka nģa bophirimela. Matlo ha a theōsa le sekhuthlo, a bona liplasi tse ngata tse sikileng le molatsoana oo ke emeng motloliug oa oona.

Go thlōga moo ra khuthla le metlala, ra fitla thlung ea Le-German la rōna, ra tekeloa tafōle, ra lula, ra ya, empa liyo e ne e le 'tsa rōna ka nthlè go kofi le tee e leng tseo re li filoeng ke Le-German la rōna. Ha re ketile go ya, ra lumelisa motsualle oa rōna, ra feta. Ra nyōlōsa moepa o mogōlō. Yuale re se re fapōgile tsela eo re nyōlōgileng ka eona. Ra tsamaéa re tsuelipana le mophoko o mogōlō, re ntse re bona mabitso a ngoliloeng mathlapeng le magageng. Mabitso ao a bontša batsamai ba yualeka 'na gore go kile ga fitla

Leselinyana la 1 Pulunguana, 1891.

bathō tulong tseo. Le 'na ka ngola lebitso teng gore mang le mang ea thla tsamaéa teng a thle a bone gore Josia Semouse o kile a fitla mona ka tsatsi la 3. 5. 1891.

Goba re fete mophoko oo, ra tlagela motse oa Kapa; matlo a lekethla leke-leke-leke. Ka èma ka talima ka nģa bochabela, ka fumana lefātše le sé na bokhuthlo, ka retelegela nģa bophirimela, ka fumana leoathle le le yualo. Ekile goya e le lona le 'nōtši ka thlas'a lefātše, athe go sé yualo, e mpa e le bokhutšoanyane ba megōpōlo eā ka. Ke lemōgile gore e ne e sé ka boomō ha moapostola Pauluse a thla rèa Medditerranean Sea lebitso la leoathle le legōlō. Ke leoathle leo a le tsamaileng hangata maetong a gae. Moapostola Pauluse o n'a sa gōpōle gore go ka ba leoathle le leng ka nthlè go leo.

Ka nako ea botlanō, mantsibōéa, ra fitla khorong. Khoro ena e mpe, éa thella e okametsoe ke mayoe a tlephileng. Tsatsi la likèla re sa le golimō-limō thabeng. Ra 'na ra theōga buthle, re ntse re phōmōla, re tsamaéa re latlegeloa ke tsela. Re ne re na le lebone le le leng fèèla, ke lekanya gore le nkiloe go Le-German la rōna. Eitse ha re bona goba tsela e latlegetse ruri, e mong oa ba leng morao (re ne re kolokile) a gōeletsa: He! He! He! E reng mothō eo a leng kapele a gotetse lebone Lebone la gotetsoa, ra 'na ra itlheka buthle-buthle. Ke ne ke latetse mothō ea kapele. Ka thella pothlo! lethlapeng; ka bona mothō enoa yualeka nōga: Tsuiliti! Ga a sa mpōlella gore re latlegile. Ebile ke mo sala morao, ke khasa ka matsogo le mangole lethlapeng, ke lemōgile gore, ha nka leka go èma, ke thla ōa; hape ka go re, lethlapa le boreleli. Tsietsi ea tlaga, lebone la fèla. Re thla etsa yuang? Ra èma le monna-matheneng, thlekelele! E mong a phasōlōga: Banna, re bōlelloa kametla goba letsatsi la bofèlo lea thla, ga go sa le le leng ka nthlè go lena re leng go lona (botle ba tšèga). Ke ha ke thla bona gore Ba-Sōthō ba tiisitse ha ba re: "Lefu legōlō ke litšègo." E mong a re: Re gōeletseng, motl'omong re thla uthluoa ke monna ea lisang moru le ledamo la motse. Ereka ha re kolokile, ga simōlla ea ka pele: He! He! He! Thusang! Ra latela ka bongue: He! He! He! Thusang! Ra thea tsèbè, re eme gar'a lefifi la bonka-ntjana. Ra phéta ra gōeletsa, 'me ra uthlua lentsue le reng: Go lōkile. Ga isa-isa, ra bona leseli le thlang le khanya gōle gar'a lifate. Eitse re e-s'o bue, monna eo a bōtsa: Le bo mang? Ra itlhalōsa. Monna eo a re felegetsa, eitse ha re kèna motseng, a khuthla.

Ra tšèla thlatse, ra re: Hurrah! Hurrah! Re tsua lefifing, re kene leseling (botle ba éa fātše ke litšègo). Tlalōso ea pōlelo eo ke go re: Re tsua timelong, re kene legolimong. Ra fumana re se re lebeletsoe hagōlō ke ba setseng hāe.

Motsōtsōng oo, ha re le mona Kapa, re 'nile ra tsua hangata go éa etsa mekete metsaneng e ka mathōko go motse oa Kapa.

Ka tsatsi la 15 Motšeanong, re sa tsua fitla motsaneng o bitsoang Wellington, ga fitla motato o tsuang England, o reng re itōkise. Thabo e bile e khōlō. Gōsasa ra thlama, ra khuthla le metlala. Eitse goba re fitle Paarl, Mr Letty a rōmela motato Graaff-Reinet go ea neng a tšepisitsoe go amōgeloa setlopheng sa the African Choir. Ka sondaga mantsibōéa, ka bona Mr Letty a kèna thlung eā ka le lekhooa le leng. Lekhooa lena la kala go mpōtsa lipōtso tse ngatanyana tsena: Ntoa ea Le-Sōthō e ne e loane yuang? Ba-Sōthō ke sechaba se yuang ntoeng? Lefātše la Le-Sōthō le yuang? Daemane le gauda le silevera li teng? Ke 'nile ka li araba pōtso tsena. Ha re le motsaneng o bitsoang Stellenbosch, e le ka la 19 Motšeanong, ga fitla motato o reng: African Choir, kenang sekepeng gōsasa. E sa le gōsasa, ra koloka go éa Kapa. Ereka ha Stellenbosch e le motsana o leng gōyana le Kapa, re fitlile Kapa ka 9.30. Ra kala go rōmela mangolo a litumeliso metsualleng, le metato go ba tsebisa gore kayenō nako e fitlile.

(*Li sa thla.*) J. SEMOUSE.

Figure 3.1. *Libini tsa Africa, V*, part 5 of Semouse's report on the "African Singers" in *Leselinyana* (November 1, 1891).

quently, given the literary templates available to the black Christian elite, to narrate such a pilgrimage meant to submit to certain conventions, to depict the journey to England as some sort of march forward, toward some promised land. *Libini* contains traces of all these things and, in a sense, like Mofolo's novel *Moeti oa Bochabela*, published 16 years later (and even Semouse's life and untimely death in 1893), could be seen as a reenactment of Bunyan's *Pilgrim's Progress*, the predominant model available for such narratives of pilgrimage.

But beyond this, the object of a piece of writing such as *Libini* was not so

much the empire as the idea of a text itself or, rather, of what it means to produce literary meaning in a global context. It was the event of the pilgrimage itself and the narrative structure emerging from it that were to produce and reproduce the universal order of reason felt to be threatened by jingo imperialism
and white settler pressure. Thus the main point about Semouse's account is that
in the same breath as it seeks to represent in literary form the empire to the
colonial subject it also validates the entire Victorian epistemology by demonstrating the capability of the colonial subject to master the terms under which
the author-subjects and text-objects in such a universal order of knowing are
created. It is these ambiguities that account for the peculiar voice and delicate
balance between disillusion and awestruck submission to the white man's world,
between outrage over settler racial discrimination and admiration for metropolitan liberalism, throughout the series of articles. And these ambiguities make
for a kind of symbolic reversal far more complex than the one in "Leeto" and
for a style very much at variance with the "conditioned, almost formulaic" tone
Tim Couzens claims subsequent writers like Bokwe and Mzimba adopted in
their travel accounts.[39]

To begin with one of the more obvious features, one of these complexities
is evident in the proportions of the series, in a certain disparity between the
sections devoted to the voyage as such and those about the imperial center. As
the following synopsis illustrates, most of the account is concerned with the
South African part of the tour and the sea voyage to England. Less than a quarter is about England and London:

| I (July 1, 1891) | Kimberley |
|---|---|
| II (August 1, 1891) | Departure from Kimberley, Beaufort West, Worcester |
| III (September 1, 1891) | Wellington, African history, Paarl |
| IV (October 1, 1891) | Cape Town, Table Mountain, Sotho grammar, Sotho history |
| V (November 1, 1891) | Table Mountain |
| VI (December 1, 1981) | Sea voyage, Canary Islands, arrival in London, first impressions of English countryside, weather |
| VII (January 1, 1892) | Portsmouth, Bedford |
| unnumbered (March 1, 1892) | Glasgow, lawsuit |

The fact that so much of *Libini* is taken up by a description of the colony and
so little is said about the voyage and England had its cause, in part, in the trau-
matic turn of events in England. More fundamentally, however, the minor role
occupied by the parts on England is explained by the formidable dilemmas that
faced an author whose education, style of mission-fashioned Sesotho, and aesthetic approach may have equipped him to make sense of a place such as Kimberley but, as we shall see more clearly in the next section, ill-prepared him to
confront one of the core predicaments of late Victorian culture and conscious-

ness: how to represent figuratively a totality so vast, decentered, and modern that it was beyond the grasp of individual experience.

Another complexity in *Libini* lies in the way African power is narrated. Thus, although much of the text is marked by an attempt to reverse, in a sense, the usual trajectory of the colonizer to the colonies, one cannot quite overlook the precarious fragility that marks this endeavor and that time and again draws the author back into the literary codes and cadences of the colonizers. Take, for instance, the following passage about African history:

> Listen to what I explain to you. Africa, on the side of the Indian Ocean, from Natal to near the Portuguese Colony, was ruled by a king by the name of Chaka. He was the lion of that whole country. That country in the West was called Embo, its ruler had a son whose name was Tshawa. One day, Tshawa and a group of young men (Iboto) and young women went westwards (the young men carrying food with them). After they left, one of the men and a woman committed adultery. According to Zulu custom, the whole group, together with the girls, should have been killed. None was to be left out, it should have been a day of total destruction, all should have been killed because of only one person. As a result, the whole group feared to return home and carried on with their hunt, down the coast to what is now known as the Cape Colony. There the Iboto met with the Bushmen (Baroa). The Bushmen named the Iboto Xhosas. Those Bushmen came from the West. I don't know their origin, I am still searching for it. Their home country is the Cape; it is there that the whites, when they came to this country, found them. They fled to the North and East of Africa. What is known is that they, like all other African nations, descended from the son of Noah, Ham. . . . The Iboto formed itself into a nation, intermarried with the Bushmen and then called itself Xhosa. That is why we find in the Xhosa language words which are called "clicks" in the white man's language. These words make the Xhosa language more difficult than those of other nations. As a result of their intermarriage with the Bushmen, we find among the Xhosa reddish people with woven lined hair like that of the Bushmen.
>
> As for the Pondos (Ma-Potho) and Fingoes (Ma-Fengu) and Ndebeles (Ma-Tèbèlè), all those living in Lesotho, and the Bakotelis (Bakwena) who rule Lesotho today, their origin is rather the same. . . . In the beginning, the Basotho were many nations; Moshoeshoe, with mercy and cleverness and power, turned these small nations into one big nation called Basotho. Among all the African nations, the Basotho are known for their ingenuity and their military prowess.

This passage from part 3 of *Libini* is the summary of a lecture Semouse gave to a Wellington hotel owner who was curious about the ethnic background of the choristers. In its polite, didactic tone it is similar to the following quote from part 4, which describes an expedition to Table Mountain:

> We woke up early in the morning and found ten whites waiting for us. We went up toward the deep valley in the South of the city. The whites began to talk to me about the nations of Africa, but I hesitated to tell them. Then they

asked me to explain the African language. I then briefly told them the follow-ing: "Our African languages are far more difficult than yours. In most cases, where for the plural you put an *s* at the end of every word, Basotho and Nde-bele add one or several letters at the beginning or inside the word. Again, as you will see, part of the word remains unchanged.

> *Sesōthō*: Singular *mothō*; plural *bathō*
> *SiNdebele*: Singular *u-mutu*; plural *a-banto*
> *Sesotho*: Singular *khòmò*; plural *li-khōmō*
> *SiNdebele*: Singular *i-nkomo*; plural *i-zi-nkomo*

"This word shows that some time ago the Basotho and the Ndebele were one nation with a common language."

When we were done with [discussing] the languages, we began talking about the Gun War of 1880. Someone asked: "What were the Basotho and the Cape colony fighting over?" Someone else remarked: "The Basotho have been drinking too much liquor and then fought among themselves. The Cape government fought against the Basotho in order to maintain order by getting in between the fighting."

They all came down with laughter. After this I began to explain to them the full story of the war from beginning to end. I said: "The Basotho have ful-filled their manly duties. Every man must fight for himself."

What makes passages such as this interesting, is clearly not the "facts" them-selves, nor even the ethnic bias and the peculiar mix of biblical imagery and his-torical evidence. It is, rather, the precarious relationship between two forms of knowledge and two practices of naming. On one hand, one senses in these lines the effort to revert, as Anne McClintock has put it, the imperial rituals of bap-tism, the Western monopoly on denomination.[40] On the other hand, in his po-tentially dissident attempt to reclaim African history for black South African readers Semouse never quite seems to escape the role of the object, the ob-served and questioned "native" who furnishes data for the imperial archive. More to the point still, what we see in these remarks is an author who, while straining himself to open up the world to African interpretation, ends up repro-ducing within his narrative the existing relations of power and modes of trans-ferring knowledge. As hard as he tries to educate his white interlocutors about Sesotho grammar or Basotho history and even where this information may be more correct than anything else that might have been available about African society and culture to the average white Cape colonialist, Semouse stays within his prescribed role as the provider of knowledge, as the Other to be known, studied, and classified. In this sense, even where he attempts to divert to the pe-riphery the knowledge gained all he achieves is the addition of another card to the imperial filing cabinet.

Finally, there are the passages of *Libini* that are entirely given over to the de-scription of the landscape. There are not many such moments, a fact that may lead one to concur with J. M. Coetzee that among black writers, save for a few passages of neoclassical pastiche in the works of H. I. E. Dhlomo landscape description and poetry have no precedent in the vernacular.[41] Nevertheless, at certain moments we do find Semouse sitting on a hilltop surveying the landscape, examining the flora. Take, for example, Semouse's brief description of Paarl:

> The following day, after washing myself, I went up the mountain; midway my knees got tired and I sat down, and admired the country. Paarl is built at the foot of the mountain, on one side stretching towards the North . . . A river called Brede river runs towards the side of the city; there are also trees. When the sun rises on top of the Drakensberg, it fills the city with shining rays.

Somewhat similar in tone is a more extended passage on Beaufort West from part 2 of *Libini tsa Africa*:

> Beaufort West is a city built in a valley facing West; it is surrounded by two hills, one in the north, the other one in the south. Near the hill south of the village there is a big water dam. The village has many kinds of trees, some with edible fruit, others for shade and wood: There are vineyards, and water runs everywhere along the sides of the streets. The inhabitants of Beaufort West are merciful people, they speak nicely with people. There are many Boers, but not farm Boers from the Orange Free State. They are French by birth. These French were driven out of France by Louis XIV.

Clearly, vistas such these are not quite the same as those of the European picturesque mode of landscape writing—no doubt, as Coetzee's work has demonstrated, one of the "great intellectual schemas, through which South Africa has been thought by Europe."[42] For instance, one of the things that distinguishes Semouse's writing from, say, earlier examples of European landscape writing such as William Burchell's *Travels into the Interior of Southern Africa* (1822) is the absence of the lone-observer-on-a-hilltop stance. Although Semouse surveys the scene from above, the landscape does not present itself as empty and, hence, there is not the urge white writers felt so pressingly to fill this emptiness with some emotional content or meaning.[43] Not only is the act of inspection presented in an almost antiheroic, casual fashion, as one of several rather mundane things going on in and around the writer's body (morning hygiene, aching knees), but also Semouse's landscapes are already bustling with activity and the observant position does not so much serve to create a phenomenological distance between a viewer and the landscape as it consists in gauging, as it were, the landscape's usefulness, its profoundly man-made character. Examining the landscape does not arouse in Semouse a sense of wonderment vis-à-vis a nature of majestic grandeur. Rather, he scales the landscape down to a measure of human usability. Trees are not works of art; they provide fruit, shade, and/or timber. And all the morning light does is shine on Paarl.

It is tempting to see a parallel here between this kind of matter-of-fact description and the thinness of landscape writing Coetzee has found in Afrikaans. The very notion of a "nature," Coetzee argues, "somehow transcending the subjection of the land to laws of ownership belongs to a social class no longer relying directly on agriculture for its livelihood, and therefore to a more economically differentiated society." Afrikaans poetry is thus characterized by "the quick notation of telling particulars" rather than by full-scale exposition, and ipso facto, Coetzee believes, the sketch is the appropriate descriptive form "for a society with considerable uniformity of background."[44] However, as his biography and a piece such as "Leeto" reveal, the countryside by the 1880s was but a faint memory in Semouse's life, one that only existed in a strangely inverted kind of correlation with the city. "Leeto," it would seem, does not enable recollection. It records a moment of amnesia: Semouse forgets Lovedale. The country simply fades against the looming presence of the diamond city. But if the disappearance of the country, both figuratively and in real terms, was the prerequisite of the global city, how was one to grasp and write this new global reality? How could a place such as London be described? And, as a corollary to this, how was one to conceive of the metropolis as the quintessential space of the modern experience? These were some of the key questions that preoccupied the imagination of colonizers and colonized alike.

### The Blind City: London and Semouse's Silence

Nineteenth-century London, contrary to the image of nineteenth-century Britain as the world's leading industrial economy, was not an industrial city. As Gareth Stedman Jones's classic study of the city illustrates, London was a major port city, an administrative center, and the commercial and financial hub of the world market. As such it remained largely apart from the textile mills, iron foundries, and coal mines of England's industrial north.[45] This feature led not only to the quite distinct forms of proletarian culture and consciousness that are the focus of Jones's book but possibly also to a specific form of literature. But discussion of this is not my objective here. For the problem here, as in the other types of global fictions examined in this book, is not what they describe but rather how the object of description comes to be constituted by the way in which it is described. The issue, then, is not London as it was but London as it was imagined by various actors such as Western intellectuals, London dockworkers, and black South African visitors.

To begin with the former, late Victorian writers such as George Robert Gissing, Henry James, and Joseph Conrad were preeminently preoccupied with the city even where the plot and characters of their work bear but a superficial relationship to the urban environment of the 1890s. In fact, by the late nineteenth century the implicit presence of the city in everyday social life had become so much taken for granted that late Victorian novelists and poets, like Baudelaire earlier, seem to have seen the city as through an "agitated veil." The urban world had become so total, its effect on every facet of social life so inescapable, that for James, for instance, London was simply "on the whole the most possible form of life" and "the most complete compendium of the world." But this view of the city as the quintessential modern form of social totality was equally indebted to and in part also stood in a tense relationship with an intellectual tradition and a discourse in which the opposition between the city and the country symbolically represented the radical transformation of nineteenth-century British society. As Raymond Williams's magisterial *The Country and the City* has shown, throughout the early nineteenth century a vastly idealized countryside had represented a paradise lost, a mythic past, while the city was seen as the preeminent symbol of a degraded present.[46] Although this dichotomy continued to permeate late Victorian letters and even though the popularity of the pseudo-pastoral imagination grew in proportion to the breakdown of the divisions between rural and urban Britain, the writers of this period found it increasingly difficult to maintain a vision of both worlds as distinct realities that could be grasped while remaining within the literary canon.

The country, for instance, enters into what Williams calls "an uneasy contract, in language, with another interest and another sensibility," with an author whose relationship with and knowledge of a rural community are no longer quite part of the community being known.[47] Writers such as George Eliot, for instance, transferred the idea of a valuing society to the past. But as Williams aptly states, by placing value in the past and by withdrawing from any full response to an existing society Eliot was left with "a set of personal relationships and of intellectual and moral insights in a history that for all valuing purposes has, disastrously, ended."[48] The aesthetics on which this retrospective gaze is based, as the reader will recognize, is of course the same as that of the panorama and the genre. It is one of the means through which modernity, from an imaginary position at the end of a process, looks upon itself as historical and outdated.

The modern urban world, for its part, is no less elusive. Although until well into the last decades of the Victorian age the image of the modern world, and here especially the city, was mediated by reference to "a condition imagined out of a landscape and a selective observation and memory," that mediation quite literally began to lose the ground on which it stood. For as the cities grew in scale and complexity, the desire "to see the true city" that had given rise to the dioramas and panoramas of the early 1800s gave way to a dramatically increased sense of chaos and urgency, to a view of the city as the unknown and, ultimately, the unknowable. It was a sense of the modern world that, as U. C. Knoepflmacher observed, at times assumed "almost schizophrenic dimensions."[49] Whereas many of the earlier writers were hoping for the rift between the old rural and the modern urban worlds to heal, their late Victorian counterparts found it ever more difficult to figuratively picture a reality so Babylonian as the modern metropolis. With the country simply having vanished, a vantage point of the literary imagination—Dickens's "rhetorical totalising view from outside"[50]—from which the city might be inspected had disappeared. The city became a space that could no longer be described in its imaginary opposition to the country.

Likewise, as the structure of these urban agglomerations changed from the old European *civitas* built around church, market square, and feudal court to something rather like a node in the giant net spun by monopoly capital, cities like London ceased to be something to be understood solely from within the uniquely British national context. Its coordinates rested elsewhere, in the vastly expanded global networks of empire and world trade. The schizophrenic dimensions, then, that the late Victorian writers began to feel were an expression of the complete disconnection from older regimes of social and spatial order that were only just beginning to be replaced by other, dimly perceived types of linkages. Henry James may have been one of the intellectuals keenly aware of this when, early in his career, he wrote that "London talks of everything in the world," because "it has taken everything in the world to make London up."[51]

To be sure, this heightened sense of globality did not fundamentally alter late Victorian writers' unfaltering belief in the centrality of London and the empire. And thus the major problem that confronted writers with even such a developed sense of the global dimensions of everyday British life as James or Conrad was to invent not only a new language to represent this new totality but also, more important, a language that, even as it wrestled with the hybridity of the metropolitan social sphere, did not in principle challenge the exercising authority of some overseeing gaze, in fact, of authorship as such. One of the answers was, as is well-known, the detective story. G. K. Chesterton, saw the city as "something wild and obvious" in which the chimney pots would appear like poetic objects to later generations just as mountain peaks had appeared to primeval man and lampposts would seem as old and natural as the trees. But while nature was "a chaos of unconscious forces," he tells us, "a city is a chaos of conscious ones." And it is here that, for Chesterton, the city assumes the function of a language, a web of meanings, encoded and to be decoded systematically. "The crest of the flower or the pattern of the lichen," he wrote, "may or may not be significant symbols. But there is no stone in the street and no brick in the wall that is not actually a deliberate symbol—a message from some man, as if it were a telegram or a post card."[52]

The point here is that while for Chesterton the city contains a "message," a semantic content that the writer must extract from the stones and bricks, at the same time the confidence in him and other writers that there is a subject, an author, capable of penetrating this web of signs and who will, in the terms of classical epistemology and aesthetics, separate appearance from essence, *Wesen* from *Erscheinung*, begins to wane. Thus (although it is not, strictly speaking, a work of the late Victorian age) in Conrad's *The Secret Agent* (1907), the omniscient assistant commissioner succeeds in solving the riddle of the anarchist bomb attack and protecting the order that Vladimir wants to destroy. But the assistant commissioner is unable to understand the reasons for Winnie Verloc's suicide. Although at the surface the totality remains decodable and known, the "darkness" that buries "five millions of lives" ultimately remains impenetrable.

The fissures that we see opening up in a work such as this between structure and experience, code and meaning, authorial ego and its Other led to another figurative procedure to express the omnipresent and impenetrable city. It is a figure that Fredric Jameson has called "monadic relativism"[53] and which Thomas Hardy appears to have had a sense of when he wrote in 1887 that London "appears not to *see itself.* Each individual is conscious of *himself,* but nobody conscious of themselves collectively."[54] What then results from this lack of collective purpose, following Jameson, is an attempt to restructure the work of art by accommodating content that must radically resist artistic figuration. In searching for the literary means to express the interpenetration of middle-class lives and the colonial network, a sense begins to take shape in these works of each consciousness being a closed world and of the social totality being the coexistence of these sealed subjective worlds.

Yet aside from this monadic consciousness there was also present toward the end of the nineteenth century an alternative concept. Raymond Williams, from whom I have taken Hardy's statement, has argued that in writers such as H. G. Wells a new consciousness, a "sense of possibility," emerged through which the cities—and within them the new organizations of the labor movement and the new institutions of education and democracy—began to lose their blindness and foresee the contours of a different society.[55] At the same time, Williams is crucially aware that this project—the liberation of the metropolitan gaze from its walled-in state—remains an unfinished one to this day. And although many now expect the completion of this project to be a matter of a politics in which the possibility of London lies as much in the future of Johannesburg as it does in the well-being of its own immigrant population and in which New York may (and indeed must) be able to give some answers at least to the questions being asked in places such as poverty-stricken Ciskei, the new metropolis, the global ecumene, for Josiah Semouse no less than fin-de-siècle English writers was hard to conceive.

This is one of the reasons why the text of *Libini* that deals with England and London occupies but a brief section of part 6 and a few sentences of the rather short part 7. In part 6, for example, Semouse first describes the arrival of the choir in England and the reactions of the crowds waiting outside the church to inspect the visitors through "binoculars" (*liferkekere*)—a taste of things to come and, like Charlotte Manye's opening statement quoted at the beginning of chapter 1, a fascinating illustration of the African reading of imperial racist ideology:

> Some said: Look at their short hair, as though they have shaved, their eyes are black and beautiful, they have mouths and noses like people.[56]

His humanity and that of his fellow Africans established, Semouse then goes on to discuss the reversed seasons in the two hemispheres before he finally closes the piece with a note on London:

> London is a very big place, I have never experienced its end, I will explain it when I have seen where it ends and have thoroughly seen its end.[57]

But this attempt to see London thoroughly never quite materializes. Part 7 of *Libini*, written in Bradford in mid-September 1891, is surprisingly laconic. Barely five paragraphs long, the column mentions a performance in Portsmouth, discusses a reception hosted there by the Duke of Connaught (who is described as being of "reddish color" and as living "like soldiers, not like kings or rulers"), and dwells for a sentence or two on the smoke-clouded towns, cotton mills, and steel works of Yorkshire before it ends abruptly on the following note of despair:

> All in all, I can say the things which I can see in this town are big and numerous, if I were to try to explain them, I would go mad.[58]

Here Semouse's account ends. Less than a month later, the madness that he had dreaded was to turn into reality when the whole odyssey ended in a fiasco. Semouse may have intuitively sensed the looming catastrophe and was perhaps too preoccupied to think much further about his *Leselinyana* assignment. We do not know. What is clear, however, is that this was a madness different from the one Semouse had expected, one that originated from within the social relations that prevailed in British towns and that Semouse, after all, may have not have been able to explain. But above all, it was a madness that ultimately silenced him *as an author* in the true sense of the word, as a modern subject whose identity was formed in direct confrontation with a world rendered in and as a text. To repeat, the point here is not the reduced language or the aesthetic paucity of Semouse's description of the metropolis but the absence of a language, of a panoramic vision, in the first place. Thus, in one sense, Semouse's inability to produce a narrative of the city, to see London "thoroughly," may be due to the failure of the tour to realize its objective of making the center see the periphery in the light of its own premises of universal reason. In another sense, however, Semouse could not experience London's end—cognitively map the city, as Fredric Jameson might say—because his encounter with the city worked from quite a different premise, from that of the colonial subject petitioning the imperial power. It was the nature of the tour, then, its character as a pilgrimage, that prevented Semouse from seeing London, from penetrating the glittering surface of its public spaces and "dream houses" of global power.[59]

After the disastrous end of the tour, Semouse's literary career was not quite over. Shortly after his return to South Africa and only months before his untimely death, there appeared an epilogue in *Leselinyana* titled "Leeto la ho khutlela Africa" (The journey back to Africa). It was Semouse's last piece of writing, and in it he spells out the details of Balmer's fraudulent behavior, his (Semouse's) rescue through James Stewart, and the stopovers at Madeira and the Cape Verde Islands. All of this is told in a somewhat listless tone, but then, at the very end, we find Semouse back on firm literary ground—the language and pastoral symbolism of the Bible:

> The favor and grace done by Dr. Stewart to the Singers of Africa is the biggest and will never be forgotten by the elders and friends of the African

Choir. Had it not been for Dr. Stewart, we would have been scattered like sheep without a shepherd.[60]

The contradiction between the passage quoted and Semouse's earlier silence about London is less surprising than it may seem. The tour, remember, was to be a pilgrimage to the source of light, the all-seeing eye, the very conscience and *theoria* of the world. Consequently, Semouse's diary offers no direct indication that the journey had awakened in him Conrad's notion that Europe "also has been one of the dark places on the earth" and that, as Frantz Fanon was to charge much later, "Europe is literally the creation of the Third World.[61] Rather, Semouse's was a journey into the heart of empire and, above all, one that was to yield and reveal a common narrative, a common history, a universal order of knowledge. Semouse was literally writing his way into the epistemic center, but once he is in it, that history can no longer be written, or only at the price of madness. What we see, then, in this early example of the African global imagination is an epistemological order in which the colonizer can panoptically see the "native," but the "native" cannot see himself.

Do we, then, conclude from all this that the process of modernization Josiah Semouse so eagerly embraced was a failed one? Was the emergent modernism of the late Victorian age with its celebration of dislocation and distance just another form of Eurocentrism that automatically condemns alternate ways of looking at the city as deficient? If, following Raymond Williams, one of the key cultural factors of the modernist shift is the emergence of new immigrant communities—communities whose only bond is their own practices—and if, as we have seen, Josiah Semouse's views of England and London lack any of the formal characteristics commonly associated with modernism (alienation instead of identification, an emphasis on formal revision rather than stable content, and so on), how do we interpret Semouse's silence?[62] The problem with metropolitan interpretations of its own modernisms as universals is perhaps not so much, as Williams seems to suggest, that it marginalizes evolving artistic traditions elsewhere as it fails to recognize the specific conditions under which writers from the periphery could not conceive of modernity other than as a move away from the narrow world of colonial oppression, racism, and slavery toward some more general and ultimately more egalitarian form of community.

And thus, I think, there was also in Semouse's text a recognition, barely discernible, of what Williams has called the "connecting process," a process, he hoped, that would pierce the "alienating screens of foreignness and race" and that would ultimately come to be seen as a common history.[63] And so we can, perhaps, also sense in Semouse's silence the first omen of a growing vigilance that this history was no longer going to be written from one center but from many different places.

# 4

## "Spectatorial Lust"

### Spectacle and the Crisis
### of Imperial Knowledge

So far I have been concerned with how Africa and Europe invented each other in various complex ways and by virtue of a number of literary forms, such as autobiography and travel writing. In this mirror dance, I argued, notions of home, person, time, and space were mediated through a series of fictional genres in which their authors' identity, social position, and historical location were defined in terms of each other's foreignness. As a result of this cross-coding and play of mimicry, however, colonizers and colonized often ended up as rather strange bedfellows, if not occupying the same social grounds being held captive by parallel aesthetic regimes, similar orders of knowledge. At the same time, it became clear how this intermingling of scripts and perspectives, for the African players in this global drama, entailed a whole series of paradoxes and ambiguities—ambiguities that not only compelled the South African musicians to travel to Europe in the first place but also intensified as the tour wore on.

The purpose of this chapter is to demonstrate how the subdued rhetoric of Semouse's *Leselinyana* articles and the guarded tone of the singers' autobiographies concealed a much tenser engagement with Europe, empire, and modernity, the focal point of which was the shows of the African Choir themselves. As I will attempt to show, the main arenas of the conflicted construction of the metropolis and the colony were the performances and, within them, the peculiar logic at the very heart of late Victorian society: the spectacle of the commodity.

## "The Music of Africa"

Before we examine some of the theoretical implications of this logic and in order to provide a textual basis for this examination, let me quote an extended passage from "The Music of Africa," a review of a concert given by the African Choir in England similar to the one shown in figure 4.1. Written by one E. Gowing Scopes, the text appeared in the *Ludgate Monthly*, a rather obscure London magazine located on the liberal end of Britain's political spectrum. In the middle of Scopes's article, the reviewer offers a detailed list of the pieces performed by the choir[1]:

"Ulo Tixo Mkulu," is the first music known to have been sung by Christian Kaffirs, and the original composition of Mtsikana, the first convert amongst the Amaxosa tribe.

"Singame wele" [We are twins], is a song and dance. The natives are exceedingly fond of singing and dancing, and this item is typical of how they spontaneously, and at any time, commence their amusements. The lead is generally taken by a bass voice, but is never begun in exactly the same way.

The choir sing a short story in the Kaffir language, giving a striking illustration of the clicks used in the native tongue. It is adapted to the music of Schumann's "Merry Peasant."

The typical Kaffir wedding song is purely native, and the harmonies have not been, in any way Europeanized; it is sung at the wedding feast by the friends of the bridegroom. The bride, whose sobs can be heard amid the general rejoicing, is finally led away by two of the guests to her husband's "mgwelo" which awaits her. At some of the marriages the festivities are kept up days and nights without cessation.

"Mgwelo engena tentyi" is a wayside Kaffir song and dance. When traveling by bullock waggon in Africa, the oxen are unyoked at intervals and allowed to graze and rest, or are outspanned—as the local term has it. This scene is supposed to take place when the Kaffirs are seated round their fires, awaiting the time for inspanning, whilst the oxen are grazing and the skoff is boiling in the "pot."

"Lutukela" is a duet, composed by a Kaffir. The style of this piece is very popular amongst the natives, they are fond of accompanying solos with their voices, and, as a rule, take the parts very clearly, without any training whatever.

Kaffirs are very fond of mimicry, and are always ready to pick up anything to imitate. An item entitled the "Kaffir Travesty," is a purely Kaffir song, and is their idea of the English street cry of "Hot Cross Buns!" Its origin is doubtful.

"Molokoda" means good-bye. The natives of South Africa, when travelling in parties, have a singular habit of singing—keeping time to the melody with their feet. Standing upon a hill, you can hear their peculiar chant when the band is miles away. "Molokoda" is a representation of the effect produced by the gradual approach and disappearance of one of these parties, who have just left their kraals to go into the towns in search of employment. Perfect stillness, on the part of the audience, is necessary during the singing of this piece.

# GRAND CONCERT

### BY THE

## AFRICAN NATIVE CHOIR.

### ᴘᴿᴼᴳᴿᴬᴹᴹᴱ

#### Part First.

| | | |
|---|---|---|
| 1. | "INTLABA-MKOSI" | Kaffir |
| 2. | "Q Qa Qa Qa," | Kaffir |

A short piece in the Kaffir tongue adapted to the music of Schumann's "Merry Peasant" giving a striking illustration of the *clicks* used in the native language. These *clicks* are considered to be the most charming part of the "*taal*" perhaps because of their being so difficult to acquire by Europeans.

| | | |
|---|---|---|
| 3. | PART SONG | English |
| 4. | "ULO TIXO MKULU" | Kaffir |

This is the first piece of music known to have been sung by Christian Kaffirs. The words and music are the original composition of Ntsikana, the first convert among the Amaxosa tribe.

| | | |
|---|---|---|
| 5. | "CHILDREN ASLEEP" | English |
| 6. | "MOTJIEVERAKATANG" | Dutch-Hottentot |

(A HUMOROUS HOTTENTOT SONG.)

This song is supposed to be a passage at arms between a native woman, who is very fond of talking, and some of her people who are taunting her for her propensity to chatter so incessantly.

| | | |
|---|---|---|
| 7. | SELECTION | English |
| 8. | "THE LORD'S PRAYER." | English |

This number is given by request. When the prayer was sung by the choir before the Queen, Her Majesty was greatly affected.

#### ◄ Part Second. ►

| | | |
|---|---|---|
| 9. | SELECTION | Kaffir |
| 10. | "MOLO-KE-DA" | Kaffir |

The natives of South Africa, when traveling in parties, have a singular habit of singing—keeping time to the melody with their feet. Standing upon a hill, you can hear their peculiar chant when the band is miles away.

*Molokeda* is a representation of the effect produced by the gradual approach and disappearance of one of these parties, who have just left their *Kraals* to go into the towns in search of employment.

Perfect stillness is kindly requested during the singing of this piece.

| | | | |
|---|---|---|---|
| 11. | Quintette, | "ON THE MOUNTAIN." | English |
| 12. | | "TYPICAL WEDDING SONG." | Kaffir |

The song is purely Native, and the harmonies have not been in any way Europeanized; it is sung at the Wedding Feast by the friends of the Bridegroom. The Bride, whose sobs can be heard amid the general rejoicing, is finally led away by two of the guests to her husband's *mowelo* which awaits her. At some of the marriages the festivities are kept up days and nights without cessation.

| | | |
|---|---|---|
| 13. | "LUTUKELA" | Kaffir |
| 14. | "SEND THE LIGHT." | English |

The words and music of this piece were composed expressly for the European tour of the African Choir, by gentlemen in South Africa who were wishful the enterprise should be a success.

| | | |
|---|---|---|
| 15. | "ONWARD CHRISTIAN SOLDIERS" | Kaffir and English |

Figure 4.1. Program of African Choir (Bernth Lindfors).

"On the Mountain" is a quintette. It was requested that the choir should give a little more English in the programme; this quintette has, therefore, been introduced in response to this request, and to please those who are so fond of their mother tongue.

"Lovedale" is a Kaffir solo with vocal accompaniment. It is another composition of a Kaffir, and describes the beauties of the country surrounding Lovedale College, Cape Colony, where seven of the choir were educated. It is also another illustration of the native fondness for vocally accompanied solos.

"Does anybody here know the Big Baboon?" is a solo and chorus. It was specially composed for the African Native Choir by James Hyde, Esq., King

Williamstown (one of the, if not the first musician in South Africa), after he had attended one of their concerts given in his town.

"Africa" is a Kaffir quartette. The London *Times*, in criticising the African Choir Concert, said—"A quartette, or rather a solo accompanied by three voices, bore so close a resemblance to Rossini's 'Cujus animam' that it is difficult to accept it as a specimen of native music at all." But this quartette is the composition of a Kaffir who had never heard of Rossini or his "Stabat Mater," and did not dream that such a selection as "Cujus animam" was in existence. It is descriptive of how the natives hum some portions of their songs.

"Good News" is another English piece, but one given in true Kaffir style.

"Send the Light" is a solo and chorus, the words and music having been composed expressly for the European tour of the African Choir, by gentlemen in South Africa who were wishful the enterprise should be a success.

Quaint? The product of a rather insignificant literary mind in an obscure magazine? Perhaps. But there is a good deal more to this piece, for a whole range of themes run through this inventory of songs whose relevance to the subject matter of this chapter may not be immediately apparent. Among other things, the reviewer reproduces typical Victorian stereotypes such as those of Africans' mimetic capabilities and their innate inability to perform higher forms of cognition. And, like the European public generally, he confuses African music and the songs of America's black slaves such as "Good News." More important than these slurs and glitches, however, is the list of song titles itself, its cataloglike character and the tone of supposed objectivity suggesting a familiarity with a series of curious items and, beyond this, a mastery of a supreme organon of global knowledge.

But the passage quoted also provides a useful overture to another fundamental aspect of the global imagination that I want to explore in this chapter. I am interested in spectacle and display as attempts to resolve the very uncertainties of late-nineteenth-century English intellectuals and members of the African middle class, accounting for these uncertainties in terms of the new scientific discoveries that unsettled existing mechanical worldviews but also in relation to the colonial encounter itself and the ambiguities it entails of sex, gender, and commodity exchange across cultural lines. What I mean will become clearer when we consider the context in which this document of late Victorian global gnosis and curiosity appears. For Scopes's list is framed by reflections of a kind not uncommon in late Victorian society, reflections about the moral foundations of the imperial order and, beneath these, about the ever more precarious relationship among order, power, and knowledge. "Let an African explorer or novelist," the *Ludgate Monthly* article begins, "Stanley or Haggard will do, write up the details, in gory language, of some sickening barbaric custom, and it will produce upon the civilized mind a sense of shuddering thankfulness that we have risen above the ignorance of these native tribes. Perhaps we have."

In our present highly cultivated state we cover ourselves with clothes, excepting only our handsome faces; walk upon level pavements that the lower classes have laid down for us, and partake of our meals from clean plates, on the strict understanding we do not put our knives to our mouths. Most families keep servants to cook and bring in the meals—it is not decent to do this sort of thing for one's self. The servants, of course, have to feed without assistance, but that cannot be helped, as it is impossible for all to be highly civilized at once. . . .

There are some weak-minded individuals who have raised the very absurd question as to whether a system of warfare that places a thousand men in an iron boat in order that they may be immediately afterwards blown into fragments by the kindly aid of a torpedo, is quite the best way of feeding the fishes or justifying civilization; in fact, whether it is a very great improvement upon some of the pastimes of barbarism from which we shrink with horror. But such reasoning as this is childish and opposed in principle to the best interests of the country. Civilization towers high above these effeminate thoughts.

The ironic tone in this passage echoes, of course, the nineteenth-century disaffection with the results of industrialization and the class antagonisms of Victorian society. At the same time, it illustrates that in the Victorian imagination domesticity, the class structure of British society, and civilization all add up to the same thing. Beyond this, the tone of the paragraphs indicates that the writer is merely introducing a rhetoric device to create a contrast with what then follows. For Scopes goes on to relate a report he had read in a Cape newspaper about a "smelling out" ceremony "among some native tribe up the country" in the course of which a young girl, having been smelled out by the medicine man of the tribe as the evildoer, was "put to death by perforating her body with seventeen assegais." And so our author promptly asks himself whether "Rider Haggardism," after all, was not more than mere fiction and missionary work more than a need of the past. But it is not long before the initial doubts about his own society return:

Is there nothing at home that compares with this strange custom? Are there not men among us given to "smelling out" their fellows, and, under the pretext of some social offence, so embittering their victims' best friends that they stab and stab again with a virulence more deadly than poisoned steel? But it is a civilized medicine man, it is the assegai of the tongue and public press.

All these grave concerns, our author goes on to state, were brought home to him on a "peaceful, Lancashire country town Sunday" during a dinner table conversation with choir director Letty that pressed on him the notion that the answer to all his doubts was knowledge. And thus, after more causerie and all manner of disparaging anecdotes about the Boers and the annexation of the Transvaal, Scopes's article launches into the descriptive part quoted previously. The piece ends on a note of optimism which must be read as a well-intentioned liberal attempt to rescue the mid-Victorian civilizing mission in view of the feverish, jingoist climate of the 1890s. Scopes concludes:

The African Choir constitute a living band of witnesses as to the power of Christian civilization on the raw material of African humanity. . . . The better one knows these men and women the narrower seems to be the gulf between our high civilization and the low barbaric life which they are supposed to represent.

In a broader perspective, Scopes's call for the maximization of knowledge must also be seen within the context of the looming epistemological and moral crisis of fin-de-siècle Europe. It was voiced precisely at the time when late Victorian society was about to lose its absolute confidence in the possibility of positive knowledge. Artists in the 1890s were feeling increasingly uncomfortable with the idea of the imitation of nature as the exclusive basis of modern aesthetic practice while new disciplines such as thermodynamics dismantled comprehensive mechanical worldviews, in turn raising serious doubts about the knowability of the world. As a result, entropy, the gradual disintegration of closed systems into increasing disorder, became a metaphor for the random and arbitrary character of all knowledge and even of social life itself.[2] Yet for many late Victorians, as Thomas Richards has shown, what the entropy of the universe really meant was the end of the British Empire.[3] As early as 1884, in a lecture aptly titled "The Storm-Cloud of the Nineteenth Century," none other than John Ruskin had warned of a storm gathering over the heads of Britons, a menace that would bring about not so much the sudden death of empire as its slow entropy in an amorphous flow of events governed by the laws of chance and statistics, by a process which he called "order by fluctuation." "The empire of England," Ruskin closed his lecture, "on which formerly the sun never set, has become one on which he never rises."

As much as thermodynamics may have shattered the belief in the possibility of a comprehensive system of knowledge, control over knowledge continued to be the single most widely believed in foundation of modern society and, in fact, of the state itself. Knowledge was inconceivable without the state just as the question of the state was a question of knowledge. In short, as Richards puts it, "the integrity of the channels of external communication was essential to the welfare of the empire."[4] Beyond this, the transformation of the public sphere of the eighteenth century into a site of and for the spectacle was the primary process that redefined the relationship between power and knowledge. It was through a network of public spaces and events like museums, world fairs, and concerts that the disjointed data were to be reordered and the waning confidence in some notion of an overarching order of things rekindled. The center of all these rituals of imperial order, however, was the commodity and, through it, a new way of looking at the world. It is this strange osmosis of the commodity and the gaze that we must examine first.

### The Organization of the View

Much research has been undertaken in recent years to unravel the logic and historical genesis of consumer society. Expanding on Marx's notion of commodity fetishism, Benjamin's concept of the wish-image, and other critical approaches to capitalist commodity production, scholars have demonstrated that modern consumer society is essentially a social order in which the commodity becomes, as Jean Baudrillard puts it, "a total *medium*," "a *system of communication* administering all social exchange."[5] What characterizes consumer society is how objects come to occupy social life in such a way that the whole society is turned into a stage for the fictions it has created for its commodities. In short, to use Guy Debord's famous formulation, modern capitalist society is a "society of the spectacle," an order that concentrates all attention, all consciousness, on the act of seeing the commodity.[6]

The roots of this society lie deep in the nineteenth century. Almost 100 years before the countries of advanced capitalism came to be regarded as consumer societies, the Great Exhibition of the Industry of All Nations at London's Crystal Palace in 1851 had inaugurated the culture of consumerism. Long before the economies of the West had begun to produce a vast surplus of goods, this first world fair had illustrated the fact that spectacle and capitalism, aesthetics and production, had become indivisible. As Thomas Richards writes, it is by the second half of the nineteenth century that the representation of the commodity had become an integral component of production. The spectacle of the commodity was no longer the distorted *mirror* of production; it was the capitalist *mode* of production. In other words, what the Crystal Palace exhibit prefigured was an economic regime that produces "signs, signs taken for wonders, signs signifying consumption."[7] And in doing so, Thomas goes on to state, the exhibition further formulated the foundations of a semiotics of the commodity spectacle. It laid down the liturgical rules (Thomas himself lists several such principles: for instance, an autonomous iconography for the object, the figuration of a consuming subject, the invention of the myth of the abundant society, and others) by which the commodity was to be worshiped. The exact details of this new semiotics of the commodity spectacle shall occupy us further in subsequent chapters. Of more immediate concern to me here are two things. First, I am interested in the imperial dimension of these "giant new rituals of self-congratulation," as Eric J. Hobsbawm calls them.[8] Second, I want to show how the production of signs as a global mode of production depended on a parallel, drawn-out process of the production of racial differences and mirror images in a broad range of related spectacles and performance genres.

Four decades after the Great Exhibition world fairs had expanded on an unprecedented scale, and by the time the Chicago fair of 1893 opened its gates these spectacles had become more than celebrations of bourgeois power and "sites of pilgrimages to the commodity fetish."[9] World fairs in the age of empire turned into major platforms of the global imagination in which the ideas of empire, progress, and the commodity all appeared rolled into one. Total events of this sort were predicated upon carefully orchestrated stagings of spaces, actors, and goods that spoke not so much of the world as it is as of how the West wished to perceive it.[10] Thus the architectural design and floor plans portrayed a humanity divided by "race"—a concept as deeply instilled in popular Western consciousness as that of "progress"—and a world in which nations occupied fixed places determined by the host country. The layout of the Turkish quarter at the Universal Exposition of 1867 in Paris, to take but one representative example, was deliberately irregular to create an "authentic" and "picturesque appearance" that was in line with Western fantasies about the Orient.[11]

The goods on display, for their part, were the tangible expression of empire as an organized system of manufactured objects rather than a set of social relations based upon domination and submission. Just as Mungo Park and his sponsors had envisaged it, commodities were to be bearers of the "civilizing mission," magically dissolving boundaries and local identities all by themselves. Along with cloth, mirrors, and clocks it was soap in particular that was thought to be some kind of "sesame," yielding untold treasures and opening up vast empires: both spiritual ones in which outer cleanliness would signal a person's inner purity and worldlier ones in which a healthy social body—like "national hygiene" a key euphemism for class hierarchy—was taken to be a consequence of personal hygiene. Furthermore, soap was also the key to a whole new form of racist ideology that Anne McClintock calls "commodity racism."[12] Soap staged a global drama in which the Victorian home became the site for the production of racial difference and fantasies of universal progress, while the colonial space in turn became domesticated.

Goods of non-Western origin were pressed into service as part of a unitary landscape of discourse and practice, creating what Carol Breckenridge has called a "Victorian ecumene," a new object-centered mythology of British global power. "More particularly, as Breckenridge's analysis of Indian artifacts at world fairs and other types of colonial collections nicely demonstrates, this new ecumene entailed more than a transformation of visual culture and a disciplining of the popular gaze. It also staged a whole typology and history of goods, technologies, and human bodies in which the colonies were said to represent an aesthetically imposing yet outdated phase of universal evolution. Contrasting, for instance, the Indian and the U.S. courts at the Crystal Palace exhibit, Breckenridge shows how the Indian pavilion featured sumptuary technologies associated with feudal power—artisanal products such as weapons, jewels, and royal paraphernalia. The display of these objects foregrounded the human body in suggesting that the royal body that used them *was* the body politic rather than a private reality. The U.S. display, by contrast, with its Morse telegraph, surgical instruments, and other implements highlighted production and associated aesthetic technologies of practicality that required but did not directly relate to the human body. By elevating objects to ends in themselves, the U.S. exhibit thus implicitly argued for a more rational and, hence, superior Western relationship to the world.[13]

Furthermore, the domesticated subjects themselves that were displayed as an integral part of the proceedings in "colonial pavilions" or "native villages" were perhaps the most prized commodity of them all. Reduced to little more than living specimens, physical embodiments of the grand scheme of things and beings produced by European imperial superiority, these flesh-and-bone images became mere stations on the revolving canvass of the imperial panorama.

Finally, along with all the imperial aplomb, these shows also provided the ideological cement needed to diminish domestic discontent and to contain radical mass action. Even if by that time very few visitors were able to afford the things on display, the sight of the amassed commodities served to rally the crowd of spectators behind the banner of progress and imperial expansion. While many commentators have been inclined to consider these and other manifestations of "social imperialism" as propaganda and a deliberate strategy on the part of the ruling classes "to address the masses,"[14] more recent research indicates that this form of social engineering was inherent in the logic of the commodity spectacle itself. For the masses not only gazed at the spectacle but also looked at themselves. For the first time, the spectacle of mass production made the crowd feel a unity, as an audience reveling in the glory of its own centrality. And thus there resulted from the combined effects of commodity fetishism and the new strategy of manufacturing popular consent what Eric J. Hobsbawm has called a "common frame of social psychology," a specifically imperialist form of popular culture that bound together the Royal Tournament and the illuminations on the seafront of Blackpool, Queen Victoria and the Kodak girl.[15]

Another major form of public culture ·concerned with the entangled visions of Europe and its colonial subjects was the series of exotic shows to which the British public had been introduced from early on in the nineteenth century. Among the Africans displayed in these spectacles, one Saartjie Baartman, touring England and France as the Hottentot Venus, gained a particularly pitiable reputation. Afflicted with steatopygia and excessively developed genitalia, the South African woman became the object of much speculation about Africans' place in the "great chain of being."[16] A similar response awaited a troupe of "Zulu Kafirs" that visited London in 1853 and that led Charles Dickens to remark that "if we have anything to learn from the Noble Savage, it is what to avoid" and that, consequently, the Zulus had better be "civilised off the face of the earth."[17] Of course, as Dickens's tirade illustrates, no matter how realistic the live performances by Africans may have been, what the British public was able to see in such shows was anything but Africans.

If then, by the mid-nineteenth century, Africa, as a concept and object of Western knowledge, had been elaborated as part of the making of Europe's self-consciousness and shaped by a cascade of narratives and other discourses of difference in which the continent had served as the symbolic antithesis to the main tenets of liberal enlightened Europe, the purpose of such spectacles of African bodies rendered up to metropolitan public scrutiny was not merely to define African identities in terms of what knowledge the West produced about them.

More important, the promiscuous mix of mirror images, that made up the consolidated symbolic world of the empire, and the peculiar racial unconscious of the world fair and the exotic show produced new modes of perception, new regimes of sensory experience. Two types of colonial spectacle—the colonial exhibition as such and the missionary exhibition—illustrate this well. The epitome of the first of these spectacles, one that had barely closed its doors before the arrival of the African Choir, was the Stanley and African Exhibition of 1890. It was in that year that Henry Morton Stanley returned from Central Africa, where he had led a "private" expedition to "rescue" Emin Pasha, the British Empire's governor of Equatoria. It was primarily because of such ventures and the publication of Stanley's best-selling books *Through the Dark Continent* (1878) and *In Darkest Africa* (1890) that the *Times*, no doubt echoing the popular mood of the time, was led to remark that "Africa in one or other of its phases is on everybody's mind and in everybody's mouth."[18] As for the content of the show, the organizers—representatives of the British aristocracy and middle class with vested interests in Africa—had placed particular emphasis on the philanthropic and humanitarian aspect of Stanley's mission and of imperialist expansion as such. As the catalog of the exhibition put it:

> Frightful wrongs to be wiped out, deeds of high surprise to be achieved, virgin countries to be commercially exploited, valuable scientific discoveries to be made, myriads of people steeped in the grossest idolatry. . . . [T]hese are some of the varied elements which have thrown a glamour and fascination over Africa and taken men's minds captive.[19]

And so on. When colonial exhibitions are compared with the second type of colonial spectacle, shows that depicted the "mission field," the differences are more of a rhetorical nature than of subject matter and ideology. Following Annie E. Coombes's careful analysis, the roots of these events can be traced to ethnographic collections that belong to missionary societies—the London Missionary Society, a mission enormously active in southern Africa, was among the first to establish a museum for its own ethnographic collection—but it was only from 1882 that missionary exhibitions were becoming regular events that promoted the activities of various missions.[20] Often these events were designed to demonstrate the African's skill as a manufacturer and thereby had to be seen as part of a broader strategy of gaining government support for the growing number of technical and "industrial" schools the missionary societies were setting up throughout Africa. At the same time, missionary exhibits disseminated a more benign image of Africa and Africans that carefully cultivated a distinctive, though by no means uninterested, position on the colonial enterprise. Of course, the strategy was a contradictory one in that it declared that colonial conquest and the redemption of the African for the "civilizing mission" were not irreconcilable projects. But because they made no effort to conceal these contradictions, Coombes concludes, such events were "distinct, both in kind and in degree, to their colonial counterpart." Because of the benevolent character of the missionary shows, they were spectacles "of a very different nature" in which the African, though still a spectacle, could be differentiated from the African displayed at the colonial exhibition.

Perhaps they were, perhaps not. While there is certainly an element of truth in this assertion at least as far as the *objects* being depicted were concerned, the available evidence might equally suggest a more complicated and simultaneously more uniform picture in relation to the viewing *subjects*. For both types of exhibitions rested on the same aesthetic of the panorama and simulation. And like the world fairs, both were important arenas for the figuration of the global spectator-consumer. Modeled, for instance, on the image of "virgin countries" passively waiting to be explored, and by means of simulated forests and an explorer's camp offering the visitor the experience of finding himself "in the heart of Africa," the Stanley exhibit actually turned the spectator into an actor in the drama of world affairs. Likewise, missionary exhibits constructed a sphere of tacit complicity with the imperialist project by putting the visitor in a mediating position between Africans (demonstrating their potential for "development") and the imperial powers. The difference between both types of spectacle, then, was probably one of degrees rather than substance in that they appealed to different strands of British colonial ideology and staged different roles for the visitors: a distanced position vis-à-vis "myriads of people steeped in idolatry" in the colonial show and a more engaging and mediating one in the missionary exhibit.

I have dwelt at length on different types of nineteenth-century spectacle concerned with visions of alterity, because they lead us directly to an aspect of modern consciousness that only becomes clear once it attains *global form*. For, I repeat, there is a good deal more to the drama of the commodity than mere social control or the production of exotic identities. The world fair and some of its associated forms like the colonial exhibit, I would argue, reveal what Stephan Oettermann has recognized as one of the key elements in the dialectic of nineteenth-century panoramic consciousness. Like the panorama—which, after all, formed one of the main attractions of world fairs—these entertainments not only liberated and directed the ascendancy to global dominance of the bourgeois gaze but also incarcerated it again.[21] Between them, world fairs, colonial shows, and missionary exhibits conjured up fantasies of a human cosmos in movement, dreams of what Jean Baudrillard has called an infinitely expandable "perspectivist space." By the same token, these entertainments attempted to again close up the space of being and evolution by confining the probing gaze that had produced these total vistas of space and time in the first place.[22] As a result, they ended up creating the spectacle of a society that not only was global but also was prevented by its very spherical, centripetal structure from seeing itself. By closing up to a *tableau vivant* the horizon and by populating it with objects and subjects to be contemplated from the center all these different types of world spectacle inaugurated a scopic regime in which the bourgeois vision ultimately ended up seeing only that with which it had encircled itself.

Furthermore, what in turn also came to be reshaped by the world fair–type spectacles was the nature of knowledge and the idea of truth as such. While the panoramic gaze may have piled up all around itself enormous quantities of pieces of reality and neatly arranged these into a total prospect, by the late nineteenth century it became increasingly clearer that there was no longer a center for all these bits of knowledge. Thus, while celebrating an immensely widened universe of people, signs, and goods, these universal rituals of auto-hypnosis also effectively masked the sharpening crisis of the new knowledge that was to unite all this immense diversity under one system of communication. Troubled by the blurred boundaries of order and chaos, fact and fiction, world fairs inaugurated a type of hypnotic, inward-turning autism that characterizes the societies of late capitalism to this day. While Michel Foucault may be correct in maintaining that this social order is not so much one of spectacle as one of surveillance in which "the play of signs defines the anchorages of power,"[23] the opposite may equally be the case. What the panoptic view reveals is everything there is; the world that opens up before it is not the real world but a world made for visual consumption, a world of commodity images. In the early world exhibitions, a world was beginning to take shape in which it is images that mediate all social existence and in which it is not the world that is being put on display but in which the world is grasped as though it were an exhibition.

A similar view is taken in Timothy Mitchell's fascinating account of the colonization and representation of Egypt in nineteenth-century world fairs and colonial politics. World fairs, Mitchell argues, did not so much exhibit the world as engineer a particular relationship between the individual and the world. What resulted from these events was not just a new vista of the Orient but also a world rendered up to individual consumption, set up before the Western eye as an exhibit. The colonial nature of the nineteenth-century world fairs thus consisted less in the fact that they celebrated the global hegemony of Western economic and political power than in the fact that they redefined the nature of knowledge. What was to be rendered in them was the idea of the "world-as-exhibition," the fact that truth was to rest on what Heidegger called "the certainty of representation."[24]

Egyptian visitors to Europe and the French Expositions Universelles of the 1860s to 1880s in turn found this obsession with the visual to be the single most important aspect of the West. "One of the characteristics of the French is to stare and get excited at everything new," an Egyptian scholar wrote in the 1820s. Other Egyptian travelers, writing later in the century, frequently commented upon their becoming the object of European curiosity and spent much time and energy describing the panoramas and dioramas and the phenomenon of *le spectacle* (for which they knew of no Arabic equivalent). All these technologies of the spectacular revealed a European preoccupation with, as one Middle Eastern author put it toward the end of the nineteenth century, *intizam al-manzar*, the organization of the view. The significance of these glimpses of the

West from outside becomes particularly apparent when set in relation to prevailing Western assumptions about an alleged lack of curiosity among Orientals, assumptions which suggest that staring and the intellectual curiosity that it
is said to express represent simply the unfettered relation of a person to the
world. Yet as Mitchell correctly points out, read against the background of
what the Middle Eastern writers of the nineteenth century found to be unnat-
ural European behavior, the Western way of addressing the world, far from
being based upon rationality, itself entails "a certain theology of its own."[25]

The question of modern Western theologies evokes, of course, Marx's famous phrase about the "theological whims" of the commodity and provides
another interesting point of convergence with the South African ethnographic
evidence. As Mitchell notes, the irony in Marx's theory of commodity fetishism
was that while it claimed the power of capitalism to rest on the phantasmagoric
misrepresentation of the actual social relations that produced alienation in the
first place, it left representation itself unquestioned. Like Marx, later theorists
of media consumption and popular culture quite unconditionally took for
granted the distinction between a realm of representation and something called
external reality. Yet, at the same time, these theorists failed to examine "the
novelty of continuously creating the effect of an 'external reality' as itself a
mechanism of power."[26] They could not see that, as Debord sums it all up, the
spectacle of the commodity "is the very heart of society's real unreality."[27]

By now it should be clear that the whole point about the "theology" of
modernity and its celebration in colonial spectacles—be they world fairs or
concerts by native choirs—was the question of the certainty of representation.
In a period of growing doubts about the empiricist foundations of the late Victorian global imagination the hegemony in Western thinking of what Johannes
Fabian calls "visualism" was more than an aspect of bourgeois empiricism.[28]
The stability of the bourgeois order increasingly depended on a system of visually verifiable truths that constantly pushed its limits outward. In an age of col-
lapsing mechanic world models, colonial spectacles set up a frame of truly
global dimensions in which European consumers were able to fancy themselves
as what Max Weber called "cultural beings" who "take a deliberate attitude toward the world" and "lend it significance."[29] The result of this was a perfectly
closed world: the order and certainty of colonialism rested on the certainty of
this distinction, while the unassailability of the society of the spectacle in turn
depended on colonialism.

### "Africa Civilized and Uncivilized": The Ambiguities of Sex and Race

To finally return to our South African–European story, not only did projects
such as the African Choir highlight the considerable contradictions inherent in
the missionary cause and the impossibility in the 1890s of reconciling the

worldly political strands of imperial domination with the more ethereal missionary project of subjugation under the divine will, but also, more significantly, it was through exotic shows, world fairs, and concerts of "non-Western" music that Western spectators were able to take up their deliberate posture and figuratively associate the object world with other spaces, other times, unfamiliar to the inquiring subject and yet familiar to it at the same time. In the following section I shall focus on dress and dramaturgy as crucial sites for staging the spectacle of imperial space and time, elaborating typologies of race and progress, and for ordering knowledge and relations of power in a time of waning certainties.

The level at which these uncertainties manifested themselves first and perhaps in the most mundane manner is the conflicts that arose within the choir itself over the entrepreneurial aspect of the tours. Judging from metropolitan and colonial press reports, by September 1891, just three months after the arrival in England, the venture had run up debts of some £1,000. And as if this were not enough, a dispute then arose about whether the managers or the choristers were to cover the losses. With the end of the whole project looming only three months after it had started, the majority of the singers appeared to be willing to continue without pay or, in any case, with very little pay, and some even stepped in with their own savings. None of this seems to have moved the managers, however, who—in spite of a court order having been invoked against them—adroitly backed out of the enterprise, leaving the choir stranded in a London hotel and Lovedale principal James Stewart and his brother-in-law John Stephen, a Glasgow shipbuilder, to foot the bill and send the remaining singers back to South Africa in the spring of 1893.[30]

But that was not all. The animosity that reigned between the Kimberley-based members of the choir and the Lovedale group, an opposition illustrated best by the antagonism between Paul Xiniwe and Charlotte Manye, appears to have been a much more critical factor in wrecking the project. The explanations proffered for this rift varied, pianist Lilian Clark somewhat predictably ascribing it to ethnic friction between Xhosa and Basotho, whereas Paul Xiniwe explained the whole disaster in the terms under which the enterprise had originally been conceived: as a political campaign against white settler paternalism. The idea of using a choir to raise funds for a technical school, he maintained, had been "simply a fine rolling phrase" to catch the unwary, and he accused the managers of having "bolstered and pampered" the Kimberley girls. Proof of this, he claimed, was the fact that the *Review of Reviews* had chosen Charlotte to give the interview I quoted at the beginning of this book. Charlotte's sister Kate, finally, adopting perhaps more of a female perspective, ascribed the conflicts to the jealousy of Xiniwe's wife, Eleanor, and the numerous gifts Charlotte was receiving from the English audience—a theory that has some merit, it would seem, given Eleanor's "business acumen" and the ambiguities of race and gender that underlay the global imagination of whites and blacks. Be this as it may, it was clear that the two women were not on the best of terms, and it thus seems no surprise that they eventually came to blows with each other in December 1891 and that consequently Charlotte found herself in a Manchester courtroom facing charges of assault.[31]

If this knot of "untoward happenings," as officious Lovedale historiography was to call the tangle of perspectives, interests, and narratives, is a fascinating demonstration of the intertwined global imaginations of Europeans and South Africans, there is one aspect of the tour that throws into even sharper relief the conflicted nature of Western and African interdependent fantasies of difference. Perhaps more than dubious financial practices, risqué amorous adventures, and embarrassing lawsuits, it was the stage dress specifically adopted for the European tour that provoked the greatest controversy and that best symbolizes the intricacies of commodity fetishism gone global.

The choir performed the first half of the program in "native" dress (such as seen in fig. 4.2) and the second half in sober Victorian dress (as for instance in fig. 4.3), and thus quite literally illustrated, as one paper had it, "Africa Civilized and Uncivilized."[32] When word about this sartorial scheme leaked back to South Africa, Lovedale missionaries immediately denounced the wearing of karosses as "mischievous" and "barbarian," blaming the managers for this decision and claiming that none of the choristers had ever worn karosses at home. "This costume would do occasionally," the *Christian Express* fretted, "but it is a mistake otherwise, and physically and morally dangerous." Morija missionary H. Dieterlen chimed in charging that the singers had "exposed themselves" to the Europeans, while choir impresario Edwin Howell, owner of London's famous Alhambra vaudeville theater and a man well versed in matters concerning gaudy dress, promptly refuted the charge, arguing that "the decision as to dress was not solely the act of the Managers, but the natives themselves were consulted and approved of the dress worn in every particular." And, he added, "they simply wear their skins over their ordinary clothing. . . . On many occasions when the Managers wished it otherwise, they preferred appearing with bare feet."[33]

Such quibbles over skins and footwear to us today may appear rather trivial. In the nineteenth century, however, such arguments over clothing, costumes, and the moral dangers of wearing animal skins bespoke a whole worldview, a smug metropolitan discourse about morals and markets, spiritual salvation, and social distinctions. But as the spectacle of commodities and the commodity of the spectacle constantly reproduced an imagined world of oppositions and dualities, the fixity and stability of the Victorian imaginary also masked the shifting nature of global relations of power itself and, within these, the ambiguity of sex and race in particular. To understand this, we have to briefly review the broad distinctions between precolonial subject–object relationships and the modern world of commodities.

In the precolonial societies of southern Africa, social life and the place within it of objects such as clothing were governed by a set of rules in which things and bodies entered into a variety of associations with each other that, while certainly being richly expressive and ( *pace* Max Weber) culturally saturated, were not mediated by commodity signs. Thus these associations did not form a code separate from the things themselves, and hence the idea of knowledge as a code or system of meanings to be applied to the material world did not exist. Nor did, correspondingly, the notion of a thing per se occur. In a sense, there even was no "nature" (and hence no "natural body")—the great signified through which the enlightened subject and its codes of operational finality came into being in the first place.[34] What was there, by contrast, were social relations that worked through numerous and complex concatenations of sameness and difference that permeated the world.[35] Similarly, the relationship between a piece of clothing and the body that it covered was not primarily one mediated by some dualism between a signifier and its signified. Rather, by wearing a certain item of clothing a person became part of a field of practice in which the bodies physical and social and the garment as "social skin" mutually actualized and inscribed each other without either of them being the primary source of meaning.

The rise of the commodity and, more specifically in our case, of the European textile industry changed all that. It not only restructured the relations of production of India, Egypt, the southern United States, and a host of other cotton-growing regions but also created new patterns of consumption within Europe itself and within this redesigned landscape of social relations, production, and consumption brought about a new sense of corporeality and bodily sensation and, in fact, of what it meant to have a body in the first place. As the work of John and Jean Comaroff on concepts of work and labor among the Tshidi Barolong of South Africa has shown, the colonized subjects increasingly came to experience wage labor as a gradual weakening of the idea of work as the primary measure of personal value.[36] Instead, industrial labor required the physical operation and interaction of bodies increasingly cut loose from any referentiality in nature. At the same time, the domestic sphere ceased to be a place where the body might reside for itself. The "house," the quintessential atom of the social universe, had become no more than a site of consumption, severed from the direct appropriation of the earth and physically segregated from the sphere of production: the mines and the factories. And it is this contradiction between production and consumption that mutilates the body. The distance of the body from the workplace only generates more need and the necessity to return to work in order to satisfy it. Unable to find a home, the body "roams" in a never-ending pursuit of satiation. Unleashed and abandoned to its devices, it eventually comes to be perceived as an afflicted, homeless thing whose pathology in turn indicates the disturbed social order.

If capitalist production reduced the body to a thing, it was through this process of reification that, paradoxically, the body was able to reenter the drama of signification. And it did so in ways that, although they may have looked somewhat antithetical, ultimately repressed the profound ambiguities

THE AFRICAN NATIVE CHOIR
WHICH SANG BEFORE H.M. THE QUEEN AT OSBORNE

Figure 4.2. The African Choir in "Native" dress (*Review of Reviews*, 1891).

inherent in modernity's relationship to the body. In the most general sense, by being disconnected from the web of echoes, traces, and similarities that made up the preindustrial world, the body became the object of a new regime of signs that were contained, ordered, and codified in the commodities used to clothe it. Commodity relations create a world in which symbols take over the role of things in the sense that order and meaning come to wholly depend on a distinction being introduced between signifiers and signified, a division in which the body of course becomes a mere referent for the commodified images of itself. Ultimately, then, what commodity production altered was not only bodily experience but also signification. Or, better still, modern industrial society reorganized the way in which meaningful life had formerly arisen out of specific contexts of practice by subjecting the relationship between things and bodies, mind and matter, to Weber's "deliberate attitude."

European missionary thinking, although largely averse to immoderate consumption, vanity, and narcissism, essentially worked from the same premise. The missionaries, already prominent interlocutors in this discourse at home, had made clothing one of the most morally charged mediums of their message. By restyling the outer shell of the "heathen," they reasoned, the inner self of the newly converted would be reformed and salvaged. But the missionary project of bodily reform was not as simple as it may seem. Nor was it passively re-

Figure 4.3. The African Choir in Victorian dress (Veit Erlmann collection).

ceived by those who were to become the object of reform. For as crisply separated as these different regimes of visuality, signification, and sartorial practice
may have been, and as much as the contention that wrecked the tour of the
African Choir seems to have revolved around conflicting notions among Britons
and South Africans about vision, seeing, and being seen, they were not as mutually exclusive as it may seem. One of the aspects of the performances where
this can be observed with particular clarity, I think, was the use of dress as a
metonymic gesture, a spectacle within the spectacle. For the whole point about
"native" dress was precisely to illustrate how much Victorian models of universal history and the chorister's own personal history coincided thanks to the "civilizing mission." The change from native dress to Victorian clothing in the two
parts of the performance was to be a serious mise-en-scène of the progressive
history of their wearers. As Kate Manye later explained, they wanted to show
"how great the change was," so that when people said "what do you spend all
the money on in the mission, . . . by seeing this difference we showed them."[37]

This allegoric device—very common in nineteenth-century representations
of racial identity and progress—was complemented by and in many ways even
depended on another metonymic strategy by which an unknown and chaotic
outside world came to be organized as a "reality" available for objective
scrutiny and classification. The photographs of the African Choir in figures 4.2

Figure 4.4. Smelling out (*Ludgate Monthly* 2 [1891–92], Harry Ransom Humanities Research Center, The University of Texas at Austin).

and 4.3 show this quite clearly. While the symmetrical positioning of the choir for the camera in figure 4.2 conforms to the standard Victorian format and thus is clearly reminiscent of the "trophy" method in museum displays of foreign implements and weapons (typically framed by two Europeans), the garments displayed in this and figures 4.4 and 4.5 convey a similar message of difference. Foremost among these items were woolen blankets such as those worn by several of the men in the back row (fig. 4.2). Blending Western forms of fashion with some modified, indigenous form of apparel, these blankets are themselves the key vehicles and symbols of the entanglement of local communities with the world economy. And, as we shall see in due course, they were the means to protest an order that reduced their owners to exotic specimens.

By the late nineteenth century, industrially manufactured blankets had largely replaced skin cloaks and similar kinds of precolonial dress throughout southern Africa. Two major differences, however, can be observed in the way in which these items were combined with other forms of European attire and, more important perhaps, in the social position of their wearers. Thus, by the second half of the nineteenth century the term "blanket" had already become firmly integrated into the lexicon of southern Nguni languages as the designa-

Figure 4.5. Ladies of the African Native Choir (*Ludgate Monthly* 2 [1891–92], Harry Ransom Humanities Research Center, The University of Texas at Austin).

tion of rural non-Christians that distinguished them from Christianized "school" people. The other major difference concerns the gender-marked use of blankets. Although men—and here especially the migrant workers—were increasingly exchanging blankets for precolonial skin cloaks and extravagantly mixed these with (and sometimes used them to cover) European clothes, it was women whose changing position in colonial society was increasingly becoming associated with woolen blankets. Although, on the face of it, they were transformations of precolonial skin aprons and cloaks and, as such, in time became key emblems in a sort of generic southern African "folk costume," the blankets were anything but a sign of the "conservativism" many South African men like to see in their womenfolk. In reality, as Jean Comaroff has argued, blankets and head scarves (worn in figure 4.2 by Eleanor Xiniwe, for instance) were the product and visible sign of a very "modern" development, what Comaroff calls the feminization of the countryside, a process in the course of which "native" women were made into guardians of the rural homestead and into premodern counterparts of European women, set apart from modern centers of production in increasingly devalued rural and domestic enclaves.[38]

But the photographs also reveal one further marker of "native" identity: the ostrich feathers and the beadwork sported by some of the men, the bracelets of some of the women, the leopard skins worn by the Manye sisters, Josiah Se-mouse and some of the other male performers, and, pointing somewhat incongruously perhaps in the direction of a generic exotic Otherness, the tiger head on the floor. The point about "native" identity is worth noting, because this was precisely what the choir's entire appearance was meant to represent. Thus choir manager Howell may not have been too far off the mark when he suggested that the choir was not wearing the dress "as in Africa." Rather, what some of the singers were wearing was a sign—a sign that stood for what, in the imperial lexicon of the late nineteenth century, was taken for Africa.

Beyond this, the "native" dress was a form of representation that at once familiarized and distanced. As an allegory and by making the part stand for the whole it made "Africa" familiar and knowable. Yet the same leopard skin, as a generic type of "African" clothing, also distanced its users from a specific locale and tradition, and in doing so it substituted representation for historical practice. Ultimately, of course, this strange vacillation rested on a type of knowledge and an "organization of the view" that could only have been possible as a result of the modern preoccupation with objects and their significance.[39]

The photographs just discussed also reveal certain elements in the sartorial scheme of the African Choir that are at odds with these rhetoric devices of familiarity and distance. For in these pictures we see the actors playing with difference in unforeseen ways that seem to hint at the subversive potential of colonial mimicry and the possibility of reversing the received subject–object relationship of the colonial order. Note, for instance, that the beadwork worn by some of the women, but most notably by Charlotte Manye, on the far right in figure 4.2, strongly resembles English jewelry of the day. Similarly, Eleanor Xiniwe (seated in the center in figure 4.2) appears to be wearing some sort of Western gown. Even more important, however, than this outright appropriation of the coded commodities of empire is the bricolage of Victorian and "African" sartorial elements in some of the women's finery. This bricolage could mean several things. First, there is the possibility, strongly hinted at in Howell's statement, that the performers, like many other Africans involved in the emerging international show business, "knowingly exploited a presentation of self and identity which reappropriated and transformed anticipated western assumptions about the African and Africa and which was calculated to have a particular effect in Britain."[40] (But, as we shall also see later on in the discussion of the Zulu Choir in chapter 6, even such seemingly innocuous play with identity could be seen as potentially subversive to imperial hegemony and therefore virulently attacked as an attempt to break up the rigid typologies of race, tribe and nation on which British global power rested.)

Second, black women in South Africa were never simply the passive consumers of foreign goods made available by the new global market. Although such strangely concocted costumes fixed women in a marginal and premodern position as "folk," it is precisely through such costumes that Charlotte Manye and Eleanor Xiniwe may have expressed, as the Comaroffs have written of women elsewhere in southern Africa, an "aura of independence and reserve": a "locally-tooled identity" that, while it might have made them hostage to a newly politicized "tradition," equally "entailed an effort to limit their dependency on the market."[41]

Third, the rapid decay of African independent power and the ensuing radicalization of the 1880s led some African intellectuals to reexamine the "heathen" past and to experiment with other expressive media by which to articulate their growing uneasiness with the imperialist variant of modernity. A decade later, as liberals in the eastern Cape began to turn to chiefs and headmen as agents of social control, spectacles of "tribal" culture—although still shunned by the missionaries—were no longer solely regarded as "heathenish" and, at the same time, came to be accepted as more than mere folklore.

Finally, the switch back and forth between Victorian dress and "native" dress also enacted a strange dialectic, reaffirming late Victorian distinctions of class, race, and gender while at the same time concealing the more deep-seated ambiguities that had created these imperial dichotomies in the first place. Here I want to quote from an interview with Kate Manye conducted by Margaret McCord in 1954, shortly before Kate's death. In it Kate talks about an English lady who suggested that the women put on powder offstage and expose their breasts while onstage:

> I told her that in Africa the heathen women in the Transkei used red powder, but they do it for the heat. They also put on dark cream on forehead, cheeks and chin in big spots for weddings and parties, and white feathers among the beads in their hair. . . . We knew they [the Europeans] were putting powder on their faces, and this stuff on their eyebrows. . . . But we did not think much, we just laughed at it. It was just their custom. But we did not mind. These people were civilized.

The issue of the exposed breasts was a more serious matter. As Kate explained:

> You see these people had seen photographs taken of heathen women with all their beadwork and so forth. But we told her that the breasts of a married woman should not be exposed, especially when she is nursing her baby the breasts should not be exposed. And nowadays we have no time for this heathen dress. You see the beads cost money and it costs much time and we do not have the time any more. We have too much work.

Clearly, the lines were distinctly drawn here between the "heathen" and "civilized," between Africans and Europeans. And yet there is another side to the story, one that speaks of ambiguity, desire, and even danger. It emerges quite neatly from the following section of Kate's account, in which she discusses the presents the women in the choir received from the British audience and the conflicts that erupted in their wake:

You see there was a quarrel between them and us. They came from the
Cape and we came from Kimberley. It was really a quarrel between Mrs.
Xiniwe and Charlotte. One night Charlotte got a present and Mrs. Xiniwe was
jealous. She said you must be wearing a charm to be made such a fuss of by
the Europeans.

The presents must have been substantial indeed. For as Kate goes on to state:

We got handkerchiefs, shawls, stockings and lots of things. I got beads and
a bracelet from a gentleman, all of silver, and two shawls from a lady, and a
five shilling piece and I got a brooch made of it, and a three shilling piece and
I made that into a brooch for my mother, and another lady gave me a bracelet
made of a snake, also silver, very pretty. . . . Others gave Charlotte presents,
she got lots, pearls from one gentleman, and earrings and a brooch. . . . We
all got presents, Mrs. Xiniwe too, but she did not get so many as Charlotte.

Kate Manye's comments must be seen in the context of a doubly unfixed position of black women negotiating a modern, cosmopolitan identity at the end
of the nineteenth century, caught between the slippery politics of cross-racial
(male) desire for dark bodies and the ambiguities of cross-cultural (female) infatuation with Western fashion. To the extent that the "native" dress revealed
an absence, that is to say the absence of "civilization," it also set forth a presence, the presence for the European viewer of a desirable black body. Conversely, as the European accouterments seemed to affirm the rationality of
global commodity exchange and its acceptance by the colonized, such patterns
of gift giving are also negated in their taken-for-grantedness—domesticated, as
it were—by the claim that they were the result of non-Western "magic." The
"native" dress and the desire it evoked in white men (Charlotte and Kate
claimed that numerous white men proposed to them during the tour) turned
the women into objects, but the appropriation of selected signs of Western
affluence by "magic," ironically, returns to them some of the agency the logic of
the spectacle denied to them in the first place.

It is these ambiguities of early global capitalism and the "spectatorial lust"
engendered by it that I believe to be the cause of a rather remarkable turn of
events in London in 1891: Kate Manye's loss of consciousness. The incident I am
referring to is reported in *The Calling of Kate Makanya*, the part-fictionalized,
part-documentary life story of Kate put together by Margaret McCord on the
basis of the 1954 interview.[42] Here McCord, whose father, Dr. McCord, directed
the hospital where Kate spent the last portion of her life, describes a fray between Johanna Jonkers and the fifteen-year-old Kate, the cause of which was Johanna's being envious of the presents Kate and "the girls from Kimberley" were
receiving from London audiences. Johanna accused Kate of wearing a magic
charm, a charge Kate first refuted as "silly." But when the squabble eventually
resulted in a more vehement brawl in the course of which Kate scratched Johanna's cheek, things reached a different level: Hours before she was due for a
solo performance at a garden party the Baroness Burdett-Coutts was giving for
the International Congress of Hygiene and Demography, Kate fainted.

What is remarkable about this incident is not so much the fact of a stressed-out adolescent swooning but the conflicting explanations subsequently offered for this unusual behavior by Paul Xiniwe, Kate's son Samuel, and her biographer Margaret McCord. "It was just a little *ufufunyane*," Xiniwe declared, for instance, "a kind of hysteria our girls get sometimes when they're afraid of bewitchment."[43] The term Xiniwe uses here, *ufufunyane*, and the translation he offers are interesting in several respects. First, *ufufunyane* is a type of malevolent possession by alien spirits that is believed to have emerged only in the 1920s in an attempt "to handle the escalating proportions of psychoneurosis often associated with failure to cope with the changing way of life in the colonial and postcolonial industrial society."[44] Second, Xiniwe's explication clearly and very adroitly plays into Victorian notions of female identity and nineteenth-century constructions of woman as a self-effacing, near invisible "something," ambiguously caught between all the solid objects of the bourgeois salon and not quite part of them.

Third, and probably most fascinating, the term *ufufunyane* was substituted in McCord's text for the original term, *isiphonso*, which Kate's son Samuel used in a letter to McCord that described his mother's problems in dealing with Mrs. Xiniwe. In what is probably its most commonly accepted English translation, Clement Doke and Benedict W. Vilakazi perhaps somewhat euphemistically suggest that *isiphonso* means "hypnotism," but according to ethnographer Axel-Ivar Berglund the cognate term *ukuphonsa* more adequately denotes a particularly vile form of witchcraft rooted in "Zulu thought-patterns."[45] In a sense, then, what these contradictory interpretations of Kate's situation might reveal is not so much the nature of the conflict and Kate's attempt to deal with it by means of a certain form of symbolic practice but how a distanced and ultimately Western gaze on such a practice generally has the potential of Orientalizing Kate's behavior as either typically female (hysteria), aberrant (hypnotism), or ethnically different (Zulu).

There is, of course, nothing inherently wrong with Berglund's attempt to interpret *ukuphonsa* within the larger symbolic framework of Zulu religious practice, but my reason for unraveling the semantics of *-phonso* and the meaning of Kate's blackout lies in the way in which it intersects with sexuality, the female body, and, above all, commodity production. What is fascinating about this little episode is not how Johanna, Eleanor, and Kate respond to the mysteries of the West (symbolized here by its wealth and the lavish gifts bestowed on them) from a position of absolute alterity but how different forms of social relations are mediated by, mirrored, and concentrated in the commodity fetish. Thus the irrationality of the commodity, its strange capability to create social identities, distinctions, and dependencies in the South African women's conflict, and the ensuing *isiphonso* intersect with and are countervailed by social relations that are essentially manipulated on the basis of a different kind of contiguity between things and people. Regardless of who was bewitching whom in our example, the point is that witchcraft accusations here are integral to Eleanor

Xiniwe's and Kate Manye's experience of the modern world and that, consistent with African beliefs, capitalism and witchcraft are seen as playing off each other within a wider discourse on moral economy. Each is equated with the dangerous appropriation of limited resources for the selfish use of individuals.[46]

In conclusion, clothes and jewelry were an immensely ambiguous symbolic terrain that could serve quite varied projects. At the very least, what the story of the African Choir and the role of "spectatorial lust" in their performances illustrate is how deeply the imperial order and the global imagination of Africans and Europeans were intertwined with the logic of commodity production and the society of the spectacle. In the next chapter we shall see how the Western faith in a unitary system of knowledge comprised every aspect of the global imagination and how numerous facets of anticolonial practice in turn expressed themselves in a form of representation that evinced the overarching, larger truth or system. At the center of this form of representation stood the nation.

5

⌁

# Symbols of Inclusion and Exclusion

*Nationalism, Colonial Consciousness,*
*and the "Great Hymn"*

Ntsikana's hymn "Ulo Thixo omkhulu" (Thou Great God) easily ranks as one of the greatest songs of religious inspiration to have come out of South Africa. Composed in the early 1820s, the "Great Hymn," as it is more commonly known, for more than a century and a half has occupied a privileged place in black South African religious symbolism. Moreover, as a result of public performances such as the concerts of the African Choir, Ntsikana's "Great Hymn" in turn also acquired notoriety as one of the first "modern" compositions in South African musical history and, as I shall argue in this chapter, a prime example of the sort of fictions about selfhood, national identity, and progress that shaped the intertwined imaginations of Europeans and Africans in the late nineteenth century. In assessing these constructions I wish to push further my inquiry into nineteenth-century panoramic consciousness and late Victorian forms of the global imagination and to elaborate on the argument made in previous chapters that the panorama of imperial time and space was an all-embracing medium, a complete system of knowledge that enabled colonizers and colonized to imagine themselves as belonging to a global ecumene of progress and civilization. More particularly, I am going to argue that even where the imagery and style of this universal narrative were contested, the linear structure itself and the idea of a rational system of knowledge remained largely unquestioned. Prophecy, art, and nationalism were three of the areas in which these continuities of colonial consciousness can be seen most clearly to be at work.

III

### The Making of a Prophet: Art and Nationalism
### in Colonial Discourse

The origins of the "Great Hymn" lie well before the 1890s, in one of the most turbulent phases of the colonizing process and, more specifically, in the emergence of an altogether new social type, the Christian "prophet." In 1795, Britain took over from Holland the Cape of Good Hope, a rather unremarkable stretch of land at the southern tip of the African continent that for a century or so had served as little more than a refreshment station for the ships of the Dutch East India Company. In the course of less than half a century Britain not only pushed the frontiers of its new overseas possession far inland but also reshaped the social architecture of the communities that had come under its sway. But these transformations did not remain confined to the new Cape Colony itself. Their repercussions were felt far beyond its borders in what was then an area occupied by a complex aggregation of independent African polities tied together by a common language, a similar cultural background, and shifting political alliances.[1]

The area around the eastern Cape in particular between 1800 and 1820 was in a state of chronic instability. Here British expansionist policies intermingled with inter-African warfare, large-scale African migrations met with massive British settlement schemes, and Christian missionary efforts competed with reshaped African cosmologies. But not only were British missionaries, African chiefs, Boer farmers, and colonial administrators in the eastern Cape embroiled in an increasingly differentiated social universe composed of classes, cultures, and "races," but also, more significantly perhaps, colonists and African societies found themselves entangled in an intricate web of mutual dependencies, competing systems of thought, and modalities of power—in a complex landscape of political relations, trade, and religion that ultimately constituted, as Clifton C. Crais has written, "ambiguous frontiers of contact."[2]

One, if not the most crucial of such ambiguous frontiers, frontier that is of particular relevance to our story, established itself around the religious beliefs and practices of the intruders. But the shape this frontier took in the eastern Cape was determined by not only the profoundly altered conditions of life and the influence of white missionaries but also, equally important in drawing and redrawing this frontier, specifically African readings of the Gospel. Here two names stand out as powerful symbols of particularly influential African responses to and adaptations of Christianity: Nxele and Ntsikana Gaba.[3] Although my main concern in this chapter is with Ntsikana, his work and historical importance cannot be fully appreciated without also taking into account Nxele's biography.

Nxele grew up on a Boer farm but, like many other Xhosa, was driven out of the colony into independent Ndlambe territory in 1812. Here he established close contacts with Chief Ndlambe, at the same time taking a keen interest in the curiously novel ways and beliefs of the advancing British colonists, then still ensconced rather unstably at the frontier outpost of Grahamstown. The propensity for theological issues was something Nxele had developed earlier in his youth when he began to show all the conventional signs of being destined to become a diviner, except for some unusual exhortations to give up witchcraft. Later, as tensions between the colonial government and the independent Xhosa chiefdoms intensified and border clashes and cattle raiding increased dramatically, Nxele's preaching assumed a more anti-European, anti-Christian pitch. Whereas previously he had incorporated some of the ideas he had learned in Grahamstown into his own syncretic blend of Xhosa belief and Christianity, in the process condemning witchcraft, polygamy, and warfare and speaking of resurrection and a Supreme Being called Mdalidiphu, Nxele subsequently married two wives and reverted to such staunchly "un-Christian" practices as *xhentsa* dancing and smearing his body with red ocher. Eventually, in May 1819, now himself already drawn deeply into the wider political arena and commanding a large following, Nxele led an attack of some 10,000 warriors on the fort at Grahamstown that was roundly warded off by the colonial troops and eventually led to Nxele's surrender several months later. Confined to Robben Island with thousands of other captives, Nxele drowned in 1820 while attempting to escape in a small boat.

Ntsikana Gaba, by comparison, was a rather more placid man who at no point in his career commanded the kind of mass following that Nxele had enjoyed. Born circa 1780 to a noble family of counselors to the famous Chief Ngqika, Ntsikana is generally considered the first Xhosa Christian. Circa 1815 Ntsikana experienced strange visions in which he saw bright rays of light striking the side of his favorite ox and a raging wind arising out of a clear sky. Neither of these events was a particularly startling phenomenon for a diviner such as Ntsikana, yet what an inner voice kept telling him was certainly a message of an altogether novel kind. "Let there be prayer! Let everything bow the knee!" the voice said, possibly echoing some of the teachings Ntsikana had heard in his childhood from the missionary van der Kemp. After these strange incidents, Ntsikana began to formulate the rudiments of an indigenous Christian theology at the center of which stood four hymns for which he had composed both the words and the music. Although these hymns, in form and content, retain much of the aesthetics, imagery, and symbolism of traditional Xhosa ritual and performance, Ntsikana's teaching—especially after he had established more regular contacts with the new mission station at Chumie (the original Lovedale)—also incorporated elements such as the regular meeting of a non-kinship-based group of believers and notions of sin and repentance. But above all, as Janet Hodgson puts it in her comprehensive treatment of the "Great Hymn," Ntsikana's new theology expressed "faith into the unknown where the supreme being rather than the ancestors held sway."[4]

Clearly, here were two conflicting notions of God's creation and white power and, correspondingly, two contrasting attempts of thinking about community, authority, and the self in a dramatically changed social universe. Biographers of Nxele and Ntsikana have persistently overemphasized both men's opposite responses to Christianity, Nxele's almost millenarian position usually being claimed by the more militant opponents of white rule and Ntsikana's more conciliatory stance providing the model for a more conservative brand of black nationalism. It is beyond the scope of this book to examine in detail any of these hagiographies. But for all their differences, Nxele and Ntsikana also had a number of things in common, particularly with respect to their social function. As diviners, both were intensely preoccupied with diagnosing the ailment that had befallen Xhosa society and driven by the desire to nourish some sense of collective identity within the framework of comprehensive cosmologies. And, as Jeffrey Peires observes, both men were operating within the same confines of Xhosa chiefly politics and the colonial frontier. They thus represent "an adaptation within the traditional religious framework of innovation and experimentation rather than a radical break away from it":

> Their different revelations were simply alternative permutations of the same stock of concepts, deriving from the necessity of fusing Xhosa religion with Christianity in order to formulate a new world-view capable of comprehending the irruption of the Europeans. . . . Nxele's nationalist theology emerged as a result of white hostility to his version of Christianity and to his patron, Ndlambe, whereas Ntsikana's pacifism was due to the political circumstances of his sponsor, Ngqika. Their popular impact depended less on their personal charisma than on the popular acceptability of their respective messages.[5]

The debate about Ntsikana's and Nxele's historical roles continues to this day. But if the resurgence in the wake of the 1994 elections of popular interest in the remains of early Xhosa chiefs and in the display of Xhosa skulls in European museums is any indication, the mythologies and stories woven around these and other charismatic nineteenth-century figures reveal less about their respective lives than, as Peires has recognized, about the "struggle for the Xhosa mind."[6] And perhaps more than anything else, the retellings and rewritings of Nxele's and Ntsikana's stories are fascinating chapters in the history of the global imagination: local variations of and early entanglements with a wide range of modern cosmologies. At the center of these modern cosmologies lie two powerful and interrelated images of personal and social identity: the prophet and the nation. Both images in time came to be applied to Nxele and Ntsikana, and since my main concern here is with the latter, a brief recapitulation of the making of Ntsikana the prophet and national figure is in order.

Historical evidence suggests that to early missionaries Nxele and Ntsikana were simply "prominent Characters" and that it was not until the late 1880s and early 1890s that some churchmen began to talk about the "prophet" Ntsikana.[7] Eventually, several decades later, and with several biographies published about him, terms such as *polofiti* and *mprofiti* had become firmly attached to Ntsikana's name and the man had become established as a figure of national importance.[8] It is interesting to note that most of these accounts construct Ntsikana's conversion to Christianity as a radical breach with Xhosa tradition and ancestor religion and as a move toward the awakening of a national feeling. Thus if John K. Bokwe, for instance, in his *Ntsikana: The Story of an African Convert*, characterizes Ntsikana's life as "a connecting link between that period of utter darkness" and the "dawning epoch of civilisation," he is of course not just subsuming Ntsikana under the great Darwinian scheme of evolution by which nature and society were said to be ordered.[9] He also provides the template that allows for Ntsikana to be brought fully into the mainstream of European mission churches and nationalist mythology. And Bokwe does so precisely at the moment, I think, when it became crucial for the white-controlled missions to combat the perceived threat of so-called Ethiopian and Zionist movements by accommodating, in theory at least, the validity of specifically African appropriations of the Gospel.

The late-nineteenth-century sanctification of Ntsikana as prophet and protonationalist correlates with subsequent attempts by scholars of South African religions to bring the growing importance of independent and Zionist religious practices squarely within the scope of the analytical apparatus of the modern state, by interpreting such practices not as "tribal" vestiges but, in the manner of the British school of functionalist anthropology, as adaptations to urban society. It is thus that the Zionist prophet, in Bengt G. Sundkler's henceforth classical definition, is no longer seen as a purely religious phenomenon but as emerging from a combination of the precolonial kingship pattern with "another strong leadership pattern within Zulu society: that of the diviner or witch-finder (isangoma)." Prophesying, as Sundkler boldly declares, "is divining, in a supposedly Christian form."[10]

The confusion we see here in authors like Bokwe and Sundkler over the *polofiti*, the diviner, the king, and the "witch-finder" is typical of a great deal of early thinking about African religious systems in general and forms of prophecy in particular.[11] It is not my intention here to offer any clarification in this matter, nor do I wish to come to any conclusion about who Ntsikana really was and how he fits in with the broader pattern of traditional religious and ritual practice. Rather, I want to put forth the notion that what all these engagements with prophecy are about is different attitudes toward the past and, through them, different ways of thinking about social order and the self. Essentially, it is as prophet that Ntsikana from around 1900 came to symbolize something beyond Christian conversion and salvation. It is in the era of intensifying racial and social tensions of the modern South Africa, I argue, that the image of Ntsikana the African prophet and that of Nxele the millenarian radical came to signify for both Europeans and Africans two opposing notions of personal identity, nationhood, and social order.

There are two areas in which these linkages among nationalism, prophecy, and ideologies of social order become most salient. The first area lies in the sphere of culture or, rather, in the peculiar way culture intervenes in the emergence of nationalist discourse. It is now a widely accepted fact that anticolonial nationalism not only took a variety of forms and was implicated within global discourses and structures of domination in a variety of ways but also emerged as a result of a particularly ambiguous relationship with the colonial state. In this regard, Partha Chatterjee has provided us with what must be the most incisive analysis of the inherent contradictoriness in nationalist thinking. Although it has now everywhere effectively wrested political power from the colonial state, according to Chatterjee, nationalism's acceptance of universal reason prevented it from dismantling a "framework of knowledge whose representational structure corresponds to the very structure of power nationalist thought seeks to repudiate."[12] It is thus, Chatterjee argues, that nationalist thought, despite its political success, is ultimately characterized by a "forced closure of possibilities," a "blocked dialectic."[13]

The questions that then arise out of this contradictoriness and that nationalist thinking poses are the following: "Can nationalist thought produce a discourse of order while daring to negate the very foundations of a system of knowledge that has conquered the world? How far can it succeed in maintaining its difference from a discourse that seeks to dominate it?"[14]

The answers to these questions, Chatterjee suggests, are overwhelmingly given in the realm of culture, especially during that phase of colonial rule when the encounter between emergent nationalist consciousness and post-Enlightenment rationalist thought produced an awareness of an essential cultural difference between East and West. It was during that "moment of departure" that nationalists would concede the superiority of the West in the sciences, technology, and other attributes of European culture, while at the same time they began to assert the superiority of the East in the spiritual realm, in the arts, and in religion. Hence a truly modern nation in Africa or Asia would combine the superior material qualities of the West with Eastern spiritual greatness and African ancestral wisdom.[15]

In reality, of course, this type of thinking was not confined to the colonies. In a sense, it might even be argued that the concept of culture was in part invented because of the colonial encounter.[16] Throughout much of the nineteenth century, knowledge in the West was equated with scientific truth, whereas culture was considered as essentially something inherent, a biological given. Both were strictly separated from each other and in themselves indivisible. There was but one truth, and the idea that there could be several cultures and many equally meaningful ways of life, although hinted at by Herder in the early nineteenth century, only gained acceptability from the beginning of the twentieth century. But while imperialist doctrine defined truth and culture as the exclusive property of the West and, in the process, declared the object of that knowledge to be the Orient, early anticolonial nationalism simply turned the whole idea of Orientalism around. The "Oriental" is still defined as unchanging and rooted in culture as depicted in Orientalist discourse, only he is no longer the passive object of Western contemplation and classification and now possesses the subjectivity to create himself. And so, while nationalist appropriations ultimately retained from Western nineteenth-century thought the essentialism and dualism contained in the idea of truth and culture, they also envisioned an order in which both ideas might be joined.

Of course, as a framework for political transformation, this sort of cultural synthesis hardly called for mass revolutionary activity. And it was not meant to. Rather, as Chatterjee correctly observes, it implied an elitist program that required the supremely refined intellect, the complete man, the charismatic leader. In other words, it is because of early nationalist attempts at cultural synthesis rather than the wholesale rejection of colonial rule that numerous possibilities open up not only for *évolués* to claim national sovereignty but also for a host of other figures to assume the role of what one might call passive innovators—figures whose authority derives both from transcendent inspirational sources and from an embeddedness in everyday culture. Prophets, I would argue, are such people. Not only do they emerge overwhelmingly in moments of acute crisis marked by the irruption of foreign powers, but also the responses they formulate against these outside forces reveal a concern with the wider moral community, its traditions, and its perceived need for inspired leadership. But whereas they do not always actively challenge the intellectual, political, and material premises of the encroaching forces of modernity, some prophets become what Marcia Wright has called "commissioning agents," figures who validate the grievances of the afflicted, provide rituals of incorporation, and sanction oppositional mobilization.[17] In other words, it is the ambiguities of the colonial order that allow nationalist elite discourse and prophetic activities to take hold of the same semantic ground. Both are frequently driven by the desire to demonstrate that it is possible for the colonized to fashion a culture that is at once distinctly local and modern.

The second area in which prophecy and prophetic authority become the focal points of colonial engagements with and contestations of nationalism is the arts. The reasons for this are obvious enough. In part they rest in the inability and sometimes reluctance of the colonial state to extend its regulative powers to the religious sphere, the arts, and other such aspects considered essential to "native life." But they also have to be sought for in the rise of a class of individuals whose intermediate position within the colonial social fabric uncomfortably sandwiched them between the colonial bourgeoisie and the indigenous masses. But above all, I would argue, the convergence of prophecy and nationalist thought in the arts is grounded within art itself. For if anticolonial nationalism, as I have said, in its formative phase thrives on making cultural difference the center of its attacks on colonial dominance, it is in the arts that nationalist ideologies find the necessary discursive structure to do so. It is in the essentially ambiguous sphere of the symbolic, the aesthetic, and even the miraculous that the nationalist program of cultural synthesis between the universalizing claims of modernity and the particularities of cultural difference and authenticity comes into its own. Basically concerned with the construction of community and the mediation of social processes in fluid and unpredictable ways that defy the rules of positive knowledge, it is the metaphorical, illocutionary, and performative components of ritual, speech, and music that by and of themselves constitute an antithesis to the denotative aspect of rationalist discourse. It is the structural difference between both modes, the rational and the aesthetic, knowledge and culture, and not any specific content of either of these domains that signifies per se the irreconcilability in nationalist thought between colonial subjugation and cultural identity.

But the juncture between prophecy, nationalism, and a new mode of expression also prompts a new type of artist. For the person destined to be in the vanguard of these merging discourses, the artist, is a curiously torn figure, inspired and solitary at the same time. On the one hand, artists possess the powers to envision a different kind of society, but one the other hand it is their very charismatic abilities that place them at a remove from the rest of society. It is this ambiguity that marks the discourse of the nationalist-prophet-artist as fragile and fraught with insoluble tensions, similar to the ones between nationalist claims to cultural sovereignty and the enlightened leadership's aspirations toward "modernization." Artists, like prophets and nationalist leaders, embody all that is essential in the people, but at the same time artists' familiarity with and control of Western forms of knowledge always place them one step ahead of the rest. And so, finally, the popular elements, after being mobilized in the anticolonial struggle, in the end find themselves distanced from the structure of the sovereign state that is supposed to emerge from this struggle.[18]

In making these sweeping generalizations about prophets and nationalism I am, of course, not oblivious to the considerable debate concerning the nature and role of prophecy in Africa, just as I am sensitive to the problems involved in views of prophecy that are derived from Weberian notions of charismatic authority. For instance, I am not suggesting that all prophets everywhere necessarily play the same social roles, nor, in fact, that they are all artists. Conversely, it would be erroneous to argue that all artists possess prophetic qualities. What I am positing merely is that it is especially in the discursive space staked out by emergent nationalism that the artist and the prophet converge, that prophetic authority and artistic authority express and assert themselves most effectively. In a sense, then, the nationalist-prophet-artist corresponds more to a cluster of potential social roles and cultural practices than to any concrete type.

Returning to Ntsikana and his work, we shall see how the "Great Hymn" for more than half a century served as one of the reference points for the debates over core elements of the nineteenth-century global imagination—debates that cannot be grasped adequately without first having a sense of the correlations between nationalism's theology and aesthetics and, of course, Ntsikana's music itself.

*B Flat or B Natural?: The "Great Hymn" and the*
*Rule of Colonial Difference*

Oral tradition has it that Ntsikana received the inspiration for the "Great Hymn" at an *umdudo* (wedding) dance he attended on or immediately after the day of his conversion experience. Further evidence suggests that the "Great Hymn" was subsequently adopted by Christian communities throughout the region and soon attracted the attention of European missionaries, who began to publish it in print as early as 1827.[19] In the form most commonly found today in the hymnals of a variety of denominations, the first couple of verses of the hymn read as follows:

> Ulo Tixo omkulu, ngosezulwini;
> Ungu Wena-wena Kaka lenyaniso.
> Ungu Wena-wena Nqaba yenyaniso.
> Ungu Wena-wena Hlati lenyaniso.
> Ungu Wena-wen' uhlel' enyangwaneni.
> Ulo dal' ubom, wadala pezulu.
> Lo Mdal' owadala wadala izulu.
> Lo Menzi wenkwenkwezi noZilimela.
>
> ──────────
>
> He is the Great God, Who is in heaven;
> Thou art Thou, Shield of truth.
> Thou art Thou, Stronghold of truth.
> Thou art Thou, Thicket of truth.
> Thou art Thou Who dwellest in the highest.
> He Who created life [below] created [life] above.
> That Creator Who created, created heaven.
> This maker of the stars and the Pleiades.

Since I shall not be concerned in the rest of this chapter with the words of the "Great Hymn," a few remarks may suffice here about the imagery and style of the hymn. According to Hodgson, several features clearly mark Ntsikana's literary style as that of an *izibongo*, a Xhosa praise poem. Like the traditional genre, the hymn is built up of a compact and richly metaphorical series of praise names of God that resonate with such staple Xhosa economic pursuits as hunting and pastoralism, as well as with notions of virility and fighting prowess. In addition, Ntsikana created a semantically dense text of piled-up words by using such established devices as parallelism and repetition, which when delivered in the manner of a traditional *imbongi* produce interesting rhythmic effects.[20] Although these are lost in the versions in which the "Great Hymn" is most commonly sung today, there are two reasons for disputing Hodgson's claim that Ntsikana deliberately contrasted his more traditional literary style modeled on the high-pitched and fast-paced *izibongo* with a "quieter and more measured" rhythmic flow of the music.[21] First, Xhosa performers do

Example 5.1. "Ulo Thixo omkhulu."

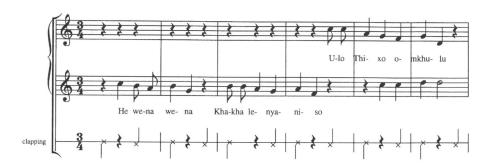

not as a rule distinguish between fully melodic chant and praise poetry, both being considered *hlabelela* (singing). Second, it is precisely the shape of Ntsikana's original composition, that is unclear in the first place.

Ntsikana did not notate his compositions, and no accurate descriptions of his music are known. Most accounts of early-nineteenth-century performances, in form and content, reiterate the statement made in 1828 by John Philip of the Church of Scotland—the first statement ever made about the hymn and its composer—that Ntsikana's hymn was sung "in a low monotonous native air."[22] Still, although we do not know what the "Great Hymn" really sounded like in Ntsikana's day and age, research carried out by David Dargie permits us to reconstruct with some degree of probability the outlines of the original work.[23]

Among the best bases for this reconstruction of the original text is "Ulo Tixo omkulu," a recording made by the eminent folk music collector Hugh Tracey in the Peddie district in 1957 (ex. 5.1).[24] Although the use of certain impolite terms such as *mlungu* (white man) in spoken asides at the end of the song suggests that Tracey's recording was made among amaQaba people with little or no contact with Christian missions, the transcription and an analysis of some of the more prominent features of this recording have led David Dargie to conclude that this performance goes back "to the early ways of singing the Great Hymn at the mission."[25] First, on the record label the song is identified as a wedding song for women (although male voices are also heard). That is to say, "Ulo Tixo omkulu" is associated with the context from which it is said to have originally emerged during Ntsikana's time. Second, save for a few minor instances of Western influence, the overall style of the performance—its cross-rhythmic patterns, call-and-response structure, hand clapping, and vocal percussion—marks Tracey's recording as a typical example of "deep"-Xhosa music. Yet the strongest indication by far of a putatively ancient origin of the song, according to Dargie, comes from the numerous correspondences between the lyrics of this example and some of the published versions of Ntsikana's original hymn. Generally, then, it is these features that lend the performance, as Dargie puts it, a "convincing authenticity."[26]

Figure 5.1. John Knox Bokwe (Cory Library, Rhodes University, Grahamstown).

Somewhat more intricate is the question of whether the melodic material in Tracey's 1957 recording, too, can be identified as Ntsikana's original composition. And it is here that we have to jump ahead by half a century to the place that by now has become rather familiar to us: Lovedale. For it is at Lovedale that Ntsikana's spiritual legacy and music have always held particular significance. After Ntsikana died in 1821 and his small congregation attached itself to the missionaries who eventually were to build Lovedale, the man once belittled as an "unremarkable household head" in time, as we have seen, acquired the posthumous status of a prophet about whom poems, biographies, and even songs were written. And like the figure of Ntsikana himself, his works became sacrosanct at Lovedale.[27]

One of those who distinguished themselves in turning Ntsikana into an icon of almost national reverence and spreading his music throughout South Africa was John Knox Bokwe (fig. 5.1)—the person who as a young boy had been so impressed by Mrs. Stewart's piano playing. Like Ntsikana, Bokwe was a leading figure in nineteenth-century Xhosa Christianity and an established idol in the

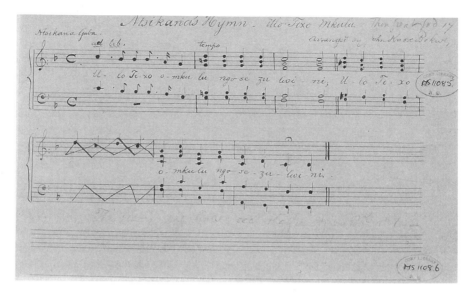

Figure 5.2. J. K. Bokwe's autograph of "Ntsikana's Hymn—Ulo Tixo Mkulu" (MS 11 085, Cory Library, Rhodes University, Grahamstown).

pantheon of Lovedale luminaries. Moreover, as one of the first Xhosa ordained ministers Bokwe was subsequently claimed as more than "a mere tribal figure," someone who himself became the object of a number of hagiographies, such as Samuel E. K. Mqhayi's *Ubomi buka J. K. Bokwe* (Life of J. K. Bokwe) (1925). J. K. Bokwe, as I have mentioned earlier, was born in 1855 at Ntselamanzi, the "native village" near Lovedale, to a family who were among the first converts of Ntsikana. Educated at Lovedale, Bokwe soon became the protégé not only of Mrs. Stewart, his piano teacher, but also of Lovedale's principal, James Stewart, who first made him a messenger and then in 1876 promoted him to assistant editor of Lovedale's in-house journal *Kaffir Express—Isigidimi Sama-Xosa* and later selected him as his own private secretary and head of the telegraph office at Lovedale. At the height of his career, in 1892, Bokwe was sent to Glasgow—following on the heels of the African Choir—to study divinity. After his return to South Africa and his ordination there, he continued working as a teacher and minister at Lovedale until his death in 1922.

Music occupied a special place in Bokwe's life. He conducted the choir at Lovedale and devoted himself to the composition of hymns and sacred songs, many of which, such as "Vuka Deborah," are still sung throughout South Africa today.[28] Bokwe's most important contribution to South African music, however, is a collection of hymns that was first published in November 1876 in *Kaffir Express—Isigidimi Sama-Xosa*, and then later again in 1885 in a hymnbook titled *Amaculo ase Lovedale* (Hymns of Lovedale). Reprinted several times, this series of Xhosa four-part hymns in tonic sol-fa contains not only Bokwe's own compo-

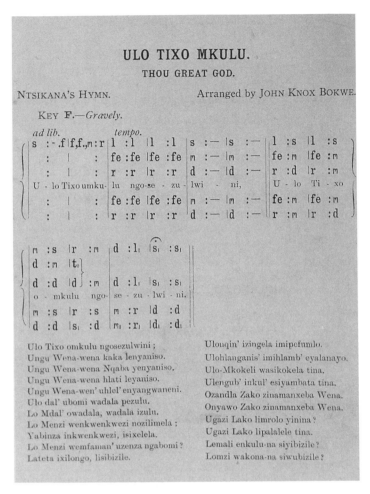

Figure 5.3. J. K. Bokwe's tonic Sol-fa score of "Ulo Tixo Mkulu" (Cory Library, Rhodes University, Grahamstown).

sitions and English hymn tunes with adapted Xhosa words but also the first printed score of Ntsikana's "Great Hymn" (figs. 5.2 and 5.3).

It is difficult to say whether this version enjoyed more acceptance in and around Lovedale than the amaQabe version recorded by Tracey. In fact, it is open to debate whether Bokwe's tonic sol-fa score is an adequate rendition of Ntsikana's original composition in the first place. The uncertainty is due not only to the lack of reliable documentation that predates Bokwe's transcriptions but also to historical evidence that suggests that Ntsikana's first converts—such as J. K. Bokwe's grandparents—reputedly sang the "Great Hymn" to two different tunes, only one of which Bokwe admitted to having memorized. In an interesting attempt to make up for Bokwe's mnemonic lacuna, David Dargie

Example 5.2. "Ulothix' omKhulu—Ntsikana's Great Hymn."

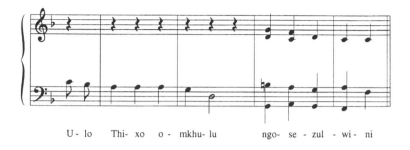

U - lo    Thi- xo    o - mkhu- lu        ngo- se - zul - wi - ni

has synoptically juxtaposed selected melodic fragments from Tracey's recorded version with Bokwe's printed score. The resultant—nonexistent—melody, he argues, might be the missing second tune of the "Great Hymn," elements of which Bokwe then incorporated into the version known to him.

Finally, to add to all the confusion, contemporary performances of the "Great Hymn" throughout the eastern Cape and as far as the Transkei—and even heavily politicized versions that surfaced during the heady 1970s—appear to have a lot more in common with yet another version featured in a recording by the Zwelitsha Choral Society under the baton of Bokwe's son Selborne T. Bokwe (ex. 5.2). While the text of this version, labeled "Ulothix' omKhulu—Ntsikana's Great Hymn," corresponds to Ntsikana's original wording, the tune on closer inspection turns out to follow rather closely one of the choral "response" lines in the Tracey recording and, to make the tangle complete, John Knox Bokwe's published score of Ntsikana's third hymn, "Ingom'enqukuva—the Round Hymn" (ex. 5.3).

Regardless of this complex layering of versions, a comparison of J. K. Bokwe's published version and S. T. Bokwe's recorded performance of the "Great Hymn" with Tracey's 1957 recording reveals a number of Western elements that are unlikely to have been part of Ntsikana's original composition. Thus, aside from a number of rather more obtrusive features such as the stolid 3/4 meter, the heavily distorted speech rhythm in bar 1, and the awkward disparity between Xhosa prosody and the melodic contour on beat 4 of bar 1 and beat 1 of bar 2, I would like to draw particular attention to two melodic and harmonic details. The first of these is a perfect fourth (b flat) in bar 1 and the second a dominant chord in bar 5. Both these are atypical of Xhosa musical grammar, based as it is on the harmonics of the musical bow, the *uhadi*. This one-stringed instrument produces two fundamental notes about a major second apart and their corresponding series of natural harmonics, some of which the player amplifies by means of a gourd-resonator attached at the lower end of the bow. Most Xhosa music is constructed—harmonically and melodically—from a selection of these overtones, thus exhibiting a hexatonic scale and a root progression or tonality shift between I and II. In a hexatonic scale based on the fundamentals

Example 5.3. "Ingom' enqukuva— the Round Hymn."

G and F, for instance, the fourth degree (b natural) would be obtained from the fifth harmonic (ex. 5.4).

As this suggests, it must remain doubtful whether Bokwe's transcription is "the only authoritative version" of Ntsikana's hymn.[29] And it is more than open to question whether an authoritative urtext can be established by means of such a comparative analysis and that, in fact, anything may be gained at all from attempting to canonize a piece of creative work that, over a period of more than 150 years of documented history, has been the object of intense re-working, appropriation, and mythologization. Rather, what an analysis such as the one attempted here may contribute is, more than anything else, a testimony to the ongoing, essentially endogenous vitality of African performance practice. The complex layering of semantic levels in a piece of expressive culture such as the "Great Hymn" serves as a reminder of the need for grounding the interpretation of meaning in concrete social processes and in the structural minutiae of the text.

Finally, something else is at issue here, too. The "Great Hymn" was not a mere "traditional" expression of the universal truth of the Gospel in the vernacular. Ntsikana's role consisted of something more than "adapting Xhosa music

Example 5.4. The basis of Xhosa tonality in the series of overtones.

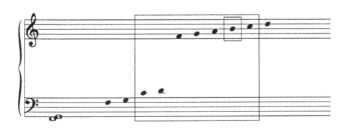

I II

for Christian worship," and thus he was more than a mere "transitional figure" who fused traditional aesthetics and a modern worldview.[30] Apart from sheer condescension, such a view suggests an inherent incompatibility of indigenous aesthetic practice and modern consciousness, just as it reproduces the basic mythology of missionization by positing a unilineal course of history from tradition to modernity, from local to universal, from collective to individual. In short, if anything is to be learned from reconstructing the history of a piece of musical fiction such as the "Great Hymn," it is that the variations and permutations to which Ntsikana's music has been subject over the course of almost two centuries bear the symbolic traces of a drawn-out and intense local dialogue with idioms and systems of meaning of a much larger scale. Like a host of related narratives and discourses examined in this book, the "Great Hymn" was a key element of the nineteenth-century global imagination in South Africa, a looking glass through which African and Europeans examined each other. And thus, leaving Ntsikana to his place of pride in the history of South African music, we now turn to some of the actors and texts implicated in this two-fold process.

I shall argue that the history of nineteenth-century European-African interpretations and constructions of the "Great Hymn" was marked by a peculiar discursive logic, by certain classificational fantasies of inclusion and exclusion or, as Partha Chatterjee has called it, a "rule of colonial difference."[31] In Chatterjee's view, the power structures and the colonial states set up in Africa and Asia during the course of the imperial project were not merely incidental to the history of modern statehood. The notion that modern forms of disciplinary power require the recognition of at least some principles of self-governance and the idea that these principles were universally applicable were vindicated precisely by excluding the colonies from the practical deployment of the theory. The point of colonial rule, Chatterjee says, was "to mark the points and instances where the colony had to become an exception.[32]

It was through three principal figures that this exception was constructed. One is that modern forms of power are applicable to all societies irrespective of historical or cultural specificities, a position which is based on a belief in the all-inclusiveness of the Western concept of reason. The second is that this concept of reason is exclusively tied to the West and cannot be exported to distant lands. The third position, while acceding to the objection raised by the second, holds that historical and cultural differences can eventually be overcome and the universality of the principle of reason restored. Although all three arguments have been associated with distinct colonial projects and imperialist ideologies, ultimately they all employ the same rule whereby the colony represents the pièce de résistance in a case to be argued in the metropolis, a rhetorical figure in a preordained narrative structure.

The implication of Chatterjee's argument for my own line of reasoning is that if modern statehood depends on the rule of colonial difference for its validation as a global truth, then the history of colonialism is of crucial interest indeed to the study of the modern state. But it is also of crucial interest to the study of the global imagination. It is this rule of colonial difference and its place within the emerging modern state in general that form the backdrop to the specific way the "parallel mutualities of colonizers and colonized" play themselves out in the framework of global culture.[33] And, finally, it is the same rule that informs the specifically aesthetic, discursive, and musical forms the global imagination of Africans and Europeans took in relation to the story of the "Great Hymn."

How, then, did this rule of colonial difference work within the context of our story? A brief look at the first accounts of Ntsikana's compositions written by European travelers and missionaries—present in the eastern Cape in ever greater numbers after Ntsikana's death—reveals that they resemble in tone and terseness Philip's statement of 1828 about the "low monotonous native air." Thus one missionary heard Ntsikana's hymn sung to what he perceived to be an "easy chant" (J. Brownlee, ca. 1822), while another simply dismissed the music as being "monotonous" (Rose, 1829). Yet another churchman detected little more than "native airs" (Kay, 1825), while traveler Andrew Steedman reported the hymn to have been sung to a "wild and plaintive melody" (1835). Of course, such statements reflected centuries of negative European viewpoints toward African music, attitudes that were shared, among others, by early commentators on Xhosa performance such as Heinrich Lichtenstein, for instance, who in 1803 maintained that Xhosa melodies "were insufferable to a musical ear" and "little better than a deadened howl."[34]

A somewhat different picture emerges from early black appraisals of the hymn. Thus Charlotte Manye's erstwhile teacher Isaac Wauchope, who learned Ntsikana's hymns from his grandmother, recounts that Ntsikana had borrowed the tune of his hymn from the chorus of a widely popular Xhosa *umdudo* (wedding) song—with one critical difference: "[T]he strain is disguised by the dropping of the main slurrings common to the vocalised Kafir song, in order to adapt it to the words, so that ideas may be expressed."[35] In the same vein, and yet another half a century later, literary scholar and Lovedale pupil Archibald C. Jordan saw the importance of Ntsikana "not in the legendary smitings by the shafts of sunrise, nor in the rising winds and readings from karosses." Of far greater historical significance was the fact that Ntsikana's "Hymn of Praise is the first literary composition ever to be assigned to individual formulation—thus constituting a bridge between the traditional and the post-traditional period."[36]

It is doubtful whether any of these statements, even though they were made by African followers and admirers of Ntsikana, adequately capture any of the aesthetic of Xhosa music as it was commonly performed in the early nineteenth century. But that is beside the point. Rather, what we have here is a strikingly persistent conception of a piece of nineteenth-century Xhosa expressive culture as an essentially modern one—a view that, like the earlier European assessments, was premised on the assumption that traditional, "primitive" music was the unconscious expression of dark collective forces and only through Christianization could it be raised to higher levels of individuality, consciousness, and cognition.

The emphasis on creativity and cognitive content as an expression of individual consciousness is complemented in early black accounts by another rhetorical figure, linked to the former in seemingly contradictory but nevertheless highly significant ways. Thus in 1858 the Reverend Tiyo Soga, another prominent figure at Lovedale, claimed that Ntsikana's hymn evoked in his small congregation "memories of the past." Some of these, he wrote, no doubt "would be pleasant, others again must have been most sad and melancholy."[37] A few years later, another report entitled "Kaffir Poetry" by an anonymous writer struck a similarly ambiguous note of black disenchantment and nostalgia. "Kaffir Poetry," first published in 1874 in Lovedale's paper, *Kaffir Express*, praises the "Great Hymn" as a genuinely African form of worship that was "sung to a wild plaintive air—irregular like the words, but without misaccentuation." But more important than this, the report goes on to state, the hymn had a powerful effect on Christian congregations, because "the Kaffirs, from the circumstances of its composition, look on it with a kind of national feeling, especially now that they droop their heads from the loss of national freedom, and the dominance of the white man."[38]

The point about misaccentuation, of course, was aimed indirectly at the white missionaries themselves and the utter disregard in mission hymnody and liturgical practice for the prosodic subtlety of the Xhosa language. Thus the critique resounded with J. K. Bokwe's efforts two years later to reconcile Western hymnody with the musical traditions of Africa. Yet read in conjunction with the rest of the commentary, the observations in "Kaffir Poetry" perhaps also suggest considerations of a broader political nature: the article advances an early, if somewhat timid, critique of the "civilizing mission" itself. But it does so in a way that bespeaks the dilemma of anticolonial nationalist thought mired in the peculiar logic of the rule of colonial difference. First, it faithfully reproduces the ideas of national progress and individual agency, the two most crucial tenets of missionary ideology. Second, it then combines these with a nostalgic reinvention of the past, thus injecting a conservative element into early African nationalist politics of resistance that was not to fully come into its own until the 1920s and 1930s. To be sure, most of this traditionalist revival was hard to articulate in verbal discourse in the 1870s. For mission converts to idolize the precolonial past would be tantamount to reverting to "heathenism." But the whole point about my analysis of the "Great Hymn" is of course that to people who seek to navigate in a rapidly expanding social universe music offered a more malleable medium than verbal discourse for anchoring personal practice and identity in meaningful space–time relationships.

Ironically, the colonial administration itself from the 1880s had begun to embark on a similar project of reorientation toward the past. For as the state sought to curb Africans' growing sense of independence and demolish their material base in a class of propertied, prosperous, and Christianized peasants, Cape officials increasingly came to rely on the mechanisms of leadership and social control embodied in the time-honored structures of Xhosa chieftaincy.[39]

Tribalism, as the vestiges of chiefly power and rural consciousness were labeled in colonial parlance, was thus no longer regarded as inimical to the civilizing mission. The missionaries and, as the previous chapter has shown, some mission-educated Africans such as Charlotte Manye cautiously followed suit.

To repeat, by the 1890s none of this had been officially sanctioned and it was not until the 1920s that such a policy shift would have been openly advocated in administration or missionary circles. At the same time, it becomes clear that the elevation of Ntsikana's "Great Hymn" in nineteenth-century Xhosa discourse from an expression of Christian faith to a monument of nationalist defiance represents an ex post facto interpretation rather than historical fact. It partakes of a specific form of nineteenth-century bourgeois consciousness in which national unity is posited as a natural condition and a wide range of fictions of collective identity conceal the fissures and cleavages that made the myth necessary in the first place. The continuity with the past that Africans perceived in Ntsikana's music in reality came out of the strangely osmotic interaction of colonial power and African opposition. In short, its presupposed authenticity is in its entirety historically produced, an invocation of the very processes that articulated marginalized idioms and hegemonic discourses, local practice, and global models.

This, then, is where the debate concerning the "Great Hymn" stood when the African Choir introduced Ntsikana's work to Europe—a debate in which music served as the powerful medium for a sustained engagement with Europe and its modern fictions about progress, nation, and the individual. Yet the debate covered more than the intricacies of Xhosa musical expression. It equally addressed the burning issues that arose from the profound upheavals during the latter half of the nineteenth century in African religious practice, cultural identity, and political consciousness. It was a controversy that echoed the "battle for the Xhosa mind," the dichotomy between Nxele's millenarian defiance and Ntsikana's moderation, and, above all, epitomized black South Africans' conflicted relationship with modernity. Moreover, within the wider arena of the black transatlantic dialogue, the early black assessments of the "Great Hymn" anticipate some of the debate over the double consciousness the jubilee songs articulated in black American culture. In due course, we shall see how these diasporic engagements played themselves out in the second tour of the African Choir, to North America. For now let us rejoin the African Choir on their tour through England and examine the British public's use of Ntsikana and his music to construct quite contrary images of Africa and, ipso facto, of itself.

Glancing over the extensive press coverage of the tour, one is struck by the sense of genuine admiration for the vocal talents displayed by the South Africans. But this positive reception—inconceivable as it would have been in Dickens's day—was less surprising than it may seem. For it dovetailed neatly with what the concerts, after all, were meant to confirm—the fulfillment in colonial everyday reality of Dickens's notorious prognosis that the Zulus had better be "civilised off the face of the earth." Consequently, for one journalist quoted by the *Ludgate Monthly* the African Choir simply constituted "a living band of witnesses as to the power of Christian civilization on the raw material of African humanity," while another critic believed that their concerts "ought to put a final end to the stale calumny that an African Christianised is an African spoiled."[40]

Yet not all sectors of the British public appear to have shared such liberal views. The music, to some critics, was simply too European. "[T]he value and interest of the pieces performed," the weekly magazine *South Africa*, for example, complained, "are considerably reduced by the inevitable European harmonies . . . suggestive rather of an English tonic sol-fa class than of savage strains."[41] And the *Musical Standard* seconded: "[I]t is pretty obvious that the South African singers have in the process of civilization adopted more or less the European scale, to say nothing of European harmonies."[42] Of course, as the dispute over stage dress discussed in chapter 4 illustrated, the disaffection was not one about musical grammar alone. Voiced though it mostly was from within more openly antimissionary and antiliberal factions of the metropolitan press, the disappointment bespoke a more deep-seated ambiguity at the heart of late Victorian imperial doctrine as such, what Renato Rosaldo has called "imperialist nostalgia."[43]

Until the mid-nineteenth century, attempts at justifying the "civilizing mission" had rested on the notion that Africans' inferiority and barbarism were to be attributed to environmental predicaments rather than to some racial deficits. The work of the early evangelical missions in the eastern Cape—just like much, although by no means all, of the colonial public discourse about "natives," colonization, and Christianization—consisted precisely in vindicating Africans' innate capacity for civilization. If whites and blacks did not occupy the same positions on the scale of racial evolution, the latter could at least hope that, given time and "proper,"—that is, white—guidance, they, too, would eventually climb the ladder of progress.

The broader changes within British society and consciousness at the end of the nineteenth century changed all that. What then came to dominate popular discourses at home and in settler society was a more blatantly racist variant of the imperialist rhetoric, one that declared Africans' "benighted" condition permanent and intrinsic. As Rider Haggard, for instance, one of the most popular writers of fiction about South Africa and author of such phenomenally successful novels as *King Solomon's Mines*, mused in 1877, civilization "produces effects diametrically opposite to those we are accustomed to observe in white nations; it debases before it can elevate." And, he went on, recapitulating his experiences in Natal and Zululand, "as regards the Kafirs it is doubtful, and remains to be proved, whether it has much power to elevate them at all."[44]

The crux that resulted from this shift toward Social Darwinism, jingoism, and "scientific racism"—a shift, recall, that had prompted the tour of the African Choir in the first place—was that it touched upon one of the nerve centers of the Victorian global imagination and that it brought into sharp relief the fluidity and hybridity of identities and social relations that were the very mark of global modernity. If, in the early days of empire, difference had been the raison d'être for the civilizing mission, scientific racism destroyed the moral justification on which imperial expansion rested. In other words, if the civilizing mission took difference as its point of departure, it was in the uppermost interest of the whole operation to efface the very difference on which it rested.

In light of these contradictions, the disappointment about the lack of "exotic" elements in displays of African identity such as the concerts of the African Choir would therefore seem to signify two somewhat paradoxical aspects of imperial practice and consciousness. On the one hand, the metropolitan disillusionment was symptomatic of the kind of nostalgia that arose when imperialism sought to erase its agency in transforming the globe. But on the other hand, the same imperialist nostalgia veiled the fact that the colonial powers had long backtracked from the promises of the civilizing mission, whatever their worth. In many ways, it might even be argued that the category "indigenous" was invented in order to soothe such nostalgia by invoking long-defunct Western fixities of place and identity, by countering the colonial world's unsettling hybridity and twofold logic of sameness turning into difference and difference becoming sameness.[45]

A vivid sense of all this emerges from a review in the *Musical Times*—along with the *Ludgate Monthly* essay discussed earlier one of the most detailed (and engaged) reviews of the African Choir. The review opens with a rhetorical gesture typical of the late Victorian obsession with an all-embracing system of positive knowledge:

> The musical capabilities displayed by the African native choir, which during the last month has claimed attention in London, must have been a surprise to many. Hitherto the African has been deemed so undeveloped as to be thought scarcely worthy of association with music, but, as in many other instances, this supposition has apparently arisen from ignorance rather than knowledge.[46]

At this point the review launches into a long list of "peculiarities" such as the lack of leading notes, an emphasis on "most elaborate sub-divisions by hand clappings," the close correlation between speech melody and vocal melody, and the frequent use of parallel fifths, neutral thirds, and augmented fourths. These and other differences serve as markers in a whole classificatory scheme of racial and temporal alterity. It is thus that, as the *Musical Times* asserts, "the notes, to their minds, have no relation to each other as with us. Hence they avoid our mi, fa, and sing the fa sharp." Ultimately, the London critic concludes his review, it is from features such as these that "a very good idea might be formed of the cradle of music."

The fa sharp that is being referred to here as a sign of primordiality is, of course, the same b natural that we have recognized as one of several salient markers of the authenticity and Africanness of the "Great Hymn." But in the

*Musical Times* it is figured as falling outside of the human realm altogether. It is a regression into something less than nature, something without "relation," without rationality. In short, it is an Other as such, the embodiment of a foreign, yet entirely knowable, reality.

To summarize, the "Great Hymn" was anything but an authentic expression of "primitive" society. Nor was it simply symbolic of African collective resistance to white domination. Rather, the truth of Ntsikana's composition was produced in the encounter of specific projects that engaged colonizers and colonized alike. Being neither the result of a mere imposition of colonial power nor the uncomplicated expression of a pristine "folk" tradition, the "Great Hymn" was, in fact, one of the many terrains on which colonialism constantly activated and reproduced itself as a cultural process, a practically mediated relationship framed by meanings. One of the truths that resulted from this process and that I have concentrated on here was a certain symbiosis of ideologies, narratives, and epistemes. Although African readings of the "Great Hymn" stressed its distance from and opposition to the white man's world, the same readings celebrated the hymn's affinity to Western notions of rationality, progress, and individuality.

Here my account of the African Choir ends or, in any case, the part of it that concerned itself with the first tour, to England. Two final aspects of this extraordinary moment in the history of the global imagination of South Africa and the West remain to be considered: the parallel tours of the Zulu Choir and the second tour of the African Choir, to North America. Both these topics—and the unique turn of events that they instigated—will be discussed in the following two chapters.

# 6

## Variations upon a Theme

### *The Zulu Choir in London,*
### *1892–93*

Natal, a British colony since 1843, was in many ways a special place. Although the process of colonization here closely followed the pattern set in the Cape, a number of significant differences in both British colonial policy and the African response to it lend the story told in this chapter—although it is but a variation upon the story of the African Choir and the larger theme of late-nineteenth-century African and European global fictions—a particular flavor.

As Colin Bundy has noted, several factors shaped social relations in the colony and mitigated the cultural pressures of white colonists on the mass of Natal's black population.[1] The first and perhaps most notable among these factors was the continuing African occupation of large tracts of ancestral lands. The second consisted in a colonial policy that in the interest of effective administration and by operating separate legal systems—one for whites based on English legislation and the other for Africans based on customary law—actively favored traditionalism and effectively blocked the growth of a sizable and modernizing black peasantry. The consequences of this policy—associated in large part with the person of Secretary of Native Affairs Theophilus Shepstone—were twofold. First, for a minority of Africans who had chosen to break with tradition, this break entailed a far greater distance from the "traditionalists" than the gap that separated mission-bred and "Red" Africans in the Cape. Second, the discourse of white colonists—economically and politically much weaker and hence more dependent on quasi-feudal relations and African produce—was colored by what Bundy has called a "febrile quality," a hysterical, delusive mood, and racially legitimized hostility toward any sign of African independent economic and political power. It is this broad pattern of social rela-

Figure 6.1. The Zulu Choir in Edendale (Veit Erlmann collection).

tions in Natal at the end of the nineteenth century that forms the background to the story of the Zulu Choir.

The circumstances of its foundation, like those of the African Choir a year earlier, are connected with Orpheus McAdoo's seminal visit to South Africa in the early 1890s. In the course of his tour the redoubtable American had also visited Durban and Pietermaritzburg, where African audiences, like black audiences in the Cape, had accorded him a particularly warm welcome, hailing his music as *okumtoti* (sweet) and predicting that it would be "remembered for a long time."[2] In addition, the remarkable success of the African Choir in the Cape and abroad provided telling proof that black South Africans, "if given the chance," were the equals not only of their American brethren but also of whites.

The members of the Zulu Choir, unlike those of the African Choir, were recruited exclusively from within one community: the Driefontein mission station near Ladysmith, one of the most prosperous and assimilated communities of *amakholwa* (believers) in the heart of Natal. The original choir consisted of leader Saul Msane; his wife, Rosaline Julia Mini; and his sister Asiana, as well as Edith Mini, Bessie Molife, Lydia Mini, Martha Molife, Hetty Kumalo, Joseph D. Mzamo, Waka Sopela, Solomon Kumalo, Joseph Kumalo, Zephaniah Dhlamini, and Josiah Tshangana (fig. 6.1). The more seasoned traveler in Natal history will immediately recognize in these names a pattern, in fact the whole story *in nuce* of Natal's black peasantry. For the Kumalo, Mini, and Molife families counted among Natal's oldest and wealthiest stock of Christianized Africans, having migrated to Edendale near Pietermaritzburg with the Methodist missionary James Allison early in the nineteenth century. Moreover, the three families for a long time dominated local African politics and led the resistance against Shepstone's "native" policy, the elders Stephanus Mini and Johannes Kumalo occupying prominent positions as "chief" of Edendale and *amakholwa* spokesman, respectively. As for Saul Msane, his biography places him at the center of the early generation of twentieth-century nationalist leaders. Born in Edendale in 1856, Msane received his education at the Healdtown Wesleyan Training Institution. A teacher at Driefontein around the time of the constitution of the Zulu Choir, Msane later occupied the position of a compound manager on the Witwatersrand, a fact which earned him the less than enviable title of Isita-sa-Bantu (enemy of the people). Despite this and a somewhat checkered career, Msane later rose to political prominence as one of the founders of the ANC and member of a delegation that was to take him on a second trip to England to protest the Native Lands Act.[3]

We shall have opportunity later on to review Msane's controversial role in the Zulu Choir. As for the tour itself, after a two-month period of training in Driefontein and with endorsements from the governor of Natal and the mayors of Durban and Pietermaritzburg, the singers set out from Pietermaritzburg in March 1892 and, after brief appearances in a number of cities of the eastern Cape and Cape Town, arrived in London on May 1. Performances in England remained confined to London throughout the summer of 1892 and, more particularly, to shows at the Horticultural Exhibition and daily appearances at the Royal Aquarium. Titled "From the Wilds to Westminster," the latter show closely followed the model of the African Choir the year before. It consisted of two parts: a first part in which, the *Weekly Dispatch* noted, "we have wild singing and dancing, ceremonies by a witch-doctor, interchange of rough courtesies by men and women in as near an approach to native costume as English decency allows, and other preludes to a fighting expedition."[4] In the second part, the company—"neatly arrayed in garments of something like english cut"—performed a variety of part songs, selections from Sullivan and Rossini, chanteys such as "Larboard Watch," and Scottish songs like "Coming thro' the Rye" and "Annie Laurie," as well as classics of the American minstrel repertoire like Stephen Foster's "Come Where My Love Lies Dreaming."

"From the Wilds to Westminster" drew but a moderate audience response, and hence it is no surprise that by October 1892 the enterprise ran into an impasse not unlike the one the African Choir had experienced the year before. To compound the crisis, choir leader Saul Msane and a small group that consisted of his wife and sister as well as Zephaniah Dhlamini and Josiah Tshangana decided to break away from the rest of the choir, allegedly on grounds of their "unwillingness to violate their Christian principles by performing in music halls." While the rest of the choir returned to Natal in March 1893, Msane and his group, reconstituted as the Zulu Christian Choir, extended their stay until August in order to earn their return passage to South Africa.

The clash between Msane and the impresarios must be briefly elaborated here. Archival evidence indicates that Msane and his group, before leaving Natal, had signed an agreement that obliged the members of the Zulu Choir to be at the service of a Ladysmith-based group of white impresarios called Holloway, Illing & Co. at a monthly wage of £20 per person.[5] Although the tour was thus clearly designed as a "strictly business venture," it is the fine print of this agreement rather than London's music halls and the Christian conscience of his compatriots that Saul Msane came into conflict with. At least, this is what the managers maintained. Msane, they claimed, had been in pecuniary difficulties and had to be advanced a large sum of money before being allowed by his creditors to leave Natal. The debt was to be repaid by deductions from his salary and that of his wife and sister, but when the managers proceeded to withhold these payments Msane accused them of breaching the agreement. Unmoved by these charges, the impresarios then found themselves accused of wanting the choir to sing in music halls.[6]

But there was more to this venture than mere quibbles over salaries and dubious offers from unsavory venues. Underlying these conflicts was a deeper-seated predicament that was inherent in the contested meanings and interpretations of modernity and, as the issue of music halls illustrates, in which questions of sobriety occupied a central position, touching a nerve center of late Victorian consciousness and, indeed, of the imperial order itself. As section 12 of the agreement stipulated, the "Natives agree to sing and perform in any Native or other costume which covers the body from the neck to immediately below the knee and it is specially agreed that they shall not be required to commit any act contrary to their profession of Christianity." Yet what precisely could be seen as contradicting Christian beliefs was open to question. H. S. Holland, a solicitor whose advice Msane sought, felt that the choir

> were legally bound by their contract to appear in Native costume, so some sort of "performance" was inevitable.
> The dance itself was perfectly innocent and had none of the associations in England which it might have had in Africa. It was made perfectly clear that they were Christians, and that the dance represented the slavery that they had already left behind, and I cannot think it had any bad effect here.[7]

Elsewhere in Natal, some observers took a somewhat sterner stance. *Inkany-iso Yase Natal*, Natal's leading mission paper, for instance, expressed regrets that the choir

> should leave under circumstances which cannot reflect credit either upon themselves or upon those with whom they have had to deal.
> Had the intentions of the promoters been better understood, and had individual members of the Choir more carefully considered the step they were about to take, they would not have signed an agreement which binds them,

although they were assured that they would not be required to do anything contrary to their religion, to exhibit themselves in heathen dress before the English public. No wonder then that they have been unable to go off in a happy frame of mind, and with confidence in their leaders. . . . We are sorry that Government, to whom, we understand, an appeal was made at the last moment, did not see any reason for delaying the departure of the troup[e] until some more satisfactory arrangements could be made; but as some of the members were Exempted Natives, while others had obtained the full consent of their parents, it was not thought advisable to interfere. . . . Do Natives know anything of the dangers of an idle life at sea? Do the girls, or their parents, realize what it means to pass twelve months in the company of a lot of single men, amidst the excitements of a life such as theirs will be? Do they realize how easy it is to fall lower, and how effectually the adoption of savage dress, even for a short while each evening, will accelerate the pace? Do they realize that, in the event of poor success or failure, the managers may be tempted to introduce the Choir to London's brilliant, but low-toned, Music Halls, where the appearance of half-naked girls will be hailed with delight? We ask, again, do these Natives realize the dangers and temptations to which they are to be exposed? No, they do not. Then most certainly they should not have been allowed to go. They should not have been allowed to decide for themselves. . . . We cannot but think that, had these men and women been made to realize the danger and temptations which will beset their way during the next twelve months, they would have declined the honour of being members of the first "Zulu Choir," or of being "presented to the Queen," or of showing the English public how like savage heathen they can become, and how unlike civilized men and christians.[8]

Although, then, on the face of it, the quarrel here, as with the African Choir, was one about contracts and money, what emerges from the comments quoted are highly dissenting notions among colonizers and colonized about modern forms of African identity in a society that had been irrevocably drawn into the maelstrom of global culture and politics. At the same time, not only do both passages reveal something of the "febrile" quality of Natal colonial politics and of the blatant racism that tainted the discourses of colonists and missionaries, but also several other issues emerge from these disputes that highlight the difficulties blacks and whites encountered in dealing with difference; issues that can only be understood by setting them in relation to the African Choir and taking into account the specific political and cultural context of Natal.

The first point to be considered here concerns the precarious position of Natal's black Christian communities. For much of the nineteenth century, *amakholwa* communities in Natal and Zululand were a hopelessly isolated minority. As late as 1880 the number of converts hardly exceeded 10,000 souls in Natal and probably even numbered only a few hundred in the neighboring areas of Zululand and Pondoland.[9] By contrast and in spite of the growing importance of labor migration, the mass of the African population remained firmly wedded to lifeways and belief systems that centered around patrilineal ancestors and their spirits and that were inextricably interwoven with a number of practices, such as polygamous marriages and divination, considered by Christians to be the quintessential signs of backwardness and savagery.

But the *amakholwa* communities were not only distanced from the much larger non-Christian African societies around them; they were also at the same time barred from full entry into white colonial society. The starkest expression of this ambiguity was, no doubt, the double legal system whereby a minority of Africans in Natal since 1865 enjoyed a qualified franchise similar to the one in existence in the Cape while the vast majority of Natal's black population was placed under what was called Native Law and, hence, the direct authority of Shepstone's "native" administration. This legal dualism was not only diametrically opposed to Cape colonial practice, but it also led to numerous conflicts between *amakholwa* and the colonial administration. Thus the franchise (often dubbed exemption) laws in practice made provision for only a handful of Africans—including the adult members of the Zulu Choir—to be exempted from Native Law. The latter, for its part, at least until its codification in 1887, was little more than an ill-defined legal system that mixed a poorly understood body of Nguni law and custom with, more often than not, magisterial arbitrariness. As a result of this dualism, Natal courts not infrequently had to deal with such cases in which a Christian couple that had failed to meet the requirements for exemption was legally bound by and tried according to the provisions of Native Law.

But this was not all. Colonial administrators such as Shepstone had made it very clear that Native Law and the "tribal system" which it perpetuated (and often created in the first place) not only played a key role in Natal's entire socioeconomic system but also were to serve as a bulwark of white rule tout court.[10] Little wonder, then, that for much of the latter half of the nineteenth century missionized Africans resented the system bitterly. Generally ignored or, at best, regarded as an anomaly by Natal's system of African administration, the members of the *évolué* class rightly suspected Native Law to be the major stumbling block in the way of their complete assimilation into colonial society.[11] Johannes Kumalo, for instance, was no doubt expressing the views of many of his fellow *amakholwa* when in 1863 he denounced Native Law in a widely reported speech before a meeting of "civilised natives":

> We have left the race of our forefathers; we have left the black race and have clung to the white. We imitate them in everything we can. . . . Look round you. You have an English house, English tables, chairs. . . . [E]verything round us is English but one, and that is the law. The law by which our cases are decided is only fit to be eaten by vultures.[12]

Kumalo was a leading spokesman of Edendale, one of Natal's premier *amakholwa* settlements. And it is Edendale that embodied the tensions and ambiguities of modernity and its Natal variant more thoroughly perhaps than any other black farming community in Natal. Between its inception in 1851 and 1891, the community outside Pietermaritzburg enjoyed what the Natal Regional Survey called a "golden age." Indeed, prosperity and economic expansion were such that by 1867 some thirty or forty Edendale families had accumulated enough capital to purchase the farm Driefontein, near Ladysmith.[13] In the following decades, the two communities not only constituted the major suppliers of foodstuffs to the nearby towns, entering into serious competition with their white counterparts, but also formed the spearhead of Natal's black political and intellectual elite. Thus, in addition to Saul Msane, Edendale produced such outstanding figures of South African intellectual life as poets Herbert and Rolfes Dhlomo, composers Reuben Caluza and Alfred A. Kumalo and political activist Selby Msimang.[14]

But no matter how far this "piece of Yorkshire," as one British visitor called Edendale,[15] may have traveled down the road to assimilation, its inhabitants were hamstrung by the same legal dualism that plagued Natal's black peasantry as a whole. Like them, Edendale and Driefontein residents were sharply aware of the contradictions of a social order that increasingly backtracked from the universal  promises that had impelled black Christians to embrace the "civilizing mission" in the first place. And thus, frustrated like black converts elsewhere in Natal by their liminal position, Edendale *amakholwa* began to explore, however cautiously, specifically local interpretations of modernity and distinctly African engagements with the new global reality.

Although this process set in somewhat later in Natal than in the Cape, it did not begin in the 1890s. Even prior to this date, Natal's black Christians, despite all their isolation and weakness, had never completely veered away from traditional society. Throughout the nineteenth century, *amakholwa* communities entertained vigorous and mostly amicable relationships with non-Christian communities, and thus polygamous marriages and other such "heathen survivals" could be found in most *amakholwa* communities.[16] Similarly, like elsewhere in southern Africa, Natal Christians had begun to turn their back on the European mainstream churches as early as 1878, when Mbiana Ngidi founded his short-lived Zulu Mbiana Congregational Church. Yet despite these early examples of the continuing resilience of the symbols of the precolonial past and for reasons which have to do with the availability until at least the Zulu War of numerous opportunities for black leadership and initiative in agriculture, commerce, and education, Zionism was slow to take hold in Natal. Full-blown independent African churches did not really emerge in Natal until the foundation in the early 1900s of Isaiah Shembe's Nazareth Church.[17]

Similarly, moves toward some kind of antisettler alliance between the black middle class and Zulu royalty, although they were beginning to gain momentum, in the 1890s were little more than sporadic and highly circumspect. After all, many *amakholwa*, including some Edendale residents, had earlier cast their lot with British efforts to crush Zulu independent military power. Thus Saul Msane's call for the return of the Zulu monarch Dinizulu, exiled on St. Helena, met with no small degree of astonishment, as did the meeting in London of the

Zulu Choir with Harriet Colenso, daughter of Natal's controversial bishop and "heretic," and herself a prominent advocate of Zulu independence of some sort.[18] It was not until after World War I, when the position of Natal's black middle class was eroding under the combined effects of disenfranchisement, dispossession, and economic recession, that such linkages between *amakholwa* and "traditionalists" were to become a pivot of Natal politics. In the 1890s, however, these relationships seldom reached the sort of more playful level such as that among the Qadi people of the Ndwedwe District, where Christians and non-Christians could occasionally join in a "heathen" song such as the following:

> Inkomidi isesikoleni,
> Sihlushwa amakholwa.
>
> ———————
>
> The Committee is at school,
> We are plagued by Christians.[19]

In most *amakholwa* communities such criticism would have been met with utter disdain and would have reinforced ever more firmly black Christians' choice to seek assimilation into the white man's world.

The second point, which follows from all this, is that the line that separates black Christians from their "traditionalist" neighbors was not only a highly conspicuous and thin one but also a line the crossing of which was fraught with numerous risks and that, consequently, became subject to a great deal of redrawing and dispute in a wide range of seemingly innocuous matters. Two of these matters, as the tour of the Zulu Choir strikingly illustrates, were music and dress. Beginning in the mid-nineteenth century, mission-educated Africans in Natal had drawn a sharp line between the music they absorbed at the missions and the complex body of songs and dances that were embedded in the traditions of Zulu society. In terms of this distinction, the former, called *imusic*, was distinguished from the latter, called *isiZulu*, by not only a different musical grammar, but also, differences in the social uses and ritual practices with which both categories were associated. Thus the core genres of *isiZulu*, categories such as *amahubo* regimental anthems and *isigekle* wedding dances, were inseparable from the world and temporal cycles of patrilineages, ancestor spirits, and rural homesteads. *Imusic*, for its part, consisted of a highly selective body of English part songs, glees, and "folk songs"—all core symbols of the Victorian romantic vision of the domestic and the rural. At the same time, the contexts in which *imusic* was an integral component and lubricant of social interaction—singing contests, school concerts, and soirees to mark the various stages of the individual's life trajectory—as much as the names of choirs singing *imusic*, names like the Motor Car Choir and Electric Light Choir, signaled, as one reader of John Dube's paper, *Ilanga Lase Natal*, put it, "an assurance of civilized advancement."[20]

Dress was an even more sensitive symbolic domain, one that possibly allowed for even less bricolage, if any, than in the Cape. While white missionaries (and their black converts) usually quoted reasons of chastity and decorum for suppressing indigenous Zulu sartorial styles which they tended to describe as "nudity," white colonists—usually less concerned about the spiritual welfare of their colonial subjects—had reasons of their own for rejecting African forms of etiquette. Until well into the 1920s they observed with deep distrust and sometimes sheer panic displays of Zulu pride and power that used the symbols of the past—including various forms of customary dress. To the same extent that colonists rejected Shepstonism as an obstacle to producing an abundant supply of cheap African labor, they usually suspected customary law and other vestiges of "tribal" society to be statements of antiwhite defiance and independent African power.[21]

For *amakholwa*, in turn, choices made in the realm of dress carried no fewer risks. As the following interchange on a related issue between a Natal colonist and *Inkanyiso Yase Natal* editors throws into sharp relief, for an African to flaunt the couture of the metropolis was a tricky enterprise, one that frequently left the wearer accused of insolence and insubordination. In the passage from *Inkanyiso* I am referring to, the editors refute a white reader's letter to the *Natal Witness* that inquired "why the members of the Zulu Choir were always being referred to as Mr, Mrs and Miss." Had the letter writer, retorted the mission paper referring to Zulu monarchs and prominent chiefs, not seen Cetshwayo, Dinizulu, or Tetelegu being addressed in the same manner?[22]

But if Natal colonists were particularly expeditious in denouncing "dressed Natives" as "cheeky," the wearing of traditional forms of Zulu garb, for its part, was no less tricky. "The so-called Zulu warrior," a *Weekly Dispatch* reporter wrote, for instance, "when brought under missionary influences, though he sings glees and choruses, does not entirely forget the wild way in which he formerly carried on."[23] Needless to say, these and similar European fantasies about an innate and immutable primitive African character often played directly into the hands of those who advocated "scientific racism" and therefore undermined *évolué* claims for equality with whites. Small wonder, then, that scores of incensed black readers of *Inkanyiso* heaped blame on Saul Msane's head for allowing "children to show off their bodies in front of whites by putting on Zulu traditional gear and by performing *ndlamu* dances,"[24] arguing that such displays of *amabhinca* (traditions) were potential "relapses" into "paganism."

Clearly, what characterizes the story of the Zulu Choir and the debates about "savages" and "pagans" is a series of variations upon the broader theme of the making of modern African identities and the global imagination of Westerners and black South Africans in the era of high imperialism. Similar to the story of the African Choir examined in the previous chapters, the tour of the Zulu Choir was subject to and validated the late Victorian global imagination. Like the performances of the African Choir, a show such as "From the Wilds to Westminster" reproduced colonial classifications of "races" and "nations," classifications in which Africans typically occupied the nether ranks. At the same time, both ventures provided metropolitan audiences with African images of the history of mankind in which Africans, no longer eternally consigned to the primeval reaches, demonstrated the fact that history, given proper imperial leadership, was progressive. And, finally, to the same extent that the disaster of the African Choir could not shatter Paul Xiniwe's, Josiah Semouse's, and Charlotte Manye's unfaltering belief in the civilizing mission as an essential part of African modernization, Saul Msane and the other members of the Zulu Choir for the rest of their lives continued to consider themselves loyal subjects of the British Crown.

But for all the similarities, the story of the Zulu Choir differs from that of the African Choir in one crucial respect. The forces at work in shaping the narratives and genres of the global imagination in Natal—the colonial state, the colonists, and to a lesser degree the missionaries and the *amakholwa*—were, each in and of itself, weaker and thus also more distanced from one another than those in the Cape. Isolated as they were, these social forces were less capable than those in the Cape of defining the contours of a modern society. Thus depending on each other to a much greater extent than in the Cape, white colonists, black peasants, and the colonial administration saw themselves as being separated from one another by a much wider economic, social, and cultural gap. Precariously ensconced in situations of relative social and economic vulnerability, few colonists, missionaries, or *amakholwa* were thus in a position to conceive of colonial society as being composed of anything other than eternally fixed racial categories.

One last press comment on the Zulu Choir may illustrate this. The following quotation is taken from the London-based journal *South Africa*, one of the leading mouthpieces of British imperialist interests. In a sneering and cynical commentary titled "From the Wilds to Westminster," the columnist writes:

> If the Aquarium Directors knew anything of South Africa, or the Zulu race, they would be plainly conscious that these performing "Zulus" have been taking a "rise" out of them. Fancy 15 fighting Zulus leaving their own country! It would be impossible to get even one to do so; and these Westminster specimens are either low, degraded Tongas, or Togt Kafirs. . . . A Zulu giving a solo in English would be a black swan. . . . The Zulus are not the "raw" article at all, but a certain manufactured product, which, though no novelty in the mother country, may be profitable to proprietors of a show, whatever it is to any one else.[25]

Zulus were either warriors or "degraded"; Christians were worlds apart from "heathens." But it is not only the uncertainties of colonial domination in Natal that account for the febrile rhetoric of the *South Africa* columnist. The "ambiguities of dependence"—the pressures of white settler society and Shepstonism on the black Christian intermediate stratum—in turn also made it far more difficult for turn-of-the-century *amakholwa* than their Cape counterparts to model themselves on some hybrid form of identity. And thus it comes as no surprise that it was to take leading *amakholwa* spokesmen such as Saul Msane and John Dube—both of them cofounders of the ANC—another two or three decades to discover alternatives to "an idealized perception of imperial middle-class society" and to elaborate a more self-conscious brand of Zulu ethnic absolutism as an essential component of the emerging global imagination of black South Africans in Natal.[26]

Meanwhile, early in 1893—by that time most of the Zulu Choir were on their way home—a successor company to the African Choir was preparing to travel to North America, to explore yet another, specifically transatlantic, form of modern consciousness. It is to their story that we shall turn in the following chapter.

# 7

## "God's Own Country"

*Black America, South Africa, and the Spirituals*

In the previous chapters I have shown how the global imagination of Africans and Europeans toward the end of the nineteenth century was shaped by inextricably intertwined aesthetic practices, fictional genres, and discourses of personal and collective identity. Blacks and whites, I argued, were reciprocally implicated in the making of a bourgeois world that was intellectually near-impregnable and whose universality was taken for granted. I have also shown that it was the purpose of the tour of the African Choir to reaffirm, in view of the rampant rapacity of settler society, the rationality and validity of this order. Finally, it became clear that the failure of the venture was attributed not so much to modernity's malcontents as to settler backwardness and swindle—the very obstacles to an enlightened global order the tours were designed to debunk in the first place. But how unassailable was this imagined world of "races," "progress," and "civilization" really? What alternative discourses, if any, were available to challenge the antinomies of modernity and to imagine forms of identities other than as subjects of empire, consumers of commodities, and viewers of spectacles? Was it possible to imagine more composite, unfinished identities? It was questions such as these that the second tour of the African Choir, to North America, was to raise and, as we shall see in this chapter, in part answer.

In what follows I shall first briefly narrate the tour itself. Following this, I shall discuss the role of the African-American spirituals in molding specifically black forms of the global imagination and in developing notions of a black ecumene at once modern and critical of modernity. More specifically, I am going to argue that the 1890s were a period of political and economic turmoil in which Africans in South Africa and African-Americans in the United States were increasingly being confronted with a situation in which, so it seemed, modernity's most progressive premises—so brilliantly instituted during the heyday of Cape liberalism and Reconstruction —were seriously threatened by a battery of Jim Crow laws, lynchings, and disfranchisement. As the century drew to a close, intellectuals, educators, and artists in both countries became convinced that, as the historian John W. Cell has written, "the two societies were traveling along the same road toward a much more competitive and troubled racial system."[1] Black Americans and black South Africans found themselves ever more engrossed in an ardent debate about the meaning of being black in the modern world. Reexamining and comparing the experience of the plantation and the colonial frontier, blacks on both sides of the Atlantic were beginning to probe the profound cultural and racial hybridity that underpinned black politics of liberation in the late nineteenth and early twentieth century.

### Hopes of Liberty: Ethiopianism, Jubilee Songs, and African Repatriation

Of all the questions raised in the ensuing period of vigorous cross-cultural query, two proved to be particularly crucial: What did Africa mean to African-Americans, and what significance did the United States have for black South Africans? Such questions were not novel, of course, and at least in the United States have invigorated in various ways the struggles of generations of African-Americans. Yet in the decade between 1890 and 1900 these questions were beginning to take on an unprecedented urgent ring. Above all, they were calling for new answers—answers that proceeded not from modernity's own ideological premises and the tenets of bourgeois rationality but from the spiritual foundations of slave culture and the traditions of the African continent. More important, perhaps, the 1890s intensified the pressure on blacks to cope with the crisis of post-Reconstruction America and pre–Boer War South Africa in ways that made it necessary to rethink issues of racial identity in more complex, cross-bred terms. Music was one, if not the most crucial, of these responses and, at the same time, was one of the most powerful mediums of the collective imagination in modernizing black societies on both sides of the Atlantic. But before I go on to explore this aspect more fully, let me quickly review the circumstances and progress of the North American tour itself.

These are much less easily reconstructed than those of the first trip, to England. One of the difficulties, for instance, lies in establishing the identities of the choir members. When plans for a second tour were first mooted, James Balmer and Charlotte Manye were apparently thinking of a group that would comprise, in addition to themselves, Marshall Maxeke, Henry C. Msikinya, Charles Dube, James Y. Tantsi, Adelaide Tantsi, and Edward T. Magaya. But, for some unknown reason, only Balmer, Manye, and Magaya remained of this original lineup (even though the others were to join them over the next couple of years at Wilberforce), while at least five or six additional members can be

Figure 7.1. The African Choir in Boston, 1893 (Veit Erlmann collection).

identified who were recruited as replacements en route to Cape Town. Among those who embarked for England were Magazo Fanele Sakie, James Nxanixani Kolombe, John Boyana Radasi, the white pianist Lilian Clark (who had also been part of the first tour), and perhaps also Thomas Katiya. In addition to these singers, several other individuals appear on a playbill and in a photograph of the choir taken in Boston, whose identities remain unknown (fig. 7.1).[2]

Whatever its final composition, then, the choir sailed to England early in 1893 and from there went on to Halifax, Nova Scotia. After several performances in and around Halifax, the group eventually worked its way down to Montreal and Toronto, offering much the same fare as during the first tour and, predictably perhaps, eliciting the same sort of reaction, typical of an audience that was, after all, predominantly white and self-consciously part and parcel of the empire. "Weird and wild," a reviewer for the *Toronto Daily Mail* wrote. "Picturesque dresses," "interesting from a philanthropic standpoint," other papers echoed. One Montreal reviewer even went as far as suggesting that whereas "the negroes of this continent . . . we have always with us, . . . the South Africans are of a very different character." Several months later, in October 1893, the tracks of the choir are lost somewhere in the cities of the East Coast, only to resurface, the following year, in Ohio. By this time the whole enterprise had apparently turned sour. What exactly happened remains unclear, but from a statement made by Magazo Sakie later in the year it appears that Balmer, once again demonstrating that he was "by no means neglectful of his own interests," had not "fully lived up to his contract in the matter of the singers' share of the profits." As a result of all this, a split occurred among the choristers sometime in September 1894, about half of the choir continuing their journey across Ohio and Pennsylvania while Charlotte, Sakie, and at least four other singers decided to cast their lot with Charles S. Morris—one of black Cleveland's "brightest young men" and a future Baptist missionary to South Africa.[3] And it is here in Cleveland, finally, that Reverdy C. Ransom, one of the AME Church's elders, opened his home to the destitute singers. Within a matter of weeks, the small group of black South Africans was admitted to Wilberforce Institute in Xenia, Ohio—the first African students to enroll at a black American institution of higher education.[4]

One of the more fascinating aspects of this rather dramatic, if somewhat sparsely chronicled, chain of events is the role of the spirituals in the encounter between black America and South Africa. In discussing this specifically diasporic form of the global imagination of black people I may be forgiven for temporarily stepping out of historical sequence in order to examine a series of events and texts that both precede and succeed the second tour of our singers. I shall first discuss the seminal tours to South Africa of Orpheus McAdoo and the Virginia Jubilee Singers and then move on to a reading of turn-of-the-century African-American and black South African religious and political thought, especially as it was articulated in and around the AME Church. Although I am going to skip over several years here—years in which our singers quietly pursued their studies at Wilberforce—the decade between 1890 and 1900, as I have said, represents a tumultuous yet coherent phase in the history of the black global imagination, one that may be conveniently studied from its end points.

Beginning with South Africa, the situation of blacks in Britain's colonial territories had been steadily deteriorating from the mid-1880s. Although still sympathetic to imperial rule, Africans from across a wide social and cultural spectrum had begun to question the way in which colonists and the colonial state slowly retreated from the "civilizing mission." Choir member Paul Xiniwe, for instance, had been involved in some form of oppositional political activity from as early as the 1880s, both as a member of the Native Educational Association and as one of the leading figures of Imbumba Yama Nyama, an organization that took its name from Ntsikana's premonition that Africans should be like "hard and solid sinew."[5] And thus what in the 1870s could still be couched in a nostalgic language in the following decade was increasingly expressed in an embittered and anguished tone. In the 1880s more than one Xhosa intellectual worried about the nation "sickening to death," while some even turned their back on the "civilizing mission" altogether.[6] As early as 1884, one Jonas Ntsiko, whose nom de plume was Uhadi Wase-luhlangeni (Harp of the nation), published a poem titled "What Salvation?," whose biting sarcasm was without parallel in African writing:

> I turn my back on the many shames
> That I see from day to day;

> It seems we march to our very grave
> Encircled by a smiling Gospel.
> For what is this Gospel?
> And what salvation?
> The shade of a fabulous ghost
> That we try to embrace in vain.[7]

Over the next couple of years the resentment about betrayed hopes and unmet promises that runs through these stanzas did not remain confined to poetry and music. A broad range of responses to dispossession, military conquest, and disfranchisement emerged in the years that preceded the tours, but it is one reaction that is of particular significance for the subject of this book: Ethiopianism.[8] Often used rather indiscriminately as an umbrella term for some kind of generic African Christianity, the name Ethiopianism first emerged in South Africa in the early 1890s, when black Christians grew ever more embittered about white-controlled churches that preached progress and incorporation while practicing restriction and exclusion. Frustrated with white paternalism and their careers hampered by white missionaries' reluctance to entrust authority to Africans, growing numbers of black ministers began to sever their inherited affiliations to European mission churches and established their own religious bodies. The first schisms emerged in 1884 when Nehemiah Tile, a Wesleyan minister in the Thembu area disaffected from the main church, founded the Tile Thembu Church. Several other churches followed in quick succession throughout the 1880s, and in 1890, a year before the departure of the first African Choir, an Anglican lay preacher in nearby Pretoria established the African Church. In 1892, in the same city, another group led by the Reverend Mangena Mokone withdrew from the Wesleyan Methodist Missionary Society and called itself Tiyopia, the Ethiopian Church, after the prophecy in Psalm 68: "Princes shall come out of Egypt; Ethiopia shall soon stretch out her hand unto God."

Into the midst of all this commotion, in July 1890, there then fell the visit of a rather unique group of people equipped with a strikingly parallel kind of message about black redemption and speaking an analogous language of racial dignity: the Virginia Jubilee Singers.[9] Although by no means the first African-Americans to visit South Africa (one estimate calculates that by the middle of the nineteenth century several hundred black Americans were scattered across southern Africa, making a living as seamen, tradesmen, and machinists), this troupe of professional entertainers was by far the most illustrious and inevitably the most conspicuous group of black Americans to have visited the country up to this point. Indirectly descended from the world-renowned Fisk Jubilee Singers, this company was led by Orpheus McAdoo, a former student of Hampton Institute, Virginia. In two record-breaking tours, McAdoo and his troupe criss-crossed the country for a total of four years, entrancing audiences from Cape Town to Pretoria and from Colesberg to Durban with a kind of music never before heard in South Africa: spirituals, the slave songs of the American South. Noted a Cape Town reviewer:

Singing such as given by the Virginia Concert Company has never before been heard in this country. Their selection consists of a peculiar kind of part song, the different voices joining in at most unexpected moments in a wild kind of harmony.... [I]n their most sacred songs they seem at times inspired, as if they were lifting up their voices in praise of God with hopes of liberty.[10]

Hopes of liberty were precisely the kind of sentiment black South Africans had been cherishing ever so fervently since the early 1890s, when the liberal premises of Cape colonial society began to crumble under the demands of mining capital and white settlers. Hence it comes as no surprise that McAdoo's performances for these audiences met with particularly sharpened sensibilities and that a list of spectators known to have heard his Jubilee Singers reads like a Who's Who of South Africa's turn-of-the-century black opposition. Saul Msane, Patrick Lenkoane, Solomon Plaatje, Henry R. Ngcayiya, Isaiah Bud-M'belle, Mangena Mokone, and John T. Jabavu at one point or another were all enraptured by McAdoo's performances and in some cases even wrote lengthy eulogies of the event. Jabavu, for instance, then editor of the weekly *Imvo Zabantsundu*, wrote the following:

It would strongly savour of presumption for a Native African of this part to venture a critique of his brethren from America, who are now visiting this quarter of their fatherland, and whose position, socially, is being deservedly pointed at on all hands as one that Natives here should strive to attain to. As African we are, of course, proud of the achievements of those of our race. Their visit will do their countrymen here no end of good. Already it has suggested reflection to many who, without such a demonstration, would have remained skeptical as to the possibility, not to say probability, of the Natives of this country being raised to anything above remaining as perpetual hewers of wood and drawers of water. The recognition of the latent abilities of the Natives ... cannot fail to exert an influence for the mutual good of all the inhabitants of this country. The visit of our friends, besides, will lead to the awakening in their countrymen here of an interest in the history of the civilization of the Negro race in America, and a knowledge of their history is sure to result beneficial to our people generally.[11]

The message was clear. Here was a group of people who were black like the South Africans themselves and who, like many Africans, were also excellent performers. More than the racial and musical affinities, however, it was the Americans' whole demeanor and, above all, their biographies that "showed the superiority of the American coloured people over the South African," as one black critic roundly asserted. McAdoo's own cometlike rise, for instance, from slavery to a university education and a career as an international entertainer was living proof of the widely held assumption, neatly expressed in one of McAdoo's student essays, that the Negro "if only given a chance of cultivation ... will show his hidden qualities."[12]

To wit, cultivation, like liberty, was one of the issues that stood high on the agenda of young Africans like Charlotte Manye, Josiah Semouse, and their peers in Kimberley's small and lively Fingo Location. And it is here perhaps more than in any other place that McAdoo's concerts in August of 1890 struck like lightning. An exhilarated Josiah Semouse wrote in a review about "Likheleke tsa America," the eloquent Americans:

> Gentlemen, I cannot find the words to describe the way in which these people sang.
> Hear! Today, they have their own schools, primary, secondary and high schools, and also universities. They are run by them without the help of the whites. They have magistrates, judges, lawyers, bishops, ministers and evangelists, and school masters. Some have learned a craft such as building, etc., etc. When will the day come when the African people will be like the Americans? When will they stop being slaves, and become nations with their own government?[13]

Others, such as young Titus Mbongwe, took things somewhat further and persuaded McAdoo to offer him a scholarship to go to Hampton Institute. Although Mbongwe was tragically killed on his way to the United States and despite the fact that scores of later applicants failed to gain admission at Hampton, there was one student who did not allow herself to be deterred. Charlotte Manye was in a class of her own. "She knew what she knew," her sister Kate recalled. During the first tour, in Sheffield, Charlotte had run into the Bohee Brothers, an African-American company owned by James and George Bohee, then resident in England as banjo teachers and traveling blackface minstrels. George had attended rehearsals of the choir and persuaded Charlotte that "England was a godforsaken country" and America was "God's own country."[14] This statement, recorded more than half a century after the tour, may not be an adequate reflection of Bohee's views, but it certainly renders some of the vastly exaggerated notions South African blacks had increasingly come to hold about America ever since the McAdoo visits. The United States was a land of plenty, the black Utopia as such—an image that was to become so deeply etched into the mythology of South African popular struggles that until well into the 1920s in parts of the Transkei *AmaMelika ayeza* (the Americans are coming) was one of the rallying cries that heralded imminent black liberation.[15]

The 1890s were an even more troubled period in the United States than in South Africa. Assailed by economic depression and searching for an identity in the face of Jim Crow legislation and white southern brutality, black Americans were grappling with what W. E. B. Du Bois famously called "the strange meaning of being black here at the dawning of the Twentieth Century."[16] And like at the Cape, the symbols and traditions of Africa played a key role in black America's quest of itself. In fact, "Africa" itself was the key emblem in this reassessment, or, as James Campbell puts it in his pioneering work on the AME Church in South Africa and the United States, it was "the literal and figurative point of departure for the construction of African-American identity, whatever one conceives it to be." In fact, glancing over the subentries on African-American images of Africa in the index to Campbell's book yields a fairly comprehensive synopsis of how Africa figured in late-nineteenth-century black American thought: as "benighted land," as "cradle of civilization," as "field for heroism" and "field of opportunity," and as "promised land."[17] But of all these imaginary Africas two stand out as fixtures in African-American discourse: the "dark" Africa whose "heathens" stand in need of God and Africa the "fatherland" to which all black Americans should ultimately return. In no institution of black society were both notions discussed more passionately than in the AME Church.

The need for some kind of missionary activity in Africa had been acutely felt by AME leaders from the start. Prominent intellectuals such as Alexander Crummell, Edward Blyden, and Martin Delany not only advocated missionary work in African-Americans' ancestral homelands but also, like several other churchmen, traveled to West Africa to lend a hand to a number of missionary enterprises that had been initiated by AME missionaries in places like Liberia and Sierra Leone. Between them, Crummell, Blyden, and Delany exerted a strong influence on African-American thinking about Africa, and finally, by the late nineteenth century, African evangelization had generally become accepted as essential for the emancipation of the black race as a whole.

Considerably less consensus, by comparison, reigned about the idea of immigration to Africa. Here, as in the case of evangelization, it was the AME Church that served as the principal clearinghouse for ideas about black immigration. Although discussions about African repatriation had flared up throughout the early part of the nineteenth century, it was not after the Civil Rights Act had been repealed in 1883 that frustrated and debt-strung southern blacks sought salvation in a rapidly swelling, if somewhat diffuse, back-to-Africa movement. Its most pronounced advocate was Henry Turner, an AME bishop, who emerged not only as the most prominent turn-of-the-century spokesman for African-American emigration but also one of America's most visible political leaders of the period. Disillusioned by the collapse of Reconstruction, Turner began to formulate a militant program of action that, while perhaps not original in its essence, did much to sharpen African-Americans' awareness of their predicament as well as to strengthen the developing relationship between black America and South Africa. (In 1898, Turner himself undertook a highly publicized journey to South Africa in the course of which he was serenaded by McAdoo's company in Johannesburg.)

Central to Turner's thinking about repatriation was—as it had been to other Pan-Africanist thinkers before him—not so much Africa itself as the argument that only a distinct national identity and the ability to maintain a nation of their own would help blacks to recover their self-respect and earn them the long-denied respect of whites. (Ironically, it was the potentially segregationist implications of this idea that Cape Prime Minister John X. Merriman claimed to have borrowed from Blyden's *Christianity and the Negro Race* and believed to be the appropriate response to Cecil Rhodes's attacks on the Cape franchise.[18])

Yet Turner's views were far from unanimously accepted in the AME Church. AME leaders held that African repatriation undermined blacks' struggle for equal participation in American national life by suggesting that African-Americans lacked the capacity to elevate themselves to the level of whites. Likewise, among the general black population reservations about Turner's ideas were widespread. Thus, to return to one group of African-Americans' firsthand experience of South Africa, the members of Orpheus McAdoo's troupe appear to have been divided on the question. McAdoo's public lectures and speeches about slavery, emancipation, and especially the dreams of an African-American Zion contributed in no small measure to acquainting African audiences with the idea of African-American emigration. And if we are to believe Semouse's report on the "eloquent Americans," they elicited the most animated response from Kimberley's black community, who saluted McAdoo's concerts with calls such as "Come back! Come back to Africa, the country of your forefathers!"[19] But while some members of his company apparently toyed with the idea of taking up permanent residence in South Africa (Will Thompson, for instance, settled in Cape Town, entering into a close relationship with Isaiah P-M'belle, Solomon Plaatje, and Henry R. Ngcayiya and, until his death in 1900, actively participating in local struggles against racial segregation in the city's public transport), others were far less enthusiastic about Turner's proposals. "There are quite enough blacks out here now," soprano Mamie Edwards, for instance, wrote home, adding that black and white cooperation would have a deeper impact on African political emancipation than black American mass emigration.[20]

In essence, of course, it was a fine line that separated such critiques of Turnerian Pan-Africanism from some of the more imperialist stereotypes about Africa that African-American racial pride and identification with the ancestral homeland were to combat in the first place. But because they feared that African repatriation might ultimately undercut African-Americans' attempts at assimilation, church leaders clung all the more tenaciously to the idea that Africans were different. To be sure, Turner had found much to admire about African civilization. But notwithstanding significant differences of opinion regarding Africa's traditions, Turner shared with his intellectual predecessors "a curious amalgam of racial chauvinism, evangelical Protestantism and Social Darwinism."[21] The image that was at the base of all these transatlantic efforts at redemption with a remarkable consistency throughout the century was that of Africa as the "Dark Continent." After all, "Come Over Here and Help Us," one of the most popular AME hymns of the period, composed by Levi Coppin (who also served in South Africa), ran as follows:

> Shall we, whose souls are lighted
> With wisdom from on high,
> Shall we to men benighted
> The lamp of life deny?

In political terms, what this ambivalence translated into was an almost unconditional support for European imperialism and, no doubt in part because of its strong stance against slavery earlier in the century, for the British Empire in particular. Thus Mamie Edwards, having visited a number of churches and schools in Kimberley run by English missionaries, in a letter to the *Freeman* was led to remark that "of all the people that God in his own divine power ever made, the English people are the people, and surely they must be the chosen ones."[22] Interestingly, it was in an area of colonial practice far less benign than the church and the classroom that she came to realize the meaning of this God-given leadership. A tour of the Kimberley mining compounds—one of mining capital's most disingenuous "innovations" for keeping workers in place and wages low—impressed on her the notion that the compounds were designed "to prevent the natives from throwing diamonds out to parties not interested in the mines or fields for any other purpose than stealing." At the same time, the measure, while bitterly resented among black miners themselves, in Edwards's eyes did little to alter commonly held paternalistic views about docile and content colonial subjects. The native, she closed her letter, was "a very good and generous kind of creature" who, "if he likes any one . . . will give his life for him." Can one think of a more striking episode to illustrate how fantasies of empire, African-American global imagination, the minstrel show, and missionary paternalism all added up to the same thing? What better example is there to illustrate the fact that Africa, as James Campbell has described it in African-Americans' encounter with the land of their ancestors, was a "strange mirror of a continent," the imaginary soil on which a profoundly troubled people regained a sense of their own identity and the confidence that history, amid the dark days of racial reaction, was progressive after all?[23]

I have discussed Ethiopianism, Orpheus McAdoo's Jubilee Singers, and the early history of the back-to-Africa movement at some length here, partly because they describe some of the ideological currents that shaped the global imagination of the African Choir but also because the South African encounter with black America and the parallel debate about African repatriation and evangelization were formative elements of South African black nationalism.[24] And finally, read against the broader background of nineteenth-century global politics, another element was at stake in these early transatlantic encounters. Underlying all these myths and entangled visions of progress, redemption, and a black Utopia was the question of what all this intense dialogue implied for African-Americans' and black South Africans' uneasy relationship with nineteenth-century modernity. If progress was possible—and the opening of the African mission and the African-American example to many offered irrefutable proof that history had not turned its back on black people in Africa and the United States—what direction was it to take? Which way would the angel of history look and whom would it take under its wings? All the human race or only some parts of it, and then perhaps more firmly than others? And, above all, what kinds of fictions were thought to be best suited to sustain this vision of progress? What musical fictions in particular? It is to the latter question that I shall now turn.

### Of Sweetness and Music Heroes

For the better part of the nineteenth century, for black people on both sides of the Atlantic modernity was a strangely Janus-faced thing. Although they were subjected at different moments in their history to a variety of socioeconomic conditions that ranged from virtual debt peonage to total enslavement, black South Africans and Americans shared a deep sense of being both inside and outside the West. Slavery, from the slave's point of view, was not external to Western civilization. It was through the plantation that slaves came to understand the meaning of modernity and gained a sense that slavery was not a premodern residue. It was through the auction block that black Americans came to grasp how enlightened rationality and ideas of inalienable human rights buttressed rather than eradicated an archaic system based on differences of race. Or, put differently, it was the overseer's whip that taught slaves that slavery was not a sideshow of capitalism. It is for this reason that it is impossible to fully appreciate the development of modern forms of black culture and consciousness without taking into account, as Paul Gilroy puts it, "the complicity of racial terror with reason."[25]

In many ways, this was true of South Africa as well. But the complexity of the black relationship with modernity was compounded here by the fact that the term "slavery" also had another, far more indeterminate ring. On one hand, the missionaries had preached that slavery was not something that had been imposed upon Africans from outside but was inherent in the "barbarous state" of African indigenous societies. Elite Africans, of course, eagerly embraced the idea, linked as it was with literacy, biblical imagery, and notions of progress, and used it to demonstrate their fitness for the new order. On the other hand, there was the historical experience of black enslavement by Dutch settlers in the Cape. Although this was only a distant memory in the eastern Cape by the time of the tours of the African Choir, choir member Johanna Jonkers appears to have come from a family of *inboekselings*—a fact which the British press never failed to mention in trying to endorse the choir's political objectives and in underlining the fundamental correspondence between empire and African emancipation. Thus slavery in South Africa, while not primarily seen as inherent to the modern condition, had nevertheless been the root image that summed up a whole range of different regimes of racial subordination and black suffering, and one cannot but concur with James Campbell's assessment that South African blacks' encounter with black America gave an additional resonance to existing concepts and familiar experiences. In calling themselves slaves, "South Africans appropriated not just words but an entire history—the history of another group of blacks who had successfully passed through a similar trial."[26]

Another major figure—no less ambiguous than slavery—for thinking about black identity in the modern world was the nation. The assumption that the struggles of black people are somehow and necessarily expressive of certain fixed national identities and particularities has had—and continues to have—wide cur-

rency among black communities in the United States and South Africa. Yet the
meanings that were attached to these notions and the struggles that they fueled
in each country differed. In the United States, nineteenth-century black nationalism took a variety of forms, but the prevailing goal was a color-blind, universal
nation based on principles of equality and human rights. But if growing numbers of blacks after emancipation in terms of these principles came to conceive
of themselves as Americans, they did so rather cautiously, not as citizens of
the United States, but as people of color who happened to live in the United
States. Consequently, to achieve and sustain their freedom they invoked the vision of America as an integrated, egalitarian society, but to energize the struggle against racial oppression they nurtured racial pride. Although this paradox
in no way led to the kind of dichotomies subsequent scholars have constructed
in trying to understand black struggles—dichotomies between assimilation and
separation, integration and nationalism—it does remain the case that African-
Americans' sense of identity was always characterized by a certain dualism.

In South Africa, early nationalist views to a certain extent resembled black
American thinking, but they also differed from it in important ways. First, referring to the liberal foundations of the civilizing mission might have been possible and indeed was current African practice in the Cape Colony. But it was
much more impractical in the Boer republics or in Natal, where liberalism had
never been recognized as part of state ideology. A second difference was that all
that black nationalists needed to do was point to demography and history in
order to prove that Africans had lived in highly centralized polities long before
the arrival of the first colonists and therefore had superior claims to independence and nationhood. Third, the relationship between nationalism and Ethiopianism or some other form of independent church movement, although complex in both societies, in South Africa was somewhat unique. Thus scholars
have commonly associated the rise of black nationalism in South Africa with
the development of Ethiopianism and independent Christian churches, arguing
that proto-nationalism was a phenomenon that was rooted in a predominantly
urban, mission-educated class of Africans. Although there is a kernel of truth in
this argument, it is one of the merits of Campbell's work on the AME Church
that it showed how varied the social constituencies, discursive styles, and political strategies of early Ethiopianists really were. South Africa's independent
churches, he argues, were not so much driven by the polite "nationalist" tradition of patient petitioning as by what he calls a "racial populism." African
Methodism in South Africa was distinguished by a militant and distinctly racial
temper that enabled blacks to perceive of themselves as people whose rights
and interests were being traduced by a powerful white world. (More than one
AME minister, for instance, is said to have urged his flock to address white
officials by their names rather than as "baas" or "sir.") But the same Methodist
orientation could equally well serve rural chiefs to stabilize their position by
providing an alternative lexicon of power outside the world of colonial administrators and white missionaries.[27]

The lesson to be learned from all this, clearly, is that both societies shared not only a common vocabulary, iconography, and a host of discursive styles but above all what W. E. B. Du Bois in *The Souls of Black Folk* has called double consciousness, a body of practices and ideas that embraced many of modernity's utopian promises and narratives and, at the same time, also fiercely resisted its discontents. It is this two-ness, as Du Bois puts it, the failure of modernity to yield true self-consciousness to black people, which African-Americans and black South Africans by the turn of the century were alive to with every fiber of their being. They not only knew, as Du Bois wrote elsewhere in his book, that "war, murder, slavery, extermination, and debauchery — this has again and again been the result of carrying civilization and the blessed gospel to the isles of the sea and the heathen without the law" but also sensed, with varying degrees of acuteness, that to gain this "true self-consciousness" they were to engage modernity from two distinct, albeit intersecting, positions. Remembering slavery, colonial conquest, and settler racism, blacks on both sides of the Atlantic toward the late nineteenth century had to interrogate the power dynamics and economic mechanisms of the modern world by using, however prudently, some of modernity's very own ideological armature. But at the same time, they had to question modernity by proceeding from resolutely oppositional, even separatist, premises, by posing against modernity's irrationality discourses of alterity and ancestral tradition. Black politics in the United States has been shaped by the choice between the two options ever since, just as black politics in South Africa can be described as the contest between a more open, integrationist nationalism and a nativist, Africanist line. And, to wit, it is these competing and intermeshed responses to modernity that have provided the predominant grid for interpreting the meaning of the spirituals in both societies.

In the United States, the sacred songs of the slaves, given their centrality to African-American consciousness and culture, have been the subject of intense and prolonged arguments over a variety of issues, such as the authenticity of black cultural expression, the roots of modern black identity in slave culture, and so forth. For the better part of the nineteenth century much of this debate took place in the highly charged context of abolitionist politics and was thus indirectly related to the more pressing issue of emancipation and some form of African-American national independence.[28] But it is also a debate that continues to have repercussions in a variety of twentieth-century arguments, such as those about the authenticity and "blackness" of African-American musical expression, and, as Paul Gilroy's *The Black Atlantic: Modernity and Double Consciousness* brilliantly illustrates, in black intellectuals' ongoing attempts to draft a provocatively antiessentialist and more self-consciously diasporic theory of modern black culture and consciousness.

Gilroy's notion of the Black Atlantic is noteworthy because it challenges exclusivist interpretations of race and nation. By taking to task the banal relativism of an "easy" postmodernism and by reassessing a number of black inquiries of modernity that invert the received relationship between margin and center Gilroy raises the question of how Utopias are conceived, how a "politics of transfiguration" is possible that reveals the hidden fissures within modernity and defiantly reconstructs its own critical, intellectual, and moral genealogy.[29] Probably the most intriguing aspect of Gilroy's departure, however, is the attempt to place black musical expression at the center of these broadly antimodern, countercultural discourses. The vitality and complexity of black transatlantic musical culture, Gilroy argues, allow us to move beyond the oppositions between essentialists and pseudo-pluralists, just as it repudiates both tidy, holistic notions of modernity and a gratuitous postmodernism. The reason for this unique feature of black musical culture lies in the specific form of communication that it enables. The brutal experience of the plantation, Gilroy maintains, produced a distinctive relationship to the body that constitutes a pre- and antidiscursive element in black metacommunication. As an enhanced mode of communication, this bodily element is most manifest in dramaturgy, enunciation, gesture, and, above all, music.[30]

While this claim reflects a broad consensus about African-American expressive culture, arguing that music is a prediscursive element risks displacing the debate on black diasporic culture and global imagination in a potentially unproductive direction. Although Gilroy is aware that modernity's ethnocentric aesthetic assumptions have consigned black musical expression to a notion of the primitive, I must disagree with him that black music makers resemble Gramscian organic intellectuals whose marginal position vis-à-vis the state and the music industries enables us to focus more clearly on the crisis of modernity.[31] Rather, in referring to Adorno's critique of Benjamin's romantic notions of authenticity discussed in chapter 1 I would suggest that music, instead of standing apart from it, partakes of this crisis. Music always coexists with other modes of communication—bodily, verbal, and others—and it is the specific configuration of these communicative modes under conditions of accelerating modernization that makes music one of the most prominent mediums of the global imagination, revealing both the unruly diasporic and the more invariable homogenizing aspects of global culture.

Nowhere was this more in evidence than in the AME Church and in its long and conflict-ridden relationship with the slave songs and, through these, the music of the African past. For instance, although black America's first hymnal, church founder Richard Allen's *A Collection of Hymns and Spiritual Songs from Various Authors*, published in 1801, to a substantial degree drew on the work of mainstream church composers such as Charles Wesley, the spiritual substance and imagery of this modestly sized collection (a much more elaborate edition was to follow in 1818) were indebted to the spirituals. Even more significant was the lack of any musical notation in AME hymnals before 1897, a fact that enabled congregations to adapt the words to a wide range of popular melodies, more sedate Wesleyan tunes, and, above all, a style of singing known as lining out. If contemporary eyewitness accounts are anything to go by, the practice of a deacon singing the first two lines and the congregation following his lead for extended periods of time must have produced a distinctly African flavor. And it is this feature that caused considerable dissension within the church, raising a host of vexing questions over black people's sense of the ancestral past and their notions of morality and sociality.

Allen, a regular participant at revivalist camp meetings himself, endorsed the lively singing and emotional atmosphere that usually characterized early AME services, acknowledging them as necessary elements of African-American worship. Others, such as Daniel Payne, the church's most formidable leader to emerge after Allen, condemned the singing of spirituals as well as such attendant practices as hand clapping, foot stamping, and the ring shout as "ridiculous and heathenish." In due course, Payne set out to reform AME hymnody along more sedate lines and, in an effort "to modify the extravagances indulged in by the people," composed several hymns and introduced instrumental music to his Baltimore congregation. Finally, by 1841, the AME annual conference resolved "that our preachers shall strenuously oppose the singing of fuge [sic] tunes and hymns of our own composing in our public places and congregations."[32]

The prominent place that the dispute over "hymns of our own composing" took up in early AME discourse may be hard for us to appreciate today. But like the parallel discussion about Ntsikana's "Great Hymn" in South Africa during the same period, the issue struck deep at early black religious leaders' sense of modern political and cultural identity, revealing perhaps the central paradox of African Methodism in the process. Throughout the nineteenth century, black church leaders and intellectuals were convinced that slavery and racial oppression were less the result of a larger, global design of exploitative socioeconomic relations than of white prejudice and whites' failure to recognize blacks' potential for modern development. And thus, ever alert to the watchful eyes of the white oppressor waiting for any signs of black degeneration, these elite members of black American society went to great lengths to meet the standards of "civilization" and "respectability"—standards to be found in matters like domestic life and forms of sociability such as music and dance. With every step, then, that they made to escape from the world of the slaveholders they also returned to at least a part of it. Or, put more abstractly, black Americans were grappling with the dilemma of how to be part of the very modernity that they had built with their own blood and sweat and, at the same time, preserve the memory of slavery.[33]

By the 1890s, the controversy over the "heathen" residues in the sacred songs of the slaves had largely subsided. But this in no way implied the end of a somewhat parallel discussion, namely, whether the slave songs were the authentic and, hence, essential reflection of a modern black identity in the United States. Even though the Fisk Jubilee Singers, the Hampton Singers, and professional companies as Orpheus McAdoo's Virginia Jubilee Singers had long elevated the spirituals to icons of black respectability far beyond the confines of the AME Church, there are at least two reasons for the continued urgency of this debate at the century's end. The first reason is that it is probably no exaggeration to say that what made the slave songs into sorrow songs and what, in a sense, even precipitated their national and international legitimacy as genuine expressions of the slave experience was the ludicrously distorted representations of blacks in minstrelsy. In other words, it was through both the prism of slave culture and white racism that black critics came to grips with the conundrum of how to be American and black.

A second reason that contributed to authenticating the spirituals was what Ronald Radano refers to as a double process of racialization and textualization. From the 1830s, a racialized, sound-filled difference had been the key reference point for white writers whose slave-song accounts worked to constrain and at the same time supply with formidable, "spiritual" power a reinvented slave music. The resultant "black music," Radano argues, thus appeared to "be less a formal continuity grounded in the vernacular than a series of socially consti-tuted expressive practices emerging from the complex discursive matrixes of post–Civil War public culture."[34] Examples of the "paradoxical double mean-ings that inform nineteenth-century conceptions of the slave songs" are to be found in a host of diaries, journals, and recollections but also in a more devel-oped effort such as William Allen's seminal *Slave Songs of the United States* of 1867. More specifically, what we see in these transcriptions and in other, text-based inscriptions of the slave songs is their authors' struggle to adequately ren-der the authenticity of the performances. And thus if the white appropriation of the slave songs into a Western culture of texts served to underscore their sameness—and through this, indirectly, the humanity of the slaves—the re-peated references to the inadequacy of the notation only enhanced the songs' foreignness.

The process that Radano outlines here is, of course, a construction of black-ness on the part of whites, and as such it is integral to the very power structures such ventures across color lines sought to deny. Yet more revealing than this is the fact that, as Radano concludes his analysis, the meanings of the slave songs, as musical constructions of the past, evolved as "an intersubjective, interracial process" in which "both racial cultures would rely on the same discourses to ar-ticulate how they imagined black music." Thus although black America would eventually hear its cultural past and discern the echoes of an ancestral world, these echoes were "saturated with textually invented 'Negro sound.'"[35] In other words, the past was now mediated by a new kind of sound, one in which Africa itself stood for an ambiguous relation of sameness and difference and in which the black continent signified the imaginary reference point for increasingly anti-thetical discourses on the racial and national makeup of the United States.

The key work of turn-of-the-century black authorship in which all this is reflected most vivaciously is, beyond any doubt, W. E. B. Du Bois's *The Souls of Black Folk*. Although not published until 1903, Du Bois's book can safely be said to have emerged from the ferment of the mid-1890s and, hence, to be closely tied to the environment and experiences that then preoccupied the South African singers. And it may equally be said that notwithstanding countless dissenting readings of *The Souls*, slave music for Du Bois, as Gilroy argues and as, indeed, the fragments of spirituals at the beginning of each chapter demonstrate, was the "privileged signifier of black authenticity." The double consciousness which *The Souls* argues is not only the founding experience of blacks in the West but also "itself expressed in the double value of these songs which are always both American and black."[36]

How, then, were the slave songs seen in South Africa, both during the tours of the African Choir and afterward? What meanings did black South Africans ascribe to the spirituals and how were these extracted from specifically musical features of the spirituals? And what exactly did black audiences in Natal mean when they spoke of McAdoo as their "music hero" (*umqhawe zasengoma*) and praised his singing as "sweet" (*okumtoti*)?[37] The answer to these questions, I submit, can be found neither uniquely in the musical text itself nor, for that matter, solely in the political reading to which the spirituals gave rise. It lies, rather, in the way in which musical practice and the interpretation of that practice by socially positioned actors determine each other.

Thus the first point to be noticed here is that both terms reverberate with a whole series of deeper meanings constructed in and through what one might call a black South African aesthetics of action. For instance, the term *ubuqhawe*, as we have seen, conveys the ability to excel in the performance of an ideal of manhood rather than the uniqueness of a heroic act itself. In this way, *ubuqhawe* is essentially a social quality, one that by foregrounding the way things are being done affirms rather than renounces the models and forms in force in a given society. The hero in black South African thinking, then, may well wield extraordinary powers, but the sources of this power ultimately reside in how well he embodies what is essential about his community.

*Ubumtoti*, sweetness, at first glance seems to denote a rather more private realm of experience. But although the term is used primarily to describe the pleasant effect something may have on the senses, it is also applied in a more general sense of goodness and thus is often used interchangeably with *ubumnandi*. What is important, however, in both cases is that the conceptualization and evaluation of a sensory experience are embedded in a more general process in which individual perceptions intermingle with the emotional experience of socially grounded events. More than gauging the effects on the senses of a thing, judging something as "sweet" enables people to position themselves in relation to others. In using the physical body as the site for making decisions about what has value and what has not, black South Africans nevertheless acknowledge the inherent social determination of such aesthetic value and thereby ultimately strive to build social harmony.

Clearly, then, the cross-connections we have seen indexed here between musical and political meaning in the context of early black South African discourses about the spirituals betray powerful continuities and ecumenes of meaning that unite South Africa and black America. Despite the conspicuous contrast between Africans' sense of the spirituals as "sweet" and Du Bois's characterization of them as "sorrow songs," these appropriations reveal a lasting concern, fundamental to blacks on both sides of the Atlantic, with power and empowerment. For all their distinctly local flavor, terms such as those discussed provide a powerful motive that links the South African appropriations with what is perhaps the most intimate, quintessential aspect of African-American sacred music: the affirmation of life in the face of adversity and the quest for the wellsprings of correct living in a world of darkness and oppression.

But these continuities also intersect with other, more locally grounded attributes that were determined by the historical circumstances of a rapidly industrializing South Africa. Regrettably, the specifically musical evidence is extremely sparse here, especially for the period between the mid-1890s and the late 1920s. What we do know, however, is that after the unification of the AME Church and Mokone's Ethiopian Church in 1898, scores of AME Church missionaries streamed into the country, carrying the spirituals into the countless congregations that were springing up all over South Africa. These missionaries in turn were followed by a considerable stratum of U.S.-educated students deeply immersed in the world of African-American religious and political thought.[38]

One figure that stands out in this regard is Francis Herman Gow, the AME Church's first South African–born bishop. Born in 1887 of Jamaican parents, Gow had returned from his studies at Tuskegee in the early 1920s to assume the principalship of Wilberforce Institute and later become Cape Town's most prominent churchman and leader of the Coloured elite. In both roles, he devoted a great deal of energy to music, especially African-American music. Thus Gow not only launched the Coleridge-Taylor Musical Society and sang in their quintet[39] but also conducted the Wilberforce Institute Singers on Columbia recordings and in a broadcast of the Johannesburg radio station.[40]

The musical activities of Gow and other U.S.-educated South Africans had, of course, quite strong political implications and were embedded in the larger contest over power. In a more general sense, however, it appears that the role African-American sacred music was beginning to play in South Africa at the dawn of the twentieth century was shaped by two interrelated cultural processes: the significant transformations black independent churches in South Africa were undergoing between the 1890s and 1920s and, in correlation with these, the rise of African nationalism during the same period.

Ethiopianism in South Africa was anything but a unified phenomenon. Nor was its relationship with the nascent African nationalist movement a simple and straightforward one. Here, as in the United States, black churches had been riven by numerous tensions, including tensions between resistance to white domination and accommodation with it. Moreover, when pressure from the colonial state and mainstream mission churches eased somewhat in the years that led up to Union, the earlier mutual reliance between the black independent church movement and black nationalist activism weakened. As a result, the relationship between the church movement and the African liberation struggle was characterized by a paradox. Or, as George M. Fredrickson describes it, the contribution that Ethiopianism in its heyday made to the protest movement

> depended more on its capacity to absorb and reshape elements of the oppressor's culture than on its ability to project an antithetical Africanist view of the world.
>
> Because they had absorbed from Western secular thought the idea that peoples have a right to self-determination, and from the scriptures brought by European missionaries special sanction for their own particular struggle, Ethiopianists had been able to begin challenging the West in more direct ways than if they had resisted Western cultural influences more successfully.[41]

It is this dilemma, I believe, that accounts more than any other factor for the distinctive place in South Africa of African-American culture generally and religious music in particular. It explains why the spirituals, from the 1920s onward, were regarded by middle-class Africans as the "civilized" alternative to what was labeled the "marabi menace," the rising groundswell of proletarian cultural forms between the two world wars.[42] Two examples, both drawn from the work of the energetic Francis H. Gow, may illustrate this. The first example is *Up from Slavery*, a musical production by Gow that premiered in 1925 at Cape Town's West Theater. Labeled a "venture of the Cape Town coloured community," the show was an attempt to put into dramatic form some of the ideas contained in Booker T. Washington's celebrated work of the same title.[43] Accordingly, among the musical fare offered in *Up from Slavery*, in addition to violin playing by Gow's wife, Louise, were a variety of African-American genres, including, of course, "Negro spirituals." But "up from slavery" here did not just mean national liberation and emancipation in the American sense; it also meant a movement away from the "heathen" past of tribalism and superstition, and thus Gow's effort was redolent of the striking parallels between early-twentieth-century African-American discourses about racial progress and the ideology of the mission-educated black elite in South Africa. Where African-Americans spoke of the vestiges of slavery, the South Africans decried heathenism; and where Booker T. Washington titled his autobiography *Up from Slavery*, South African ANC president R. V. Selope Thema began his with the words: "The story of my life may be summed up in the phrase 'Up from barbarism.'"[44] Ultimately, however, both meant the same thing. The essential idea in both types of discourse was the belief in the need for a black elite guiding the way to racial progress and, perhaps even more important, a precarious combination of archetypal Victorian conceptions about a universal standard of "civilization" with the more Herderian notion that each race or nation would develop according to its own "genius."[45]

As far as the spirituals were concerned, of all the texts that were circulating in South Africa in the 1920s none illustrates this ambiguity better than an article, "The Miracle of Negro Spirituals," by James Weldon Johnson, which appeared in the black elite paper *Umteteli wa Bantu*. "The Spirituals," the distinguished intellectual and author of *The Book of American Negro Spirituals* (1925–27) boldly commences his article, "are purely and solely the creation of the American Negro." The Negro had brought with him from Africa his native musical instinct, to be sure. But what was it, Johnson asks,

> which led the Spirituals to rise above the base of primitive African rhythms and go a step in advance of African music through a higher development of harmony?
>
> Why did not the Negro in America revive and continue the beating out of complex rhythms on tomtoms and drums while he uttered barbaric and martial cries?

The answer to this, Johnson writes, is Christianity. The miracle of the creation of the spiritual is that "it was by sheer spiritual forces that African chants were metamorphosed into the Spirituals." But this metamorphosis, Johnson concludes his article, does not appear to have extended to the words of the spirituals. Of these, he contends, not so much can be said as of the music. Because the Negro bard in the United States had to work "under mental limitations," the spirituals are "trite" and characterized by "monotonous repetition." Nevertheless, they were not altogether devoid of an "appealing simplicity." In fact, they had "real poetry, the naïve poetry of a primitive race."

The fact that these musings were published in a Chamber of Mines–sponsored paper—ironically, edited at the time by Charlotte's husband and Wilberforce graduate Marshall Maxeke—illustrates how neatly Johnson's argument captured the black elite's own ambivalence toward a past (and more often than not a present) that, while it had laid the foundations of black culture and music in the modern world, was also irredeemably "barbaric and martial." Moreover, the American's reflections appeared at a time when the black elite in South Africa was becoming sensitive to the rising tensions between an emerging radical Africanism and old-style accommodationist nationalism. If black leaders, increasingly faced with unremitting state repression and intensifying mass radicalism, wanted to preserve their class privileges and leadership role, an all-out attack on Africa's "barbaric and martial cries" would not have guaranteed them a mass constituency. Conversely, challenging Western cultural hegemony seemed even less fruitful, given the overall imbalances of power. The task, then, that many black intellectuals set themselves was to rework Western hegemony so as to make whites reconsider their racial prejudices, and to refashion African tradition so it would "rise above the primitive base."[46]

Again, it was the cultural achievements of black America that were believed to be part of the answer. Jazz, for example, in Selope Thema's view was "the contribution of our race to the enjoyment of mankind." But unlike Johnson, who appeared to see the spirituals as the exclusive warranty of black self-empowerment, with little or no relevance to white America, conservative black nationalists in South Africa such as Selope Thema found it necessary to continually stress the importance of engaging white people's attention with displays of black aptitude. Hence the fact that "the white world has become madly in love with dances that are of Negro origin" showed that the "soul of the race," far from being torn asunder by the cruel life of the plantations, had become a "gift of the jungle to the civilized world" and that "the white world is gaining something from the black."[47]

Spirituals, and here I offer my second example, were another such gift. Like jazz, their origin was in Africa. But it was the United States and the encounter with Christianity that had ennobled the spirituals, turning them into a vehicle of cross-racial dialogue. In many ways, it was through the spirituals that the entire project of black racial vindication was ultimately invested in the benevolence of whites. Indeed, this seemed to be the whole point about public performances of spirituals in South Africa such as a live broadcast in 1927 by the Wilberforce Institute Singers under the direction of Francis Gow. As an anonymous reviewer of the event wrote: "[T]he African has the gift of song." But, the reviewer wondered, if through the spirituals the black slaves had "endeavoured to awaken the conscience of their masters" and if "to day the children of the slaves are making themselves felt in the fields of art, science and literature," wouldn't the spirituals in Africa have the same effect as they did in the United States? "Will they teach the European to humanise his attitude towards the African?"[48]

Arguments such as these dominated black South African discourses until well into the mid–twentieth century, and it was not until the sharpening class conflicts of the apartheid era that alternative perspectives on black America emerged—perspectives that made it possible, for instance, for black South Africans to identify the spirituals as the commensurate expression of a more global movement toward black liberation, one that reverberated with a growing concern among black intellectuals on both sides of the Atlantic with what Paul Gilroy has called a "more general order of subaltern experience."[49] Part II will examine these shifts.

# 8

## Interlude

The songs, texts, and narratives that I have examined in the first part of this book not only were part of a drama that shaped the destinies of a handful of South Africans but were also embedded in a dramaturgy of much wider dimensions—a scenario so powerful and deeply implanted in the rituals, objects, aesthetics, and power relations of the colonial world that it affected the thoughts and actions of a wide range of actors on both sides of the imperial divide, making them appear almost indiscriminately embroiled and kept captive by one another's social and symbolic worlds. At the same time, there was another side to our story, one that became apparent in the intense and ongoing quest among people of color on both sides of the Atlantic for alternative forms of the global imagination. These were diasporic discourses and phantasms of belonging that refuted the idea of cultural homogeneity and at times even allowed themselves to be inspired by the antinomies and discrepancies of a modernity both perilous and liberating. Both these strands of the nineteenth-century Western and African global imagination were to remain powerful intellectual legacies throughout the following century, reviving old and creating new forms of Western dominance as well as nourishing the struggles of people against racial oppression and social inequality. But above all they were discourses that continued to shape the lives of the South African singers as they themselves went on to live into the twentieth century.

With the exception of some members of the second North American tour who might have permanently settled in the United States, the majority of the singers returned to South Africa. It is here that several of them came to play important roles in the life of their communities and in the national political arena at large. Paul Xiniwe, for instance, apart from becoming a prominent businessman and politician in the Transvaal branch of the ANC, together with W. D. Soga launched the newspaper *Izwi Labantu*, which he edited until his death in 1902.[1] Saul Msane, for his part, rose to prominence as one of the cofounders of the ANC, and it is in that function that he subsequently revisited Britain as a member of a delegation protesting the Native Lands Act of 1913. And, in a remarkable revision of the more reticent position he had evinced in 1892 vis-à-vis "heathen" Zulu practices and symbols, he later increasingly turned toward the Zulu monarch and the precolonial past as a bulwark against the rapidly deteriorating social position of the African elite.

Charlotte Manye was the only woman of both choirs who was to leave a brilliant record of public achievement in a world that was still by and large a man's world. She gained a reputation as one of the female leaders of the ANC and as a leading force in the AME Church's Mite Missionary Society and a host of other black welfare organizations. She died in 1939—like the rest of her class, politically marginalized and economically deprived.[2] Finally, Kate Manye went on to live a more tranquil life, but like her elder sister she devoted most of her adult life to social work, attaching herself to Dr. James McCord and his Zulu hospital in Durban until her death in 1955.[3]

All in all, then, it was but for a brief moment in their lives that Paul Xiniwe, Saul Msane, and the Manye sisters were able to put into practice at least some of the visions of justice and enlightened leadership which their tours had enacted. It was not long before much darker forces would close in upon them, their class, and, in fact, their entire social universe. Yet despite the setbacks and the humiliation inflicted upon them, the Christian worldview and faith of these men and women in the correctness of "British civilization"—both Charlotte and Kate Manye later in their lives often proudly referred to their encounter with Queen Victoria—remained unshaken and, in many ways, was even fortified by the experience of twentieth-century semislavery.[4] But whatever their achievements, trials, and illusions, it was to take another 100 years for Semouse's, Xiniwe's, and both Manyes' hopes of liberty to be fulfilled. One may speculate about the difficulties these men and women might have experienced along the way in grasping the momentous changes of the world which they had opened up for themselves. No doubt they would have been utterly appalled by a country in which not only was their own class effectively annihilated but also by 1948 the majority of its population had, in fact, been reduced to disenfranchised, third-rate citizens. And perhaps they would have even sensed a certain continuity that linked their labors with the bitter struggles raging in the 1980s to overturn an odious regime desperately holding onto power by means of guns, prisons, bureaucrats, and crafty persuasion. It is to this world of the 1980s, the last years of the apartheid era, that we now turn, leaping ahead by almost 100 years from a world of colonial certainties and total fictions to an era of waning confidence, ambiguous realities, and fragmented identities.

# "DAYS OF MIRACLE AND WONDER"

*Graceland* and the
Continuities of
the Postcolonial World

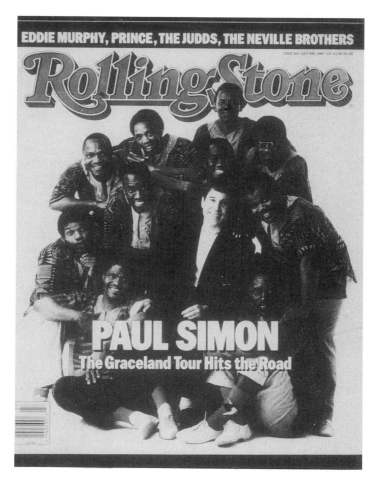

Paul Simon and Ladysmith Black Mambazo on the cover of *Rolling Stone*. (Photo by Mark Seliger from *Rolling Stone*, July 2, 1987. By Straight Arrow Publishers, Inc. 1987. All Rights Reserved. Reprinted by Permission.)

Paul Simon's *Graceland* now ranks as one of the most influential albums in late-twentieth-century pop music history, paralleled only by such megahits as Madonna's *Like a Prayer* and Michael Jackson's *Thriller*. Moreover, unlike few other pop productions of the 1980s, *Graceland* has been the object of fierce political controversy. One of the disputes it sparked arose over Simon's politics, his noncompliance with the U.N.-proclaimed boycott of the apartheid regime in particular. Implicit in the charge that by recording in South Africa Simon had done a disfavor to the liberation struggle was another one that reflected some of the deepest concerns of black activists on both sides of the Atlantic. Simon, they claimed, had appropriated for his own gain and deracinated from its native soil what seemed to be the inalienable essence and one of the most powerful symbols of black South African cultural identity: the music. This position enjoyed considerable purchase among black communities in both countries, and thus, no sooner had the album in the fall of 1986 earned Simon a Grammy, one of the international music industry's most coveted awards, than media attention seemed to focus more on what Simon had not contributed to the album bearing his name than to what, in fact, he had. And indeed, at least half the tracks on *Graceland* owed as much to the work of several dozen mostly African performers as they did to Simon's own efforts. Although the U.S. pop star was unusually candid in foregrounding the collaborative nature of the project, he quickly found himself suspected of being more of a facilitator than an originator or, worse, of reviving his flagging career by capitalizing on the vibrant musical heritage of a people struggling for its freedom. "It is the Black man's job," one South African critic griped, "to help the White man do his thing."[1] In the United States, critics on the left called the LP "turbid," while *Newsweek*, in a somewhat more conservative assessment, spoke of the music as being "unlikely hybrid."[2]

Of all the musics blended into the album, it was perhaps that of Ladysmith Black Mambazo, an established and revered male choir from Durban, with its wrenching grandeur, that seemed to mark most clearly this space of the "Other" into which Simon had allegedly intruded. Although not explicitly political itself, the velvet vocal textures and soaring harmonies of lead singer Bhekizizwe Shabalala and his ten-men group seemed to symbolize both the tremendous energy and determination of a nation reclaiming political and social equity and the ancestral depths from which sprang black people's right to be different. In short, the music of Ladysmith Black Mambazo embodied everything that was essential about South Africa's oppressed black masses—their traditions, travails, tribulations, and aspirations.

In a sense, then, by opening to performers grieving decades of racial oppression the power of his material and institutional resources, one of America's leading pop stars seemed to have done precisely the opposite of the white man's thing. But had Simon thereby also illuminated "the power relations be-

tween Western artists and their sources of inspiration from the 'Third World'?"[3]
Or was the album perhaps not about the politics of race at all? There are good
reasons to believe that Graceland was situated somewhere in the middle of
these conflicting claims. It was the first in a series of major interventions by
U.S.-based artists that engaged the apartheid regime from an explicitly liberal
stance. Like Richard Attenborough's movie Cry Freedom (1987) and Chris Menge's
movie World Apart (1988), Simon's project ostensibly deployed what Rob Nixon
has called the "convention of the innocent abroad," mediating radical Third
World politics for a mainstream U.S. audience.[4] And like these big-budget ventures, Graceland softened the more strident tonalities of the antiapartheid struggle by stressing the idea of cross-cultural dialogue and by evoking in its predominantly Western and white audiences the hazy feeling of some universal
ecumene of human rights and free enterprise.

Setting aside for a moment, then, the politics of big business and grassroots
opposition, how liberal and dialogic was the album's message really? Consider,
for instance, the words of "Diamonds on the Soles of Her Shoes," no doubt one
of the most riveting songs on the album and one of two in which Ladysmith
Black Mambazo plays a pivotal role and its lead singer, Bhekizizwe Shabalala, is
credited as a cosongwriter.

> Awa awa,
> akucwayele kile kanjalo.
> O kodwa ezinsukwini uzongenelisa namhlanje.
> Zanamuhla sibona kwenzeka kanjalo amantombazane ayazondla.
> Awa awa sibona.
> Kwenze ka kanjani?
> Awa, awa amantombazane ayeza.
> ─────────
> Awa awa,
> it is usually not like that.
> Oh, but in the days ahead, she is going to satisfy me, today.
> Today we are witnessing that the girls are self-reliant.
> Awa, awa, we see.
> How does it happen?
> Awa, awa, the girls are self-reliant.
>
> She's a rich girl
> She don't try to hide it
> Diamonds on the soles of her shoes.
>
> He's a poor boy
> Empty as a pocket
> Empty as a pocket with nothing to lose
> Sing Ta na na
> Ta na na na
> She got diamonds on the soles of her shoes.

It does not take much to realize that what these lyrics signify at the structural level is, if not a dialogue across cultures, something like the copresence of two speakers expressing themselves in two different languages. And as, indeed, my translation of the opening lines in isiZulu shows, the difference that is being articulated here is a more pronounced one, hinting at two fundamentally divergent notions of social order. On the one hand, the title and the English lyrics of the song appear to convey something of the spectacular opulence and hallucinatory character of late-twentieth-century consumer society. But on the other hand, this stands in stark contrast to the Zulu section in which Shabalala voices his perplexity ("awa, awa") at the unusual state of gender relations in Simon's story.

The score of "Diamonds," at first glance, seems to corroborate the contrasts manifested at the textual level. The song begins with Ladysmith Black Mambazo singing a smoothly flowing a cappella introduction in the typical *isicathamiya* close-harmony style of migrant workers—a style unlike anything heard in previous encounters of Western mainstream pop with African music. But then, at some point in the a cappella section, Simon unobtrusively blends in with the flow, extending almost seamlessly Shabalala's last line about the self-reliant girls with "She's a rich girl. . . . " Following this, a carefully balanced back-and-forth of musical parts establishes itself in which the lead part frequently alternates between Shabalala and Simon, and both at times chime in with the chorus in the manner of a typical African call-and-response pattern. In short, the music disavows what the words proclaim. It erases the opposition signaled in the first three stanzas by enfolding, as it were, within a single affective idiom two totally opposed regimes of truth.

What, then, is one to make of a kaleidoscope such as this, Simon's and Shabalala's pulsing sound texture of difference and sameness, exclusion and incorporation, background and foreground? What can we learn from the strangely intertwined images of glittery New York and a gender-troubled Zululand, and what do the peculiarly parallel and yet distinct yearnings for the land of grace and for female submission reveal about the experiences of actors as radically apart as a Brooklyn-born pop superstar and a black South African migrant worker turned Grammy Award winner? And reflecting back on the story told in part I, what do a Xhosa Christian hymn, late Victorian London, colonial shows, b flats, and b naturals have to do with Zulu wedding songs, the New York of the 1980s, and international megaevents? And what, finally, do the continuities and discontinuities among these periods, genres, and aesthetics tell us about the global imagination of South African migrant workers and about how First World consumers and African-American performers recast the world after colonialism?

Questions such as these, I believe, cannot be answered without a consideration of the aesthetics, sound, and style of some of the musics that lend *Graceland* some of its distinctive flavor and that have since moved on to invigorate other cross-cultural alliances and global musical encounters. And so, deviating from the structure of part I, I am not concerned in the chapters that follow with the events surrounding the production of *Graceland*. Instead I examine some of the discourses and practices on which the album draws, most notably the aesthetics of world beat (chapter 10) and the history and ideology of *isicathamiya* music (chapter 11). In addition to these, I also look at several productions after *Graceland* that have involved Ladysmith Black Mambazo, such as a video documentary on the life and work of its founder, Bhekizizwe J. Shabalala (chapter 12), as well as two Broadway plays (chapter 13). In the final chapters, chapters 14 and 15, I examine the racial ambiguities of black and white cover versions of the *isicathamiya* classic "Mbube" and the appearance of Black Mambazo in Michael Jackson's video *Moonwalker*.

# 9

## Figuring Culture

*The Crisis of Modernity and*
*Twentieth-Century Historical Consciousness*

One notion that influences a variety of key constructions of the twentieth century is based on the assumption that the period from around 1918 to 1989 can be distinguished from the previous century in terms of the growing instability of bourgeois power and that modernity—a form of intra- and inter-societal relationships invented in the eighteenth and consolidated in the nineteenth century—has reached something like its zero hour, a point of no return. Culture, as an arena for both this crisis and the attempts to stabilize it, can be said to be a key factor in this process. And, ironically, it is the role of culture in twentieth-century historical consciousness that links the era between 1918 and 1989 to the late nineteenth century in interesting and often neglected ways.

Current thinking about the twentieth century may differ from contemporary thought about the earlier century in that the sense of newness and radical disjuncture that permeated early-nineteenth-century popular culture and consciousness has given way to a more pessimistic feeling of déjà vu and even of regression. Still, at the same time as the twentieth century represents a moment of sharpening crisis, the idea remains crucial to a range of writers as dissimilar as Max Weber, Ernest Mandel, Sigmund Freud, and Eric Hobsbawm that both centuries are part of a relatively coherent, if somewhat irrational, order of things and that the way the one led into the other is to be construed not as the unfolding of universal reason, but in terms of some sort of fatal causality or sequentiality. The specific theoretical formulations of this old-in-the-new vary considerably, but the peculiar linkages between the twentieth and the nineteenth century are almost uniformly seen to be grounded in some sort of "factual" constancy.

Thus some of the major paradigms of twentieth-century thought such as classical Weberian sociology and Marxism seek to recuperate a notion of historical continuity based on some fundamental "truths" of historical process. In most post-Weberian modernization theories, for instance, one such truth is a dynamic of persistent renewal and development—a dynamic that, although far from being without its internal contradictions, propels societies along some sort of an imaginary vector. In other words, precisely where modernity casts itself as constantly moving away from tradition toward a stage of ever-greater rationalization and differentiation it keeps remaining the same. Similarly, although in a lot of Marxist approaches the Victorian age is represented as the apex of modernity—albeit distorted by the rules of capitalist production—and the twentieth century, by contrast, appears to be characterized by something like a sense of finality (consider, for instance, Mandel's notion of late capitalism or the somber images of catastrophe, massacre, nightmare, carnage, and cataclysm that recur throughout Hobsbawm's monumental *Age of Extremes: The Short Twentieth Century, 1914–1991*)[1];—both centuries are firmly placed under a common, almost historicist logic. In both Marxist and modernization theories, then, historical processes that spanned the nineteenth and twentieth centuries and the crisis to which they have been subject are understood as one evolutionary totality. They are construed as being tied together if not by reason, at least through some sort of essential correspondence or as fundamentally being characteristic of *modern forms of social order and social process.*

There are, of course, numerous problems with such views, but perhaps the most consequential is that they are homemade. They essentially derive from Eurocentric notions of historical process and global order and thus ignore the uncanny resistance culture puts up against Western ideas of rational development. More important, what such constructions of the twentieth century fail to realize is three things. First, post-Weberian and Marxist views of late modernity do not adequately register the fact that, as Arjun Appadurai puts it, the modernity that we now find ourselves to be part of is a modernity "at large, irregularly self-conscious, and unevenly experienced."[2] The trajectory that is traced by such notions of global process posits Europe as a given referent in historical knowledge. And as a corollary of this, while Europe is comfortably imagined as the cradle of modernity, its crisis stems from beyond its borders and much less often from within them. This is not to deny, of course, that Hobsbawm, for instance, is aware of the fact that the world at the end of the twentieth century is clearly "no longer Eurocentric"[3] and that, like many others, he acknowledges the multiplicity of meanings and diverse politics of memory competing in the postcolonial world. But what is lacking in both Hobsbawm's account of the "short century" and other recent Marxist writings, let alone modernization theory, is a sense of the fragility of claims that attempt to explain social processes in the total terms of a world that has the West as the subject of all other histories.[4]

Second, the concept of twentieth-century modernity as one in crisis is contingent on the reverse notion of modernity as an initially stable project. Yet as an exciting body of recent historical work has shown, and as I have indeed argued in chapter 1, the outcome of early modernization processes was far from certain. The nineteenth century in particular was itself shot through with numerous irrationalities, magicalities, and fetishes. In fact, one might argue that the strange career of the modern in the West was possible precisely because so much of it existed only at the level of ideology, as a result of a perceived antithesis between an enlightened West and a recalcitrant, backward Rest.

Third, modernity, even by the least parochial views, cannot be described anymore as European specialty. What a great deal of recent critical writing has alerted us to is the extent to which the making of modern Europe has had many partners outside Europe. Europe—as a concept—developed as much through the ambiguities and tensions of the colonial encounter as it did in Europe itself. It is, by this fact, no less an imaginary entity than the "Orient" itself, that most exoticized Other of the West.

In expanding on these critiques and in seeking to describe what I believe to be crucial to an understanding of the global imagination in the late twentieth century in the second part of this book I pursue a different line of reasoning. My concern is not with the periodizing of world history, nor do I have much to say about the contemporary crisis of modernity per se. Rather, my interest is in the way in which ideas of social process reflect and are shaped by a form of imagination that was beginning to emerge in the late nineteenth century and that— although thoroughly translocal and transnational in scope—was not merely an extension of Western master narratives. Rather, as I stressed in my discussion of the late nineteenth century, this imagination, despite the nineteenth-century fixation with distinctions of race, nation, and class, was characterized by a blurring of boundaries, genres, and styles and by the coming into existence of a series of mutual dependencies, ambiguities, and mirrorings that enfolded Europe and the West in like manner.

As a way of opening the discussion of my argument, in this chapter I shall broaden the analysis of nineteenth-century bourgeois cultural forms by making two complementary sorts of argument. First I shall suggest that the twentieth century shares with its predecessor a concern with the making of a global order whose very essence consists in the messy entanglement and at times parallel articulation of different idioms of power, concepts of historical process, notions of selfhood, and constructions of racial identity. But precisely because it proceeded from such shifting and hybrid cultural grounds, this order was an uncertain project from the start. The idea, then, of modernity as an initially secure moment of Western history unexpectedly running into difficulties at the fringes of the First World sometime in the late twentieth century in my account is replaced with that of the past two centuries as a relatively contiguous stretch of history, one that is kept together less by a chain of stages that moved from periods of stability to moments of crisis than by the profound tensions, contradictions, and mythologies that have beset societies, nation-states, and classes around the world since and because of the emergence of the colonial world. Implicit in this view of nineteenth- and twentieth-century modernity as some sort of historical entropy is a contrapuntal move that aims at destabilizing comfortable notions of a fixed non-Western world. Like Dipesh Chakrabarty and other scholars coming out of the Subaltern Studies project, my aim is not merely to "provincialize" Europe but to problematize "Africa" at the same time as I dismantle the "West," to deconstruct the notion of tradition at the same time as I query the idea of modernity.[5]

Second, I shall suggest that it is in culture that people in the two eras sought to recuperate a sense of security and communality. Implicit in this is the notion that stylization, figuration, and a more general aestheticization of life are not the hallmark of the postmodern turn toward the cultural but, as I pointed out earlier, are rooted in the aesthetics of world fairs, the early shopping arcades of Paris, and the panorama. Hence I cannot accept Scott Lash's distinction between turn-of-the-century modernism as the product of cultural differentiation favoring discursive modes of signification—modernist art distancing itself from reality, modernist critiques of realist epistemologies separating the theoretical realm from the real world—and postmodernism as a process of dedifferentiation favoring a figural mode of signification.[6] For as we have seen, the rudiments of the more recent aesthetics of the sensory, the impact, and the atmospheric lie in certain forms of late-nineteenth-century popular culture and here especially in the strangely cross-mirrored encounters between a putatively knowledge-driven, "differentiated" modern West and a supposedly archaic, mimetic, and "dedifferentiated" colonial Other.

All this is not to deny the considerable discrepancies that exist between the two centuries. For instance, compared to its predecessor, the twentieth century cannot be said to have been a century of the genre. Similarly, it might be argued, the twentieth century was a century of sound and not, like the nineteenth century, one of sight.[7] Although there may be many more areas in which such broad distinctions can be made, I see the parallels between the two centuries by far outweighing the differences. Thus, in my view, the twentieth century, like the nineteenth century, was quite clearly an age of fiction. In an oddly inverted sense, it was a truly panoptical era in that it was images that supervised people rather than humans who controlled images. A continuous logic and aesthetics of the surface links the panorama of the nineteenth century and the WYSIWYG and cyberspace of our time. Thus what is truly "post" about the postmodern is perhaps not so much that the days of the panoramic gaze are over but that they are not. What had began in the mid-nineteenth century was brought to a conclusion in the late twentieth century. It was then that the lives and thinking of large numbers of people were beginning to be wholly enclosed, structured, and even governed by the images they had created for themselves and of themselves.

I am using this rather stark terminology because I wish to highlight a number of differences between Arjun Appadurai's argument about the "work of the imagination" and my notion of the global imagination. Like Appadurai, I recognize in contemporary imagination an "organized field of social practices" and a "key component of the new global order."[8] I disagree with him in linking this role of the imagination primarily to the rise of the electronic media of the twentieth century and, more important, in separating imagination from fantasy in the attempt to free the imagination in the contemporary world from some of the negative, individualistic, and phantasmagoric connotations fantasy, play, and consumption carry in bourgeois society. The consumption of the mass media may well move images "into local repertoires of irony, anger, humor, and resistance" and thus become "a staging ground for action, and not only for escape."[9] What is less clear is whether the new "communities of sentiment" that crystallize around and are being moved into action by the consumption of such mass-produced images constitute a new type of community, with a greater degree of freedom and the capability for more solidarity at the same time.

Regrettably, Appadurai remains ambiguous about the matter, ostensibly because he wishes to relinquish the prognostic powers of social theory. In reality, I would assume, he has this cautious stance in common with other writers for whom the triumph of the symbolic in the twentieth century contains both a mythological and a liberating element. Zygmunt Bauman, for instance, drawing on the work of Richard Rorty and Kant's notion of the aesthetic community, argues that the best the search for synthesis and its basis in the idea of the sublime may achieve is the building of "clouds of community." Based upon a maximum consensus as these lifestyle communities are, they nevertheless lead to more fragmentation.[10]

Similarly, for French sociologist Michel Maffesoli the contemporary world is an "imaginal world" in which the symbol has reverted to its original meaning, that of a binding element, a mythological ingredient that "throws together" those who believe. But instead of a moralist critique of the spectacle and the "religious" role of the image—a critique that according to him would be based on a rather limited notion of a purely rational real—Maffesoli proposes a more positive way of looking at this "imaginal world." He advocates a mode of analysis that "allows us to think of the real by starting with the unreal." Style and figure are crucial elements of this type of analysis. Their impact on social life at the end of the twentieth century is profound and of almost utopian power. The figure, Maffesoli says, induces "a specific enthusiasm, an ecstatic enthusiasm, or an emotional intensity . . . that was at the origin of the revolutions of times past, and it is quite possible that it may also be at the origin of the painful gestation, through which we are living now, of the sociality yet to come."[11]

The notion of figure Maffesoli uses here draws on a what I consider to lie at the heart of current critical theory: the concern with mimesis and the shift in late modern Western thinking from an epistemology of representation to an aesthetic of presentation.[12] But it also refers to what the French sociologist, rather problematically, I think, calls the "postmodern form of the social link."[13] Figure and style, in Maffesoli's view, are more than a mere superstructure, more than an embellishment of the bourgeois private sphere. Rather, they refer back to a truly general conception of life in late modernity, one in which the individualism and social differentiation of modernity are replaced with what he calls a "mass subjectivity," an "all-out relationism." Generally, what this decline of individualism in the late twentieth century implies is a shift from the social toward an "empathetic sociality," a move toward the truly global, a "holism" which, as Maffesoli puts it, "envisages everything in interaction and in its totality."[14]

Several points can be made here. First, we must ask ourselves whether Maffesoli's celebration of style, viewed against the background of the rationalist fear of the image, is not simply a misreading of the nineteenth century in that it ignores the nineteenth-century infatuation with the panorama, the commodity as fetish, and the spectacle in general. Second, the notion of figure as some arabesque form of sociality in late modernity is attendant, of course, on the corresponding idea that the bourgeois self and the social contracts in which it is anchored and that constitute it themselves represent some sort of groundwork— an assumption that is increasingly losing purchase as a host of poststructuralist scholars have begun to unravel the myth of the bourgeois ego and to chart the fuzzy boundaries of gender, age, class, and race intermeshing in the modern self.[15] Third, we must raise an objection to Maffesoli's all-too-eager espousing of the image in that the notion of figure as being opposed to ground and as enabling communication appears to have a lot more in common with the way sociality was conceived in nineteenth-century consciousness than his analysis admits. After all, the figurative was the predominant form in which the nineteenth century masked the discrepancies—the ruins, as Walter Benjamin and Dolf Sternberger would have put it—of the capitalist order. Figure, in the sense of an emphasis in high modernity on the superfluous and the useless, could even be said to be at the heart of the capitalist social logic. Given that in consumer society the use value of objects is gradually extinguished by pure exchange value and that social relations are governed by objects, figure becomes the form under which commodities take on a life of their own and begin to develop a culture of their own. Figure is all that is left of culture under late capitalism.

In sum, figure and style—and everything else that comes in their wake, such as play, irony, etc.—may not be the harbingers of a new sociality after all but, rather, the symptoms of decay. But figure may also (and here I wish to move from these introductory remarks to the discussion of some of the post-*Graceland* manifestations of the global imagination in the work of Ladysmith Black Mambazo) be fruitfully seen as being both expressive of other forms of social organization that resist modernity's utilitarianism and at the same time caught up in the commodification of everyday life under late capitalism.

## 10

# Hero on the Pop Chart

*Paul Simon and the Aesthetics of World Music*

St. George, so the legend goes, was a high-ranking soldier under the Roman emperor Diocletian. Born in Cappadocia of noble Christian parents, from whom he received a careful religious training, George organized a Christian community at Urmia in Persian Armenia, and it is said that he even visited Britain on an imperial expedition. Later in his life, however, George clashed with the emperor when the latter began his massive campaigns of anti-Christian persecution. In the course of these George was arrested and, after being tortured, was finally put to death on April 23, 303.

The historical basis of this legend, as the *Encyclopedia Britannica* of 1910 tells us, "is particularly unsound, there being two claimants to the name and honour." However, the compendium goes on to state:

> [M]odern criticism is not unwilling to accept the main fact that an officer named Georgios, of high rank in the army, suffered martyrdom probably under Diocletian. . . . The great fame of George, who is reverenced alike by Eastern and Western Christendom and by Mahommedans, is due to many causes. He was martyred on the eve of the triumph of Christianity, his shrine was reared near the scene of a great Greek legend (Perseus and Andromeda), and his relics when removed from Lydda, where many pilgrims had visited them, to Zorava in the Hauran served to impress his fame not only on the Syrian population, but on their Moslem conquerors, and again on the Crusaders, who in grateful memory of the saint's intervention on their behalf at Antioch built a new cathedral at Lydda to take the place of the church destroyed by the Saracens. This cathedral was in turn destroyed by Saladin.[1]

I have opened this chapter on Paul Simon with the St. George legend or with what, after all, is little more than the more recent philological explication of a conglomerate of rather cryptic texts, because the replica of a painting that adorns the album cover of *Graceland* depicts, of course, the saint as he was imagined by a fifteenth- or sixteenth-century Ethiopian artist. More specifically, I am intrigued by the unusual cover artwork because the image of the martyr establishes a particularly emblematic link between Paul Simon, the popular music and culture of the late twentieth century, and a specific story. This link is crucial not only because the East African effigy is unlikely to have been selected randomly for one of the most influential world beat albums of the 1980s but also because the cross-reference that is being hinted at on the cover is one between the author of the album and a narrative of a special kind: a myth in the full sense of the word, an ancient heroic tale about a man's exploits and defeat. And, beyond this, the album cover indexes a structural relationship between several of the key areas and problematic issues of global cultural production. The representation of a key figure in Western and Eastern mythology on the album jacket, I believe, creates a symbolic dialogue between Europe and its Other that turns on a close linkage between the fundamental predicaments of such domains of modern life as individuality, authorship, and narrative.

It is these linkages that this chapter seeks to explore. Rather than rehearsing some of the well-known arguments about the place of *Graceland* within the antiapartheid struggle and, more broadly, an antihegemonic politics of culture, I am going to limit myself in the following tentative analysis to questions of aesthetics and the production of cultural texts. Although, then, there is no denying the fact that *Graceland* was one of the most controversial political interventions in the mid-1980s, ambiguously caught between the Reagan-era politics of "constructive engagement" and the transformation of the cultural boycott from a reactive instrument of protest and punishment in the 1960s to a tool of the affirmation of black cultural achievement, my approach is a slightly different one.[2] I shall put forward a reading of the album and more specifically of the role of Paul Simon in its production that will engage with the problem of what Renato Rosaldo has called "imperialist nostalgia."[3] Rather than denouncing Simon's work as false consciousness or a rip-off, I shall unravel its aesthetic premises in a whole range of twentieth-century social and technological transformations.

More specifically, the argument I advance in this chapter is the following: in an age of unparalleled uncertainty and ambivalence—a time in which only the vaguest hopes can be entertained for the continued existence of human life in its known form—the Western global imagination and artistic sensibilities have become increasingly alert to the play of differences that governs world politics and culture. While at times this play of differences is felt to be a vital, inspirational force, at other times it is perceived as a profoundly unsettling aspect of contemporary culture. But regardless of how acutely late modern artistic production and consciousness register these tensions, what speaks through even the most articulate, self-reflexive texts and performances, such as *Graceland*, is a desire for certainty, for what Edward Said calls a "new inclusiveness."[4]

The causes of this peculiar late-twentieth-century form of the panoramic, monadic mind are diverse and, apart from the dramatic advance in the technology and aesthetic of simulation and the fictional discussed in the previous chapter, in part reside in the changed role of the middle class in general and of artists, intellectuals, and what Pierre Bourdieu calls the "new cultural intermediaries" in particular. These changes in turn engender and are expressed in specific mirror images of the Western self and in certain figures of the Other whose place in the global imagination of the West shares with those of the late nineteenth century several things. Most notable among these is the turbid persistence of fantasies of an abused and defenseless Africa and, directly linked with these, a certain heroic image of the West and the individual.

But this enduring Eurocentric stance is possible, I shall argue, not because of any intact legacy of imperialist practice and thinking—a legacy that clearly has been severely damaged not least as a result of the anticolonial struggles and, in South Africa, of the antiapartheid campaign. Rather, it results from the very technological means of the global imagination in the late twentieth century and the new forms of social relations mediated by these technologies. Generally speaking, the interplay between the digitalization of the media and the dynamics of consumer society has profoundly altered on a global scale traditional notions of identity, personhood, and society and led to an aestheticization of social relations. The musical equivalent of this aestheticization lies in what Peter Wicke has called a medial aesthetics of music, in a new type of referentiality. For contrary to the commonly held view that world beat is the voice of difference, articulating an Other and its distance from the Western self, I propose to explore the notion of world beat as an "empty" semantic field, as a form of cultural practice that rests on completely altered notions of truth, meaning, and Utopia and that replaces these with what I call an aesthetics of the sono-dramatic. The ability to create these events and the experiences that flow from them are closely connected with the economic power of the advanced countries of the postindustrial world and the concentration in them of the most developed information technology. Western hegemony in the late twentieth century is no longer a matter of "materially" subjecting the periphery to the cycles and economic interests of the center, but of manufacturing sense, of producing amid the rampant discontinuities of the postcolonial world a sense of connectedness by injecting into the seamless, medial flow "realities" and actualities that have been generated by purely electronic means.

Finally, to reconnect all this with our analysis of Paul Simon, *Graceland*, and South Africa, I shall examine two kinds of text and the ways in which the paradox of an all-inclusive and yet centrifugal aesthetic of late modernity is encoded in them: Paul Simon's biography and the myths that have been constructed of the singer's life; and the album *Graceland* itself and here especially the track "Diamonds." Both texts not only exemplify Simon's own search for identity but also are emblematic of the attempts of significant sectors of the middle class to refashion themselves as cultural intermediaries and to reach some state of grace and redemption.

## "New Inclusiveness," Cultural Intermediaries, and the Crisis of Liberalism

In part I we saw how, during the heyday of the scramble for Africa, a number of as yet relatively invisible but highly significant developments in science and technology were beginning to call into question the notion of a comprehensive system of knowledge. It is within this context, I argued, that such forms of late-nineteenth-century spectacles as the tours of the African Choir and Zulu Choir have to be seen. These and other global spectacles were part of the self-congratulatory pathos of the center laying claim to the periphery and the right to represent it. But more important, they also offered to the metropolitan public (and to a lesser extent to the colonial elite) the sensory immediacy of a knowable, all-encompassing totality. Now in the 1990s, almost a century later, it is clear that it is precisely this holistic, perspectivist space of modernity and the mechanical age that has corroded and dissolved into a world without synthesis, as Robert Musil once called it. Ironically, the recognition among societies and individuals around the world that we are indeed all sitting on the same planet and this is the only world at our disposal is also accompanied by an uneasy feeling that this very world is splintering into hundreds and thousands of smaller worlds—all equally removed from a common center and all connected among each other in myriad ways, through what Gilles Deleuze has famously called a rhizome. But is it possible to conclude from this, as more than one critic has claimed, that the days of the panoramic gaze are over, that the world has indeed become unsurveyable?[5] Or do fantasies of a world made in the image of Europe linger on in the West, at some subliminal level of late-twentieth-century forms of the global imagination?

It is perhaps one of the greatest strengths of Edward Said's book *Culture and Imperialism* that it shows how modernism derived much of its revolutionary impulse from a hitherto-underestimated response to the external pressures on Western society and culture. But far from confronting the illusion of empire head-on, the modernist aesthetic registers the imperial dawn in cryptic ways, at the level of formal dislocation and disruption. When European society finally did take due account of the crumbling global order, says Said, it did so in texts that conveyed "an ironic sense of how vulnerable Europe was" and that were expressed in a new encyclopedic form. This form had three distinctive features. First, there was a circularity of structure. Second, the new encyclopedic form rested on one of the strongest hallmarks of modernism: the juxtaposition of the familiar and the alien, the commonplace and the exotic. Third, and perhaps most important, was the irony of a self-conscious form that conceived of reality as something held together by a single creative will. Spatiality here turns into a matter of aesthetics when the ability to tell stories and to write histories from an all-inclusive single vantage point wanes in direct relation to the crumbling order of imperial domination.[6]

In a more general sense, one might argue that the emergence of a new kind of spatiality is also embedded in the decline of a specific aspect of bourgeois power, namely, that of a form of power that laid claims not only to distant lands but also to representation as such. The bourgeoisie not only ruled the world but also claimed the exclusive right to explain it. Yet at a time when such claims are being challenged by a host of competing epistemologies, it is the monopoly on explanation that Western bourgeois thinking seeks to restore, not imperial rule as such. While some of the early-twentieth-century high modernist expressions of this new inclusiveness are well known, the crucial point to be made about Primitivism, Vitalism, Exoticism, and so on is the extent to which they succeed in incorporating into the West's total vision the symbols of difference that are supposed to be the very negation of the West. Like some of the later developments in music such as New Age, they incorporate the Other as the off-center representation of that which carries modern Western subjectivity to new levels of universality. And finally, the irony here is that the allegory contained in modernist representations of practices as opposites and critiques of our own belongs to the same order of knowledge as the nineteenth-century genre. Beneath all the celebration of disjuncture and juxtaposition, it stems from a desire to fetter and to regroup around its own axis the unruly forces of difference.

How, then, does all this play itself out in late-twentieth-century artistic production? The image of St. George on the album cover of *Graceland*, I argued at the beginning of this chapter, corresponds to a particular vision of the individual and the artist in the late twentieth century. Here I want to expand on this hypothesis by suggesting that this vision has to be seen in relation to the crisis of the music industry in the late 1970s and, more specifically, the crisis of liberalism and the musician-artist during the period immediately prior to the collapse of the bipolar world. While this crisis has commonly been attributed to a number of profound shifts in the technology, production, and consumption of popular music, somewhat less attention has been given to the ways in which such shifts were themselves encoded and grounded in constructions of rock and pop history as manifestations of individual performers' identities and the transformations these underwent in the 1980s. One of the areas where these changing constructions become particularly evident is the relationship between discourses about pop stars and the actual recordings. What appears to characterize this relationship, according to Will Straw, is the paradox that while in the 1970s mainstream performers' individual identity provided the dominant grid through which new records were marketed, the proliferation of discourses about pop celebrities in the 1980s is in inverse proportion to the importance of the musical message itself. In other words, while in the 1970s there existed a relationship between the musician's identity and his or her recordings that required a certain interpretive link be made between discourse and music, in the 1980s and despite a tremendously increased amount of information, such discourses seemed to have only a limited effect on the way in which stars and fans were locked into the turnover of the pop charts.[7]

This shift, one might argue, in itself indexes not just a change in the role of performers and of the songwriter-musician as a culture hero but also a decline in the functional centrality of cultural intermediaries in the 1980s and more generally of liberalism as the basis for the construction of modern selves. If it is correct that modernity opens up the project of the individual and if liberalism, simply stated, is the ideology that determines the nation-state and a free market economy to be the contexts in which that project comes to fruition, it is precisely the triumph of neoliberalism shortly before and after the Fall of the Berlin Wall that challenges the emancipatory promise on which liberalism rests. It is through the generalization of, if not the material, the aesthetic premises of consumer society that some of the coordinates of the autonomous, self-reflexive individual have been called into question. At the moment when the ideal *Persönlichkeit* turns into the perfect consumer and ethics is replaced by lifestyle, liberalism is at its lowest.

But other pressures were coming to bear on liberal notions of the self in the mid-1980s and more particularly on the role of liberalism among First World middle-class consumers. Globalization, understood here as declassification and deregularization, pushed further modernity's proliferation of competing value spheres and, as a result, cast unprecedented doubt on any notion that seeks to substantiate an absolute ethics and its basis in a rounded self. The ideal of personality, to turn Simmel's phrase on its head, no longer has the roundness of the image of the world.

In terms of pop history, the crisis of liberalism entailed a series of marked shifts. In the 1970s, hero ethics may be said to have been epitomized by particularly emblematic figures such as the Paul Simon of "Bridge over Troubled Water" and "Sounds of Silence"—in other words, by a Paul Simon whose whole persona and music are defined as the expression of an authentic individual standing his ground, apart from and in opposition to society. To understand such a musician's music meant to understand and therefore rely on the appropriate information about that musician's personality, history, and worldview. As a result, the interpretation of a performer's choices and life trajectory and how he or she imparted these to a series of songs called work became the single most important move in defining the performer's brokerage role. In other words, the interpretive act the 1970s consumer was asked to perform corresponded to the self-interrogation to which the modern individual is routinely subjecting him- or herself. In the 1980s, by contrast, as hero ethics turned toward the aesthetic, the emphasis in mainstream pop and rock shifted from interpretation as a means of determining the social practices of cultural intermediaries to something I would call lateral reception. That is to say, the very identity and social role of cultural intermediaries such as the Paul Simon of *Graceland* is now a matter of the linkages that performers and their audiences establish between different musical practices—linkages in which the performer, as Straw puts it, functions as a "point of continuity," a "point of coherence of a number of strategic operations upon the field of popular/musical culture."[8]

Lawrence Grossberg, in a discussion of the place of rock in what he calls the "liberal consensus and everyday life," makes a parallel argument, suggesting that the emergence of rock was deeply tied to an ideology of pluralism and mobility of postwar U.S. consumer society and that it was only as a result of the sustained attacks that rock elicited from the conservative mainstream that it was politicized, "behind its back."[9] But even then, Grossberg argues, all that politicized rock achieved was to rock the boat of culture and everyday life. By the 1980s, all this changed. As the compromises that constituted the postwar liberal consensus began to unravel themselves, the optimism of the boom years faded and a radically different model of mobility that was centered on the accumulation of wealth gained acceptance, the culture industries, too, changed their tune. It is thus that, beginning in the 1980s, the music industry was driven less by the need to create individual hits than the need to produce stars who "can move across media to produce markets." Rather than a hit or an album, it is the star him- or herself who becomes the primary commodity, "delivering the audience to a particular market or product appeal."[10]

Returning to Paul Simon, the real paradox, then, that is reflected in his post-1970s career (as also, of course, in the career and work of artists like Peter Gabriel and David Byrne) would appear to be the following. On the one hand, there is the recognition—often more explicit in the lyrics and professional practices of the figureheads of world beat than in mainstream rock or pop celebrities—that no artist can any longer legitimately substantiate a master narrative (about the individual, human rights, and so on) amid the polytheism of values and partial standpoints. On the other hand, there is precisely an attempt to cast aside any suspicion and reflection about the possibility of an absolute ethics by holding onto some of the former liberal stance, by reviving, if only in attenuated form, the myth of the individual standing his ground in a world of shifting alliances and values. On a superficial reading, one might even be tempted to accept Charles Hamm's assessment that *Graceland* was the "late-blooming product" of the folk revival of the 1950s and 1960s, attaching itself more or less directly to a number of "good causes" similar to the ones espoused by liberal humanists of the era.[11] The only problem with this reading is that whatever form liberalism may have taken in the 1980s, it was not so much discredited by the doubtful practices of performers who, as Hamm puts it, used South African music "as a means to enhance their own careers as entertainers"[12] as it was by the problem of upholding a vision of freedom and liberal humanism at a time when it was the centrality of Enlightenment Europe itself that had become the issue.

It is this ambiguity, then, that accounts for the emphasis in promotional material, interviews, and the album cover on Paul Simon as a songwriter, the man with a personality, a biography, and perhaps also a cause. But it is also the same ambiguity that critics have been grappling with in describing Simon's lyrics as "introspective and cerebral," "unflappably reserved," "strangely disembodied," and "compellingly dreamlike."[13] And, finally, it is an ambiguity that is reflected in one of the most powerful determinants in the work of cross-cultural mediators like Paul Simon. This is the fact that artists become cultural entrepreneurs in their own right, involving themselves in curatorial, promotional, and collaborative efforts across different cultural spheres. But this mixing of roles, as Steven Feld has suggested, not only results in the blurring of genre lines between real "world music" and "world beat"[14] but also suggests that performers have themselves become what Jacques Attali calls the "mold within which reproduction and repetition take shape."[15] The superstars of world beat move across genres to produce new markets as they become tutors in the mastering of techniques of mobility and self-presentation in a global environment. They become exemplars in the endless work of self-stylization that allow the individual to become expert at maneuvering the enormously widened arena of traditions and values and to elaborate criteria for allocating meaning without venturing into judgments or hierarchies of value.

It seems clear, then, that the global practices of the new cultural intermediaries, clearly driven as they are by a sense of displeasure with the incompleteness and malcontents of modernity, still do the work of the West. Even by critically acknowledging the shaky grounds on which rested the bourgeois ego's ascent to global power, Simon reinvents liberalism. His attempts to reposition the individual toward a place of centrality, in spite of all the widening of the expressive field, also restore to modernity some of what is absent from it. World beat productions such as *Graceland* fill up the West's gaps and absences, making it more complete.

### Postmodern Aesthetics and the Sono-Dramatic

One of the assumptions that distinguishes a more enlightened brand of musicology from some of the discipline's more parochial concerns rests on the idea that music's meanings are not intrinsic to the work of art but are constituted in the social and cultural practices of individuals engaging with music in a variety of ways. Music, according to this view, is inherently a social process. But this relationship between music and society cannot be conceptualized in terms of some structural homology whereby certain musical features reflect or are determined by some social structure. It does not consist in relating consciousness to a reality but in setting up networks of mediation. As John Shepherd and Peter Wicke succinctly put it: "The question, then, is not that of understanding the relationship between 'music' and 'society.' It is that of understanding the constitutive features of music as a social process in relationship to other, equally non-reducible realms of social process."[16]

One of these features, according to these authors, is that of the sounds of music being a "medium." Derived from the world of science, the term "medium" is used to mean an agent in which processes take place, but which remains unaffected by the processes themselves. The concept of medium is useful because it allows us to understand the production of musical meaning as being socially negotiated but not arbitrary. As a medium for—rather than agent of—the construction of meanings, sound restricts and facilitates the range of meanings that can be constructed through it. In this, the concept of sound as the material medium of music is different from that of sound as a signifier. Sounds in music have implications beyond the brute presence in music, beyond the arbitrary connection of signifier and signified.[17]

These implications are best understood, Shepherd and Wicke suggest, by examining the "technology of articulation" that links the materiality of sounds and the creation of affective meaning. To cite the example the authors use to illustrate this point, the motor rhythms of the bass guitar riff in the Rolling Stones' song "Satisfaction" can be said to reference macho sexuality. But this form of sexuality, Shepherd and Wicke write, is not first constituted socially and then in some way imparted to a set of sounds. Rather, the motor rhythms of "Satisfaction"

> are themselves taken to constitute socially and culturally the form of sexuality in question through their very articulation. They are taken at the time of their articulation to occasion in individual subjects as socially and culturally constituted the structure of feeling of this form of sexuality in a manner specific to themselves, a manner which cannot be reduced to the manner in which other, similar and comparable forms of sexuality are constituted socially and culturally through media other than music.[18]

The articulation of affect and sonically mediated practice in "Satisfaction" is powerfully stated here and in its specific social and historical context undoubtedly quite concisely so. It will be complemented here—and therefore also challenged in a sense—by the concept of an aesthetics of the sono-dramatic, the idea, that is, that the globalized and rampant musics of late modernity *are* arbitrary indeed and no longer mediate, as Shepherd and Wicke suggest, culture-specific processes of appropriation of the external world. The notion of music as a medium, then, is enlarged by the claim that world beat not only has become a neutral ground, incapable, like all music, of shaping the processes of meaning construction, but also no longer has the capacity that Shepherd and Wicke seem to be willing to grant all music of "shaping the material grounds and potentials for meaning construction" themselves.[19]

The notion of music as a form of sono-drama goes back to the assertion, possibly first articulated by the Viennese critic Karl Kraus during World War I, that the modern media are based on a kine-dramatic logic, that it is not that events create news, but the message generates the events it is supposed to relate. Of course, Kraus's concept of the kine-dramatic was above all meant to destroy the illusion that modern media—he was thinking mainly, I believe, of the role of the press in the war propaganda—had anything to do with the transmission of content. The news, Kraus lamented, was the event or part of the event itself, thus redefining the real as the fictitious that is being realized.

In many ways, Kraus's thought anticipates Gregory Bateson's and Marshall McLuhan's later thesis that what media disseminate is not information but redundancy and that, consequently, metaphors of transmission and tripartite sender-message-receiver models are inept for a theory of communication and an aesthetic of global media.[20] But Kraus's concept also resonates in the work of Murray Schafer and Jacques Attali and even some of Paul Virilio's views. All these authors, without explicitly referring to the Viennese critic, have broadened Kraus's concept by introducing the notion that the kine-dramatic logic of the media extends to all realms of social life. The operational velocity of the media, Virilio argues, for instance, destroys not only the duration of information but also everything that has duration. The media attack everything that used to be, in the past, a material and spiritual bulwark against disappearance and death when communication meant staying and life.[21] Likewise, Schafer expresses a certain anxiety over what he calls the schizophonic effects of technology that separate original sounds from their reproduction, the result being that "machine-made substitutes are providing the operative signals directing modern life."[22]

The notion of music as a sono-dramatic element not only critically expands Shepherd's and Wicke's concept of medium but also turns a central assumption of interpretive anthropology and ethnomusicology on its head: the hypothesis, namely, that symbolic practice and social action mutually constitute and index each other as meaningful forms of existence, that social life is all a stage, and that, conversely, theater and ritual are not mirror images but different modalities of social practice. In contradistinction to this, the concept of the sono-dramatic works from the notion that sound produces action. It postulates that action is not in sound and sound not part or a consequence of action (which on a purely pragmatic level [you have to press the keys to be able to hear something] it undoubtedly is), but rather action is an aspect of and supplement to sound. Put differently, sound is not *about* an event or a context; it is the event itself, albeit not in some reified sense of a frame in which sound *takes place*, but rather as a space in which other things—meaningful as they, too, are—also occur. Put in more basic terms and with regard to world beat, the point about the sono-dramatic role of music is that questions of aesthetic content or taste here become irrelevant and are replaced with a concern for pure aesthetics, for what Alfred Schutz called syntony.

At this point I must elucidate a number of misunderstandings that might be provoked by my notion of music as a-semantic and based on an aesthetics of the sono-dramatic. The objection could be raised, for instance, that I am granting technology and mass-mediated music overproportionate power to reduce listeners to passive consumers. Or one might point out that it is precisely one of the effects of the globalization of musical aesthetics that world beat emerges as a "distinctly subversive practice" that latently contributes "to the dismantling of the subject of Western popular music, a subject whose identity rests squarely upon the political economy of empire."[23] While I am making no such claims, my use of the term "a-semantic" is not meant to convey a sense of moral panic either. I do not believe, like Attali, that the message has become "banalized," and I do not share Schafer's nostalgia for an innocent age before the advent of the mass media. Music in global culture is not any more banal or emptied out of meaning than any other kind of music in different kinds of social settings and historical periods. What makes such musics a-semantic is the transformation that has occurred in the meaning, as it were, of meaning. Meaning itself recedes into the *spaces between* different spheres of meaning. Difference itself is the meaning; it is the fact that different cultural repertoires are being put into global circulation. Global musical sounds, then, do not speak. World beat is not a messenger. Rather, it is action—action that mediates nothing but action.

It is not that there are no longer any individuals who seek for musical meanings a place in other realms of meaningful practice. It is simply that this search takes on the rhythms of consumer society, becoming more hectic, Sisyphus-like, and with fewer reliable guidelines. In fact, it becomes work itself. The task that globally connected, albeit locally situated, audiences are now asked to undertake does not so much provide entertainment and relief from the strain of production as it engages them in the ceaseless labor of having to look for places of meaningfulness somewhere in the endless chain of signifiers.

Returning for a moment to the introduction to "Diamonds on the Soles of Her Shoes" and my brief analysis of it at the beginning of part II, the point at which the aesthetics of the sono-dramatic and the a-semantic is syntactically and stylistically configured is, I think, primarily in two areas. One is the linguistic plurality of the song, the fact that for U.S. audiences at least the lines sung in isiZulu mean just that: they are at the zero degree of difference. They *are* pure Otherness.

The second area in which the emptiness of "Diamonds" becomes apparent is vocal timbre. One of the ways (which I shall explain more fully in the following chapter) in which *isicathamiya* history is frequently conceptualized by South African migrant audiences is the vocal registers and timbres prevalent during a given historical period. Thus *mbube, isikhwela Jo, isithululu,* and *cothoza mfana,* while they often index the type of movement that accompanies various vocal styles, all may be distinguished from one another on the basis of the vocal characteristics being displayed. For instance, while the historically earlier *isikhwela Jo* is characterized by high-pitched, almost yelling sounds, *cothoza mfana* and *isicathamiya*—the style sung by Ladysmith Black Mambazo—generally feature more soft-touched, low-intensity vocals. Ironically, however, both types of vocal delivery are said to be variants of specific ways of expressing maleness, of asserting certain gendered notions of the ideal social order under oppressive and distraught conditions: the rustic *isikhwela Jo* coming more out of precolonial domains of male power like warfare, the more polished *isicathamiya* emphasizing urbanity as a privileged domain of male migrant accomplishment.

Paul Simon's vocal style, by contrast, although on the surface it may resemble the more feminized-sounding timbres of the South African group, could suggest an altogether different set of gender roles and ways of positioning the Western male subject. On the one hand, Paul Simon's open, sometimes thin and whining voice, in the Western context, may well index somewhat archetypical images of masculinity such as that of the "boy next door." In other words, it may be read as a denial of the machismo of hard rock. On the other hand, one might agree with John Shepherd's assessment that the head tones, the light and thin vocal timbre of the vulnerable male, essentially reference "an appeal for emotional nurturance" of women and therefore do not "abdicate the supposed supremacy of traditional rationality."[24]

It is difficult to imagine how black South African audiences of the late 1980s might have decoded Simon's vocal timbre.[25] Yet despite Bhekizizwe Shabalala's lavish praise for Simon's voice, I would venture to suggest that South African male audiences and *isicathamiya* aficionados would have found it difficult to align the U.S. pop star's vocal qualities and white middle-class need for "nurturance" with their own choral version of asserting masculinity in the strictly patriarchical terms of precolonial Zulu gender hierarchies and a patrilineal homestead economy. Thus it stands to reason that the difference of vocal timbre that separates Paul Simon and Ladysmith Black Mambazo, although it certainly suggests something about the meaning of each of these within their respective cultural spheres, in the juxtaposition in "Diamonds" may, in fact, mean only itself. Just as the difference between English and isiZulu in the introduction is constructed as one between two different codes, the materiality and graininess of the two vocal utterances are made to enter into some sort of neutral relationship. Although audiences in the West and South Africa will inevitably link Simon's and Shabalala's voices each in and for itself to their respective owners' histories, they do not necessarily connect the difference of vocal production to the difference between those histories and what it might suggest about the contradictions of rapidly changing gender roles in an interconnected world.

## Elvis, Redemption, and the Unity of Musical Form

It is ironic that while Paul Simon's album can be seen as one of the prime examples of the aesthetics of the sono-dramatic, denoting pure difference and absolute global flow rather than any concrete set of meanings, it may also suggest the opposite: an aesthetics of identity and authenticity. Just as "Diamonds" appears to signal the abdication of the subject, it slips back through the back door of a new aesthetics of identity. The root figure for this aesthetics is Graceland, Elvis Presley's Memphis mansion. In fact, as one of Simon's biographers puts it:

> For too many years, *Graceland* had symbolized the first lost promise of rock and roll; by the spring of 1987 its name offered the possibility of the dream being reborn. *Graceland* had become synonymous with the rhythms of resistance, it gave the triumphant sound of black South African music a foothold in the market-place of the world and, in doing so, focused attention on the bitter struggle of a nation to reclaim its home.[26]

The passage is from *Paul Simon: Still Crazy after All These Years*, a biography of Simon by Patrick Humphries published in 1989. Patrick Humphries is a seasoned journalist and biographer (his previous work includes books on Bruce Springsteen, Alfred Hitchcock, Bob Dylan, Tom Waits, and Simon and Garfunkel) and thus a man who plays a considerable role in the construction of celebrity. Moreover, his biography is itself part of a discursive tradition and concurrent practice of what Antoine Hennion calls "the production of success."[27] And, above all, Humphries's text is an attempt to root late modern pop production in some kind of historical project.

At the level of content, for instance, this attempt may be seen in Humphries's assumption that *Graceland* is a more complete, reborn version of Elvis Presley's music. But it is also reflected in the peculiar, if not altogether atypical, misreading of several other factors. For instance, there is the notion that South African music is "triumphant" rather than mournful. Then, there also is the strange juxtaposition of the global marketplace with the nation that raises the question of how a nation can find its "home" in something as rampantly disordered and unhomelike as the global market. The most telling level, however, at which this strategy of authenticating Simon takes place is in the circular rhetoric figure that underlies *Still Crazy after All These Years*. Thus the book begins with an introduction in which Humphries describes Elvis Presley's Memphis mansion, Graceland, and the pilgrimage millions have made to the "spiritual home of the King" after his death. In 1982, the author goes on to relate,

> Paul Simon and his young son Harper were among the visitors—like so many others of his generation. Simon felt that the impact of Elvis on his own life and music had been incalculable. It was thanks to Graceland, and all it stood for, that Simon felt that he had a "reason to believe / We all will be received in Graceland."
>
> Abbey Road will be linked forever with the Beatles, Asbury Park with Springsteen, and Big Pink is inseparable from the Dylan mythology; even more than these, Graceland has always held a uniquely powerful place in rock iconography. In 1986, however, it came to mean more than just the empty shrine of the dead Elvis. . . . *Graceland* has now become the most controversial album of the 80s, a fact which Simon himself could hardly have foreseen as he followed the well-trodden track to the hallowed Memphis mansion.[28]

Compare these opening remarks with a quote from the book's last two paragraphs:

> It was Thomas Wolfe who wrote "You can never go home again"; but everyone tries and with *Graceland* Paul Simon came back to where it all began. . . .
>
> Hairstyles and attitudes may change, but Paul Simon is still driven by the same thing, which bodes well for more of the magical music which has filled his life so far. Late in life he has had "a shot at redemption"; as the 80s draw to a close it will be fascinating to see how he uses it.[29]

Clearly, the formal bracket that is created here by the texts quoted has one major function, that of grouping Humphries's biographical narrative around a

Example 10.1. Middle parts in the introduction to "Diamonds on the Soles of Her Shoes."

altha + thena

a- wa a- wa

subject, a center that is both stable and in motion. It is a subject Simon's biographer constructs here that is "driven by the same thing" but is also one that is born and "reborn." In short, it is an individual whose subjectivity is *ongoing*, in a state of constant *becoming*. It also is clear that this rhetorical figure, in all its retrospective closure and restless drive toward some future beyond the 1980s, really reflects the anxiety and the nostalgia of the middle-class individual caught in the fluctuations of late modern risk society.

In closing my discussion of Paul Simon, biographic narrative, and the aesthetics of world beat, let me return one last time to "Diamonds" and suggest that the Janus-faced sensibilities of the late modern middle-class individual are articulated in more than literary form and, in a sense, "below" the macrolevel of the politics of stardom. They are traceable at the microlevel of musical form. Thus while at one level the introduction undoubtedly is a prime example of the often-noted "blend" and "flow" achieved in *Graceland*, at several other levels tensions are observed between an attempted formal closure, African style, and the impossibility of such closure within a rock mold.

Beginning with the layering of vocal parts in "Diamonds," it conforms with the standard rules of *isicathamiya* polyphony. There are three such layers: a bass part (*bhes*) sung by the majority of singers, two falsetto parts called *thena* and *altha* sung by one or two singers each, and a lead part (*faspathi*).

Each of these three layers moves in cycles of eight beats, entering at different moments of the cycle. The middle layer of *altha* and *thena* in "Diamonds," strictly speaking, consists of a short motif of only four quavers sung in parallel thirds ("awa, awa") (ex. 10.1). Yet here, as in many *isicathamiya* songs, the two parts are prolonged, as it were, by moving in parallel octaves with the bass (ex. 10.2). The solo part, finally, is usually distinct from the refrain, but in "Diamonds"—where it is sung by Paul Simon—it frequently runs parallel (usually in fifths) with the bass part (ex. 10.3).

None of this is in any way exceptional, and hence it is in perfect agreement with the rules of *isicathamiya* grammar. But the formal integration in these first couple of cycles can be said not only to be guaranteed by the groove Ladysmith Black Mambazo is establishing but also, in a sense, to even be enhanced by the way in which Simon and the choir take turns in singing the solo line or, rather, how both blur the line between solo line and choral response. The point at which this occurs is when the line "empty as a pocket" is sung for a second

Example 10.2.  Middle and bass parts in the introduction to "Diamonds on the Soles of Her Shoes."

time—bringing the choir back to the foreground and replacing the "awa awa"—and the song continues with the words "with nothing to lose."

Things take a different direction, however, when Simon sings, "Sing ta na na," and the chord changes to A. What then appears to be put into place is a more Western song format complete with a I–IV–V chord progression and an organization of vocal parts that abandons the polyphonic layering of the beginning and turns everything else into an accompaniment of Paul Simon's solo line (ex. 10.4).

After this section has been repeated twice, the song returns to the cyclic pattern of the beginning, except that now the lyrics are "diamonds on the soles of her shoes" and it is Paul Simon who sings the chorus. While this sort of equilibrium would appear to cast considerable doubt on readings that accuse Simon of having used the South African musicians, the ease and naturalness referenced by all this role switching and framing of Western song elements in an overall *isicathamiya* structure can also be seen in a more ambiguous light. Perhaps this becomes nowhere more apparent than in the disjuncture between the recorded track of "Diamonds" itself and the published score in the *Graceland* songbook.

Transcribed and arranged by John Curtin, the score contains numerous inconsistencies that can be read as the somewhat inept attempt to interpret "Diamonds" as a piece of mainstream rock and, in this sense, as offering useful

Example 10.3.  Lead part in the introduction to "Diamonds on the Soles of Her Shoes."

Example 10.4. Western song format in the introduction to "Diamonds on the Soles of Her Shoes."

glimpses of one Western listener's way of deriving a sense of internal coherence from a set of disparate and supposedly free-floating musical practices. There are two such moments I want to focus on here. The first is the point at which Paul Simon comes in with, "She's a rich girl." The problem here for Curtin apparently consisted in preserving the independence and cyclicity of Simon's solo but at the same time compressing both his line and the choral response into the corset of a Western 4/4 meter. Thus, in order to allow the

Example 10.5. Introduction to "Diamonds on the Soles of Her Shoes," in *Graceland* songbook, transcribed by John Curtin.

downbeat to fall on the main syllables, Curtin changes the time signature from 4/4 to 2/4 and back (ex. 10.5).

The second is toward the end of the introduction (ex. 10.6). Here, in suggesting fingerings for the closing section on "diamonds on the soles of her shoes," Curtin suggests a I(E)–IV(A)–V(B) cadence as the harmonic framework. Perceived with a Western ear, the chord movement could indeed be interpreted as oscillating between I and V, with a subdominant being hinted at intermittently. In reality, of course, things are somewhat more indistinct. While perfect cadences are common in *isicathamiya* and can be traced to the strong admixture of Christian hymnody in the genre, "Diamonds" is much less easily classified as falling within this category of songs. Much less easily, at any rate, than "Mbube," for instance, one of the classics of the genre composed in the mid-1930s (see chapter 14). The reason for this ambiguity is that the "chord" structure in "Diamonds" might be better understood as a form of root progression in which the tonal material of the three chords E–B, A–F♯, B–F♯ is derived from the third and fourth partials of only two shifting fundamentals: A and B. The only note that is not accounted for by this sort of bow music–derived harmonic progression is the F♯, occurring with the root A. The fact that it is sung in the introduction by Paul Simon might suggest that the Western-trained singer is thinking of his melodic line in terms of the I–V progression implicit in the harmonic framework of the song, rather than—as African performers inevitably would—in terms of a root progression. In this interpretation, then, the F♯ could be seen as Vv or as a suspension of E.

In conclusion, the issues embodied in the lyrics, vocal textures, and microstructure of "Diamonds on the Soles of Her Shoes" are embedded in the larger processes that both shape and are contingent upon the aesthetics of world beat. While the effort to recenter the Western subject in times of crumbling geopolitical orders and epistemological certainties entails a number of practical and symbolic operations squarely situated in the matrix of late-

Example 10.6. Introduction to "Diamonds on the Soles of Her Shoes," closing section.

Example 10.6. *(continued)*

*(continued)*

Example 10.6. (*continued*)

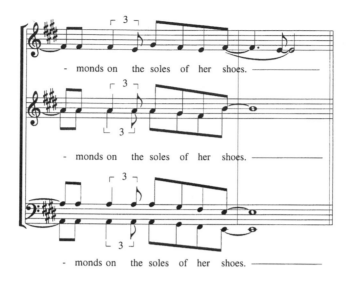

twentieth-century consumer culture, it is Ladysmith Black Mambazo and the tradition of *isicathamiya* choral music that clearly provide the bedrock for such reworkings of Western middle-class consciousness. Whether or not this basis itself is as foundational, congruous, and grounded as the collaboration between Simon and the South African group suggests will be the subject of the following chapter.

# II

## Fantasies of Home

### The Antinomies of Modernity and the Music of Ladysmith Black Mambazo

Few musics of South African origin have attracted more international acclaim in recent years than the music of Ladysmith Black Mambazo. And unlike other African musical styles that have become established components of the global music industry, the a cappella choral music known as *isicathamiya* has come to be regarded as one of the most powerful expressions of Africa's musical heritage and, what is more, as one of black South Africans' most resilient statements of defiance against apartheid. The fact that traditional expressive forms emerge as part of a broader narrative critical of modernity and that these forms then themselves constitute some new master discourse that makes modernism look like a curiosity cabinet is in itself a historical phenomenon, one that is rooted as much in the shifting notions of tradition as in the crisis of modernity itself. For instance, as my earlier discussion of the place of musical aesthetics in late-twentieth-century Western thought has suggested, the figures and fictions that have enabled Western intellectuals to both celebrate difference and disjuncture and at the same time express a deep yearning for wholeness and certainty, in a paradoxical move, led many pop performers back to one of the founding gestures of modernism: the search for truth elsewhere, on the edges and the margins, on the other side of the circular canvas. And, I concluded, it is within such attempts at recasting the world after colonialism, that non-Western music comes to play a special role. In order to pursue this line of argument further and to ground my analysis more firmly in the tangle of texts enmeshed in *Graceland* I am going to examine in this chapter the making and meaning of *isicathamiya*, the tradition of male a cappella choral music and dance out of which comes the music of Ladysmith Black Mambazo and the introduction to "Diamonds on the Soles of Her Shoes."

But first let me return briefly to the Simon biography by Patrick Humphries discussed in the previous chapter. The chapter "All Around the World," which reviews the *Graceland* tour of 1987, ends with the following sentence: "Black African music was one of the strands which Elvis Presley wove into rock and roll in Memphis' Sun Studios in 1954; but Paul Simon went back even further and introduced the world to the music in a purer and more recognizable form."[1]

I am quoting this short passage not only because it neatly summarizes the position which music critics around the world have adopted vis-à-vis Simon's encounter with South African music but also because it reflects a view in the West about Africa, its culture, and its musical traditions that, in its persistent exoticism, stands in a direct line with some of the earlier forms of the Western global imagination examined in part I. It is within this discourse about roots and purity, I shall argue in the following pages, that *isicathamiya* plays a key role as an emblem of redemption and authenticity. But in outlining the historical trajectory and current practice of *isicathamiya* here I shall question the construction in the post-*Graceland* debate of *isicathamiya* performance as the unmediated and authentic expression of a mythic African past. In fact, I shall maintain that, although the songs within the genre voice a quest for identity and security in a dramatically changed social universe similar to Paul Simon's songs, *isicathamiya* performance is driven by the same dilemmas of the modern world that also trouble Western middle-class sensibilities. Ladysmith Black Mambazo's songs constitute an African discourse about Africa, to be sure, but at the same time these songs represent an attempt to both reject and embrace modernity as part of the same gesture. The search in *isicathamiya* performance for an identity and some kind of rootedness in indubitable space–time structures, although it flows from a deep sense of alienation and from the bitter experience of being part of modernity and at the same time excluded from it, is deeply caught up with modernity and some of its specifically global fictions. With every step they dance and with every note they sing, the search for what *isicathamiya* performers call home, as much as they may seek to return migrant workers to a primordial Africa, a land of redemption and wholeness, draws them ever more inexorably into the West and the modern world. If we are to grasp this dialectic of absence and presence and, more specifically, to comprehend the role of *isicathamiya* in the making of *Graceland*, the first thing we have to consider is its history.[2]

*Of Coons, Churches, and Competitions:*
*The History of* Isicathamiya

*Isicathamiya* emerged at the turn of the century out of the experiences and struggles of isiZulu-speaking migrant workers in Natal. Fleeing desperate living conditions in the countryside, growing numbers of males were drawn into South Africa's burgeoning industrial economy, where they took up employment in the harbor and railway yards of Durban, white households, or the embryonic manufacturing industry of the Witwatersrand. *Isicathamiya* was born of the encounter between these two worlds—the world of rural homesteads, warfare, ancestor spirits, and wedding ceremonials on the one hand and the realm of factories and urban popular culture on the other hand. Certainly these worlds rested on two vastly different sets of images of personal identity, sociability, and aesthetic value. At the same time, during the formative period of *isicathamiya*—a period that stretched from around World War I to the mid-1930s—both spheres were also associated with and constructed through specific performance genres.

Thus social relations in the countryside centered around a body of danced song and sung dance that celebrated and ritually constituted the lineage as the quintessential unit of meaningful human existence, both for itself and in relation to other lineages. Within this larger body of genres, wedding songs (*izingoma zomtshado*) occupy a central position. Of the enormous variety of songs and dances that accompany the highly intricate and lengthy process of Zulu marriage negotiations, betrothal, and the final wedding ceremony, the ones called *isigekle* and *ikhetho* were the most crucial in shaping early *isicathamiya*. Performed by the bride's and by the bridegroom's parties, respectively, *isigekle* and *ikhetho* were characterized by a formation of dancers in a single line and by vigorous polyphonic singing in call-and-response. Also crucial was *ukubika ibala*, a dance more commonly encountered at Christian weddings, when the bride's party, *umthimba*, led by a "conductor," entered the homestead of the bridegroom to escort the bride to her new home.

Present-day *isicathamiya* performance to a substantial degree is indebted to these three main categories of wedding song. At the level of lyrics, for instance, as we shall see in a moment, a significant portion of *isicathamiya* songs either directly derive from wedding songs or otherwise elaborate on gender issues, problems of parental authority, and other such questions as arise from the profound transformations that affected rural households in modern South African society. Similarly, the single straight line of performers is the principal choreographic formation in both early and contemporary *isicathamiya*—a constellation which, like some of its rural models in wedding dances, is frequently called *imashi* (march), reflecting the impact on Zulu society of Western and particularly Christian notions of social order. Finally, within their sonic structure, too, *isicathamiya* songs share some of the characteristics of rural wedding songs, notably the call-and-response form and a strong admixture of Christian hymnody. Wesleyan hymns have had a pervasive influence on many traditional genres from very early on in the nineteenth century, but in wedding songs the missionary impact is most clearly felt in a certain squareness of the melodic contour and metrical form. In fact, the influence of Western hymns has been such that the older generation of *isicathamiya* practitioners, when referring to the wedding component of old-style *isicathamiya*, still prefer to talk about *ameleki* (American)—the hymns, religious imagery, and prac-

tices of the American Board of Missions, the earliest and for a long time predominant Christian mission in Natal.

But more than these structural correspondences, what determines the close
relationship between wedding songs and dances and *isicathamiya* performance,
past and present, is the role of these genres as symbolic mediators between two
closely connected realms of the precolonial social world: the worldly and the
sacred, the public and the private, the male and the female. For these dances are
more than mere embellishments of the ritual proceedings. They are the wedding itself. Dancing (*ukusina*) solemnizes and sacralizes a marriage, and thus the
most common question asked in determining the stage of the ceremonial
process, characteristically, is, "Umakoti usesinile?" (Has the bride danced?)

Another subcategory of rural performance on which early *isicathamiya* practitioners drew was the songs and dances associated with warfare. Dating back
to the time of Shaka and in some cases even earlier, regimental war anthems
(*amahubo empi*) remained an important element of group cohesion even in
colonial and postcolonial times, serving in contexts as diverse as tourist entertainment and trade unionism. Beyond this, when singing such songs performers
form single lines as in an *impi* (regiment) marching into the field, and thus
much of the social organization of *isicathamiya* choirs is metaphorically predicated on the world of precolonial Zulu military power.

If by the 1920s the voices and narratives of the countryside had lost none of
their resilience, South Africa's cities offered no less rich an arsenal of genres for
migrants to draw upon. By far the most potent urban influences on early *isicathamiya* were the songs and dances associated with the minstrel and vaudeville theater of the nineteenth century. Up until the turn of the century, minstrel shows had been without any doubt the most popular form of stage
entertainment in South Africa, and although essentially a grossly racist genre
pandering to white colonial anxieties, burnt cork shows met with no small degree of enthusiasm among the country's black population. Inspired by the seminal tours of Orpheus M. McAdoo's Jubilee Singers in the 1890s and drawing
on "Coloured" adaptations of blackface minstrelsy, scores of local minstrel
troupes in towns and on rural mission stations familiarized migrant laborers
with the genre. What attracted these audiences to songs such as "Oh! Susan-
nah," ragtime dancing, and the figure of the "coon," besides the novelty and hi-
larious drama embodied in these core symbols of the minstrel stage, were two
things. Minstrelsy, and here especially the "coon," provided images of urban so-
phistication and modernization and by simultaneously deriding black elite idio-
syncrasies offered a means of distancing oneself from modernity's discontents.
Black audiences knew that not all black people were boisterous and mischievous, but they also knew that some were. And thus the image of the "coon,"
once it was wrested from the exclusive domain of white supremacist discourse,
became a tool of intracommunal criticism, a way of dealing with an increasingly differentiated social environment. The "coon" and the dances and vocal
style of the minstrel stage, in the minds of early *isicathamiya* performers, all

added up to *isikhunzi* (literally, coons), the earliest known proto-style of *isi-cathamiya*.

Wedding songs, regimental war songs, and the minstrel repertoire in the beginning may have arisen from two diametrically opposed worlds, but by the turn of the century such forms of popular performance had long since become entangled with one another. In fact, one of the most striking historical lessons to be learned from the rise of a performance tradition like *isicathamiya* is how inextricably meshed different social worlds and forms of imagination already were in the early history of modern South Africa and how the expressive genres that emerged from this intermixture were anything but primordial, undiluted, or ancient. Thus, by as early as the 1920s, ragtime choreography had become a major influence on some of the long-entrenched rural wedding dances like *ikhetho*. In fact, *ukureka*, as Zulu speakers came to name the new urban dance style, in time became an umbrella term for Christian wedding dances in general. And as if to underscore the modern connotations of *ukureka*, an accompanying genre of wedding songs was created, called *amakhoti* (chords).

Conversely, urban performance genres were more than just the modern echoes of the "tribal" past. Zionist ritual, to name but one example especially relevant within the context of *isicathamiya*, is tooled on the symbols and rituals of the rural and the precolonial world in ways that convey a sense of stubborn insistence, a deliberate attempt amid the experiences of urban deprivation and alienation to refashion the self to more accustomed designs. As Caesar Ndlovu's research on the parallels between *isicathamiya* performance and Zionist ritual has shown, *isicathamiya* singers and dancers are mostly *amaZayoni*—adherents of black independent Zionist churches—and as such consider their performances as analogies of and commentaries on ancestor worship and Zionist church ritual. Thus both *isicathamiya* singers and *amaZayoni* use the term *um-lindelo* (waiting time) when referring to the warm-up section of the competitions, when everybody awaits the arrival of the judge, and all-night religious services and the anticipation that precedes the arrival of the Holy Messenger.[3] Similarly, the circling around with fast, shuffling steps in both Zionist prayer meetings and *isicathamiya* performances is called *isifekezeli*, a form of choreography associated with homeward motion and with the search for a sanctuary amid the chaos of the modern world. In short, both types of urban performance, rather than merely representing varying degrees of urbanization or positions on an imagined rural–urban continuum, intercede between some of the contrarieties engendered by the modern world—oppositions between the sacred and the profane, between the past and the present—and seek to transcend them in ways that furnish people with the power essential for correct living.[4]

The heterogeneous blend of styles and traditions I have described here characterized *isicathamiya* during a first, experimental period, which lasted until the mid-1930s. Following this early initiatory phase, a second period of maturity can be established, one that is now generally regarded as the classic era of *isi-*

*cathamiya* performance and that extended into the late 1960s. Its pioneer and principal moving force was Solomon Popoli Linda. Born in 1909 in the vicinity of Pomeroy in the poverty-stricken labor reserve of Msinga, Linda was steeped in the traditions of *amahubo* and *izingoma zomtshado*. But as a boarder at the nearby Gordon Memorial School he also came into contact with Western mission culture, with its choir contests, hymns, and strangely antithetical notions of social order. Both these traditions furnished him with the necessary competence to compete with other early choirs in Johannesburg, a task Linda excelled in first as a member of his uncle's choir and then from the mid-1930s on as leader of his own group, the Evening Birds. The real breakthrough, however, was not to come until 1939, when Linda, now working as a packer at the new Gallo record pressing plant, was discovered by talent scout Griffith Motsieloa. Gallo was then South Africa's premier record company and the plant at Roodepoort the first of its kind in Africa. And thus when the company in 1939 released Solomon Linda's composition "Mbube" (Lion) not only did the record become South Africa's first "hit" and Linda's choir *isicathamiya*'s uncrowned kings, but also the word *mbube* became synonymous with the whole genre of male a cappella choral singing. All this demonstrates that Linda's career and *isicathamiya*'s classical period were deeply tied up with the rise of South Africa's recording industry and, through it, the expansion of the country's nascent manufacturing industry.

In performance, all this expressed itself in quite paradoxical figures: a series of innovations and modernizations and, at the same time, a new, redirected sense of the past and the countryside. Thus Solomon Linda was the first choir leader to make it a point that his singers appear onstage in uniform dress and in line with the latest trends in urban fashion. The Evening Birds sported pinstriped three-piece suits, Florsheim shoes, and hats and indulged in a fast-paced, energetic choreography called *istep* that made performers look like resolute men defiantly walking the streets of the white man's city. Another more Western and hence urban element in Linda's songs is manifest in a tune such as "Mbube." After a short introduction reminiscent of the metrically free, pentatonic *ihubo*, the choir launches into the main section of the song, in which only a few elements are retained of deep-Zulu musical grammar. The harmonic framework is a plain $I–IV–I\frac{4}{6}–V^7$ progression in four bars, the solo vocal line moving strictly in synchrony with this triadic structure. (For a full analysis of "Mbube" see chapter 14.)

Despite all these symbolic turns toward the urban sphere, Linda also remodeled a number of core musical icons of the rural world to fit the new *mbube* style. Among other things, he strengthened the bass section of his choir, a move which not only departed from the *isikhunzi* principle of one singer per voice part but also implied a return to more rural, precolonial forms of male performance, with their preponderance of deeply sonorous bass registers. By far the most persistent and potent expression, however, of *isicathamiya*'s place within the culture and consciousness of South Africa's black migrant workers is in a certain Janus-faced notion of male identity that is encoded in these symbolic layers. For, on the one hand, suits, *istep* dancing, and booming basses all signaled the indomitable desire to mark the urban space with a presence, to assert a notion and practice of manhood that directly challenged white assumptions of black workers as noiseless, almost self-effacing, and ill-clad "labor units." Song texts, on the other hand, worked within the same overall poetics of manhood, if only in a different direction: by incorporating a great deal of self-praise. I have shown in chapter 2 how southern African verbal arts and the idea of the person intertwine in *izibongo*, the praise name. In African thinking, I noted, the making of a man was not so much a self-reflexive, introspective process by which an individual sought to determine his value and position in society through the inspection of his inner riches. It was rather that a man was able to build his name by looking outward, by acquiring the preeminence of a hero (*umqhawe*), and, finally, by accumulating wealth in people through the construction of ever more proliferating bonds and affiliations.

The contrast between this heroic notion of individual being and Western ideas of rootedness and existential depth can hardly be more pronounced. As can, of course, the contrast between the parallel ideas of the name and performed identity. Throughout southern Africa, praise names are often eloquent and compellingly rich compositions that at once constitute what Hoyt Alverson has called "meaning structures for thinking about the self" and road signs on the path toward the building up of personhood.[5] *Isicathamiya* song texts, one might argue accordingly, simply extend this practice to the tribulations and insecurities of labor migration, racial oppression, and urban life, by shifting the object of praise from the precolonial hero to the networks of "home-people" and workmates that migrants from the same rural district or the same factory construct in town and that form the social basis of most *isicathamiya* choirs.

Another method briefly to be considered here of male empowerment through the skillful manipulation of language consists in the juxtaposition of textual elements from seemingly disparate and disconnected semantic realms. *Mbube* performers such as Linda often interlaced *izibongo*-style eulogy with cryptic and ostensibly nonsensical phrases, a fact which Western observers have usually found to be an indication of detribalization and poetic impoverishment. Yet what conventional analyses of lyrical "content" fail to reveal is the crucial fact that the resultant patchwork of sounds and images is not meant to convey a meaning in the first place. Migrant performers, as Jonathan Clegg has pointed out, are interested in the tensions that result from the profuse overlapping of multiple and blurred semantic fields.[6] Theirs is a concern with the stylistic process of "building up significance," not with significance as a value in itself. What *isicathamiya* choirs communicate, then, is not meaning as such —words or images referring to some content—but rather the ability to *give* meaning. To weave together praise poetry, proverbs, snippets of TV beer commercials, and fragments of Zionist hymns is to move into style, to create *sym-*

*bolon* proper, binding elements that bring into relationship with one another different experiential domains of masculinity in the modern world. Thus, ultimately, what *isicathamiya* performance in general and song texts in particular achieve is what Michael Herzfeld, writing about the poetics of manhood in Crete, calls a "stylistic transfiguration of action." The performance of these texts focuses the attention not on *what* men are and what they do but on *how* they do it. Being a man and a hero, someone who commands the respect of friend and foe alike, is the same as showing how good one is at being such a man. In short, it is the ability to manipulate style rather than to define content that indicates male identity.

Solomon Linda's Evening Birds dominated South Africa's *isicathamiya* scene until the early 1950s—the last recording was made in 1954—against increasing competition from choirs such as the Durban Evening Birds and Maktshwa's Choir and despite the fact that other groups were beginning to experiment with alternative styles such as *isikambula*, *isikhwela Jo*, and *'mbombing* (bombing). In essence, all these were structural variations on the *mbube* model, the only difference being a vocal texture that favored extremely high-pitched, almost yelling sounds—vocal explosions not quite unlike the exploding bombs migrant performers were able to watch in World War II newsreels and, like these, icons of virility and manly belligerence. Most postwar choirs adhered rather strictly to this aesthetic, thereby increasingly cutting themselves off from the transformations in South African society at large and the situation of migrant labor and culture in particular. As a result, it was not until the early 1970s that *isicathamiya* began to take due account of these changes and that a third phase in its history commenced.

Two broader developments account for this change of direction: the mounting crisis of grand apartheid and its "homelands" in conjunction with the growing confluence of migrant and township cultures, on the one hand, and the expansion of radio broadcasting, on the other hand. While it is certainly true that the rise to power in 1948 of the Afrikaner-dominated National Party led South African society to an even more troubled future of racial conflict, the hardening politics of labor coercion, segregation, and rural resettlement also met with mounting popular resistance—the Durban strikes of 1973 and the Soweto uprising of 1976 are two of the examples that come to mind here. But, more important perhaps, by the mid-1970s, as all sorts of economic and political crises compounded, the ruling oligarchy felt impelled to generate some legitimacy for the reigning order and to initiate a process of reform from above, part of which consisted in making radio and television more attractive to black mass audiences as a means of reinforcing existing class and political cleavages within black society.

Finally, important shifts also took place in the situation of migrant labor itself, especially in the mining industry, the core of South Africa's migrant labor army. Although frequently inimical toward permanently urbanized black communities, migrant workers bore the brunt of apartheid repression and, correspondingly, in time came to espouse the same unitary worker consciousness as the township dwellers and even formed the vanguard of militant opposition to the system.[7] Furthermore, as Dunbar Moodie has convincingly argued, it was a number of significant increases in mine wages in the early 1970s that enabled migrant workers to consider themselves as "professional miners whose families continue to reside in the countryside" rather than as farmers working to fund rural homesteads.[8] One of the most dramatic consequences of this "purposive organization of life-worlds," as Moodie calls it, was that the idea of the kin group and the rural homestead acquired new meaning. Although a remarkably elastic network of relations even in precolonial society, in the political economy of the labor reserve traditional kinship systems were constantly dissolved and remolded and thereby became phases in a developmental cycle that equally included other types of household compositions like the nuclear family.[9] At the same time, as the rural homestead ceased to be the center of migrants' socio-moral universe and came to resemble more an offshoot in what was essentially a world dominated by urban ways, migrants' culture and consciousness experienced a marked shift toward more urban-based forms.[10]

The rapid expansion of radio broadcasting in South Africa was the second factor in shaping the evolution of *isicathamiya* performance during its third phase. The development of broadcasting services for the major African languages had been one of the apartheid regime's top priorities after it came to power in 1948, and when the South African Broadcasting Corporation's black stations, dubbed Radio Bantu, went on the air in 1962 it was by far the most powerful broadcasting service on the entire continent, reaching up to 97 percent of the country's black population. The goal of Radio Bantu was to propagate the apartheid mythology of "separate development," obtain black South Africans' assent to the idea of the "homelands" as a blueprint for development, and goad them into a work ethic compatible with the demands of capital. To accentuate these broader political objectives, in the early 1960s, a vast amount of traditional music, sustaining as it allegedly did apartheid engineers' hygienic vision of separate "tribal" identities, was recorded in the field and broadcast regularly on all the vernacular services.[11] Even though toward the end of the decade this scheme was broadened to include other types of popular music (provided these did not put in question, by content or association, the goals of Separate Development), *isicathamiya* remained the favorite of both broadcasters and listeners. With its nostalgia for the countryside and dislike of the city, *isicathamiya* seemed ideally suited to serve the interests of state and capital and, in fact, contributed nicely to what early broadcasting officials had termed the media's role in the "strengthening of native home life."

At the studio level, this policy was scrupulously overseen by two highly influential broadcasters: Yvonne Huskisson and Alexius Buthelezi. Well versed in matters concerning Zulu and Pedi music, these two individuals were responsible, as one official apartheid organ put it, for making "a contribution towards preserving the identity of the Black peoples."[12] In addition to being music director of Radio Bantu, Huskisson published *The Bantu Composers of Southern Africa*, a patronizing Who's Who of sorts that emphasized South African black composers' pristinely discrete ethnic identities.[13] Buthelezi, for his part, compiled a compendium of *isicathamiya* choirs and, more important, hosted a weekly show called *Cothoza Mfana*.[14] Based on a tune by Gershon Mcanyana and the Scorpions that cautions the choir to tiptoe (*cothoza*) while in the studio, Buthelezi's show proved enormously successful with listeners and in time became the premier national showcase for fledgling *isicathamiya* choirs. Between them, these concerted efforts at "preserving" alleged ethnic identities not only helped to canonize and fossilize what in historical practice had been highly intertextual, crossbred genres but also contributed to the survival of a genre which by the 1970s was rapidly losing hold in the emerging culture of "urban displacement." In fact, as Bhekizizwe Shabalala once remarked, had it not been for "some radio personalities who very much liked the style," *isicathamiya* in the late 1960s "would have really nearly died."

All this implies, of course, a paradox—the fact, namely, that the emergence of *isicathamiya* as a genre of the Zulu core was in reality the product of a prolonged entanglement with the forces of modernity, especially with the media. At the same time, I must stress the fact that this state-sponsored construction of "tribal" identities was never simply a matter of downright imposition from above or docile acquiescence from below. The charge, levied by many an observer, that the osmosis in *isicathamiya* among media, homelands ideology, and rural nostalgia veered dangerously close to an exoneration of the apartheid regime and its lackeys is of course a serious one—one that needs to be carefully considered in the light of the deepening political crisis of the 1970s and 1980s. But it is also an accusation that needs to be addressed by unraveling *isicathamiya*'s own aesthetic logic, beyond the narrow academic dichotomies of hegemony and resistance. If, as I would argue, the development of *isicathamiya* in the 1970s and up until 1986 has to be seen within this framework of the politics of "homeland" and "displaced urbanization," it is nevertheless true that the genre posed its own hybrid aesthetics against apartheid's doctrines of racial purity. Perhaps this is nowhere clearer than in the music of two of the undoubtedly preeminent *isicathamiya* choirs after Solomon Linda's Evening Birds: the King Star Brothers and Ladysmith Black Mambazo.

The King Star Brothers had been established in Johannesburg in the early 1960s from a group of young men from the Transvaal town of Standerton, an area that for a long time had known more down-tempo and middle-register forms of vocal performance. As their first SABC recordings of 1963 reveal, it was the King Star Brothers who introduced a less compact, less densely textured sound into the prevailing *'mbombing* style of the time. Ladysmith Black Mambazo for its part had only been founded in the late 1960s, but after a series of SABC appearances in 1970 and the release of their first album, *Amabutho*, in 1973, the group soon outstripped the King Star Brothers in popularity. After a rapid succession of several gold records in the mid-1970s, Bhekizizwe Shabalala decided to transform his choir into a full-blown commercial enterprise—the first *isicathamiya* group to function solely within the music industry, outside of the conventional circuit of competitions. Underlying this cometlike rise, however, were far-reaching changes in a number of areas that relate to performance style. The first of these was a new choreography that incorporated key elements of a dance style called *umgqashiyo*, which had been popularized in the mid-1960s by the all female band Mahotella Queens and had been a favorite with migrant audiences ever since. The second innovation consisted in the introduction of a certain element of chronology and narrative sequentiality into song lyrics. Whereas the majority of *isicathamiya* song texts, as we have seen, build up significance and metaphorical density from the almost formalist juxtaposition of images and thereby, as performance, correlate with the parallel processes of name and personality building, Shabalala in many of his songs chose to foreground himself as a fully constituted author, a knowing subject empowered to take a deliberate stance toward the world as one standing in need of elucidation.

Last, the third and perhaps most important innovation in the music of Ladysmith Black Mambazo was in the domain of sound texture. Having greatly refashioned the poetic structure of *isicathamiya* performance, Shabalala felt that when performing, just as "when talking to a person who is sitting next to you, you don't have to shout." So he decided to "bring the range down" by getting his choir to sing what were essentially *'mbombing* and *isikhwela Jo* tunes in feathery, velvety voices. The outcome of this was *isicathamiya*, a sound audiences in South Africa came to treasure as *pholile* and *kumnandi*, calm and sweet.

On a superficial reading, the new direction Shabalala had given to *isicathamiya* performance in these three key areas may not be readily identified with revolutionary politics and antiapartheid bravado per se. But what critics of Ladysmith Black Mambazo's alleged political abstinence tended to overlook in their search for politically explicit lyrics appears to be the fact that Shabalala's reshaping of migrant choral music cut against the grain of some of apartheid's most entrenched mythologies not by openly denouncing them but by undermining their aesthetic premises. Shabalala's music, primarily through the cross-linkages it maintained with *umgqashiyo* and *mbaqanga*, bridged migrant culture and township culture in ways that countered apartheid engineers' limited sense of social fluctuation and their attempts to curb it by inventing artificial and eternally fixed social and racial categories. At the same time, Shabalala's work thoroughly deconstructs the notion that, rather than being vehicles of a self-conscious urbanity, black innovation and cultural leadership had to serve "tribal" interests and identities. The individual author speaking through many of his songs, although he rarely articulates himself as an "I," is one who squarely positions himself at the intersection of a wide range of social worlds and experiences, adroitly navigating among them.

My account of *isicathamiya* history would be incomplete without mentioning at least briefly the possibility of a fourth phase, one that began with the release of *Graceland*, coincided with the end of apartheid rule, and may well continue into the present moment of the reconstruction of South African society. Although it may be premature at this point in time to anticipate what precise contours *isicathamiya* performance is eventually going to take in the "new South Africa," what the opening chapter of *Graceland* and Ladysmith Black Mambazo seems to indicate is that the future story of *isicathamiya* will be ever more conjoined with other stories and other musics elsewhere on our planet. At the very least, what the further course of *isicathamiya* will prove, as indeed my entire historical sketch suggests, is how questionable it is to imagine, in the manner of Humphries and other authors in the West, the genre as being encapsulated in some sort of cultural quarantine of timelessness and uncontaminated authenticity. Instead, as my short synopsis here indicates, the future will reveal the "Orientalist" legacy inherent in such a stance, by bringing to the fore the fundamental historicity of *isicathamiya* and by highlighting a number of interlocking themes in its rich history of hybridity and intertextuality—themes woven into songs long forgotten and into others, truly global ones, like "Mbube" and "Diamonds on the Soles of Her Shoes."

The first of these themes is the troubling feeling of rupture that pervades the genre, a rupture not just of all established social ties—of high and low, male and female, the home and the world—but a radical discontinuity of time as such. At least, this is what appears to be the meaning of such a desolately taciturn song as "Anginamali," by the Empangeni Home Tigers:

Namhlanje kimi, kukude emuva, kukude phambili.

Today, for me, the past is far and the future is far.

What migrant workers seem to register in verses such as these, as well as in the angered and mournful sounds of *isicathamiya* generally, is not just the condition of migrancy. It is, above all, migrants' growing loss of agency and sense of continuity. Something more is at stake in a song such as "Anginamali." than placelessness, something more existential and so utterly disquieting that it must inevitably belie any Western fantasies about an Africa at one with itself and the inner sources of human existence.

The second theme that runs through my account is the intermingled boundaries of class, ethnicity, language, and genres that mark *isicathamiya* performance. From its inception in the 1920s the genre has been staying on a radically syncretic course, boldly restating the intermingled character of South Africa's social and cultural landscape. Early *isicathamiya* performers, contrary to the prevailing and apparently indelible image of migrants as politically conservative and culturally introspective, eagerly sought to assimilate the old with the new, the indigenous with the foreign, the home with the diaspora. They sang of the wisdom of Shaka but to a tune borrowed from the Christian missions; they modeled their choirs on the image of precolonial war regiments, but the dances bore the elegant mark of the urban flaneur.

Another theme, related to the former, is the symbolic complexity of the genre at the microlevel. Not only do *isicathamiya* songs and dances defy simplistic notions of performance practice as a homogeneous expression of a monolithic consciousness of migrant workers, often the vocal timbre, sound texture, lyrical genre, and choreographic and sartorial style also belong to different semantic orders even within the same song. In fact, competition, dissension, and conflict are of the very essence in *isicathamiya* performance, a fact to be borne in mind not only in light of Ladysmith Black Mambazo's velvet-textured sounds and topical lyrics but also because it is precisely the more strident tonalities of *isicathamiya* that are being excised from contemporary discussions of *Graceland*. By portraying the music of Ladysmith Black Mambazo as the happy alternative to apartheid's unyielding cruelty or, alternatively, as the bold war cry of a proud nation of warriors, Western observers have ignored the creative work of performers struggling to alter the received tropes of Zuluness and, as Rob Nixon has observed, to extricate themselves from the near-monopoly of Inkatha (now called the Inkatha Freedom Party) over a contrived ethnohistory conventionally narrated through male warrior triumphs.[15]

By far the most crucial theme, however, that underlies all these symbolic journeys across social, political, and cultural boundaries and in many ways works against the grain of the brazenly conflictual construction of male identities is, quite paradoxically, the attempt in *isicathamiya* performance to bound and bind the individual within some presumed harmonious and intact world, to construct a tightly sealed realm of habitus and local moorings. The root image of this vastly idealized, fictitious world is that of the home, *khaya*. An immensely multilayered term in the Zulu lexicon, *khaya* denotes a dwelling, an inhabited place, the homestead, a place to which one belongs, or simply the members of a family. The term thus appears to translate not so much a location as a set of relationships in space and time; it conveys a sense of what it means to live in a society in which everything flows from within and is mediated by the lineage.

*Isicathamiya* performance reflects and at the same time enacts migrants' nostalgia for the "home" in a variety of ways. For instance, apart from the fact that most choirs consist of a combination of men from the same kin group and/or the same rural area, *isicathamiya* choreography, through the association with wedding dances, evokes potent images of domestic unity and, by celebrating basically iniquitous gender relationships, of social control. Conversely, a song text like the following (sung, ironically, to a tune reminiscent of the Top Notes' and Isley Brothers' classic "Twist and Shout") stands for the acute sense of dislocation and yearning for the family at home that is voiced in many songs:

> Nisibona silapha siphuma kude.
> Siphuma le ebunzimeni.
> Silapha nje sizulazula
> senziwa yindaba zokuhlupheka.

Sashiya abazali nezihlobo zethu.
Thina sihamba sifuna imali.
Ngihlupheka, ngihlupheka, ngihlupheka.

---

As you see us here, we come from afar.
We come from afar.
As we are here, we are roaming around
because of suffering.
We left our parents and family.
We travel in search of money.
I suffer, I suffer, I suffer.[16]

Clearly, as these sorrowful lines show, *isicathamiya*, notwithstanding a ready acceptance of the city and its forms, is tantamount to homecoming. Its practitioners are homeward bound. But this "return to the whole"—to paraphrase a key concept in James W. Fernandez's work on metaphor and performance—is more than the goal of all symbolic practice.[17] In a society that inflicted upon its black majority the vagaries of a Fordist economic regime and a ruthlessly oppressive minority rule, this retrieval of an imagined past also takes on quite specific meanings. And thus, in a broader sense, the homecoming of *isicathamiya* can be seen as part of a much more comprehensive semantics of social order, one that extends migrants' retrospective quest beyond the realm of the personal and the family into the political and public sphere.

The ultimate expression of this imagined world of orderliness and cohesion, the embodiment and source of all material wealth and spiritual value, is *ilizwe*, the Zulu nation, the Zulu country. It is manifest above all in countless song texts that bemoan the loss of Zulu independent power, invoke the grandeur and wisdom of Shaka, and, on occasion, express support for the present king, Goodwill Zwelithini, and Chief Gatsha Buthelezi. Of course, this confluence of the desire for security and the notion of the Zulu nation as the "home" and foundation of all meaningful human existence cannot be taken at face value as the natural disposition, as it were, of the Zulu "people." Rather, it must be placed within the broader context of twentieth-century South African politics and the apartheid system in particular. For as a closer look at the political history of ethnicity in modern South Africa reveals, the idea of a Pan-Zulu ethnic and cultural identity is a recent and, what is more, exceedingly contested construct. It resulted from the intense and interested labors of the black intelligentsia and white ideologues in the 1920s and 1930s and, beyond this, continued to be a major element of antiapartheid politics of the 1980s and of the present postapartheid era.

Thus if *isicathamiya* performers, in the course of battling an oppressive, alien system, have developed complex tactics of defense that draw on a truly cosmopolitan range of traditions and if these same choices are often represented in the West as expressions of an authentic African, Zulu identity, we are dealing with more than just a contradiction. And we have to do with more than the fact that these performers, by adhering to the "Orientalized" images of warlike and yet somehow childish members of something called the "Zulu tribe" the state has concocted of them, appear to be doing exactly what the system expects of them. Rather, we are dealing with one of the core ambiguities of the black experience in modern society. The tension that becomes apparent in the uneasy shifts between an almost modernist cosmopolitanism and a self-styled nativism is part of what Paul Gilroy has called the politics of transfiguration. They are immanent within the utopian desires that are expressed, as he puts it, "on a lower frequency," in a partially hidden public sphere.[18] Working under the nose of the oppressor, *isicathamiya* performers, much like black popular artists in South Africa in general, have laid claim to the entire range of modern expressive means white South Africa has withheld from them and at the same time invoked alternative social relations by deliberately retreating from modernity into tradition.

In other words, migrant workers and performers, through a genre such as *isicathamiya*, have been able to author complex and multiply determined identities—identities that were not given from time immemorial but historically produced in the uneasy confrontation with the West, the world system, and the forces of modernity. Conversely, I have shown how the disembedding logic of modernity prompted a reverse process—that of finding, amid the rampant ambiguities and insecurities of modern South African society, certainty and deliverance in a feeling of belonging and being at home. And as I said at the beginning, this search for identity links the music of Ladysmith Black Mambazo to Simon's soul-searching mission in interesting ways. The overall picture, however, that emerges from my discussion is that of a form of symbolic practice quite inauthentic and rhizomic itself, one that stands in a tense relationship with the forces and processes that made it. It is a picture of a long and venerable tradition that, although it is no longer part of the past, still speaks to the past. And by the same token it is a representation of a creative practice that, although it cannot be placed within the Western mainstream, does not stand outside the West. Rather, the music of Ladysmith Black Mambazo has all the discrepancies, failures, and figures of both tradition and modernity available to it.

## 12

# Dream Journeys

*Techniques of the Self and the Biographical*
*Imagination of Bhekizizwe J. Shabalala*

If the music of Ladysmith Black Mambazo, as I have argued in the previous chapter, has engaged modernity and the West in a variety of ambiguous ways—rather than enclosing itself in its own universe, distanced from the modern world—where does this leave us in terms of the process which I call the global imagination and the interdependence of Western constructions of Africa and of African representations of the West? What conclusions are we to draw from this for the extraordinary part *Graceland* played in what Rob Nixon has called the "vexed sense of half-shared histories" of South Africans and Americans?[1] Furthermore, if Western middle-class identities in the late twentieth century are formed in a world of risk, fluctuation, and uncertain boundaries and emerge coded by discourses of race and Otherness, what contrasting images of Europe and the modern world influence the making of African identities? What allows us to chart postcolonial African selves in Africa alone rather than in the interplay of Africa and the West? Above all, if the technologies and practices employed to produce such cross-indexed and double-mirrored identities—the fanzines, videos, package tours, television documentaries, digital samplers, pop albums, and home pages—are globally disseminated, what can we deduce from this for the kinds of selves situated at the margins of the postcolonial world? And, finally, what do these practices tell us about the concept of the African individual, its uncertainties, contingencies, and trajectories?

This chapter seeks to provide some tentative answers to these questions. Concentrating on the life story and self-representation of Bhekizizwe Shabalala in a series of biographical texts, I pursue the inquiry begun in chapter 2 on personal identity, knowledge, and (auto)biography and seek to bring together a set of issues that have been crucial to my argument throughout this book. More specifically, I shall argue that the construction of an African global actor such as the leader of Ladysmith Black Mambazo is determined by a logic similar to the discourses invested in the persona of Paul Simon. Put another way, just as the making of Paul Simon is refracted and made problematic through discourses of Africa, Bhekizizwe Shabalala's construction of himself is embedded in a complex and often difficult relationship with the West. The identity of neither performer exists of and for itself. As the one takes Africa as one of his individuality's reference points, so the other draws on core Western myths of the self to imagine himself. As Simon cultivates his authority as a cosmopolitan artist and world cultural intermediary by evoking the authentic and primordial, Shabalala affirms his selfhood as an African by making available to himself the conceptual categories and modes of representation ordering bourgeois society in the West.

Of course, the point of this chapter is not merely to compare and contrast the two types of discourse of personal identity and state their similarity and divergence. Rather, it is to explore how in the context of the postcolonial world of the 1980s such discourses and the identities that emerge in relation to them can no longer be understood as independent projects. In attending to the tensions, fissures, and shifts that result from the intermingling discourses of the biographical imagination I stress the profound interdependence of such projects and how they restate and cut across the dichotomies of Africa and the West, tradition and modernity, "them and us."

The evidence for my argument comes from three related sets of texts. The first is *Journey of Dreams*, a documentary about Bhekizizwe Shabalala, his music, and his life story.[2] Produced by Shabalala's New York–based agents, Night After Night, and directed by David Lister, *Journey of Dreams* was shot in 1988, just months after the release of the Grammy-winning album *Shaka Zulu*.[3] Although it was never shown in public, the film is one of the more sustained elaborations to date about one of South Africa's most successful composers and performers.[4] As a supplement to this, I shall also refer to Alex J. Thembela and Edmund P. M. Radebe's *The Life and Works of Bhekizizwe Shabalala and the Ladysmith Black Mambazo*, a volume of 70-odd pages that discusses Shabalala's life, his ideas, and his music.[5] Finally, the third set of texts, discussed mainly in the third section of this chapter, is Shabalala's work proper, the vast body of songs now assembled on well over 30 albums. Like all *isicathamiya* songs, these songs are rich in autobiographical detail, even if in their content they do not offer ready clues as to what holds Shabalala's life together.

In juxtaposing these texts I make four contentions. First, Shabalala's spectacular rise from impoverished migrant worker to international star—typical of many world beat exponents as it clearly is—exhibits all the predicaments and deadlocks of the modern self acting on a global level. Hence one of the aims of biographical productions such as I examine here and, in fact, of all practices of selfhood is to attach such unsettling personal experiences and forms of being to a secure project of identity. In other words, I take it as axiomatic that the concern with the self, personal identity, and forms of autobiography is not peculiar to the West. Nor is, in fact, an underlying sense of inchoateness that often prompts such personal quests in the first place peculiar. Quite to the contrary, as I have shown in the previous chapter, the experience of a torn self and the damaging effects of racial oppression upon a person's sense of self are fundamental to the lives of millions of black South Africans and to migrant workers in particular. The need to ask a question such as "Who am I?" stems from this experience and leads to autobiographical searchings that seek to anchor the self in a more authentic ground, in a beginning, and also in a deeper unity with other selves.

Second, I concur with Nikolas Rose that what characterizes modern selves is not so much the specific meanings used to interpret contemporary human existence as a variety of "machines"—pedagogic machines, consuming machines, bureaucratic machines—that administer, presuppose, and assemble a particular psychological relation to ourselves, a particular mode of evaluating, disclosing, curing, calibrating, and making sense of the self.[6] One of these machines, I argue, is an aesthetic machine. Operated by the entertainment industry, this machine engages human beings on the condition that it is through certain aesthetic practices—or, at any rate, certain forms of popular culture such as pop songs, biographies, and video documentaries—that they relate to themselves and narrate themselves as individuals crafted in certain supposedly unique ways and wedded to particular "lifestyles" based on personal choice.

Third, although these stylizations of the self are always socially mediated and meaningful, they are by no means determined by one firmly circumscribed cultural context alone. That is to say, Bhekizizwe Shabalala's self-searching is narrated in a symbolic framework in which a number of meanings and images of personhood rooted in Zulu culture—the hero, the warrior, the dreaming individual communicating with the ancestor spirits—converge with key stereotypes of the Western biographical imagination and the industry's star system: stereotypes such as that of life as an advancement and journey, of manhood as the display of competitive powers, and so on. Yet the fact that the contrasting experiences of performers troubled by memories of their ancestral homelands and those of an African superstar of world beat adroitly manipulating global markets, high tech, and the grammar of celebrity intersect and partially erase one another in these texts does not imply that they uniformly query dominant Western discourses of the self.

Fourth, I posit that there are striking parallels between the kinds of questions Shabalala asks himself and those the members of the African Choir posed a century earlier. Although Shabalala's engagement of Africa and the West and the distinct way he positions himself within the overall framework of what I have called the global imagination of Western and African performers contains a more personal, introspective element and at the same time displays a stronger sense of racial pride than the African Choir, he and individuals like Paul Xiniwe,

Charlotte Manye, and Josiah Semouse share a solid footing in techniques and discourses of the self that at least in part are derived from and amenable to bourgeois structures of domination.

## Life Stories, the Music Industry, and the Aesthetics Machine

"You see, when I just get up and walk on the stage to get the Grammy and see the multitude of people in that hall, first of all I was asking myself: Who am I? What am I coming here to do, because of what?" It is with these words that Bhekizizwe Shabalala opens *Journey of Dreams*, and, at first glance, the film seems to be just that: the unvarnished account of Bhekizizwe Shabalala in search of answers to these questions, beginning with his childhood in Natal and early musical experiences in the 1960s, moving on to the first recording session in 1970, and culminating in the encounter with Paul Simon and the subsequent triumph of *Graceland* in the late 1980s. But woven into this chronicle is a series of statements and observations in which the filmmakers implicitly address a range of general topics central to the global imagination of contemporary black South African performers and, of course, Western filmmakers themselves.

A sense of this strategy immediately arises from the first section of the film, after the opening passage quoted at the beginning of this section, during which the camera takes us to Shabalala's birthplace, somewhere in the Natal midlands. Here, in the hills and fields of Ladysmith, Shabalala discusses two of the inspirational sources he draws on for his music: the countryside and its sounds, primarily, and the singing and dancing that accompanied the ritual activities of his father, a *nyanga* (diviner). Following this, Shabalala proceeds to an explanation of the name of his group, Ladysmith Black Mambazo, the Black Ax from Ladysmith, and of his teaching method. This exploration of the beginnings then leads into a sequence in which the choir is seen recording the song "Hello, My Baby" in a Johannesburg studio. What is interesting about this part of the film is how the encounter with technology and the market is glossed as the almost seamless continuation of Shabalala's rural origins. The secret of "precision a cappella singing," producer West Nkosi declares in a bold re-reading of African-American musical history (not to mention other American vocal traditions), is that "the rhythm, they've got it in their blood. The American market likes it because it is something unusual to them. They have never had a group singing without any instruments backing it up."

The next section strikes a slightly different note. It develops around a cluster of themes crucial to African life under the brutal conditions of apartheid: themes such as labor migration, the hostile urban environment, and the alienation of the migrant worker from his family and ancestral traditions. There are three narrative units here and, within these, three songs that illustrate these themes. First, we see images of a train—pulled here by what resembles more a vintage engine than the current electric models—and migrant labor compounds, while in the background Ladysmith Black Mambazo performs "Stimela" (Train), one of the group's earliest songs. In the following sequence the film takes the spectator to Nicholson Hall, one of several multipurpose halls Durban *isicathamiya* choirs use for their weekly all-night competitions. Here the choir is shown onstage performing "Hello, My Baby."

All this is interwoven with a narrative of Bhekizizwe Shabalala's frustration about the boisterous, "almost vaudeville" style of singing prevalent in the 1960s and his search for new means of expression. Of critical importance here are Shabalala's dreams—retold many times and illustrated in the video by a young boy dreamily gazing into the distance—of children floating around the skies and teaching him to sing in heavenly harmonies. I would like to dwell for a moment on the role of dreaming because of the prominent place of dreams in the documentary and, even more so, in *Life and Works*. Here, in a chapter titled "The Great Dream," authors Thembela and Radebe provide a detailed synopsis of three dreams that shaped Shabalala's career in significant ways.[7] The first dream is the one of the singing children in the sky. The second dream—less familiar perhaps to Ladysmith Black Mambazo listeners—is of his maternal grandmother, a former Mazibuko. In the dream she told Joseph to organize the Mazibuko boys and form what is now known as Ladysmith Black Mambazo. The third and probably most startling dream was a vision of Bhekizizwe's father, who appeared with a bundle of wooden sticks as are used in the construction of Zulu traditional cattle enclosures. While Thembela and Radebe interpret the first two dreams as presaging important career decisions, they remain rather cryptic about the meaning of the third dream. Bhekizizwe was struck by the dream, they write, "because he was already trying to find a way of convincing his mother to agree on leaving the original place of residence." But (and here the authors seem to want to change the subject) they then state that "we will leave the story of Joseph's family at that," only to go on to discuss how the group's numerous weekend engagements got them into trouble at their workplace and how, by 1972, all of its members had resigned from their work in order to "devote their full attention only to singing."[8]

To return to *Journey of Dreams*, the next section of the film is based on the song "Nomathemba," one of Bhekizizwe Shabalala's earliest hit songs and a key text, as we shall see in this and subsequent chapters, in his autobiographical imagination in general. The performance is illustrated by a mix of images that depict Zulu maidens merrily doing the wash in a rural stream, a group of *ingoma* dancers, scenes of urban hustle and bustle, and, finally, Nomathemba herself on a bus, sporting flamboyant dress and sunglasses. The story of Nomathemba, as the commentator explains, is of course "a parable of the predicament of the migrant worker who is cut off from his community and has little hope of ever having a normal family life." But the story also merges here with the other elements—the dreams and Shabalala's attempt to reformulate *isicathamiya* aesthetics—into a metanarrative whose real subject matter is the nostalgia for a different kind of social order.

Little wonder, then, that after this episode the film returns to the theme of Shabalala's deeper sources of inspiration. Here images of Ladysmith Black Mambazo are juxtaposed with further shots of *ingoma* dancers while West Nkosi, talking about the group's first album, *Amabutho*, asserts that Shabalala's music is "our traditional music." This sequence then leads into a section in which footage from the South African television saga *Shaka Zulu* is interspersed with still more images of *ingoma* dancers and of Ladysmith Black Mambazo, now in "traditional" animal skins, singing material from the *Amabutho* album. The voice-over narration in this section runs as follows:

> When Europe was on the brink of the Victorian age, Shaka Zulu was the most powerful man in southern Africa. He forged the Zulu nation into an awesome fighting force, controlled almost the entire eastern seaboard, and put a stamp on the national character for centuries to come.
>
> For poetic reference, Bhekizizwe Shabalala had the most dramatic legend in all African history to draw upon. Here, in the praise song "Amabutho," Ladysmith Black Mambazo pays tribute to the ancestral regiments of Zulu warriors.

It is sentences such as these that clearly group the video within the long history of Western attempts at figuring Europe through the management of images of Zuluness. The fact that this image of Zulu barbarous nobility is only marginally less clichéd than other commercial representations of the celebrated Zulu king is perhaps due to the fact that the filmmakers enlisted Barry Leitch as a cultural adviser. Leitch in the late 1980s and early 1990s was active in a similar capacity at Shakaland, a peculiar crossbreed between hotel, cultural center, and theme park located in the heart of Natal dedicated to documenting Zulu tradition. Originally built as a film set for the TV saga, Shakaland has been praised as a worthy didactic effort to impart genuine understanding of and respect for Zulu culture and history. Yet, as the preceding passage demonstrates, *Shaka Zulu*, Shakaland, and, by extension, *Journey of Dreams* are about more than the idolization of Shaka as the ideal Zulu male. What the predominantly Western or white audiences gain through products such as these, in the words of Carolyn Hamilton, is "a new and more sophisticated authority over 'Zuluness' . . . in an increasingly volatile and unknown world."[9]

The figure of Shaka does not loom quite as large in *Life and Works* as it does in the video, but a sense of the enormous significance for Shabalala of Zulu tradition emerges from the chapter titled "The Man, the Group and Their Music." Here, in the first of two paragraphs on "cultural roots," Thembela and Radebe highlight Shabalala's love of Zulu culture and his respect for the various cultures and languages of the world. To exemplify this, in the second paragraph they talk about the Zulu concept of *isoka*, the young fop. It is out of his great respect for traditional culture, the authors claim, that Shabalala discusses his relationships with numerous ladies—at one time he is said to have won the favors of almost thirty women—without shame. But these exploits, the authors go on to state, in Shabalala's mind are not the same as those of a Don Juan: "In the true Zulu culture it was a real virtue for a young man to fall in love with several maidens."[10]

With its unabashed gender bias, the paragraph recalls the section in Alfred Xuma's biography of Charlotte Manye discussed in chapter 2 where the author praises Charlotte's modern education and liberal views while at the same time stressing her adherence to traditional customs such as *ukuhlonipa*. And like Charlotte, we are told, Shabalala does not recognize any contradiction between Christian religion and African culture. Although he separated from two of his three wives upon converting to Christianity, this was not "because of Christian prescription," but because of "the usual problems based on the cultural roots and complicated by the exigencies of a culture in transition."

*Journey of Dreams* tells a parallel story of the intertwining of Shabalala's personal history, ethnic pride, and the modernization of Zulu society. The Zulus of the present, we are told after the Shaka Zulu–Amabutho episode, were transformed from a tribal people to an integral part of a multicultural society. And, the commentator continues, as the discovery of minerals and the subsequent industrialization transformed South African society, so in 1984 Bhekizizwe Shabalala himself "was due for a musical transformation." It was in that year that he met Paul Simon.

Not only did the meeting with Simon mark a turning point in Shabalala's life and career, but also the collaboration was the beginning of a new synthesis between Africa and the West. "Through *Graceland*," the narrator says while Simon and Ladysmith Black Mambazo are seen performing "Diamonds on the Soles of Her Shoes" at Harare's Rufaro Stadium, "music audiences around the world discovered something entirely new: the rare and hypnotic sound of Africa, presented in familiar packaging. The response made *Graceland* Simon's biggest ever solo album. And Africa itself applauded."

Africa may have applauded, but the film also makes it quite clear that Africa did not have to wait for Simon to discover its "hypnotic" sound. Africa itself had its own stars, its own music industry. And thus, while Simon pays tribute to Shabalala in the somewhat sugary "Under African Skies," in one of the most striking collages of the film images of rural Zululand are juxtaposed with shots of Shabalala's numerous gold records and other industry awards. And again, as scenes of *isicathamiya* choral competitions and jackets of Ladysmith Black Mambazo albums blend into one another, the commentator praises the group as Africa's best-selling artists, "bigger than the Beatles, bigger than Michael Jackson."

In *Life and Works*, the tale of a proud, and yet exotic, authentic Africa carrying a spiritual message to the West is retold in slightly different terms. Here authors Thembela and Radebe reiterate the familiar from-rags-to-riches-story, telling of the "rural farm boy from Ladysmith" whose "spirituality catapulted him into and took him to all the four corners of the world." To that effect, press clippings are quoted that applaud the music of Ladysmith Black Mambazo as displaying "indigenous African sentiment rooted in tribal traditions" and a "delightful simplicity and charm that's utterly non-showbiz."[11] And again, as in the video, there then follow a long list of international tours and awards and a collection of assorted facsimiles that show, among other things, the Grammy nomination certificate of 1987 and a letter by Chicago's Mayor Richard M. Daley proclaiming May 20, 1992, Ladysmith Black Mambazo Day.

Paul Simon, Chicago, Grammy Award—the picture of the U.S. music industry painted in the film and the book not only lacks any critical dimension but also is revealing in another respect. Thus while the camera follows Ladysmith Black Mambazo around the streets of New York and to Carnegie Hall we are told what this new experience was really all about. "Whole new audiences," the narrator says, and a "vastly different" industry awaited the South African group. As did a new type of business, he goes on to state, one in which the competitors—here we catch glimpses of Grace Jones and other African-American pop icons—and the admirers were often one and the same. Despite its brevity and although Lister does not elaborate on the point the phrase is interesting because of the way it enshrouds the complexities of black entanglements with the U.S. market and turns difference into sameness, newness into the ever-same. At the same time as the section celebrates the market as the culmination and fulfillment of a dream, it appears to bemoan this same market as the cause of the submerging of black expressive culture by the logic of exchange value. At least, this to me is one of the meanings suggested by the reference to Ladysmith Black Mambazo's African-American supporters who might revert the law of the market in the name of a black global ecumene.

*Journey of Dreams* ends on a pensive, rather placid note. While we observe Ladysmith Black Mambazo singing hymns in their home church in a Durban township, Bhekizizwe Shabalala talks about his faith and how he first brought the choir into the church and then converted his mother, an avowed *isangoma* (healer-diviner). The final sequence has Ladysmith Black Mambazo performing "Homeless," the song that audiences and critics have come to interpret as Shabalala's most touching and, at the same time, most compelling political statement. As the mellifluous harmonies of the song roll on and the group appears in traditional loinskins and headdresses, shots of Shabalala are interspersed with a rural scenery of thatched huts and cattle kraals and, as if to contrast the nostalgia for the ancestral homelands with South Africa's troublesome present, scenes of urban township life.

Although, as I said, it was never released, Lister's documentary has met with the expressive approval of Bhekizizwe Shabalala. As did, of course, *Life and Works*. Yet both the book and the video are not unproblematic. For instance, by suggesting that Shabalala's music has no prehistory and that the product of his creativity is abstracted from natural sounds Lister repeats two of the most hackneyed clichés about Africa. Similarly, describing *isicathamiya* competitions as impromptu events that developed from "crystal clear inspiration" uncritically accepts dominant stereotypes of African music as spontaneous "folk" creations.

Furthermore, at several moments the filmmakers chose to insert a number of postproduction shots that raise questions about the embarrassing manner in which Africa is still being imagined at the end of the twentieth century. Thus when Shabalala talks about his father's work as a diviner, and the images shown are those of a dim, torch-lit hut with a shadowy figure crouched before a huge pot boiling on a fire while several women are dancing in the background, we witness the effects on the American imaginary of two centuries of minstrelsy nonsense. Similarly, several scenes that illustrate Shabalala's youth show an idyllic countryside and a young boy merrily tilling a field. What the scenery does not show is the fact that Shabalala grew up on a white farm in a family of destitute farm laborers. Above all, images such as those of rootedness in ancient religious practice and ethnic identity leave unexamined the contradictions and multifocality of current Western and African identities.

Thembela and Radebe similarly depoliticize Shabalala's work by positing Zuluness as a stable reference point of identification and by refusing to acknowledge the conflicted nature of cultural and ethnic politics in the period that led up to the historic elections of 1994. Similarly questionable is the neglect to counterbalance some of Shabalala's more overt paternalism, if only by critically attending to the gender bias embodied in his music and by admitting into their discourse alternative, female perspectives on Zulu tradition.

I offer these comments not with the intention of assessing the artistic merits of Lister's work, let alone because I wish to determine whether the film or the book depicts the "real" Shabalala. My interest in this chapter is not with unraveling the person behind the text or with the question, troubling anthropologists and sociologists, of what the quandaries are of, as Georg Simmel skeptically put it, a "perfect cognition" of the Other. Nor do I concern myself much here with the problem of whether, in Clifford Geertz's canonical formulation, "the Western conception of the person as a bounded, unique, more or less integrated motivational and cognitive universe" is a "rather peculiar idea within the context of the world's cultures."[12] Rather, what I want to highlight are the shared ideas and assumptions about personal experience, the discourses and social constellations within which it becomes possible, desirable, profitable, and plausible to talk about an individual, an artist, in certain exoticizing, romanticizing, or otherwise essentializing ways. What is at issue are the techniques of the globally connected, aestheticized self and, perhaps more fundamentally for our purposes, the politics at play in the production of new fixed subjectivities, new repositories of knowledge about Africa, and, finally, in reordering the relationships between Africa and the West at the end of the bipolar world.

Of particular relevance in this regard are the ways in which these social relations and discourses are determined by the modus operandi of what I have called the aesthetics machine and here especially how this machine is managed by the transnational music industry. If modern selves, as Nikolas Rose has argued, are seen as the embodiment of private worlds and emotional interiority, it is not because psychology has revealed them to us as such but because modern selves are always already "constituted by our linkage into 'public' languages, practices, techniques and artifacts."[13] There are several implications of this notion of the "assembled self" for the production, representation, and marketing of artists' identities. First, the notion is essentially a double inversion of the classical bourgeois theory that radical subjectification results in great art. Rather, it presupposes that art as a machine sets up the idea of the self as a self-reflexive, aesthetically pleasing whole enveloped by an aura of singularity in the first place. At the same time, speaking of art as a machine renders obsolete the idea that a work of art mediates between a subject—an author, a composer, and so on—and a truth, by making subjective experience itself the sole repository of truth.

Second, and perhaps even more important, this definition of the aesthetic does not limit itself to the arts. Key to this broadened concept of aesthetics is the idea—crucial to late modernity—that the crafting of modern selves differs from other regimes of self-making in that it is no longer the rules of cognition and ethical conduct that form the basis of good, truthful living but the realm of the sublime, of apperception, and of the sensory. While this hypothesis needs to be seen in the context of the aestheticization of life in Western consumer society, its implications reach far deeper than the often-stated fixation in the advanced countries of the West with design and surfaces. Central to this argument about aesthetics as the ethics of modern human existence proper is the view that the modern ego models itself on an epistemology of *Erscheinung* rather than *Wesen*, that the play of form is more important in the shaping of a life than the actualization in a person's biography of an interior, a character, or spirit.[14]

Third, and here we are dealing with an implication that needs to be explored in more detail, such public languages of the aesthetic—languages like pop songs, biographies, interviews, charts, and promotional materials such as T-shirts and music videos—are not so much of interest at the level of meaning: what style has value, which song lyrics capture best the mood of the moment, and so on. Rather, what we need to find out is how such languages are placed within, reinforce, or enable certain global power structures and regimes of truth and how these structures in turn hold the "speakers" of such languages in complicity with the whole system of authority and subordination itself. We have to ask, for instance, how the discursive engagement through biographies with world beat performers implicates Western and Third World readers within a whole set of relations of mastery and dependency or, conversely, how it is possible to maintain structures of domination by defining the terms, genres, and circuits of circulation of public languages rather than by enforcing the contents of such languages.

The basic mechanism here, to be observed with particular clarity, I think, in discourses about artists' lives, is one in which a discrepancy is perceived between the artist as an invented product, on the one hand, whose every move and appearance, let alone musical utterance, is the outcome of complex processes

of technological mediation and marketing strategies, and the real person behind this mask, on the other. Biographies—along with live concerts and other
promotional products—seek to close this gap. But this endeavor is complicated
by a contradiction. As public language, biographies are based on a peculiar logic
in which a star is authenticated by a circular movement, one in which his public facade or the products associated with his image are invested with a presence
by referring to an absence. The star's persona gains truth and validity to the extent that it can be linked to what it conceals: his or her real, inner self. And vice
versa: the making present of the genius behind the work, of the undivided and
hidden self, only highlights further its vacuity and absence. Of course this sort
of biographical quid pro quo, as Simon Frith has pointed out, works particularly well with the pop musician-interpreter, whose real, material voice reveals
the person behind the public mask, and rather less well with the musician-com-
poser, whose identity is veiled behind compositional techniques and therefore
becomes the stuff of a special academic discipline (musicology), accordingly.[15]

Be that as it may, it is the circuitous character of biographical discourses that
reflects the perverse relationship generally of use value and exchange value in
popular music under late capitalism. The strange closure of such discourses is
the sign under which the relations of authority that engender such music are
figured, and it is the sign that accounts for the sway of the aesthetics machine
over the imagination of modern selves. That is to say, the extent to which biographies and all the other aesthetics machines succeed in making this conundrum plausible determines their authority. Like ethnographies, biographical
machines function not because they set up a correspondence with a reality, an
object (for there is no such object) but through formal, artlike coherence within
themselves.[16] It is for this reason that the production of credible stories of personal identity not only requires an audience practiced in the biographical interpretation of selves and that the peculiar tension between public image and private self be constantly kept alive but also, more important, requires a canon of
forms. The credibility of these stories does not so much demand, in Antoine
Hennion's terms, "meaningfulness" and expressive content that is as genuinely
"true to life" as possible as it necessitates certain literary conventions—the
major techniques of Western narrativity and literary realism, such as linearity,
the distanced, all-knowing author, the allegorical gaze, and so on.[17]

Numerous examples of all these techniques and forms can be found throughout Journey and Life and Works, and I shall return to some of them later. For the
moment, the question remains how all these contemporary Western theories
of the aesthetic self are linked to images of Zulus in loincloths and tales of divine Providence. What does the nostalgia for Shaka Zulu and ukuhlonipa have
to do with Western selves—of Paul Simon, say—ever alert to new possibilities, perpetually self-stylizing themselves, and always on the move? Clearly, one
of the objections that might be raised against my line of reasoning is that the
representations of Bhekizizwe Shabalala in such texts as Journey and Life and
Works do violence to a tradition of thinking about the self that differs funda-

mentally from that of the West. Or are there discourses of the self that oppose the logic of the aesthetics machine and that, while not completely disconnected from modern notions of personal being, engage the West from a position of alterity? What, for instance, can we learn from Shabalala's songs, from both their lyrical content and the way they emanate from performance practice? It is to these questions that I wish to turn in the following section.

### The Battle in the Heart of London

One of the most poignant moments in *Journey of Dreams*, in my view, is at the beginning of the video, when Bhekizizwe Shabalala talks about his father, Jonathan, the healer and diviner. Jonathan's medicine, Shabalala states with inimitable charm, was bitter. His music, by contrast, is sweet. The assertion is disarmingly succinct, because no one who has ever heard Ladysmith Black Mambazo will want to deny that the smooth and silken choral harmonies that seem to enfold and soothe the listener are among the most polished a cappella singing currently available. But Shabalala's construction of himself as a prophet, a visionary, and a healer does not quite accord with all aspects of his creative work. It hides a profound disparity between sound texture, performance practice, and, more often than not, song lyrics. Like *isicathamiya* generally, the music of Ladysmith Black Mambazo translates some of the conflicted entanglements of African performers with modernity and the global reality of the twentieth century and, through these, wrestles with competing claims made on the self in a world of shifting boundaries and hybrid identities.

At the most general level, what might be said about Shabalala's songs is that they talk about the person, to be sure, but not necessarily about an ego in the bourgeois sense. While his early songs are all about the collective identity of the "boys from Ladysmith," it is only in his later work that there begins to emerge a discourse centered on Shabalala's own personality. While this shift clearly indicates the way in which he adopted key elements of the industry's star cult, it would be a mistake to locate this encounter with the West only at the level of the authorial voice. Throughout Shabalala's career his autobiographical quest expressed itself in many forms: literary ones, musical ones, and danced ones. By far the most prominent, however, of these mediums of self-fashioning is not at all at the level of the text: it is in the kinds of practices that underlie the composition and performance of *isicathamiya* songs. Three of these I would now like to examine more closely. The first is the social organization of *isicathamiya* performance and performance roles within the context of all-night competitions, the second is the role of dreaming in Zulu everyday practice and art, and the third is traveling. While the latter two are quite visibly reflected in the title of the video, constructions of the West in the organization of *isicathamiya* performance are less obvious.[18] They are to be deduced primarily from the competitive setting in which such performance occurs.

*Isicathamiya*, I have said, is embedded in an intensely competitive environment: it has for a long time been performed and still is being performed in weekly all-night competitions; its choreography incorporates a great deal of military symbolism; and its choirs unite "home people" from the same rural district while its songs accordingly boast of their regional and group identity. But this ethos of fierce rivalry, like the notorious "faction fights" among migrant workers and "homeland" dwellers, is not a holdover from the ancient past, much less the result of some supposedly innate Zulu belligerence. Rather, both are the product of modern society, not its antithesis. They are expressions of what Ian R. Phimister and Charles van Onselen have called the "political economy of tribal animosity," a complex and decidedly modern set of social relations governed by the rules of capitalist production and bitterly contested in strategies and symbols anchored in the countryside.[19]

We owe a trenchant analysis of some of these strategies to Jonathan Clegg, whose work on *ingoma* dance teams has revealed striking correspondences between urban migration, farm labor, precolonial lineage, and district organization and the ritualization of conflict in competitive dancing.[20] Basically, Clegg's argument is the following: After the military regiments had become dysfunctional in the wake of the destruction of the Zulu kingdom in 1879 and former ancestral lands had been carved up by white farms, competition between different districts (*isigodi*), once a source of social cohesion, could no longer be controlled by conventional, legitimate means such as *umgangela* (stick fighting). What had formerly been a playful contest between youths from different districts increasingly turned into serious confrontations between people competing for employment and other resources on white farms that spanned two or more precolonial districts. In an attempt to mitigate such violent conflicts, Clegg concludes, migrant workers around the 1920s began to organize *ingoma* dance competitions that translated the rural antagonisms and alliances into the language of the urban environment. By staging these competitions dancers provided a form in which the tensions of migrant existence could be dealt with in less harmful ways than through armed "faction fights."[21]

But even *ingoma* dance competitions never quite evaded the ethos of power, physical strength, and violence that sporadically stirred even the most placid-minded performers to agitated expressions of local pride. Thus *ingoma* dance events in Durban in the 1920s routinely pitted segments of the more radical and urbanized group of stevedores and members of the somewhat less urbane class of domestic workers against one another in dogged altercations. Not surprisingly, such fights frequently led to serious bloodshed and eventually provided the justification for a harsh and lasting clampdown in 1931 on certain forms of *ingoma* dancing and other somewhat rustic leisure activities popular with migrant workers. It is out of this juncture of white "reformist" urban politics and militant African opposition, I would claim, that *isicathamiya* choral competitions emerged in the 1930s and 1940s, satisfying the need among South Africa's most urbanized migrant population for the legitimate expression of regional and group identity. Or, as "Intselelo," a song by the Empangeni Home Tigers, puts it:

> Nants' intsele lo.
> Awuviki!
> Asigadli ngazagela baba.
> Asigadli ngazagila, sigadla ngengoma.
> Uyawazi yini lamabutho?
>
> ———
>
> Here is a challenge.
> Shield yourself!
> We are not attacking with assegais, father.
> We are not attacking with assegais, but with song.
> Do you know these warriors?[22]

Competitions, then, are not only at the core of *isicathamiya* performance but are also the social mechanism through which migrant workers resolve the contradictions of urban life. The social organization of migrant workers' performance events in terms of mock faction fights is not the sign of some presumed Zulu rural anachronism; it is an indication of the antinomies of modernity and indeed of figuring the West itself. Ultimately, then, what emerges from this discussion of *isicathamiya* competitions is a notion of the self that is more than an imitation of the idea of the modern individual as a self-fashioned, aesthetically coherent whole. Yet, at the same time, this notion of the self is based on an idea of personhood that is not diametrically opposed to that of the West. Rather, the image of the warrior-migrant-performer invokes the West as one of several, interconnected points of reference.

One the most fascinating images in this regard of the self encountering the West and redefining its identity in that encounter is found in the song "Homeless," often cited as one of Shabalala's and Simon's most expressive and personal songs because of its romantic imagery of the "moonlight sleeping on a midnight lake." Yet in the middle section of the song (authored by Shabalala and often omitted from published scores), almost in passing, Shabalala strikes a more prosaic, almost aggressive note.

> Chorus:
> Yith'omanqoba.
> Esanqoba lonke izwe.
> Yith'omanqoba.
> Esayibamba phakath'eNgilandi.
> Awuzwe baba,
> yith'omanqoba.
> Esayibamba phakath'eLandani.
>
> ———
>
> Chorus:
> We are the conquerors.

> We conquered the whole country.
> We are the conquerors.
> We fought the battle right in England.
> Listen, Father,
> we are the conquerors.
> We fought the battle in the heart of London.

The last four lines not only are a reminder of the circumstances under which the song emerged—the first trip of Ladysmith Black Mambazo to London—but also, more important, convey a sense of how Zulu notions of social oganization merge with one of the most persistent icons of Western power and the imperial order. They illustrate the symbolic importance London has held from the nineteenth century within what one might call Zulu Occidentalism. No other emblem—with the exception perhaps of Queen Victoria herself—has occupied such a prominent place in Zulu constructions of the West and indeed of power itself.

The broader metaphoric significance of London as power—and through it Shabalala's conceptions of the West—needs to be emphasized, because as Robert Thornton has argued, Zulu imaginations of Europe and Europeans differ radically from Western reifications of Zulus.[23] While the colonizers saw the Zulus as being unified by a statelike polity and, as a result, came to think of Zulu as a name for some special kind of Africanness and a form of primordial autochthony and power, the situation for the Zulus was different. Having long developed complex notions of power of their own, Zulus simply came to consider the different varieties of European arrivals—British missionaries, Boer farmers, Portuguese merchants, and agents of imperial rule—as yet another modality of power that required different modes of access. The most important distinction, Thornton argues, Zulus made between these forms of white power was that between the power of the "outside," generalized as a source of goods and moral authority and personified by Queen Victoria, and the power of the "inside," generalized and experienced as a form of virulent racism and exclusiveness.

I have dwelt on "faction fighting," *isicathamiya* competitions, Zulu notions of power, and the place of London as the key symbol of the West in the autobiographical imagination of Bhekizizwe Shabalala because these motifs highlight a concept of the person that differs from Western notions and, at the same time, intersects with them at several levels. For one, these motifs refute the ideology of the communal, "tribal" roots of individual creative practice, so central to Western constructions of African expressive traditions and, indeed, the continent itself. The point is important because the person that is being constructed in this intermixture of images, styles, and practices does not conform to stereotyped versions of the African as being driven by the timeless forces of habitus and tradition, just as it does not merely replicate the ways in which members of Western consumer society like to think of themselves as being engaged in a permanent battle to maximize their resources and in a never-ending quest for the inner foundation of their being. Rather, competitions, images of power, and violence play such a crucial role in Bhekizizwe Shabalala's self-imagination because they are about the pivotal position in black South African discourses of the self of the *umqhawe*, the hero, and the transformations this idea is undergoing in late modern culture.

In the discussion of hero ethics and heroism in southern Africa in chapter 2, I argued that what differentiated bourgeois individualism and heroism was the fact that the hero in the preindustrial societies of southern Africa was essentially a social creation rather than, like the Western individual, a being seeking fulfillment outside socially prescribed roles. The African hero, I said, excelled at the performance of a given social role, and instead of viewing a rift between personal identity as a performed and identity as a preexistent, given entity, an *umqhawe* sees no such disparity. He *is* what he appears to be, and hence there is no need to penetrate the thick layers of concealment, acting, and pretension felt to obscure, in Western thinking at any rate, the real, inner self. Hence, what identifies the question that opens the documentary on Bhekizizwe Shabalala—"Who am I?"—as a key question in the modern discourse of the self is not the enormously rich terrain it may open up for intense soul-searching; it is the fact that it merely stands in for a hero question. It allows modern subjects to play at being a hero.

Dreams are the second medium of self-fashioning that underlie *isicathamiya* performance. Fusing powerful conceptions of personal being—performing and composing—the significance of dreaming stems from the deepest layers of Zulu thought on what it takes to be a person. At the same time, dreaming is one of the areas in which personhood and modern life are enmeshed with each other in the most unconscious and hence most inextricable manner. An example briefly referred to in the previous section may illustrate this.

We have seen how dreams have been one of Bhekizizwe Shabalala's most powerful creative resources and, more generally, how such dreams have marked critical turning points in his life. In this regard, I related a series of dreams and their interpretation in *Journey of Dreams* and *Life and Works*. The dream of the father urging Bhekizizwe to build a cattle enclosure is the most interesting in the series, and I would briefly like to return to it for a more developed interpretation. In Alex Thembela and Edmund Radebe's discussion of the dream, recall, the visitation prompted a vital career move, namely, the decision to quit factory work and become a professional performer. While this reading confirms the Zulu theory of dreaming as a form of communication with the *amadlozi* ancestor spirits in which these offer moral guidance, it ignores the fact that this move deeper into the white man's world and Shabalala's refusal to build an *umuzi*, a rural homestead—the ultimate goal of migrant labor strategies and the completion of all meaningful male endeavor—does not actually counteract the advice of the *amadlozi*. In a sense and quite paradoxically, Shabalala's severing from wage labor and the full integration of Ladysmith Black Mambazo into the alien sphere of recording studios, A&Rs, and charts is implicitly tied to a homecoming of sorts. The fascinating aspect of Shabalala's dreams, then, to me lies not in their embeddedness in supposedly traditional ways but in how a conscious move to engage with the West on the terms set by the music industry is rendered in the more customary ways of making sense of life trajectories and how a radical and uncertain shift in Shabalala's biography is controlled by placing it in the more familiar framework ancestor religion makes available to the interpretation and rationalization of personal choices.

But there is another sense in which dreaming becomes an important field in which Shabalala's autobiographical imagination and the crafting of modern selves intermingle. This is the role of the pop industry itself as some kind of dream machine, producing commodities that in reality are what Walter Benjamin called wish-images: fantasies of bliss and redemption, sonically encoded. At the very least, what such dream images invoke is the desire to acquire an identity similar to the one of the star him- or herself who produces them. It is here that my last point comes into play, the role of travel in Bhekizizwe Shabalala's life and, concomitantly, the image of the journey in Zulu culture and in Western regimes of self-fashioning.

Again the question here poses itself of whether in the form in which it is put forward in Lister's documentary the image of the journey is not, in fact, directed at Western audiences, evoking in them specifically modern desires of both retrieval and evasion, arousing fantasies about the ideal self and its trajectories, and also resonating with current theoretical concerns with boundary crossing, postmodern nomadism, and placelessness. For clearly, the idea that life itself resembles a journey, that travel is a metaphor for human existence in the sense that it is aimed at reaching a point of finality and completion in some otherworldly destination, is an idea rooted deep in Western thinking, particularly in Christian notions of pilgrimage and salvation.[24] And as we have seen, it is one that played a significant part in shaping the consciousness of modernizing Africans in the nineteenth century through the intermediary of texts such as Bunyan's *Pilgrim's Progress*.

But beyond this, several other dimensions are crucial to specifically modern analogies of travel and life. First is the idea, rehearsed in a deluge of romantic travel literature, of a return, closure, and even redemption effected by travel. Second is the idea, strongly embedded in the Protestant ethic, of modern man as an inner-worldly pilgrim whose wanderings become a necessity in the desert of modern life and, by the same token, leave traces, assume the form of a path, and, in short, become invested with meaning.[25] Third, and perhaps even more important as a notion that links travel and life in a specifically Western sense, often existing alongside with the former, cyclic conception, is narrative, especially writing. Central here is the conception of writing as somehow delineating or proceeding on some sort of axis, a line with a beginning and an end point. This idea of the aim-orientedness and linearity of writing, in combination with the importance of memory in both travel and writing, is then usually associated with the key tenets of bourgeois thought about the individual, such as the belief that evolution is the prerequisite of historical consciousness, which in turn is the sine qua non of freedom itself. In fact, the association is such that a meaningful life in Western thinking not only presupposes travel-like, goal-searching directedness but, also like travel, only becomes recognizable as such when it can be remembered, narrated.

At the same time, these linkages between travel and authorship, writing and subjectification, in the Western imagination are not unproblematic. As my discussion of Josiah Semouse's travel diary in chapter 3 has shown, such linkages since about the turn of the century have become increasingly embroiled in the crisis of panoramic knowledge and imperial supremacy that was affecting the twentieth-century bourgeois subject. Generally, what has become problematic in the relationship among travel and writing, knowledge of the Other, and inscription is not so much the legitimacy of colonial conquest and the complicity of writing with the European hegemonic project as such but the tenacious reliance of the bourgeois concept of the ego on what Michel de Certeau has called the "work of returning." Modern travel writing, he argues, from about the sixteenth century has exhibited the attempt to reduce difference to sameness, to turn the entirely Other into an "exteriority behind which an interiority, the unique definition of man, can be recognized."[26] If we are to believe de Certeau, we might say that, ultimately, the Western syllogism of travel and life is due to a strange operation by which the coming into being of a subject depends on the acknowledgment of the a priori existence of such a subject. Or, put differently, an otherwise unknown and uncertain reality, the self, acquires an identity by way of getting scriptural control over the unknown.

Of course, I am not suggesting that all these analogies and parallelisms of life, narrative, and travel in Western thinking have been interpreted in the same way at all times and in all places. But the fact that such analogies are culturally salient at all in the West and not in Zulu culture needs to be taken into account when looking at the distinctions and intersections between Western notions of being and constructions of Bhekizizwe Shabalala, the dreamer and traveler. As I have shown in chapter 11, travel and migration in the minds of South Africa's black population do not carry pleasant connotations. Quite to the contrary, as a form of popular expression such as isicathamiya so aptly illustrates, the idea of a journey is first and foremost associated with the alienating system of capitalist production and racial oppression and thus symbolically configured in a variety of ways. At the level of song lyrics, for instance, such migratory existence is registered in the formal structure of these lyrics rather than in their content. As I have outlined in chapter 11, the seemingly illogical succession of verses is the result of a conscious effort to render the experience of dislocation and shifting perspectives in nonlinear forms.

There are many more levels at which the migrant experience of dislocation and urban space is being configured, several of which I have discussed extensively elsewhere.[27] Here I would simply like to point out that what characterizes certain bodily forms of spatial enunciation such as istep (a type of "walking" choreography in which the performers briskly make two steps forward and two back) and *isikhambula* (gambling, a style of *isicathamiya* that mirrors the way in which choirs shuttle between different competitions in one night) is a profound ambiguity. These forms convey a sense of movement and travel in which somewhat more ancient forms of corporeal experience clash with modes of bodily behavior and perception as are generated by the city, machine work, and capitalist labor relations. The example of *isikhambula* is particularly instructive here because there are a number of striking discrepancies between the meaning of *isikhambula* and the way Shabalala's "entry into the international arena" is represented in *Journey* and *Life and Works*. *Isikhambula* was the name for a mode of performance prevalent during the 1940s and 1950s, and although it is rarely practiced today, the term reflects something of the uncertainty, instability, and velocity of modern urban life—a poignant early Zulu metaphor for Western risk society and, to paraphrase Walter Benjamin, for the inability of the worker and the gambler to achieve a sense of completion, to make use of experience.

Needless to say, none of this is reflected in the discussion of Shabalala's international tours in *Journey of Dreams*. Quite to the contrary, as we have seen, the terse pathos of the term *isikhambula* here is erased by a romantic discourse of international stardom and a mythology of glamour in which volatile markets and global media are not antithetical to the fullness of personal being but, rather, the essential condition of it. Shabalala's life: the romance of a dream come true.

In closing this chapter, I would like to elaborate briefly on my third hypothesis—namely, that striking parallels exist between the way the production of imperial subjects and the formation of postcolonial African identities were both tied to a project of inscription and an ideology that saw individual advancement and freedom of expression as intimately linked to systems of social discipline and collective association like the nation, the institutions of modern government, and discourses of ethnic identity. The political implications of this argument are not just, as Nikolas Rose correctly suggests from a somewhat Foucauldian perspective, that the most fundamental aspect of modern politics of subjectification is that ideals of autonomy have precisely become allied with programs for regulating subjects in the name of their freedom.[28] More important perhaps is the fact, strikingly confirmed by stories like these as well as research elsewhere, that these controlled bourgeois subjectivities were constituted every bit as much at the colonial frontier as they were in the metropolis.[29] It is as a result of the very forms of knowledge, discourses of identity, and practices of subjectification that enabled the members of the African Choir to imagine themselves as players actively manipulating and inflecting the global scheme of things that these same individuals made themselves available for the regulatory endeavors of the modern state.

It may be overly harsh to suggest that the same may hold true of Bhekizizwe Shabalala and other stars of the contemporary world beat scene, especially when, in a country like South Africa, such arts of memory as biographical self-fashioning are an integral part of the struggle of black people to reclaim the past from the silence of an oppressive regime. But even where he appears to foreground discourses of alterity and authenticity, by making his experiences available so that they may be recast in the terms required by the aesthetics machine, Shabalala at least in part yields to the lingering dichotomies of the imperial world—dichotomies grounded less in the persistence of relations of domination than in the minutiae of the biographical imagination and techniques of the self.

In the remaining three chapters I shall explore how a postcolonial politics of identity may be possible that works within some of the parameters set by the global culture industry while at the same time renouncing the restrictive effects on the individual of modernity by evoking black traditions of intraracial communication. And again, as with the spirituals discussed in chapter 7, it is in music and performance that these contending engagements with the postcolonial order can be recognized best.

# 13

## Songs of Truth and Healing

### *Searching for a New South Africa*

From a local perspective, the change ushered in by South Africa's first free elections in 1994 was a truly momentous one. But seen from a more global vantage point, it could be argued, what the historic event represents is, in many respects, more the end of an old era than the beginning of a new one. The elections that ended three centuries of white domination and brought an ANC-dominated coalition to power was the climax of a story, the provisional end point of a long narrative thread that had been spun out of a variety of fictions, of both national and racial identity. But the 1994 elections spoke of continuity in another sense as well. To many, especially in the West, they seemed to offer irrefutable proof that one of the West's best-selling myths, that of the universality of representative democracy, was still worth telling. Finally, and perhaps most important, the historic balloting unleashed, in addition to all the euphoria, a collective act of painful retrospection, a teeth-gritting penitence of almost religious dimensions.

Two events, situated before and after the vote, seem to illustrate this situation of liminality particularly well: the 1992 Chicago production of a play called *The Song of Jacob Zulu* and the meetings of the Truth and Reconciliation Commission (TRC), set up in 1994 to investigate politically motivated acts of violence committed under apartheid. Although there is no direct link between them, both undertakings can be fruitfully seen as part of a broader movement toward a global, antiessentialist, and irreducibly pluralist politics, one that draws on the universalist message of human rights and reconciliation. However, this new politics and the work of artists, writers, and performers that flowed from it cannot be contemplated in isolation from the process of transformation in the "new South Africa," especially from some of its more distinctively local cultural underpinnings. Drawing on the powerful symbols and traditions of black intracommunal identity and transatlantic racial solidarity, the play and the TRC are also expressive of a new politics of memory and a fervent search for a postapartheid identity. The precarious equipoise of Western-style constitutionalism and African ethnic exceptionalism that characterized the South Africa of the early 1990s, I argue in this chapter, is augured and mediated at a variety of levels in a piece of fiction such as *Jacob Zulu*, as well as in the discourses that surrounded and came out of the TRC.

*The Song of Jacob Zulu* was written by Tug Yourgrau, a young white playwright who had left South Africa as a child and has since lived in the United States.[1] Premiered at the Steppenwolf Theater in Chicago in April 1992, the play won the Bhekizizwe Jefferson Award for Best New Work and garnered nominations for several prizes, including six Tony Awards. The play tells the story of Andrew Zondo, a young student who planted a bomb at a Natal shopping center that killed four people and injured many.[2] The action takes place during Jacob's trial in an imaginary courtroom of the Supreme Court. In a sequence of short scenes we see Jacob Zulu, alias Andrew Zondo, enact a series of flashbacks that illustrate the key stages of his life story leading up to the bomb blast.

The son of the meek Reverend Zulu, Jacob spends his youth in Imbali, near Pietermaritzburg, quietly pursuing his high school studies and avoiding political activism—that is to say, until he gets drawn into the school boycotts of the early 1980s and eventually ends up being recruited into the ANC. From this point, the story is one about the making of an Umkhonto we Sizwe guerrilla. While still at Imbali, Jacob is caught distributing ANC pamphlets and then tortured by the police, who try to extract the names of his comrades from him. Promising to cooperate, Jacob is released from prison but manages to escape across the border into Mozambique. Here he becomes witness to an air raid on Maputo by the SADF (South African Defense Force) in the course of which two of his closest comrades are killed. Shattered by the experience, Jacob decides to join Umkhonto we Sizwe and to undergo military training in a guerrilla camp in Angola. To make him prove that he is not an *impimpi*, an informer, the Umkhonto commanders in Angola soon send him back to South Africa to plant a bomb in retaliation for an SADF attack on the homes of South African exiles in Lesotho. As he is seeking out a target to strike, Jacob's sights fall on a South African Airways office in a mall near the small coastal town of Shaka's Rock. Yet unsure about whether civilians would be hurt, he decides to postpone the act and returns home. Here a dream reminds him of the tragic death of his older brother Philip in 1976. Although Philip was critically sick with pneumonia, the ambulance that was supposed to rescue him came several hours late—too late for the boy to survive. The day after Jacob has the dream he explodes a limpet mine in the shopping center.

The closing scene has Jacob delivering a final, painfully remorseful statement before the judge passes the death sentence on him:

I wish to say first that the ANC never gave me instructions to kill innocent people. And I'd like to say to those people who lost their family members because of what I did, I am sorry. If I could give part of my flesh to those who remain, I would do it gladly. . . . You see, people die all the time. Even when their breath does not stop, they die inside their heart. And I hope that my life is a lesson to my brother Martin and to all the youth. (*Pause*) That is what I wish to say.

Here the scene changes to reveal Jacob standing under the gallows awaiting his execution. The curtain drops on the entire cast joining in the national anthem, "Nkosi Sikelel' IAfrika."

As tragic as this story is, it is not an unusual one. As Yourgrau writes, *The Song of Jacob Zulu* is sung for the victims of all races killed in the struggle for a free South Africa.[3] And thus it is a highly allegorical play—allegorical because the figure of Jacob Zulu stands "for the whole generation of young black South Africans who have been sacrificed to history, who are unschooled and potentially explosive,"[4] but allegorical also because the process of reconciliation that the play argues for (and whose real-life dramatization in the Truth and Reconciliation Commission it in many ways even anticipated by two years) is itself about something else. It is about the essential matrix and root figure of bourgeois identity: the nation, probably the most persistent type of global fiction examined throughout this book.

### Call and Response: Ubuntu *and the Nation-State*

Technically speaking, the Truth and Reconciliation Commission was one of the key statutory bodies set up in the wake of the 1994 elections to foster the democratic development of South African society. More specifically, its task was to examine cases of political violence and under certain circumstances, such as an admission of guilt by the perpetrator, to recommend amnesty. Yet at a deeper level, the TRC was about considerably more and decidedly less than justice—more because the work of the commission has progressed alongside the debate over South Africa's new draft constitution and has spawned an even more impassioned debate about the role of a liberal "state of right" in displacing nationalism and in defusing ethnic conflict, less because constitutionalism, state building, and the creation of what is termed a "culture of human rights" with the help of the TRC are "drawn into the services of a reformulated nationalist imperative in the 'New South Africa.'"

Such, at least, is the conclusion Richard A. Wilson arrives at in considering the discourses on power, nation building, and identity that have surrounded the TRC hearings from the beginning.[5] If we are to believe Wilson's shrewd analysis of the issues at stake, law is not above other value systems. It is a form of social consciousness enmeshed in historical and social processes and, hence, caught between other, competing normative discourses. In short, it is a "language of power" and as such overlaps with other idioms of power. One of these idioms is tied up with and comes out of state power. Given the history of the apartheid state and the formidable obstacles that hamper the consolidation of a postapartheid legal infrastructure, the new, legally constituted state has become the primary terrain for the exercise of new forms of political power and for propelling the transformation of South African society into a fully developed democracy. But this emphasis on the state is not without its problems. It places an undue emphasis on the new bureaucratic class that runs it and on their attempts to seek legitimization through identifying the constitution with popular conceptions of culture, community, and nation.

Wilson provides conclusive evidence that under conditions of continued material disparity between blacks and whites, some militant version of Black Consciousness ideology is likely to gain prominence in such discourses about the future reconstruction of South African society along constitutional and more equitable lines. One example of this linking of human rights with national identity and communal welfare is *ubuntu*, a concept increasingly being deployed in South Africa as an umbrella term for all sorts of exclusivist, Africanist agendas. Another somewhat more elastic and ethnically less constricted metaphor for state-initiated reform projects and nation building is reconciliation. Like *ubuntu*, reconciliation prior to 1996 figured prominently as a maxim in the interim constitution, while December 16 was officially declared a Day of Reconciliation, thus replacing the highly contentious Dingaan's Day of the apartheid era.

Truth commissions, finally, like the South African TRC, are another example of how embattled bureaucracies use past human rights abuses as part of the legitimization of the present order. And as Wilson aptly states, a body such as the TRC does so by sharing with nationalist narratives a similar form, an emphasis on the narration of a revised official history as one of a shared, nonethnically marked nation. Typically, its reports enact a radical break with a past that is being seen as one of a pariah nation. But unlike other newly constituted nations, here it is an unspeakable, evil past, a repressed internal Other, that is the pariah and that is being ritually excised through an operation such as the TRC hearings. Another way in which these testimonies serve more the cause of nationalism than that of justice is in the synecdochic emphasis on a few cases that are made to stand for all victims of apartheid—a rhetorical device that is at the basis of all nationalist discourse.[6]

Clearly, then, postapartheid South Africa seems to be characterized by a strange Janus-faced mood, by a symbiosis between constitutionalism and nationalism, rainbow-pluralism and Africanism. In short, its present is both a future that has not quite arrived and a past that has not quite died. How, then, is this interregnum configured in a piece of work such as *The Song of Jacob Zulu*? What can we learn from a play such as this about the continued hold over the collective imagination of South Africans of notions of power and social order that are both a product of colonialism and antithetical to it? Here it is instructive to consider briefly the circumstances that drew Tug Yourgrau and Bhekizizwe Shabalala into the collaboration that finally led to the production of *Jacob Zulu*. For not only is Wilson's reading of the TRC strikingly illustrated by a number of elements from the play, but also Yourgrau's account of his first encounter with Shabalala reveals a whole series of correspondences and parallels:

> So it was that on a chilly March morning in 1991 I found myself at the coffee shop of the Holiday Inn in Somerville, Massachusetts, a blue-collar town north of Boston, waiting to see Bhekizizwe Shabalala, the founder and leader of the group. I encountered a small, brown-skinned man with a big smile and a gentle voice, swaddled in a large parka. He ordered tea with lemon, and we sat down to talk. Bhekizizwe liked the idea of the play, its antiviolent theme, very much. We sang the hymn "Jesus Loves Me" together in Zulu: "Wangithand uJesu lo. . . ." (I'm a Jew, but I'd learned the song as a child). Bhekizizwe harmonized. I was thrilled. Then Bhekizizwe came upon Andrew Zondo's name in my notes. He blurted out that this boy was his cousin! He and his group knew the father and had sung in the family church. Both of us were astonished. I heard in my head the sound of the planets realigning themselves. "We must do this," said Joseph. "He is my cousin."[7]

Ultimately, what resulted for Yourgrau from the collaboration that then began was not just a career as a playwright and screenwriter. (He has since returned to South Africa to work on a TV documentary for the SABC titled *The New South Africa: A Personal Journey*.) By working with Bhekizizwe and "the guys," he was inspired by "a sound of angels come to ground. I was able to reenter, as it were, the world of my childhood and, in a vital way, to make it right and whole."[8]

Two fascinating themes emerge from this scene of a South African–born liberal South African Jew and a Grammy Award–winning black church minister from Durban singing a Zulu hymn in a Massachusetts hotel. One of these is the odd sense of some New Age spherical harmony that speaks through Yourgrau's voice. The other is that of a strong religious sentiment of redemption—a redemption, however, that is more directly linked to a rather worldly discord between a privileged upbringing as a white child and black nurses who taught the young Tug Zulu hymns. Although the way such childhood memories and the half-hidden, seductive place they occupy in the white male racial imagination would merit a whole dissection of its own, what is striking here is how these souvenirs are juxtaposed with the family memories of Bhekizizwe Shabalala. To Shabalala, it appears, the story of Jacob Zulu, alias Andrew Zondo, recalls a different kind of wholeness, one that is redolent of the intimate connection he perceives between kinship ties and his church. The commitment to family that speaks through Shabalala's excitement, like Yourgrau's nostalgia, comes out of experiences of loss and exile. But unlike Yourgrau's they are experiences rooted in a long black history of dispossession, of a loss of ancestral moorings, and of an exile within one's own country.

The perhaps most telling scene of *Jacob Zulu* in this regard is scene 3, where Jacob's father attempts to persuade the legal counsel of his son's Christian convictions and enacts a flashback to the time when he baptized his son:

REV. ZULU   What a day, what a time, what a day, what a time! Brothers and Sisters, today Jacob's sins will be washed away in the blood of the Lamb!

CONGREGATION   Hallelujah! . . .

REV. ZULU   Jacob, Jacob, Jacob, do you accept into your heart Christ Jesus as your Savior?

JACOB   *Yebo [yes], Baba, yebo.*

REV. ZULU   I baptize you in the name of the Father, of the Son, and of the Holy Ghost.

(*The* CONGREGATION *explode with shouts of "Hallelujah!" and "Amen!"* REV. ZULU, MRS. ZULU *and the* CHORUS *hug the dripping, shivering boy.* JACOB *is exultant. . . .*)

UNCLE MDISHWA   We brought the *iskhumba sembuzi* [goatskin].

REV. ZULU   *Haikona!* [No!] No, no! Take that thing off him!

AUNT MIRIAM   Hezekaya! What has got into you? We all put on the goatskin. You put it on.

REV. ZULU   That was before I heard the Word of the Lord.

AUNT MIRIAM   And now it is Jacob's turn. Do you want the ancestors, the *amaDlozi*, to get angry with the boy? . . .

REV. ZULU   No. This is a House of the Lord. There's no place here for this superstition. . . .

MRS. ZULU   Hezekaya, I understand how you feel. But this is Jacob's day. Let him have his way.

REV. ZULU   (Pause) Oh, all right. . . .

JACOB   (*Starts singing and dancing around in the goatskin.*)

The act of cleansing we witness in this scene in many ways repeats elements from the biography of Bhekizizwe Shabalala, who only converted to Christianity in his adulthood and, as we have seen in chapter 12, is now an ordained minister in what in academic parlance would be called an independent church. Beyond this, the cultural bricolage in the scene is iconic of the deep yearning shared by millions of black South Africans to embrace a fuller, more African spiritual life, to somehow merge the Gospel with the beliefs and practices of traditional ancestor worship.

I do not wish to minimize the importance of such strategies in coping with the profoundly unsettling effects of apartheid on both blacks and whites, nor do I deny the role that nonviolence and Christian faith played in ending racial oppression. All I am suggesting is that despite all their differences, Yourgrau's and Shabalala's attempts at dealing with the past share a certain form. Both seem to look upon the story of Jacob Zulu with an autobiographical eye of sorts, as a structuring device for renarrating personal identity in a moment of trauma and transition. At the same time, by framing this narrative in scenes of nostalgia for childhood innocence, conversion, and purification they rehearse an elementary mnemonic technique, a ritual gesture that is also emblematic of the current South African politics of memory and national renewal.

As it is, interestingly, of past endeavors at redeeming Africa from the "claws of evil." A striking example of these is *For Unkulunkulu's Sake* (For the Almighty's sake), a play produced in 1913 by students of Hampton Institute, Virginia, and directed by the South African Madikane Cele.[9] A distant relative of John L. Dube, the first ANC president and director of Hampton's sister college, Ohlange Institute, Cele was among the growing number of South African students who, following in the footsteps of Charlotte Manye, came to the United States in search of higher education. Among his numerous activities at Hampton—he recorded a series of Zulu songs for Natalie Curtis-Burlin—the production of *For Unkulunkulu's Sake* was by far the most important.[10]

The play consisted of four acts. The first act presented an idyllic village in the African forest, with a chief and his cooking wives. Upon this "quiet domestic scene" suddenly bursts a band of warriors accompanied by a white trader who introduces his "spirit water" to the villagers. Although the villagers readily accept the new drink, the trader quite inexplicably leaves behind him "a deep-seated prejudice against all white men," while the warriors "dash off on the war path." The second act shows a "witch doctor" uncovering a theft that had occurred, no doubt, because of the white man's intoxicating water and, in the process, condemning an innocent person—a plea, as the *Hampton Student* reports, "for a more enlightened religion." The third act is even more gruesome. Here the witch doctor is seen trying in vain to rescue a valued warrior from death, insisting as a last resort on the sacrifice of the chief's favorite son. At the last minute, to the strains of the Lutheran hymn "A Mighty Fortress" and "For the Nation's Honor," salvation comes in the shape of a "missionary who has just come among them." His superior medical skills restore the warrior to health and generally herald the beginning of "a new era for that tribe." The last act, set in 1920, after the chief's son has returned and established "a little Hampton in the heart of Africa," shows the fruit of all these missionary labors: "a happy Christian home amid scenes of industry and thrift."

Imperialist kitsch, to be sure. Yet there is a case to be made here for a number of potent continuities—continuities in how American conceptions of Africa were shaped in the early twentieth century by religious sentiment and how a Chicago audience of the 1990s was to view the birth of a new South Africa. Continuities, too, in the way African music was used to index primordiality. Yourgrau's script is certainly a powerful reworking of the Zondo case, but the strongest element by far in *Jacob Zulu* is the music of Ladysmith Black Mambazo. And, I argue, it is the layer at which and through which the complex intermingling of the images of liberation, nation building, and repentance is mediated. In terms of dramaturgy, the part played by Bhekizizwe Shabalala and his choir could be compared to that of the choir in Greek drama. The group is

Figure 13.1.  Scene from *The Song of Jacob Zulu*. (Photograph copyright 1993 Jack Mitchell, used by permission of Arcade Publishing.)

onstage throughout the play, commenting on the events, exhorting Jacob to confess, or simply miming the courtroom audience or the police breaking up a student protest rally (fig. 13.1). In the final scene before Jacob's hanging, the group with Bhekizizwe Shabalala in the middle is seen as it leads the entire cast in a rousing rendition of the national anthem, "Nkosi Sikelel' IAfrika."

The fact that the music is an integral part of the proceedings onstage is underscored by a second, equally suggestive soundscape offstage. Thus scenes in the Shaka's Rock shopping mall are set to tinny Christmas carols, signaling "white area," foreignness, and affluence. *Mbaqanga* music blares from a boom box in a house near Piet Retief where Jacob spends the night just before he escapes to Mozambique. Finally, a musical bow, *ugubhu*, is heard playing the night before the bomb blast as Jacob lies awake in his bed. Of course, what the succession of these examples might suggest, among other things, is that Jacob's life journey, his song as it were, is a progressive moving away from the province of white power into the collective body, the black nation. It is a musical reconstruction of identity that is being orchestrated through this soundscape, one that guides Jacob from the "stinking little shops" of Shaka's Rock ("This is what they do to our history?" he muses) to a realm of ancestral roots signaled here by the arcane sounds of deep-Zulu bow music. At the end of this trajectory, at the precise moment when Jacob's identity quite literally is about to disintegrate under the gallows, the nation arises triumphantly to the strains of "Nkosi Sikelel' IAfrika."

While these musics, then, in the broadest sense and following James W. Fernandez, have a metaphoric function, basically predicating an image on an inchoate subject and thereby providing him or her with an identity, the music sung by Ladysmith Black Mambazo appears to be much more determined by the requirements of performative syntax and the causality of action.[11] It directly intervenes in the plot, shaping the characters, metonymically moving them into metaphoric predications. An example of this is found in act 2, scene 5. Here we see Jacob in his cell the night before the final verdict. Ladysmith Black Mambazo, clad as *impi* warriors with traditional headdresses, shields, and spears, enters and wakes Jacob from his dreams, in which the *amathongo*, the spirits of the forefathers, have come to him. As Jacob paces around the cell, telling his story—his real story, which he can tell neither his parents nor his lawyer—the following exchange unfolds between him and the singers-warriors-spirits:

(CHORUS MEMBERS *dance in pairs and small groups all about the stage, eventually surrounding and waking up* JACOB. *The* LEADER *shouts the names of the different regiment each pair of warriors represents.*)

LEADER    Khiphinkuzi! [Drive the bull from the kraal!]
          Uphondo Iwendlovu! [Horn of the elephant!]
          Untaba yeZulu! [Mountain of Heaven!]
          Mkhuphulangwenu! [Lift the crocodile!]
          Umanukelana! [Fight till the blood stinks!]

CHORUS    The warriors have gathered
          A council of elders.
          We're ready to listen.

LEADER    Speak from your heart,
          Speak the truth.

JACOB     When my superior told me to retaliate for the nine martyrs killed in Lesotho, I knew I had to prove myself. But where could I strike? Pietermaritzburg? Durban? No, too many people in those places know me. So I got a map and I looked on it . . . and I saw it. Itshe likaShaka, Shaka's Rock. Where the Zulu regiments fought the enemies of Shaka. I must strike someplace *there*.

LEADER    Bayede!

CHORUS    Sikidi! [Finish them off!]

LEADER    Bayede Baba!

CHORUS    Bayede, bayede, bayede Nkosi!

LEADER    When Shaka, the great king of the Zulus
          Wanted to kill his enemies . . .

CHORUS    When Shaka, the great king of the Zulus
          Wanted to kill his enemies . . .

(*The* LEADER *passes his assegai to* JACOB.)

JACOB     When Shaka, the great king of the Zulus, wanted to kill his ene-
          mies, he sent his impis to catch them up like the horns of the buf-
          falo. They took them high on the rock and drove them down into
          the sea.

(*The* CHORUS *thrust with their spears, then raise them.*)

CHORUS    Ngadla, ngadla! [I have eaten!]
JACOB     I took a bus to Shaka's Rock. . . .

The subtext of this scene is located at two levels, both of which mediate and
reveal the kind of allegorical linkages that I have outlined among nationalist-
Africanist discourse, reconciliation, and the story of Andrew Zondo: a metaphoric level and a metonymic one. The mediation working at the metaphoric
level links Jacob's narrative with the heroic Zulu past primarily through the
ability of musical genre to reference multiple and overlapping fields of meaning. The songs or parts of the songs that Ladysmith Black Mambazo sings here
are drawn from a cluster of regimental anthems known as *amahubo*. Deriving
mostly from the time of Shaka, these songs are considered by many as the epitome of Zulu musical expression and collective identity, having influenced a
wide range of forms, including Zionist church hymns and *isicathamiya* songs.
The general effect, then, that performances of *amahubo* have in a great number
of contexts, past and present, is to conjoin in one rich sound image notions of
Shaka, Zulu military power, and African political autonomy and, beyond these,
visions of the ideal social order.

Far more important, and perhaps much more subtle and therefore imperceptible to international audiences, than the metaphoric operations driven by the
music is the way sound works as a metonymic device, how sound achieves semantic density by movement and by dramatic concatenation. Jacob's words and
the singing of the warriors-spirits blend into each other in a fashion reminiscent of the call-and-response structures prevalent in African musical traditions.
Thus the associative syllogism of Shaka, power, and national liberation that at
one level is configured by means of the formal properties of musical genre and
style at another level is deepened and rendered more affective by what one
might call structure in motion. The irresistibility of such interplay between
metaphor and metonymy, its persuasive power, as it were, resides in the fact
that it assumes, as Fernandez puts it, the mission of metaphor in expressive culture: namely, to accomplish affective movement in inchoate pronouns.[12] Put

differently, cultural forms such as this microscene are not mere mirror expressions of given identities and emotions. It is through small bits of fiction such as this scene in a prison cell that the politics of memory and the search for a new identity in postapartheid South Africa are most engrossingly figured and mediated.

It is tempting at this point to close my account of a piece of work that, for all its deficiencies and the many questions it raises, is a moving tribute to the spirit of cross-cultural understanding that is so crucial if the new South Africa is finally going to wrest itself from centuries of hatred and violence. But as so often in life and art, there is a postscript to be made. The postscript here is titled *Nomathemba* and is a supplement of sorts to *Jacob Zulu*, a second play involving Ladysmith Black Mambazo that premiered in Chicago in 1994.[13] Like its forerunner, *Nomathemba* is a story about reconciliation, a reconciliation of a different kind. And, above all, it is a story about power.

## Nomathemba *and a Postscript*

The idea to extend his composed work into a more fully developed theatrical format came to Bhekizizwe Shabalala while he was working on *Jacob Zulu*. (In many ways, a scenic element has, of course, always been part of Shabalala's idea of what *isicathamiya* is about and to a certain extent has even been present in his nightly dream visions.) In collaboration with Steppenwolf Theater director Eric Simonson and playwright-poet Ntozake Shange a script was then worked out for, as Simonson puts it, "a hybrid kind of folk opera" based on one of Shabalala's earliest and most popular songs of the same title: "Nomathemba."[14] First issued on the 1973 album *Amabutho* and since rerecorded on the internationally best-selling album *Shaka Zulu*, "Nomathemba" tells the story of a young woman named Nomathemba who abandons her rural home and fiancé to go to the city. In the play this idea, following Simonson, is transformed into "a simple story with a clear message. Nomathemba's character, as well as the title of the play, is also a metaphor for the people of 'New South Africa's' continued search for hope and renewal in their country."

The theme of the town woman who relinquishes her customary duties toward her kin and husband is, of course, one of the fixtures of black males' anxiety and disenchantment with *modeli*, the "modern times." It stems from a long history of exploitative gender relations in which women were the primary producers of wealth and labor power, but it also reflects the tensions and intergenerational conflicts produced by capitalist labor migration. Throughout much of the twentieth century, women were essential in keeping intact what was left of the rural homestead economy and in ensuring the production of male labor power. Women's labor complemented their men's ability to earn urban wages and thereby indirectly worked toward men's prestige as heads of households. Consequently, even the most innocuous sign of a lessening commitment on the part of women to a rural lifestyle was perceived as a threat to social harmony and male authority as such.[15]

The patriarchal bias in migrant workers' rejection of supposedly immoral town women and *modeli* is a recurrent theme in *isicathamiya*, equivalent in significance to other images of the lonely worker in town pining for his sweetheart at home, of the train as a predator destroying bonds of kinship, and so on. Yet as is so often the case with Bhekizizwe Shabalala, this sort of pastoralism is presented with a twist. In the play, Nomathemba's lover, Bongani, is described as a "proud, handsome, boastful young man" who also undertakes "a journey of hope . . . to discover himself and the true value of his feelings for Nomathemba." As Simonson sees it:

> He thinks she has left only because he failed to pay her dowry, or "bride-price"—but, of course, we know this is not the case. He takes off after her, and Ladysmith Black Mambazo and their leader, Bhekizizwe Shabalala, sing to Bongani as he travels in search of her from city to city, asking him, "Why does Nomathemba love you?" He is not able to express why. He can think only of material things he gives her, but keeps searching, writing her letters that she does not answer. He goes from rags to riches in the city, and is also disenchanted by the way people treat him when he is desperate and penniless. In one scene he has fallen into a dream where he sees Nomathemba all in white, making the afternoon meal. In the dream, he shows her the fields and farm he will cultivate for them, and wakes up knowing that he cannot live without her. He becomes humble, and finally prays for forgiveness for his boastful ways, if only he can find his Nomathemba. Finally, the spirit of his country comes to him (in the form of Bhekizizwe Shabalala) and tells him he has proven his love for Nomathemba by searching endlessly for her, and should return home to wait.

Bongani's meekness is, of course, a far cry from the kind of response expected of a Zulu male whose woman has abandoned him, just as it is plainly at odds with the real crisis of black masculinity brought about by apartheid, unemployment, and the legacy of Bantu Education.[16] Yet this forgiveness and the peculiarly reversed situation in which it is the man who returns home and waits in a sense resonate with a certain repentance in many *isicathamiya* songs—a repentance romantically imagined as being required of youthful rebels who submit to parental authority after they have experienced the hardship of migrant labor and city life.[17]

And so the syllogistic circle of reconciliation and male power, national unity and gender inequity, completes itself. As Tug Yourgrau worries about young black South Africans who are "unschooled and potentially explosive" and Bhekizizwe Shabalala in *Nomathemba* and in "Diamonds on the Soles of Her Shoes" is troubled about women's independence, we are left wondering indeed about that strange thing called history: a history, Yourgrau fears, that "will claim many more victims before a free South Africa comes into being."

# 14

## Communities of Style

### Musical Figures of Black Diasporic Identity

W hen Nelson Mandela, just released from 27 years' imprisonment, visited Detroit on a historic first tour of the United States, he surprised audiences there with a striking familiarity with soul music and Motown. The music of Marvin Gaye, Mandela told a jubilant crowd, had provided solace during the long and lonely days of his incarceration. His choice could not have been more apt. For not only were, for an older generation of black South Africans, the names of Percy Sledge, Otis Redding, and Wilson Pickett household words (Sledge even visited South Africa in 1970, followed by a stream of black American musicians such as Tina Turner, Clarence Carter, and Brook Benton), but also their music struck at the heart of the affinities black communities on both sides of the Atlantic perceived between soul and the struggle for civil rights. It is in this sense, then, that Mandela in his Robben Island cell, like millions of black listeners in South Africa and the United States had accepted soul "as an expression of black consciousness."[1]

As significant as soul may have been for a generation of increasingly impatient young South African blacks, it was certainly not the only and not the first black style of transatlantic significance. Beginning with Orpheus McAdoo's performances of spirituals during his historic tours of the 1890s, African-American music has been immensely influential in shaping a broad range of black South African styles. Of these, the so-called "township" jazz was certainly one of the most accomplished, incorporating as it did the music of vocal swing groups such as the Mills Brothers and Ink Spots as well as other black American interpretations of Tin Pan Alley. But even in later decades, African-American and African-American-influenced styles such as the twist, disco, and, as we have seen, soul worked to consolidate the intense

246

interchange that had existed for several decades within the broader field of black politics and culture.[2]

The same is true of the reverse direction in the musical two-way traffic between the United States and South Africa. But although here the music of Ladysmith Black Mambazo may have outstripped all other black South African musical traditions previously introduced to U.S. audiences, it by no means represents the first category of South African music to become a major international success. Nor are the members of the group the first South African performers to have gained direct personal experience of black American music. They were preceded by a long and unbroken chain of black South African musical presence in the United States—a succession that began in the 1890s with the African Choir and continued through the twentieth century with Madikane Cele's Hampton cylinder recordings of 1913 and Francis Gow's studies at Oberlin College, followed by Reuben Caluza's work with Nathaniel Dett and his tours with the African Quartette in the early 1930s. The series of visitors reached a sad climax in the early 1960s with the involuntary exodus of the country's most brilliant jazz musicians, people as renowned as Hugh Masekela and Abdullah Ibrahim, and others, now less well remembered, like Caiphus Semenya and Letta Mbulu.

As crucial as these firsthand encounters with the music of black America were in fostering black self-respect in South Africa and in energizing the struggle against apartheid, the transatlantic dialogue is likely to intensify even as a new, democratic South Africa is beginning to take more definite shape. The work of Ladysmith Black Mambazo in the wake of *Graceland* is perhaps the most telling indication of the direction this conjunction might take. And so, in keeping with the overall theme of part II of this book, I shall examine in this and the following chapter a series of transatlantic projects in which the music of Ladysmith Black Mambazo played an integral part. More specifically, I shall look at the collaboration of the group with two of black America's most celebrated artists in two highly distinct pieces of black creativity. The first is *Do It A Cappella*, a television show hosted by filmmaker Spike Lee that featured a number of black vocal harmony groups, while the second—discussed in chapter 15—is Michael Jackson's video film *Moonwalker*.

Both productions raise a wide range of questions on a variety of topics, from the representation of racial identity and dance to the black body, black masculinity, and the role of repetition in black cultures. In what follows I shall discuss these and several other topics, but in doing so I am going to concentrate especially on the question of what these cross-linkages between black musical genres and questions of identity mean in relation to what I have called the global imagination of Africans and African-Americans. Thus the problem I am addressing is, on one level, what these interactions tell us about what Eugene Genovese has called "the ambiguity of the black experience as a national question" and, on another level, what black identities are being constructed through these musical dialogues between Africa and the diaspora.[3] And, finally, I want to probe the processes of performance mediating such racial ecumenes, focusing especially on the ambiguities of cross-cultural "borrowing," repetition, and commodity form.

### "Wimoweh" and the Dynamics of Cross-Cultural "Borrowing"

Spike Lee is now widely acclaimed as one of America's leading filmmakers. But critics also reckon with him as a major intellectual force, prominently intervening in such films as *Do the Right Thing, Jungle Fever*, and *Malcolm X* in some of the most heated debates over issues of race, morality, and gender. One of the less celebrated of Lee's interventions is *Do It A Cappella*, a filmic "tour" of mostly black vocal harmony styles that premiered in the PBS *Great Performances* series in 1990 and was subsequently released on compact disc. The show involved a number of well-known and also less well-known African-American acts such as hip-hoppers True Image, the veteran Persuasions, and the six-piece gospel group Take 6. Equally represented were the white doo-woppers Rockapella and, possibly in implicit recognition of the globality of black musical intercommunication, the Anglo-African female sextet Mint Juleps and Ladysmith Black Mambazo from South Africa. As for the latter group's participation, it consisted in a rousing performance of the South African national anthem "Nkosi Sikelel' IAfrika," a performance of the song "Nansi Imali" (renamed "Phansi Emgodini" on the CD) from the 1981 album *Phansi Emgodini* (In the mines), and a joint performance with the Mint Juleps of "The Lion Sleeps Tonight."[4] It is a reading of the latter that I would like to concentrate on here.

The fact that these two groups teamed up under the auspices of one of America's most controversial filmmakers is not accidental. Spike Lee's cinematographic work and political vision, as most critics seem to agree, is tainted by a strong dosage of racial exclusivism and neo-nationalism, by what Michael Eric Dyson calls "a static conception of racial identity."[5] While it is hard to disagree with these critics, a glance at a piece of work such as *Do It A Cappella* might also reveal a more nuanced picture. For, as I shall argue, what we can see taking place in many of the songs assembled on Lee's compilation is what I would call endotropic performance, the sonic construction of a black communal identity by way not of tightly bound ideological constructs but through the shared experience of style. Performances such as I am examining here create a black ecumene of listeners not by delineating crisply separated, racially defined orders of meaning but by focusing attention on the act of communication as such. Such performances are essentially phatic; they do not concern themselves with a meaning but with what goes on when black people converse with each other in certain ways and thereby mark themselves as different.

The argument that I sketch here intersects with the intriguing attempts by Henry Louis Gates Jr. to broaden the concept of signifying from a form of ver-

bal abuse in black American folklore and everyday practice to a general principle of African-American aesthetics. Signifyin(g), according to Gates, is more
than the dozens, capping, or naming. It is a pervasive mode of communication
under which are subsumed several other rhetorical tropes, including metaphor,
metonymy, metalepsis, hyperbole, and also irony and parody. Although it tran-
scends the realm of politics, signifyin(g) is a language of blackness that enables
the black person to communicate behind masks, in a linguistic universe
shielded from white control. In short, signifyin(g) is "the black trope of tropes,
the figure for black rhetorical figures."[6]

Gates's notion of signifyin(g) includes occasional references to music and
so, not surprisingly, has found ready acceptance among scholars of African-
American music, informing work on funk, pop, parody and irony in jazz, and
also techniques of troping in the blues.[7] While I do not deny the importance of
irony and parody in a great many African-American performance traditions, I
am reluctant to grant signifying in music the same general status as a governing
aesthetic principle as it has in Gates's theory of African-American literary criticism. The principal reason for this is the fact that distinctions between, say, ordinary and figurative uses are much more problematic and much less clear-cut
in music than they are in language. Regardless of the specific meanings of figuration in Western music, no apparent case can be made for a general rhetoric
of music. Indirection, in its most general sense, is the very essence of musical
performance.

Despite its limited applicability, then, outside the literary field, the point
where Gates's concept may be usefully applied to musical analysis is in the
more extended and "thicker" meaning of signifyin(g) as repetition that aims
at foregrounding the signifier itself. For signifyin(g), as Gates suggests, self-
consciously advertises its rhetorical status. By organizing its syntagmatic structure around repetition, refiguration, and variation, signifyin(g) discourses foreground styling rather than the mimetic representation of novel content.[8] Or,
put another way, while in standard English usage, *signification* denotes meaning,
in the black tradition it denotes *ways of meaning*.[9] In a broader sense, one might
even argue that what signifyin(g) constitutes is a black semiotics proper, a vernacular science of the sign and the paradigm. But whereas Gates seems to limit
this definition of signifyin(g) to relations between texts, to the kinds of double-
voiced shifts and displacements that obtain when one text tropes another, I
would suggest that this formal principle is also key to black performance even
within the same piece of music or within a single performance.

What does this mean? At the broadest level, African performance and all diasporic musical styles that flow from it are characterized by repetition. There is
a wide spectrum of forms in which repetition occurs, from the cyclical recurrence of short patterns to the polyrhythmic interlocking of several such contrasting cycles and larger call-and-response structures.[10] The most important
characteristic, however, of the cyclic structure of African music and the main
point where it differs from Western types of repetition lies in the fact that repe-

tition must be thought of here as *practice*.[11] The cycles of African music focus attention on how things are being done rather than on what externalities are being signaled and pictured by them. African music works by implication, not by explication. It emphasizes manner rather than matter, and temporal flow is more important to it than static representation. Or, as ethnomusicologist and drummer John M. Chernoff puts it in what is still one of the best discussions of African rhythm and musical aesthetics:

> African music is a cultural activity which reveals a group of people organizing and involving themselves with their own communal relationships. . . . The aesthetic point of this exercise is not to reflect a reality which *stands behind* it but to ritualize a reality that is *within* it.[12]

Yet these features of African musical performance exceed purely aesthetic or technical concerns. Embedded in them are some of the cardinal principles of African ethics and social conduct. Repetition in African (or, for that matter, any non-Western) performance, as opposed to what is suggested by the massive misinterpretations of "primitive" music in Western philosophical dogma and pop ideology, does not aim at a loss of the subject. It is seldom trance-inducing and does not as a rule serve to remove social inhibitions that supposed weigh down individual spontaneity as in the West. Quite to the contrary, the repetitiveness of much African performance calibrates and stabilizes; it fosters mediated involvement and community building. The cycles and recurring patterns of African music require and effectively promote composure rather than self-abandonment and ecstasy. Music making in Africa, in Chernoff's phrase, "is above all an occasion for the demonstration of character."[13]

I am not stressing these distinctions idly here. It has not been my intention to compare two idioms that are in themselves rather incompatible. Nor did I wish to dispute the fact that in Western music, too, repetition plays a significant role. Rather, what I want to describe is the discursive field in which musical differences become associated with certain notions of racial exclusivity or, alternatively, in which the manipulation of musical form is seen as being completely subordinated to the interests of the music industry. In fact, for the majority of scholars concerned with demonstrating the uniqueness of black musical traditions, it seems that the question of repetition has been reduced to the same *sine qua non* it has been for Theodor W. Adorno and other Marxist authors for whom repetition manifests the regressive tendency of the culture industry. James A. Snead, for instance, in a sweeping treatment of repetition in European and black cultures, gravitates dangerously toward a static view of musical practice and black identity.[14] And so does Tricia Rose in her work on rap music. Rose takes issue with the Frankfurt School and correctly argues that by naturalizing dominant cultural forms such views silence black music makers' choices and become complicit with racism.[15] Yet what precisely makes certain "cultural priorities" black and not others is not easily deduced from a description of the divergent practices and compositional choices of performers who happen to be either black or white without also drawing attention to the way such critical differences are culturally mediated and erected on the ever-shifting grounds of class and race relations.

This has several implications for my contention that black ecumenes are communities of style. The most important of these is the notion that the "blackness" of iterative musical structures, their unique status as a vernacular semiotics of sorts, is determined by complex notions of personhood and communal ethos and by historically determined practices of intercultural exchange. I concur with Richard Middleton's estimation that critical differences between black and European musics are never given. They must be placed in the dialogic relationships between Africa, the diaspora, and also Europe. In other words, even though communities may seek to establish themselves around markers of racial identity, such coalescence of sound and society is never stable. Central to my argument, then, is the question of how such aesthetic differences and definitions of personal identity are historically determined, sonically mediated, and infallibly caught up in a vortex of racial ambiguity. I want to explore how specific uses of repetition frequently come to reflect and sustain a dialectic of racial feeling, a slippery politics of cross-racial desire and repulsion. Most of all, I am fascinated by the semantic shifts and revisions that arise from cross-racial handlings of repetition and from the layering of different modes of reiteration in crossover musical styles.

As an example of the kind of codings across racial lines I have in mind I would like to refer to Eric Lott's incisive discussion of mid-nineteenth-century minstrel sheet music.[16] Drawing on the findings of Hans Nathan that from the 1840s multiple repetitions of brief phrases had become the chief structural principle of minstrel music, Lott argues that these willed attempts to approximate the effects found in slave songs were more than "handicraft" devices deployed by the burgeoning music industry to disguise the alienated character of its product. They were performing "fairly direct kinds of cultural work, of both class and race." Although tied to heterogeneous audiences, by using racial meanings as a cover for class conflict minstrel music helped to "represent" plebeian theatergoers.[17] At the same time, this potentially "insurgent" impulse, by girding itself with a chimerical, performed "blackness," was channeled into a kind of "bland, albeit racialized, gentility." In the final analysis, what the repetition found in minstrel music represented amounted to a "plundering of black music," an act of dispossession whose outcome was a "hesitation between types, a tension between circularity and teleology, a wink at the counterfeit alongside a nod toward 'blackness.'"[18]

Lott's hypothesis would deserve careful ethnographic substantiation, especially with regard to the way these different types of repetition together constituted a variable field in which different "racial effects" were being brought forth. It may be worth testing Lott's assertion that the minstrel show staged conflicted (white) racial subjectivities by vacillating between what he calls the "libidinal" and "ego" functions of musical repetition. The emptying out of the self achieved by the rapturous, cyclic motion of short repeated phrases in the minstrel show immersed white spectators in blissful experiences of boundary crossing into realms of racial Otherness. Intermeshed with these were the more extended strophic structures associated with European folk music and the concomitant enjoyment of selfhood, both of which translate feelings of racial mastery.[19] Lott's main concern is of course with a specific, historically determined set of racial subjectivities turning on the power imbalances of slaveholding antebellum America and attendant white crises of identity. But by attending to the discourses and logic of racial exchange, his analysis also usefully tackles the more general question of how performance provides an arena for the construction of precarious racial identities.

Returning to "Mbube" or, rather, to "The Lion Sleeps Tonight," what an intervention in black cultural politics such as Lee's compilation illustrates is how a corresponding set of black racial feelings is girded by the ambiguities of cultural and musical form and how the construction of black ecumenes can be and inevitably is complicated by a jumbling of racial signifiers that simultaneously negate and call forth exclusivist, essentialist views of black difference. The musical shifts that underlie "The Lion Sleeps Tonight" configure tropes of blackness and whiteness and through these index the social constellations they encompass. In order to gain a sense of these complicated reversals and inversions, and before entering into a detailed structural analysis, a few words about the song's origins are in order. "The Lion Sleeps Tonight" is based on one of the great South African classics of all time: the hit record "Mbube," released in 1939 on the Gallotone label. Not only is Solomon Linda, its composer, recognized as one of the great figures in the history of black South African music, but also his work (he and his choir, the Evening Birds, between 1938 and 1954 released slightly over 40 songs on the Gallotone label) represents the apex of what should be properly called the golden era of *isicathamiya* performance and of a genre that bears the name of his most celebrated composition: *mbube*.

Readers familiar with the history of American popular music are likely to associate "The Lion Sleeps Tonight" more with Pete Seeger and the Weavers, the folk revival of the 1960s, and perhaps also the Tokens. And indeed, as we shall soon see, it was the cover versions of "Mbube" by these two groups that later had a considerable impact on endotropic black reworkings of Linda's song. But before I go into some of these, we need to get a better idea of the song's main structural elements. And thus in what follows I shall dissect "Mbube" into several strands that I believe are crucial to the fabric of the song and the genre as a whole. These components are located at different levels of musical organization—some pertaining to form and melodic structure, others having to do with sound texture and the groove—and I shall make no attempt here to bring these levels into some form of hierarchy (just as I do not mean to suggest that these parameters reflect a priori assumptions about what constitutes musical structure). As primary evidence of my analysis I refer to Linda's 1939 Gallotone recording, even if its relative brevity—the whole track lasts barely three min-

utes—and the instrumental backing of banjo, guitar, and piano distorts somewhat the musical essence of Zulu male a cappella singing. But I shall also take
into account general aspects of *mbube* musical grammar as evinced in other period recordings and in more recent live performances of "Mbube."[20]

The first feature I would like to examine is the division of "Mbube" into two
sections: an introduction set in a metrically free style and the main body of the
song. The introduction is further subdivided into a solo of a few notes sung by
Linda and a closing formula sung by the choir. Harmonically and quite literally
speaking, the introduction "leads into" the tonality of the main body of the
song and is, in this sense, an emphatic gesture that directs the attention away
from itself to what follows. Thus its function differs markedly from that of a
great many *isicathamiya* performances in which introductory sections tend to
be longer and, above all, almost independent of the main song itself. Moreover,
in live performances such preludes are usually marked by stiff, immobile body
postures of the choir and feature lyrics that contain elaborate self-praise.

The second notable component is the distribution of the vocal parts and the
formal alignment of the material that is assigned to them. There are four parts,
called soprano, *altha* (alto), *thena* (tenor), and *bhes* (bass). The soprano part is
sung by the leader, while alto and tenor are sung by one singer each. The bass
part is taken by the remaining singers and consists of a fairly busy ostinato pattern whose strong triadic structure suggests the harmonic framework of the
song: I–IV–I$_6^4$–V$^7$ (ex. 14.1). The pattern is repeated 17 times and thus under-
pins—with a rallentando during the last cycle—the entire length of the main
body of the song.

Alto and tenor, for their part, frequently provide filling parts, moving in parallel fourths or thirds (ex. 14.2).

The soprano, finally, sings three distinct melodic patterns, A, B, and C (ex.
14.3, ex. 14.4, and ex. 14.5), each with its own variations.

Example 14.1. "Mbube," bass pattern.

Example 14.2. "Mbube," *altha* and *thena*.

The third element of "Mbube" is the vocal registers and, in correlation with these, the timbral qualities of the recording. From the outset, *isicathamiya* choirs have been modeled on Western mixed choirs, soprano and *altha* substituting the female voice parts that were lacking in the all-male environment of migrant labor compounds. But this act of mimesis was mediated by a complex set of aesthetic and cultural connotations that reached beyond the organization of performance roles. For instance, a synonym for *bhes*, the bass part, is *doshaba*, those who sing the do. In calling themselves *doshaba*, *isicathamiya* performers explicitly link the organization of a choir with the idea of Western tonality, and thus what singers such as Linda's Evening Birds were engaged in was, in the full sense of the word, a re-presentation of Western musical practice as an articulated whole of performance style, aesthetics, and social practice.

The fourth element is the multipart organization of the vocal parts, here especially the responsorial relationship between the chorus and the leader. What is striking here is the absence of what David Rycroft has identified as the main principle of Nguni vocal polyphony: the nonsimultaneous entry of the vocal parts.[21] There exists in the recording under consideration a fit between the solo vocal line and the chorus so closed and fixed that it is impossible to consider this synchronism as the complete overlapping of "call" and "response." The reason for this is that the lead singer's part, in the terms of Western functional harmony, is contingent on the chordal movement of the chorus. Throughout the 17 cycles the beginnings of Linda's solo phrases coincide with the first notes of the choral response, and in all cases it is the tonic that is being stated or implied in all four parts.

Example 14.3. "Mbube," pattern A.

Example 14.4. "Mbube," pattern B.

Example 14.5. "Mbube," pattern C.

Despite the absence of a recognizable call-and-response structure, the possibility must also be taken into account here that Linda's contemporaries were reconceptualizing the I–IV–V cadence as a "riff" of sorts, a form of traditional root progression—a projection several authors have found to be common in a variety of urban genres influenced by early mission hymnody and Western popular genres such as *mbaqanga, marabi, thula ndivile,* and many others.[22] Yet on the basis of the evidence at hand I hesitate to speak of a root progression in Western guise here, because there is nothing in "Mbube" that would permit us to understand these chord sequences as "*linear* multi-part structures."[23] For instance, the Western cadence cannot—not even theoretically—be reduced to a progression based on the two roots b flat and c, substituting, as it were, the seventh degree of the dominant seventh and the fifth degree of the tonic and the first degree of the subdominant, respectively. Above all, what is lacking here to create the effect of a root progression is the "perpetual motion" that is achieved by the movement of unresolved harmonies. Instead, leading notes at the end of the solo phrase produce a distinct cadential effect.

The regularity exhibited by the responsorial structure moving in synchrony with the basic harmonic framework is enhanced by the fifth and last feature of "Mbube": the pairing of basic phrases and their syntactic arrangement in an overall symmetry. For instance, each cycle consists of four bars, and each bar contains one chord. Moreover, two of the three melodic patterns sung by the lead singer (A and B, viz., B') are grouped in strict binary fashion, while the third pattern, C, occurs only once at the end, thus somehow forming the symmetrical counterpart to the silent cycle 1. Thus the overall architecture of the song presents itself as in example 14.6.

Example 14.6. "Mbube," song form.

| Introduction | |
|---|---|
| solo, chorus | bass pattern |

| 1 | 2 | 3 | 4 |
|---|---|---|---|
| A | A | B | B |

| 5 | 6 | 7 | 8 |
|---|---|---|---|
| A | A | B | B' |

| 9 | 10 | 11 | 12 |
|---|---|---|---|
| A | A' | B'' | B'' |

| 13 | 14 | 15 | 16 | finis |
|---|---|---|---|---|
| A' | A'' | C | B | rit, chord |

Example 14.7. "Mbube," solo.

Paired phrases such as AA, BB, and so on are also found in Nguni music, but here a Western song structure is clearly implied. And thus it matters little whether the cycles, repetitions, and cultural symmetries I elucidated in my little semiotic analysis (for every concern with repetition ultimately requires a science of the sign) can be classified, according to Middleton's scheme, as belonging to the musematic, the discursive, or some more general type of repetition.[24] The point is that none of the features I have pinpointed here qualify "Mbube" as the founding text of a genre that is now generally accepted as belonging to the Zulu traditional core. And it certainly is not, as one observer of the 1939 recording session echoed white mythology, the fortuitous result of an on-the-spot improvisation, "with that natural feel for harmony inherent in the African."[25]

But how can one hear a song such as this with an intraracial, endotropic ear when obviously so much of it appears to be so different from anything commonly associated with African musical traditions? One way of tackling this question would obviously be to listen for traces in "Mbube" of Zulu musical tradition. And indeed, upon closer inspection, we will find that there are several elements in Linda's recording that disrupt the non-African regularity exhibited in the five areas of musical organization discussed previously. Thus, with the exception of the first occurrence of the lead singer's solo, Linda always anticipates the main beat of his line by a fraction, as, for instance, in example 14.7.

Other features include the large descent in melodic pattern A and the descending fourth of pattern B, both attributes "Mbube" shares with the melodic contour and intervallic structure of Zulu music as a whole. Similarly, the timbral textures of booming basses and male falsetto voices, apart from indexing a Western mixed choir, in an endotropic perspective, suggest specific—and not necessarily gendered—notions of emotional intensity and active participation.

By far the best way, however, of tracing these specifically African elements is by considering the fine grain of the temporal organization, the minute spaces, displacements, and "participatory discrepancies," to use Charles Keil's terminology,[26] that disrupt the closure of Western harmonic form and phrase structure.

Example 14.8. "Mbube," solo.

Of fundamental importance here is a tension between the squareness of the repetitive groundwork and a certain laggard motion that toward the end of the recording seems to slow down the overall tempo, as if trying to hold back the cyclic iteration. Technically, this is achieved by two things. First, beginning with cycle 14 (2'05) the middle parts and the bass replace the more lively pattern of triple quavers with stodgy-sounding crotchets. But pushing against this flattening effect are a few almost imperceptible moments when these crotchets seem to fall behind the beat by a few split seconds—an effect that David Rycroft has called "near miss" and that gives Zulu music its unique majestic ring. Second, during the last two or three cycles Linda's solos become less contoured, the melodic phrases turning into mere traces of their first occurrences at the beginning of the song (ex. 14.8).

Clearly, then, "Mbube" exhibits a number of ambiguities, if not antagonisms, that do not permit us to comfortably link the song to a specific African essence or to view it as the product of black submission under the dominant culture. But what is the song really? A parody of Western music? An acceptance of the dominant culture and the music industry? Answers to these questions are crucial to an understanding of black diasporic interpolations of "Mbube," but they are difficult to give on the basis of a structural analysis alone. Rather, as I argued in chapter 11, a genre such as *mbube* in itself offers a medium for working through the complex experience of moving in and out of multiple social contexts and identities while at the same time offering a symbolic universe for the construction of personal identity and character.

Linda's "Mbube" reflects all these conflicting strands of the migrant experience in ways that are located within its very syntax and, more important perhaps, in the chain of signifiers it brings to the fore. Here it becomes apparent why in my analysis of "Mbube" I was not concerned with determining "parent cultures" or degrees of acculturation and authenticity but with the ways in which such permutations create a realm of discursive complicity, a sphere of inclusive exclusivity in which the terms of primal reference, mimetic representation, and longing are inextricably jumbled. "Mbube," I argue, is not concerned with setting up a separate code or with ironically counterposing its own universe of authentic truth against the dominant code. Although such signifyin(g) techniques are not entirely absent from black South African performance, Linda does not parody the rigidity of Western mass-produced musical forms. Rather, his song subtly inflects the received structure and uses it as a mask behind which to focus on the chain of signifiers. The repetitiveness of "Mbube," its sameness, even where it seems to be cast in a Western mold, underscores a statement of black difference, thus drawing attention to the process of signification, rather than meaning itself.

To what extent does all this apply to the performance of "Mbube" by the Mint Juleps and Ladysmith Black Mambazo? In order to answer this question, a more prolonged digression will be necessary. We have to consider some of the cover versions that emerged after Linda's 1939 recording, especially two early U.S. versions that proved particularly influential in determining later black South African and African-American handlings of Linda's song. The first version is a Decca recording made in 1952 under the title "Wimoweh" by Pete Seeger's Weavers, accompanied by a big band under Gordon Jenkins.[27] Seeger claimed that the Weavers learned the song from Linda's record and that he played the notes "almost as I learned them."[28] Problematic as such claims to authenticity undoubtedly on many levels are, in the case of the second cover version, "The Lion Sleeps Tonight" by the Tokens, they are almost impossible to sustain. Backed by Neal Sedaka's band and sung to new lyrics by producers Hugo Peretti and Luigi Creatore, the Tokens' version not only topped the charts for three consecutive weeks in 1961[29] but also turned Linda's original song into a pop song along the lines of Tin Pan Alley, and, as we shall see, subjected "Mbube" to yet another process of racial interpretation.

"Wimoweh" and "The Lion Sleeps Tonight" have since witnessed countless revivals. From Bert Kaempfert, whose 1962 album *A Swingin' Safari* was one of the best-selling albums of its time and made tunes such as August Musarurgwa's "Skokiaan" and Lemmy "Special" Mabaso's pennywhistle tune "Little Lemmy" world famous,[30] to a Mande version by *kora* player Mory Kante, to a punk deconstruction of sorts by the German band Ledernacken and a Danish parody, a multitude of artists have tried their hands at some cover version or other of Linda's song.[31] In what follows I shall make occasional reference to these and other covers, especially those by black performers, such as Miriam Makeba's 1960 recording that featured the Chad Mitchell Trio and a 1965 Columbia recording of the Manhattan Brothers, then South Africa's leading black vocal quartet and internationally known for its 1960 appearance in the musical *King Kong*.

To begin my discussion with the first feature of Linda's song—the division into an introduction and the main body of the song—both the Weavers and the Tokens omit Linda's introduction, as do, in fact, all other versions with the exception of that of Miriam Makeba, who sings an introduction akin to the original version. (Incidentally, her version is also the only one that credits Solomon Linda as the composer of the song.)

Example 14.9. "Wimoweh" and "The Lion Sleeps Tonight," bass part.

As for the second element—the distribution of parts and the material assigned to them—both the Weavers and the Tokens retain the basic quaternary structure of a bass providing some sort of ground pattern, two middle voices, and the falsetto lead singer. Some variation, however, does occur in the melodic material of each of these parts. Thus in both cases the original I–IV–V pattern (ex. 14.1) is essentially left unaltered, but as in most subsequent versions the first bar sounds more accentuated and marchlike (ex. 14.9).

Similarly, both the Weavers and the Tokens make use of middle parts singing the familiar pattern of triple quavers (ex. 14.2), though with the words changed from the three syllabled *i-mbu-be* to the four syllabled *e-wi-mo-weh* the rhythm shifts to a brisker upbeat pattern (ex. 14.10).

Finally, as in Linda's original there is in both the Weavers' and the Tokens' version a high-registered or falsetto lead vocalist singing a combination of the three melodic patterns A, B, and C. Although the overall ratio of permutations and variations is greatly reduced, it is in the shape of these patterns that considerable variations are observed (ex. 14.11). Thus pattern A in the Weavers' version differs from Linda's rendering in that Seeger here introduces a figure that undulates slightly between c and b♭ and that became one of the melodic hallmarks of subsequent cover versions (a, b)—a deliberate attempt, perhaps, at translating into sound Seeger's rather surprising (mis)reading of the solo line in "Mbube" as a "flowing descant which often bears no direct relation to the time of the remaining parts."[32] Another method of rephrasing pattern A found in most versions is the elimination of microtonal inflections and their substitution with more stultified, immutable melodic fragments abstracted from the original phrase. Thus both Bert Kaempfert's version (c) and the Manhattan Brothers' version (d) compress pattern A into a c' held over almost two bars before it suddenly leaps to the octave below.

Pattern B (ex. 14.12) retains much of its original shape in the Weavers' version (a), including the anticipated beat. Yet in the recording by the Tokens (b) the

Example 14.10. "Wimoweh" and "The Lion Sleeps Tonight," middle parts.

e - wi - mo- weh  e - wi - mo- weh  e -

Example 14.11. "Wimoweh" and "The Lion Sleeps Tonight," pattern A.

pattern is reduced to a short motif of a descending fourth that occurs only once at the end.

Finally, pattern C (ex. 14.13) is subject to the most far-reaching revision. Unlike Makeba's version, where C hardly figures at all, the Weavers' version preserves much of the original melodic contour, while the Tokens (variation a) "level" the rhythmic structure and, perhaps more important, conclude the four-bar phrase on the second degree and not on the subdominant, as in Linda's original version.

The changed contour of pattern C must be seen in close relationship with

Example 14.12. "Wimoweh" and "The Lion Sleeps Tonight," pattern B.

Example 14.13. "Wimoweh" and "The Lion Sleeps Tonight," pattern C.

the fifth and last feature I singled out in my analysis of Linda's "Mbube": the overall architecture of the song and its pop song–like division into binary phrases. It is in this area that the two cover versions diverge most prominently from the 1939 recording. Generally speaking, what the Weavers', the Tokens', and most other versions have in common is the prominent role assigned to melodic pattern C, which, as we have seen, in Linda's original recording only occurs once, at the end. In most cover versions, C becomes the central melodic element, a hook that is repeated with little or no variation at all. Moreover, the Tokens rework the pattern so as to expand it to a Western eight-bar phrase divided into two sections, the second of which typically begins on the dominant—thereby suggesting "narrative" flow—before it reverts to the sameness of the first four bars (ex. 14.14).

Equally in keeping with Western models is the bipartite AA, BB form, although the Tokens in particular seek to conceal the relentless cycle of static phrases behind a number of ornaments such as an obbligato solo voice, a soprano saxophone pattern, "fills" such as drum triplets, and "breaks" that sound like "hop hop" (ex. 14.15).

Example 14.14. "The Lion Sleeps Tonight," enlarged pattern C.

Example 14.15. "The Lion Sleeps Tonight."

The pop song structure becomes even more evident at the macrolevel, where the binarism of unvarying phrases is subsumed under the typical Tin Pan Alley ABABCB format. The Tokens divide the song into four cycles of 16 bars each, with a "bridge" of eight bars after the third cycle (played by soprano sax and the obbligato voice) and a "fade-out" of eight bars after the fourth cycle. Each of these cycles is further subdivided into two sections of eight bars sepa-

Example 14.16. "The Lion Sleeps Tonight," song form.

| 1 | 2 | 3 | 4 |
|---|---|---|---|
| C | C | - | - |

| 5 | 6 | 7 | 8 |
|---|---|---|---|
| C | C' obbligato I | A | A |

| 9 | 10 | 11 | 12 |
|---|---|---|---|
| C | C' obbligato II | A | A' |

| 13 | 14 | 15 | 16 |
|---|---|---|---|
| - obbligato II saxophone | - obbligato II saxophone | C | C' obbligato I |

| 17 | 18 | 19 | 20 |
|---|---|---|---|
| B obbligato I | A obbligato I | C | C (fade) |

rated by the "hop hop," thus creating the impression of contrast or of solo and refrain (ex. 14.16).

The analysis I have undertaken here leads to two conclusions. First, it has become clear that in the hands of Western mainstream pop musicians the micro-dynamics of African repetitive musical forms undergo fundamental shifts. Second, the difference that results from these shifts is not primarily of interest at the level of the signified but as the site of specific encounters between socially and culturally determined processes of signification, mimesis, and duplication. What I am interested in, above all, is the racial underpinnings of such mass-mediated practices. Although one might possibly conceive of some generic Africanness or "happy safari" feeling as one of the meanings commonly invested in "The Lion Sleeps Tonight," of greater interest to me here are the racial pressures and social tensions that help to produce and shape the syntax of such covers.

It is here that the Tokens offer a fascinating clue to the complex interplay of racial fear and fascination occasioned and reflected by "The Lion Sleeps Tonight." "We were embarrassed by it," member Phil Margo recalled the group's reaction to RCA's decision to release the song.[33] The remark is revealing. Embarrassed by what? By the inane minstrel lyrics about lions in the jungle and peaceful villages? By Mitch Margo's trite falsetto? Whether the Tokens' embarrassment confined itself to matters of musical taste or was motivated by political awareness is not clear. What *is* clear is that the Tokens took the song for a "folksong" and that they were familiar with Makeba's version and also with that of the Weavers. And so, I would suggest, what Phil Margo's embarrassment really was about was a sense of guilt, a tacit admission of the industry's and the group's complicity in the plundering and counterfeiting of black culture.

I do not make this charge lightly. The ownership of cultural capital is a matter of considerable importance to black South Africans whose repercussions were even felt in black nationalist interventions in the debate about *Graceland*.[34] More significantly, I want to argue, what makes certain forms of intercultural "borrowing" so vexing and guilt-ridden is not so much the fact of theft posing as some more legitimate form of exchange as it is the way such mass-mediated transactions of cultural capital between Africa and the West are cryptically configured in shifts of musical form and how, at the same time, these shifts gloss over the power imbalances of such transactions.

I use the somewhat undetermined and ambiguous term "transaction" advisedly here. For as another look at example 14.15 shows, the "breaks" and "fills" the Tokens use for veiling the deadly monotony of their version are false currency. They are, as Carol J. Clover puts it in a parallel discussion of white appropriations of black dance in film, "the 'memories' that surface in the process of 'forgetting,' as though in a perverse bargain, they must be admitted *in order* to be overridden."[35] In the same breath as the drum triplets and the "hop hop" shouts remember the "folk" origins of "Mbube," they forget them. Thus, regardless of their intended meanings—"tom-toms," "savages," whatever—their function is indeed purely nominal. They pretend to restore in a token act of equal exchange to the original a racial authenticity that they denied to it by counterfeiting it in the first place.[36] This, I believe, is the true reason for the popularity of a song such as "The Lion Sleeps Tonight." It is the inscrutability of these racial encodings, their character as a social hieroglyph, that explains the grip a Tin Pan Alley remake such as the Tokens' cover version of "Mbube" has on Western audiences.

After this excursion into the music industry's racialization of musical form I now return to Spike Lee, the Mint Juleps, and Ladysmith Black Mambazo. As we have seen, black South African performers have always been keenly aware of the parallels between their own vocal traditions and African-American forms of harmony singing, even though the opportunities for such intercultural comparisons may have been few prior to the 1950s and such staple genres as African-American gospel quartet singing remained altogether unknown in South Africa. And as the recent work of Ladysmith Black Mambazo after *Graceland* demonstrates, their interest in black American vocal traditions deepened as the group came into contact with African-American performers. One such significant encounter was a concert in September 1990 at the Civic Center of Bessemer, Alabama, called "Home of the Heroes."[37] The event featured a number of African-American gospel quartets such as the Fairfield Four, Four Eagle Gospel Singers, and Birmingham Sunlights and highlighted the striking parallels between black gospel music and *isicathamiya* from South Africa. Other experi-

Example 14.17. "The Lion Sleeps Tonight," Mint Juleps.

ences include the joint appearance with Marvin L. Winans in a recording of "Leaning on the Everlasting Arm" on the album *Two Worlds, One Heart* and, of course, the joint appearance with the Mint Juleps on Spike Lee's TV show.

As for the latter performance, it is characterized by two partly contradictory, partly complementary tendencies. Ladysmith Black Mambazo, for instance, throughout the performance hardly swerves from Linda's original, maintaining the basic simplicity and brittle balance described earlier between Western four-square regularity and African circularity. The Mint Juleps, by contrast, follow the format firmly fixed by three decades of covering, at best underpinning, Linda's basic structure with somewhat richer harmonies such as sweet-sounding parallel thirds.

Furthermore, the Anglo-Africans broaden the concept of Western-style narrativity by adding a variant of the Tokens' pattern C on the minor relative. Although in performance this pattern follows A, it is structurally akin to earlier Western cover versions by the Tokens and other groups in that it props up—or, rather, waters down—the "African" four-bar pattern to a standard pop song eight-bar phrase (ex. 14.17).

These Western revisions are further accentuated by the overall imbalance in the entire performance between the two groups and, hence, between echoes of Linda's original and Western cover versions. Thus although Ladysmith Black Mambazo starts the song, they slip into the background in the middle of the song, only to reemerge fully in the final part of the performance in a way that comes very close to the Linda original.

Yet in spite of all these imbalances, "The Lion Sleeps Tonight" has something of a recuperative effort. Not only was Lee's TV project as a whole framed as a nostalgic search for the good old days of doo-wop in Brooklyn, but there is discernible in the collaborative venture of the Mint Juleps and Ladysmith Black Mambazo a clear attempt to arrive at a certain integration, to achieve what Paul Gilroy has called "diasporic intimacy." This endeavor is noticeable at several moments in the performance, but especially when both groups disrupt the binary syntactic structure of AA and CC, by first polyphonically juxtaposing A and C and then launching into a spirited interlocking of different variants of B (ex. 14.18).

To wit, this innocent little device leaves intact the Western idea—present in

Example 14.18. "The Lion Sleeps Tonight," Mint Juleps and Ladysmith Black Mambazo.

earlier cover versions but also to a lesser degree in the original "Mbube" itself—of highlighting contrasting melodic patterns as a means to achieve narrative progression and lyrical density. But at the same time the juxtaposition of these melodic patterns is entirely located on a metacommunicative level. The patterns confront each other not so much as different orders of meaning—orders which, as we have seen, are difficult to connect to the hybrid jumbling of musical matter present even in Linda's song—but as two profoundly related and yet highly distinct ways of signifying: repetition as a commercial process represented here by the "hook" and repetition as practice, as the African mode of interaction required for the demonstration of character. In this way, the overlaying of patterns seeks to draw attention to itself. It is a self-referential move that foregrounds the process of communication itself and the pleasure of endotropic listening that it affords.

Clearly, then, the Mint Juleps and Ladysmith Black Mambazo are not merely invoking tradition, restating an authentic, unproblematic original. Rather, they seem to acknowledge the fact that while modern mass cultural reworkings of black traditions are produced, in Gilroy's phrase, "in the long shadow" of black ancestral traditions, they also occur "in the jaws of modern experience." But above all, it is not a racial signified itself that is being envisaged by these creative labors. It is rather, as Gilroy states, "the rituals of performance that provide prima facie evidence of linkage between black cultures."[38]

To conclude, diasporic performances such as "The Lion Sleeps Tonight" by the Mint Juleps and Ladysmith Black Mambazo provide eloquent proof of the impossibility of seizing upon music as a means to sustain an organic blackness. They support the notion that black ecumenes operate within an impossible logic of sameness and difference. Black diasporic cultural formations often emerge in complicity with the dominant culture, feeding on the sediments of a long history of "borrowing" and crossover. At the very least, like every attempt at inflecting or keeping at bay the language of power by means of irony, parody, or satire, such black stylings, even as they play with the canon of forms, always contain a restatement, an affirmation of form, and thus constitute an ambiguous dance with power.

# 15

## Dances with Power

### Michael Jackson, Ladysmith Black Mambazo,
### and the Ambiguities of Race

Of all the superlatives that are routinely attached to Michael Jackson's name, none appears to surpass those connected with his alleged racial features, with the complete whiteness of his skin and the utter thinness of his lips, or the profound blackness of his music. In fact, not only has no other performer divided public opinion more sharply over questions of racial identity than Jackson, but also, in a country prone to chronic fits of amnesia over its most deep-seated troubles, the most striking aspect about Michael Jackson, quite ironically, appears to be the gulf that separates African-American assessments of his music from those of white critics, especially those whose writing springs from a concern with cultural critique and the co-optation of the country's black superstars by the multinational media. Phillip Brian Harper, for instance, in a discussion of black crossover acts of the 1980s, has argued that African-American musical forms and perceptions of African-American culture are consistently being manipulated to suit industry interests. More specifically, he maintains, the production of crossover success is determined by black performers' ability to blur the line between strictly musical production and visual appeal, Michael Jackson's rise to superstardom having been due in large part to his early appearance on MTV.[1] The visualization of Jackson or, as Harper prefers to call it, the synesthetic interplay of television appearance and musical product "was both a means to and an indication of his status as a crossover performer." Beyond this, the role of synesthesia within the music industry demonstrates the dependence of MTV on categories such as "black" music—categories that crossover is supposed to render meaningless in the first place. For one of the functions of the "blackness" of Michael Jackson's music is precisely to define the more "mainstream" forms of pop on which the industry so vitally depends.[2]

Rather more typical of black decodings is an assertion such as the one by Michael Eric Dyson that Jackson's performances reveal a postmodern spirituality, a "festive choreography of religious reality" that "communicates powerful religious truths and moral themes."[3] During live performances such as that at the 1988 Grammy Awards ceremony, Dyson says, Jackson transformed the stage into a "world-extending sanctuary" on which he enacted rituals of religious ecstasy, moral courage, and spiritual passion that were rooted in black America's richest traditions.[4]

Neither reading, taken as an absolute, is unproblematic. Both fail to recognize and sufficiently thematize the interdependence of the commercialization of black music and its communal, counterhegemonic legacies. But both positions also overlap in that they stress the body as the primary site for the racialization and deracialization of Jackson. Thus Harper attributes Jackson's phenomenal popularity with "mainstream" audiences to the television *exposure* he had gained since 1983. Given the context in which it is used, the term "exposure" carries somewhat doubtful connotations. It patently recalls the early days of blackface minstrelsy, when black performers such as the celebrated William Henry Lane, alias Juba, not only gave "correct Imitation dances of all the principal Ethiopian [white] dancers in the United States" but also perversely, in order to dispel doubts about the authenticity of white minstrel "representations" of blacks, chose to "give an imitation of himself."[5] It is perfectly within this logic of minstrel mimicry that the desire a black performer such as Jackson evokes in white television viewers is constructed as being spurred not by the fact of his crossing over but rather by the opposite. The object of that desire is the result of Jackson being represented as an "imitation of himself," as the product of an irreducible racial condition, now made all the more irrefutable by being rendered up to public view.[6] Jackson enjoyed the video success he did, *People* columnist Albert Goldman writes, because he's "got Bojangles in his bones."[7]

The same bones resurface in Dyson's account of Jackson's 1988 Grammy show, this time in quite a different ritual of racial anatomy. What became visually apparent during this event, Dyson tells us, was the religious nature of Jackson's performance:

> Jackson spun and fell on his knees, dramatizing his message of the dialectical relationship between personal change and social transformation. Back on his feet, Jackson pleaded once more for the world to change. . . . Jackson, with new vitality breathed into him, "got happy" again, turning several times, spinning joyously, and spontaneously jumping up and down, shaking his hands, and doing a complex walk-skip-jump movement.[8]

All this spinning, jumping, and shaking, as Dyson is crucially aware, must of course be seen as part of the African-American "confrontation with debilitating forms and uses of embodiment" under slavery. Reduced to a mere object, a commodity, the slave's body became the site of difference par excellence and its redemption in rituals of purification and sanctification the center of African-American religious practice.[9]

Figure 15.1. Michael Jackson in "Smooth Criminal" (Michael Jackson, *Moonwalker*). (Courtesy of Epic Records.)

Present-day inscriptions of the body in black performance are determined by processes far more complex than either Harper or Dyson suggests. They are neither purely restorative endeavors nor determined solely by the interests of the music industry. Rather, we have to acknowledge what Susan McClary and Robert Walser call the "cultural contradictions of the black body" and black popular musicians' attempts to deal with these contradictions in "creative and rhetorically powerful ways."[10] And so in what follows I shall examine the collaboration of Michael Jackson and Ladysmith Black Mambazo, concentrating on how Jackson's full-length video *Moonwalker* figures the more visceral, unspoken levels of the black experience by foregrounding body styles as the primary site of black identity work. The two segments of *Moonwalker* I am particularly concerned with here are "Smooth Criminal" and "The Moon Is Walking." Both segments are set in a retro mode. In the first segment, the scene is a 1930s club (the name of the club is Club 30s), in which Michael Jackson baffles a motley crowd of mobsters, pimps, and prostitutes by a display of spectacular dancing and actual gun power. Appended at the end of *Moonwalker*, as the credits begin to roll, is "The Moon Is Walking," the segment that features Ladysmith Black Mambazo. Dressed in suits and hats that match those of the club scene and appearing in a brick-walled room similar to the one in "Smooth Criminal," the South African group is seen performing a classical *isicathamiya* routine which is

Figure 15.2. Ladysmith Black Mambazo in "The Moon Is Walking" (Michael Jackson, *Moonwalker*). (Courtesy of Epic Records.)

interspersed with brief quotations from "Smooth Criminal" shown earlier in the film.

### Criminals, MTV, and Black Body Styles

Although they do not immediately succeed each other, the fact that "The Moon Is Walking" is strewn with quotations from "Smooth Criminal" suggests the close parallels Jackson wished to highlight between elements of his dance style and that of the South African performers. Of these, the parallels between the body postures are perhaps the most striking. Both Jackson's dance troupe (fig. 15.1) and Ladysmith Black Mambazo (fig. 15.2) have their arms firmly pressed against their bodies, and both acts kick their legs high in the air, wobble their knees, and lift up their trouser legs. Musically, too, strong resemblances are observed in the way both songs are constructed around a repetitive two-bar bass pattern. Even if these correspondences cannot be proven to have resulted from concrete historical contacts between African-American and South African dancers, it is clear that black performers at the end of the twentieth century are no less fascinated by the continuities and parallels between their respective expressive traditions than their predecessors in the 1890s.

As intriguing as they may be, these structural similarities in themselves do not help us understand the embodiment of black racial subjectivities and their mediation in mass-produced images. Nor is their semantic referent, the "content," of much assistance in decoding these processes. To be sure, *Moonwalker* and many other Jackson films play on a host of themes fundamental to African-American life. And Jackson does address in them a whole range of stereotypes about black people, and as the censoring by the media of the car window smashing scene in *Black or White* illustrates, he deconstructs them in ways that, as Carol Clover has written, have "all the force of a return of the repressed."[11] Nevertheless, even if Stuart Hall's dictum holds that the body for African-American musicians has been and frequently still is the only cultural capital, the canvas of representation, the question of what it is precisely that is black about Jackson's films bears repetition.[12] Or, as Kobena Mercer asks in his analysis of *Thriller*: "[W]hat is it that makes this young, *black* man so different?"[13]

Image or body, mimesis or physis, clearly the problem with Jackson's racial difference and, by analogy, with the "black" in *Moonwalker* and popular culture in general is that it requires a fuller understanding of the interplay of video aesthetics, racial politics, dance history, and popular music. Regrettably, the present state of research on African-American and South African dance offers scant ground for considering the discourses at play in a more integrated, theoretically informed fashion. The literature on African-American dance, for example, although rich in thematic scope and documentary evidence, insufficiently problematizes the active role of such dancing in the production of race. The myriad forms of African-American dance are predominantly seen as expressions of fixed racial identities, and not much attention has been given to the contested areas and strained relationships between different racial worlds.[14] Similarly, very little headway has been made since the emergence of music television in the research on the relationship between music and motion, aurality and visuality. Although the literature devoted to music video and television has grown tremendously over the past ten years, the bulk of this work has limited itself to questions such as media policy, the production of stardom, music video and postmodernism, sexuality and gender, and narrative realism.[15] By contrast, there is a pressing demand for structural analyses of actual videos, here especially of full-scale dancing and the interplay of images and soundtrack, as there is, even more urgently perhaps, a need for ethnographic studies of the production and consumption of such videos.

In South Africa, similar lacunae exist. Serious scholarly attention to dance has long been overdue, and it is only since the 1980s that an exciting body of new work has begun to tackle the complex relationships among music, social practice, body politics, and dance. The central insight that results from a series of fine studies on dance genres as varied as Zulu *ingoma* dancing, Pedi *Kiba* female dances, and the religious dances of the Nazareth Church is the notion that, like its African-American counterpart, black dance in South Africa has been caught up in ambiguous power relations. On the one hand, it is located at the heart of black people's efforts to redeem the body from a set of alienating and repressive practices and to remake a social universe undone by colonial conquest, capitalist transformation, and racial oppression.[16] On the other hand, as these studies also show, such dances deal with the contradictions of urban life in ways that do not always challenge the hegemonic order head-on.

What this suggests, clearly, is that we not only need to develop both theoretically and methodologically the study of black dance and body politics in both countries but must also realize, at the very least, that African and African-American dance is not simply the immediate embodiment of given social and racial identities. Instead, it may be worth pursuing Susan McClary and Robert Walser's suggestive lead that what black performers have accomplished has primarily been to "enact recodings of desire through music and images."[17] Gender and sexuality for these authors are the primary objects of these recodings of desire, and in many ways, of course, they are correct. Yet in a broader sense one might suggest that what is being constituted by these bodily reformulations is a subject in the first place, endowed with the capacity to make meaning. Even if these meanings are always gendered and, as I shall show, culturally specific, the point that interests me here is how such processes of identity formation and recoding of desire are determined by certain idioms of power. While many of these idioms stem from the formal and aesthetic legacies of black dance traditions on both sides of the Atlantic, the focal point at which these different African-American and black South African stylizations converge in the two segments of *Moonwalker* is the very specific image of the badman. One of the key figures of black American and South African social life and the dialectical image, as Benjamin would have said, par excellence of a racially divided society, the badman in both contexts helps to project a whole series of ambiguous conceptions of social order, personhood, power, and morality.

It is not necessary here to go into the role of the badman in black American folklore and consciousness and to point to the continuity between, say, the trickster and the criminal outwitting a hostile and oppressive white world.[18] Far more important are the social and racial tensions that quite literally and tangibly came to clash on the gangster's very skin. And it is here that remarkable parallels exist with the figure of the gangster in South Africa. Thus substantial historical research has shed light on the liminal position different categories of black criminals have occupied in South African society over the course of the past 100 years, illuminating the complex intermingling of urban criminality, migrant labor organization, ethnicity, and politics. Thus the early *isitshozi* and *indlavini* gangs that were operating among Mpondo migrant miners played an important role in shaping workers' perceptions and in sharpening ethnic conflict among miners.[19] Similarly, the early-twentieth-century *amalaita* gangs of domestic servants, although primarily concerned with adapting traditional forms of youth organization to the new conditions of urban life, at times provided the basis for more serious challenges to local political authorities.[20]

Equally indeterminate images corresponded to the intermediate social position of the black South African gangster. The organization of the *amalaita*, for instance, was modeled on the hierarchies of Zulu precolonial polities, complete with the traditional system of ranks and titles. At the same time, the nostalgia that expressed itself in these reminiscences of a glorious past was shared by the more law-abiding sectors of the population for whom the criminal, despite all the terror he instilled, was in many ways more a herald of social reconstruction rather than the harbinger of anarchy. Likewise, the historically younger type of the urban thug, the *tsotsi*, was both the source of horror and the object of admiration. The embodiment par excellence of antithetical power and manly bravado, the *tsotsi* was romanticized for defying the white man's law and, above all, envied for outdoing white South Africa in what probably constituted its most vulnerable basis of class and racial privilege: the monopoly on representation. For class and race rule in South Africa depended not only on the physical coercion of dark-skinned bodies. Equally crucial was the ability to control the images used to represent the order in place and, more particularly, those that symbolized racial difference itself. Of these, the commodity signs of burgeoning consumer society and the emerging fashion industry were perhaps paramount. The consumption and imitation of U.S. goods and lifestyles—cars, clothes, movies, jazz records—were important indicators of black male accomplishment, the ultimate cachet of racial pride.[21] They signaled a refusal to submit to the impoverished notions whites had of blacks' sense of identity and, paradoxically, suggested a desire to fortify laboring bodies by the consumption of their own commodified images.

The black dandy not only was a symbol for class differentiation within U.S. and South African society at large but also symbolized the growing divisions within black communities themselves. Especially in South Africa, dapper clothes came to be seen as an additional resource in the competition for security within an oppressive capitalist world. A three-piece suit and a hat distanced the more évolué workers from the lower-paid sectors of the migrant workforce and thus implicitly served to express their wearer's acceptance of the commodity sign as the basis of the entire system of social distinction.[22]

If the ability to make meaning as the basis for identity work in black cultures generates specific social categories like the gangster and, within these, reproduces the larger contradictions of capitalist society, even greater emphasis is placed on the process of signifying as such. The idiomatic manipulation and stylization of the body in themselves constitute a source of empowerment. Indeed, at first glance what *Moonwalker*—like *Thriller* and several other of Jackson's *Short Films*—is about is spatial mutation and bodily stylization. Over the course of 90 minutes, we see spaces blend into each other, images and sounds quote and cross-reference each other. But above all we observe Jackson slipping into about a dozen different roles, shapes, and objects. He turns into a motorcycling Brer Rabbit (or Bugs Bunny?) first, outwitting tourists and the police, then into a car and back again into the real Michael Jackson. Toward the end of

the film, in a spectacular computer-animated sequence, Jackson even trans-
mutes into a spaceship. In a sense, Ladysmith Black Mambazo, too, appears to
undergo a metamorphosis. Their usual stage personae as Zulus and committed
Christians in "The Moon Is Walking" turn into those of suit-wearing Chicago-
style gangsters of the 1920s. In other words, the disembodiment and transmo-
grification of Michael Jackson into the otherworldly and futuristic is mirrored
by Ladysmith Black Mambazo reincarnating in another time and another social
role.

One might argue with Kobena Mercer that all this ambiguity, ultimately, enacts "spectacles of racial and sexual indeterminacy."[23] And yet these shifting
identities to me do not indicate the fracturedness of the postmodern condition,
and there is more to them than the two-dimensionality of the TV image.
Linked with them are specifically racial *ways of meaning*, specific endotropic
uses of the body that reject the commodity form as they embrace it. "Smooth
Criminal" and "The Moon Is Walking" are black dances with power because
they empower the dancers "tricking" mass culture, but they are also dances
with power in that the dancers give themselves over to a playful encounter with
that very culture. The sense of wonder and the extraordinary generated by the
special effects in *Moonwalker* and the lyrics of "The Moon Is Walking" stands
for the awe the consumer is supposed to feel in view of Michael Jackson and
Bhekizizwe Shabalala as media products, as stars-as-image.[24] But at the same
time, as Mercer points out, Jackson's love of "camp," the supernatural, the exaggerated, and the hyper questions dominant stereotypes of black masculinity.[25]

### Tapping, Repetition, and the Commodity Form

How, then, can we locate this dance with power in our two segments of *Moon-*
*walker* at the level of form, in the chain of signifiers? And in what syntactical aspect of the choreography in particular? How can one show that structured
physical motion encodes the ambiguous identities of black performers incorporating the power structures at the same time as they are confronting them? As
in music, I suggest, quoting and repetition are the essential techniques to be examined here. Bracketing here the debate about the repetitiveness of pop music
and music video's alleged break with realism and narrative, I shall resume the
point made earlier in my discussion of "Mbube" that repetition, in the hands of
black performers, must be understood as formal revision, as signifyin(g).[26]

In *Moonwalker*, formal revision occurs mostly at the macrolevel. The song
"Smooth Criminal" and video material from the clip are repeated no less than
four times, each time with a signal difference. The first two times the video images are in what I would call real time—that is, the time spent watching corresponds to the time passing during the actual dancing. The third time, when bits
of video material from "Smooth Criminal" are quoted in the "Moon Is Walk-

ing" segment, they are mostly in slow motion. Finally, the fourth time, when the credits roll at the end of the whole film, the accompanying images appear more blurry and as if in time-lapse. In one sense, one might argue that what these different layers of psychological time and modes of repetition are meant to achieve is to both produce and conceal what Wolfgang F. Haug has called the "appearance of use value," the promise in pop music and music video of some additional use value elsewhere in other videos, another LP. The only difference from the music video based on the three-minute single format is that here the repeated segments and cuts of "Smooth Criminal" use music and images interchangeably in order to hook the consumer. In another sense, it is perfectly conceivable to see the choreography of the first two repetitions as an attempt to make the advertised product doubly attractive by presenting the identical product (sound) in two different packings (video). Thus the first time the dancing is more open, focused on solos, and the movements generally seem to be directed more to the progression of the plot. During the repetition the choreography is more formal and features more corps de ballet action in the center of the room. In addition to this, there is a high degree of correspondence between the music and the dance not only in the rhythm but also at the level of gestural gestalt.

Despite all this, I am reluctant to reduce the formal structure of this segment to the serial logic of commodity production and advertising strategies. There is more to "Smooth Criminal" and "The Moon Is Walking" than predictability and Benjamin's "time of Hell." This becomes particularly evident at the moment when the camera leaves the club to turn to Jackson's little friend in the alley demonstrating that everything Michael knows he took from him.[27] Not only does this scene gracefully pay homage to black adolescent street culture, but also the directors deliberately invert the mimetic hierarchy as it were — the anchorage of power in the social ordering of copies — and thereby draw attention to the play of signifiers itself.

In "The Moon Is Walking," similar processes of stylization are observed. This segment has two parts. In the first part, the group is seen singing an introduction in isiZulu similar to the one that opens Linda's "Mbube." Movement here is limited to a few hand gestures that illustrate aspects of the lyrics and later, while the introduction moves into the main body of the song and the performers are slowly getting into gear, slaps on the thighs. Yet as the bass line is gradually being foregrounded and the lead singer's part reduced to a minimum, the song settles into a groove (or, as *isicathamiya* performers say, is *vuthiwe*, getting "cooked"), and the main section of "The Moon Is Walking" starts.

This section is composed of 29 cycles of 16 pulses each. It begins with two cycles without movement, and it is not until cycle 3 that the singers begin executing a simple walking step in time with the main beat of the song. "Walking step" here means that the gait is more animated than in plain walking and that at times it resembles more a jumping on the spot. While engaged in this

Example 15.1. "The Moon Is Walking," cycles 15–18.
Top row: Only the corner points of these foot and arm movements are indicated here. Feet touching the ground are marked by X. Bottom row: feet; l = left foot, r = right foot.

**15**

| X |   | X |   | X | X |   | X | X | XX | X | XX | X | XX | X |   |
|---|---|---|---|---|---|---|---|---|----|---|----|---|----|---|---|
| l |   | r |   | l | r |   | l | r | rr | r | rr | r | rr | r |   |

**16**

| X | X |   | X | X |   | X | XX | X | XX | X | XX | X |   | X | X |
|---|---|---|---|---|---|---|----|---|----|---|----|---|---|---|---|
| l | r |   | l | r |   | r | rr | r | rr | r | rr | r |   | l | r |

**17**

|   | X | X |   | X |   | X | X |   | X | X |   | X |   | X |   |
|---|---|---|---|---|---|---|---|---|---|---|---|---|---|---|---|
|   | l | r |   | l |   | l | r |   | l | r |   | l |   | r |   |

**18**

|   | X | X |   |   | X | X | XX | X | XX | X | XX | X |   | X | X |
|---|---|---|---|---|---|---|----|---|----|---|----|---|---|---|---|
|   | l | r |   |   | l | r | rr | r | rr | r | rr | r |   | l | r |

type of footwork, the performers keep the rest of their bodies immobile, and only the angled arms sway back and forth on the beat. This pattern continues through to cycle 15, when the performers launch into spirited tapping (ex. 15.1). In cycle 20 the walking step is resumed, but in cycles 21–22 the singers turn to the left by 90 degrees so as to show their sides, and wave their hats (ex. 15.2).

There are several contradictory ways of dancing with power here that deserve closer attention. The first is the walking step. Called *istep* in isiZulu, it has to be placed within the broader context of Zulu dance and the dualism that characterizes uses of the body in *isicathamiya* choreography. Elsewhere I have argued that the ambulatory character of *istep*, its proximity to walking, celebrates "the body finding its proper place in the normative space of the engineers of the apartheid city." *Istep* does not pose a spatial enunciation of its own against the rigidity and orderliness of the segregated city, and thus, unlike some of the rural influences on *isicathamiya* discussed in chapter 11, it does not permit dancers to rehabilitate their unhomed bodies and to recover their capacity for symbolic representation beyond the white city.[28]

The second way is the tapping. It is executed here on the right foot and with the sole coming flatly down on the floor. The rest of the body remains fairly immobile, with the torso bent forward slightly and the hands clasped in front of the stomach. Although the exact origin of tap dancing in South Africa is un-

Example 15.2. "The Moon Is Walking," cycles 20–29. (Bottom row: video image, LBM = Ladysmith Black Mambazo dancing, J = Michael Jackson.)

**20**

| x |  | x |  | x | x |  | x | x |  | x |  | x |  | x | x |
|---|---|---|---|---|---|---|---|---|---|---|---|---|---|---|---|
| r |  | l |  | r | l |  | r | l |  | r |  | l |  | r | l |

... J (as inmate) ...

**21**

|  | x | x |  | x |  | x | x | x |  | x | x | x |  | x |  | x |
|---|---|---|---|---|---|---|---|---|---|---|---|---|---|---|---|---|
|  | r | l |  | r |  | l | r | l |  | r | l | r |  |  |  |  |

... LBM ...

**22**

| x |  | x | x | x |  | x | x | x |  | x |  | x |  | x |  |
|---|---|---|---|---|---|---|---|---|---|---|---|---|---|---|---|

...

**23**

| x |  | x |  | x |  | x |  | x |  | x |  | x |  | x |  |
|---|---|---|---|---|---|---|---|---|---|---|---|---|---|---|---|

... J (running across open space) ...

**24**

| x |  | x |  | x |  | x |  | x |  | x |  | x |  | x |  |
|---|---|---|---|---|---|---|---|---|---|---|---|---|---|---|---|

... (in airplane) ...                    (face) ...

**25**

| x |  | x |  | x |  | x |  | x |  | x |  | x |  | x |  |
|---|---|---|---|---|---|---|---|---|---|---|---|---|---|---|---|

... LBM                    J (whirling) ...

**26**

| x |  | x |  | x |  | x |  | x |  | x |  | x |  | x |  |
|---|---|---|---|---|---|---|---|---|---|---|---|---|---|---|---|

...                    LBM ...

**27**

| x |  | x |  | x |  | x |  | x |  | x |  | x |  | x |  |
|---|---|---|---|---|---|---|---|---|---|---|---|---|---|---|---|

... J (being pulled out of club) ...

**28**

| x |  | x |  | x |  | x |  | x |  | x |  | x |  | x |  |
|---|---|---|---|---|---|---|---|---|---|---|---|---|---|---|---|

**29**

| x |  | x |  | x |  | x |  | x |  | x |  | x |  | x |  |
|---|---|---|---|---|---|---|---|---|---|---|---|---|---|---|---|

Example 15.3. "The Moon Is Walking," phrase shift, cycles 15, 16, 18.

15

| x |   | x |   | x | x |   | x | x | xx | x | xx | x | xx | x |   |
|---|---|---|---|---|---|---|---|---|----|---|----|---|----|---|---|
| 1 |   | r |   | 1 | r |   | 1 | r | rr | r | rr | r | rr | r |   |

16

| x | x |   | x | x |   | x | xx | x | xx | x | xx | x |   | x | x |
|---|---|---|---|---|---|---|----|---|----|---|----|---|---|---|---|
| 1 | r |   | 1 | r |   | r | rr | r | rr | r | rr | r |   | 1 | r |

18

|   | x | x |   |   | x | x | xx | x | xx | x | xx | x |   | x | x |
|---|---|---|---|---|---|---|----|---|----|---|----|---|---|---|---|
|   | 1 | r |   |   | 1 | r | rr | r | rr | r | rr | r |   | 1 | r |

clear—instances of *isicathulo* (shoe) tap dancing are reported from as early as World War I—intricate footwork is generally not part of what have been called "stamping" dances of the southern Nguni.[29] Nevertheless, the tap here does not completely merge with its Western mass-mediated models either. In fact, one of the more fascinating aspects of the tapping sequences in "The Moon Is Walking," one that harkens back to a sphere outside of commodity fetishism, is their temporal organization and the use in them of what David Rycroft has called "phrase shift."[30] What this term refers to is a phenomenon common in much African traditional performance, the fact, namely, that whereas the relationship between the call and the response remains stable within each repeated cycle the position of the musical phrases within either the call or response may shift. Obeying this principle, the dancers repeat a certain pattern several times and also modify it slightly, but above all, they shift its position within the cycle. (In order to bring these shifts out more clearly, I have in ex. 15.3 notated only the core tapping movements.)

Here, as in Jackson's transformations, serializations, and simulacra, what the subtle phrase shifts in the Black Mambazo tap sequences foreground, clearly, is the act of giving meaning. At the same time, through such rhythmic cycles black performers involved in diasporic projects distance themselves from the commodity form and the West by grounding such acts in the social forms and traditions of Africa. By chosing Ladysmith Black Mambazo as the closing act of his film, Michael Jackson on one level issues an engrossing (and bodily engrossed) statement of cultural difference and rejection. But this does not mean that, on another level, such recuperative projects escape the risk of reification. Because they are tied to specific culturally salient notions of black identity such as the badman, such projects are ambiguously caught up in the symbiosis of vernacular, counterhegemonic traditions and mass-produced fetishes.

The question, then, that students of black diasporic engagements with capitalism, modernity, and mass culture need to address is to what extent such bodily encoded and globally enacted ambiguities of black identity provide the basis for imagining alternate conceptions of social order. What the present study, along with the work of other scholars, has tried to suggest is that it is the very partiality and incompleteness of diasporic forms of the global imagination that endow black interrogations of modernity with transcending power.[31]

$$16$$

# Epilogue

## *The Art of the Impossible*

One way of reading the history of political ideas, as Peter Sloterdijk has suggested, is to see in them a series of attempts at resolving a dilemma: the paradox, namely, that the longer we undergo experiences with those of our own kind, the more evident it becomes that we do not get along with them. Therefore, Sloterdijk concludes, all known forms of politics have consisted in the art of the possible, in the ability to conceive of the widest possible community—primal horde, tribe, nation—and to ensure its survival through the successful manipulation of all-inclusive, collective imaginations and autohypnoses.[1] But, Sloterdijk cautions, the price man has to pay for achieving this goal is high, too high. In the age of hyperpolitics everything reaches a point of no return: raw materials without return, species without return, atmospheres without return, and, ultimately, human beings without return. And so, Sloterdijk concludes, in the age of the "last" people it is time to reconsider smaller forms of association in which man must learn anew the oldest art, that of reproducing man through man.[2] When all known political forms fall apart, he seems to suggest, when the supraorders of empire, the nation-state, and Eastern bloc and Western bloc disintegrate, it is time to think about new, more small-scale models for what is humanly possible.

In this book I have chosen a different line of reasoning. At the very least, what I hope to convey by the analysis of processes of globalization and the role of music in the global imagination of black South Africans, African-Americans, and Europeans is the idea that the autohypnoses, fictions of identity, and global order of the nineteenth and twentieth century, with all their contradictory intermixtures and mirrored affinities, are important if we want to formulate the rudiments of a politics of the twenty-first century. Although Sloterdijk's analysis is compelling, I do not think that the answer to the world's relentless drive toward ever vaster, ever more all-embracing forms of association lies in a new paleo-politics. Rather, I have been interested in opening up the full potential of the globalizing world by exploring musics that are at large, ubiquitous and unfettered, and by stressing the disjunctures and ambiguities of racial, national, and/or personal identities that emerge in their wake. I did not wish to reduce complexity to simplicity, hybridity to authenticity, but rather to explore the rudiments of a future politics and cultural practice as the art of the impossible.

One of these rudiments, and it is here that in the past 15 chapters I have sought to intervene in the name of a specifically musical practice of the impossible, is in the distinct forms of signifying practice developed over several hundred years within the Black Atlantic: the myriad forms of cultures and diasporic connections among Africa, the Caribbean, Europe, and the United States, and, most important perhaps, the specific black modernities that emerged from them. My question, then, has not been what truth may reside in any given musical style—and, hence, what forms of truthful living might possibly be constructed through and out of it—but rather whether the truth about Western music, pop music, Ladysmith Black Mambazo, and Michael Jackson—the truth about South Africa and the West—might not turn out to lie elsewhere, in their inescapable relatedness with each other and with all the other musics: Paul Simon's *Graceland* and Ntsikana's "Great Hymn," the Tokens' "The Lion Sleeps Tonight" and the Mint Juleps' version of "Mbube." Put another way, while there may well be some justification for the sort of strategic essentialism implied in musical constructions of modern black political cultures as pure and unified, the question is how such fictions of black solidarity may invigorate the politics of the impossible. The answer, I believe, cannot lie in a retreat into the insular, the social uterus, or the "psychospheric synchronization of the horde," as Sloterdijk calls the first forms of the humanly possible.[3] Rather, it is through the recognition of the irrevocable complicity and interdependency of people, technologies, cultural topographies, and musical practices in the last two centuries that we may begin to get a better sense of a world that is now truly one.

# Notes

## Introduction

1. Marilyn Strathern, ed., *Shifting Contexts: Transformations in Anthropological Knowledge* (London: Routledge, 1995).

2. Jean-François Lyotard, *Le postmoderne expliqué aux enfants: Correspondance, 1982–1985* (Paris: Galilée, 1986).

3. Nicholas Thomas, *Colonialism's Culture: Anthropology, Travel and Government* (Princeton: Princeton University Press, 1994), p. 24.

4. Nicholas B. Dirks, Introduction, *Colonialism and Culture* (Ann Arbor: University of Michigan Press, 1992), p. 6.

5. John A. Hobson, *Imperialism: A Study* (Ann Arbor: University of Michigan Press, 1965), p. 215.

6. Walter Benjamin, *Gesammelte Schriften*, vol. 2 (Frankfurt: Suhrkamp, 1989), p. 309.

7. Dolf Sternberger, *Panorama of the Nineteenth Century* (Oxford: Basil Blackwell, 1977), p. 83.

8. Among the best examples are Peter Manuel's informative *Cassette Culture: Popular Music and Technology in North India* (Chicago: University of Chicago Press, 1993); Christopher Waterman's study, *Juju: A Social History and Ethnography of an African Popular Music* (Chicago: University of Chicago Press, 1990); Jocelyne Guilbault, *Zouk: World Music in the West Indies* (Chicago: University of Chicago Press, 1993); and Thomas Turino, *Moving Away from Silence* (Chicago: University of Chicago Press, 1993).

9. Anthony Giddens, *Modernity and Self-Identity: Self and Society in the Late Modern Age* (Stanford: Stanford University Press, 1991), p. 18.

10. Michel Foucault, *Discipline and Punish: The Birth of the Prison* (New York: Pantheon, 1977), p. 31.

11. For a more comprehensive treatment of the politics and aesthetics of "world music" see Veit Erlmann, "The Politics and Aesthetics of Transnational Musics," *World of Music* 2 (1994): 3–15.

12. Ann L. Stoler, *Race and the Education of Desire: Foucault's History of Sexuality and the Colonial Order of Things* (Durham, NC: Duke University Press, 1995), p. 209.

13. Paul Gilroy, *The Black Atlantic: Modernity and Double Consciousness* (Cambridge: Harvard University Press, 1993), p. 36.

## Part I

1. *Review of Reviews* 4, no. 2 (September 1891): 256.

2. Quoted in *Imvo Zabantsundu* (February 4, 1892); James Stewart, *Lovedale, South Africa* (Edinburgh: Andrew Elliot, 1894), p. 70.

## Chapter 1

1. Anthony Giddens, *Modernity and Self-Identity: Self and Society in the Late Modern Age* (Cambridge: Cambridge University Press, 1991), p. 32.

2. Roland Robertson, *Globalization: Social Theory and Global Culture* (London: Sage, 1992), p. 59.

3. Fredric Jameson, *Postmodernism, Or: The Cultural Logic of Late Capitalism* (Durham, NC: Duke University Press, 1991), p. 411. Anthony Giddens, writing about the transformation of self-identity and day-to-day life under globalization, similarly speaks of the "intersection of presence and absence" (*Modernity and Self-Identity*, p. 21).

4. Eric Hobsbawm, *The Age of Revolution, 1789–1848* (New York: New American Library, 1962), p. xvi.

5. John Stuart Mill, "Civilisation," in *Collected Works of John Stuart Mill*, vol. 18: *Essays on Politics and Society* (Toronto: University of Toronto Press, 1977), p. 117.

6. Friedrich Nietzsche, *Beyond Good and Evil*, in *The Complete Works of Friedrich Nietzsche*, vol. 5 (Edinburgh: T. N. Foulis, 1909), sections 223–24.

7. Ernst Bloch, *Erbschaft dieser Zeit* (Frankfurt: Suhrkamp, 1962), pp. 382–83.

8. Walter Benjamin, *Das Passagen-Werk* (Frankfurt: Suhrkamp, 1982), p. 493.

9. The *Passagen-Werk* has not been translated into English. For an intelligent introduction to it, see Susan Buck-Morss, *The Dialectics of Seeing: Walter Benjamin and the Arcades Project* (Cambridge: MIT Press, 1989).

10. Benjamin, *Passagen-Werk*, pp. 175, 177.

11. Ibid., p. 676.

12. Ibid., pp. 1010–11.

13. Quoted in ibid., p. 168.

14. Theodor W. Adorno, *Briefe und Briefwechsel*, vol. 1 (Frankfurt: Suhrkamp, 1994), p. 141.

15. Ibid., pp. 142–43.

16. Dolf Sternberger, *Panorama of the Nineteenth Century* (Oxford: Basil Blackwell, 1977).

17. Ibid., pp. 53–54.

18. Ibid., p. 83.

19. Ibid., p. 84.

20. Ibid., p. 98.

21. Ibid., p. 119.

22. Benjamin, *Passagen-Werk*, p. 660.

23. Ibid., p. 48.

24. Walter Benjamin, *Berliner Kindheit um Neunzehnhundert* (Frankfurt: Suhrkamp, 1986), pp. 14–17.

25. Victor G. Kiernan, *Marxism and Imperialism* (New York: St. Martin's Press, 1974), p. 111.

26. Edward Said, *Culture and Imperialism* (New York: Knopf, 1993), p. xx. Other notable works that do not ignore the reality of empire are Ann L. Stoler, *Race and the Education of Desire: Foucault's History of Sexuality and the Colonial Order of Things* (Durham, NC: Duke University Press, 1995); and John Comaroff and Jean Comaroff, *Of Revelation and Revolution: Christianity, Colonialism, and Consciousness in South Africa* (Chicago: University of Chicago Press, 1991).

27. Said, *Culture and Imperialism*, p. 12.

28. Ibid., p. 22.

29. Ibid., p. 25.

30. Ibid., p. 24.

31. Ibid., p. 164.

32. Ibid., p. 163.

33. Ibid., pp. 80f. For an excellent discussion of ideas of home in England and Africa see John Comaroff and Jean Comaroff, *Ethnography and the Historical Imagination* (Boulder: Westview, 1992), pp. 265–95.

34. Eric Hobsbawm, *The Age of Empire, 1875–1914* (New York: Vintage, 1989), p. 59.

35. Sternberger, *Panorama of the Nineteenth Century*, pp. 173–74.

36. Said, *Culture and Imperialism*, pp. 221–22.

37. *Industrialisation and Social Change in South Africa: African Class Formation, Culture, and Consciousness, 1870–1930*, ed. Shula Marks and Richard Rathbone (London: Longman, 1982), pp. 9–10.

38. Comaroff and Comaroff, *Ethnography and the Historical Imagination*, p. 260.

39. Terence Ranger, *Dance and Society in Eastern Africa 1890–1970: The Beni Ngoma* (London: Heinemann, 1975), p. 166.

40. Bernard M. Magubane, *The Political Economy of Race and Class in South Africa* (New York: Monthly Review Press, 1979), p. 55.

41. See, for instance, some of the essays in *Power and the Praise Poem: Southern African Voices in History*, ed. Leroy Vail and Landeg White (Charlottesville: University of Virginia Press, 1991); *Hidden Struggles in Rural South Africa: Politics and Popular Movements in the Transkei and Eastern Cape, 1890–1930*, ed. William Beinart and Colin Bundy (Berkeley: University of California Press, 1987); and David Coplan, *In Township Tonight! South Africa's Black City Music and Theatre* (New York: Longman, 1985).

42. Comaroff and Comaroff, *Ethnography and the Historical Imagination*, p. 37.

43. I am thinking here in particular of the pioneering work by Arjun Appadurai and the contributors to his edited volume *The Social Life of Things: Commodities in Cultural Perspective* (Cambridge: Cambridge University Press, 1986), as well as Nicholas Thomas, *Entangled Objects: Exchange, Material Culture, and Colonialism in the Pacific* (Cambridge: Harvard University Press, 1991); and Daniel Miller, *Modernity: An Ethnographic Approach. Dualism and Mass Consumption in Trinidad* (Oxford: Berg, 1996). For the Zimbabwean context see Timothy Burke, *Lifebuoy Men, Lux Women: Commodification, Consumption and Cleanliness in Modern Zimbabwe* (Durham, NC: Duke University Press, 1996).

44. Keletso E. Atkins, *The Moon Is Dead! Give Us Our Money!: The Cultural Origins of an African Work Ethic, Natal, South Africa, 1843–1900* (Portsmouth, NH: Heinemann, 1993); Isabel Hofmeyr, *We Spend Our Years as a Tale That Is Told: Oral Historical Narrative*

*in a South African Chiefdom* (London: James Currey, 1993). Also see Robert J. C. Young, *Colonial Desire: Hybridity in Theory, Culture, and Race* (New York: Routledge, 1995).

45. Hofmeyr, *We Spend Our Years as a Tale That Is Told.*

46. Ibid., pp. 109−110.

47. Ibid., p. 128.

48. Ibid., p. 130.

49. Ibid., p. 131.

50. Ibid., p. 133.

51. Nietzsche, *Good and Evil*, section 262.

52. Hofmeyr, *We Spend Our Years as a Tale That Is Told*, pp. 139−59.

## Chapter 2

1. Michel de Certeau, *The Writing of History* (New York: Columbia University Press, 1988), p. 80.

2. Ibid., p. 100.

3. Ibid., p. 102.

4. Anthony Giddens, *Modernity and Self-Identity: Self and Society in the Late Modern Age* (Cambridge: Cambridge University Press, 1991), p. 54.

5. John Iliffe, *Africans: The History of a Continent* (New York: Cambridge University Press, 1995), p. 187.

6. Pierre Bourdieu, *The Biographical Illusion* (Chicago: Working Papers and Proceedings of the Center for Psychosocial Studies, no. 14, 1987).

7. de Certeau, *The Writing of History*, p. 79.

8. Friedrich Nietzsche, *Beyond Good and Evil*, in *The Complete Works of Friedrich Nietzsche*, vol. 5 (Edinburgh and London: T. N. Foulis, 1909), sections 223, 224, and 262.

9. Bourdieu, *The Biographical Illusion.*

10. John Comaroff and Jean Comaroff, *Of Revelation and Revolution: Christianity, Colonialism, and Consciousness in South Africa* (Chicago: University of Chicago Press, 1991), p. 61.

11. James Wells, *Stewart of Lovedale: The Life of James Stewart* (London: Hodder and Stoughton, 1908), p. 16.

12. John Comaroff and Jean Comaroff, *Ethnography and the Historical Imagination* (Boulder: Westview, 1992), p. 173. There is a tremendously rich literature waiting to be explored. Among some of the as-yet-unpublished diaries concerned with some of the people and places discussed in this book, one might mention Mini Stewart's "Diary of a Trip to South Africa 1886" (Cory Library, MS 9597).

13. Ibid.

14. James Clifford, *The Predicament of Culture: Twentieth-Century Ethnography, Literature, and Art* (Cambridge: Harvard University Press, 1988), pp. 110, 104.

15. "Literary Notes," *Imvo Zabantsundu* (December 24, 1896).

16. *Anthropology and Autobiography*, ed. Judith Okely and Helen Callaway (London: Routledge, 1992), p. 4. For a useful summary of the biographical method in anthropology, see also Lewis L. Langness and Gelya Frank, *Lives: An Anthropological Approach to Biography* (Novato, CA.: Chandler and Sharp, 1981).

17. Marshall Berman, *All That Is Solid Melts into Air: The Experience of Modernity* (New York: Penguin, 1982), p. 17.

18. Comaroff and Comaroff, *Ethnography and the Historical Imagination*, p. 254. See

also John L. Comaroff, "Competition for Office and Political Processes among the Barolong boo Tshidi" (Ph.D. dissertation, University of London, 1973), chap. 5.

19. Comaroff and Comaroff, *Of Revelation and Revolution*, pp. 213–30.

20. Daniel P. Kunene, *Heroic Poetry of the Basotho* (Oxford: Clarendon, 1971), pp. xvi, 1. For discussions of Zulu auriture, see also Elizabeth Gunner, "Songs of Innocence and Experience: Women as Composers and Performers of Izibongo, Zulu Praise Poetry," *Research in African Literatures* 10, no. 2 (1979):239–67; and Carol Muller, "Nazarite Song, Dance, and Dreams: The Sacralization of Time, Space, and the Female Body in South Africa" (Ph.D. dissertation, New York University, 1994).

21. For a succinct discussion of heroism and Weber's notion of personality, see Mike Featherstone, "The Heroic Life and Everyday Life," in *Undoing Culture: Globalization, Postmodernism and Identity* (London: Sage, 1995), pp. 54–71.

22. Kunene, *Heroic Poetry of the Basotho*, p. 62.

23. Quoted in David Coplan, *In the Time of the Cannibals: The Word Music of South Africa's Basotho Migrants* (Chicago: University of Chicago Press, 1994), p. 59.

24. Eugene Casalis, *The Basuto, or Twenty-three Years in South Africa* (Cape Town: C. Struik, 1965), p. 307.

25. Stephen Kern, *The Culture of Time and Space 1880–1918* (Cambridge: Harvard University Press, 1983).

26. Stanley J. Tambiah, "The Magical Power of Words," *Man* 3, no. 1 (1968):175–208.

27. Stanley Trapido, "'The Friends of the Natives': Merchants, Peasants and the Political and Ideological Structure of Liberalism in the Cape, 1854–1910," in *Economy and Society in Pre-Industrial South Africa*, ed. Shula Marks and Anthony Atmore (London: Longman, 1980), p. 247.

28. Partha Chatterjee, *Nationalist Thought and the Colonial World: A Derivative Discourse?* (Minneapolis: University of Minnesota Press, 1986), p. 168.

29. Edward Said, *Culture and Imperialism* (New York: Knopf, 1993), p. 273.

30. Alfred B. Xuma, *Charlotte Manye (Mrs. Maxeke), "What An Educated African Girl Can Do"* (n.p.: The Women's Mite Missionary Society of the AME Church, 1930), p. 9.

31. Charlotte M. Maxeke, "The Progress of Native Womanhood," in *Christianity and the Natives of South Africa*, ed. J. Dexter Taylor (Lovedale: Lovedale Press, 1928), quoted in James Campbell, *Songs of Zion: The African Methodist Episcopal Church in the United States and South Africa* (New York: Oxford University Press, 1995), p. 284.

32. Shula Marks, "Patriotism, Patriarchy, and Purity: Natal and the Politics of Zulu Ethnic Consciousness," in *The Creation of Tribalism in Southern Africa*, ed. Leroy Vail (London: James Currey, 1989); Deborah Gaitskell, "Housewives, Maids, or Mothers: Some Contradictions of Domesticity for Christian Women in Johannesburg, 1903–1939," *Journal of African History* 24 (1983):241–56.

33. *Industrialisation and Social Change in South Africa: African Class Formation, Culture, and Consciousness, 1870–1930*, ed. Shula Marks and Richard Rathbone (London: Longman, 1982), p. 226.

34. T. D. Mweli Skota, *The African Yearly Register* (Johannesburg: R. L. Esson, 1931), p. 109. Skota reproduced most of the information on Xiniwe almost verbatim from a much older source published in 1887: *Lovedale Past and Present: A Register of 2000 Names* (Lovedale: Lovedale Press).

35. James T. Campbell, "T. D. Mweli Skota and the Making and Unmaking of a Black Elite" (Johannesburg: University of the Witwatersrand, History Workshop, Feb-

ruary 9–14, 1987), p. 2. Most of my account of Skota and *The African Yearly Register* relies on Campbell's paper. Other early examples of autobiography are Everitt Segoete's largely autobiographical novel *Monono ke Moholi ke Mouane* [Riches are mist, they are vapor] (Morija, Basutoland: Morija Press, 1910).

36. Skota, *African Yearly Register*, p. 109.

37. Campbell, "T. D. Mweli Skota and the Making and Unmaking of a Black Elite," p. 5.

38. Skota, *African Yearly Register*, pp. 101, 67.

39. Robert A. Hill and Gregory A. Pirio, "'Africa for the Africans': The Garvey Movement in South Africa, 1920–1940," in *The Politics of Race, Class and Nationalism in Twentieth Century South Africa*, ed. Shula Marks and Stanley Trapido (London: Longman, 1987):209–53.

40. Quoted in Campbell, "T. D. Mweli Skota and the Making and Unmaking of a Black Elite," p. 220.

41. For recent work on the reinvention of Shaka, for instance, see Carolyn Hamilton, *Terrific Majesty: The Powers of Shaka Zulu and the Limits of Historical Invention* (Cambridge: Harvard University Press, 1998); and Leroy Vail and Landeg White, eds., *Power and the Praise Poem: Southern African Voices in History* (Charlottesville: University of Virginia Press, 1991), pp. 64–70. On the early period of African-American and black South African contacts in the 1920s, see Tim Couzens, "'Moralizing Leisure Time': The Transatlantic Connection and Black Johannesburg, 1918–1936," in Marks and Rathbone, *Industrialisation and Social Change in South Africa*, pp. 314–37.

42. B. Ntsikana, *The Life of Ntsikana: His Prophecies and His Famous Hymn* (Lovedale: Lovedale Press, 1902); John K. Bokwe, *Ntsikana: The Story of an African Convert* (Lovedale: Lovedale Press, 1914). For parallel attempts in black autobiography in the 1930s, see Gilbert Coka's autobiography in Margery Perham, *Ten Africans* (London: Faber and Faber, 1936), pp. 273–322.

*Chapter 3*

1. Mary Louise Pratt, *Imperial Eyes: Travel Writing and Transculturation* (London: Routledge, 1992).

2. Among the numerous publications on this aspect, see, for instance, Jan Nederveen Pieterse, *White on Black: Images of Africa and Blacks in Western Popular Culture* (New Haven: Yale University Press, 1992); Philip Curtin, *The Image of Africa: British Ideas and Action, 1780–1850* (Madison: University of Wisconsin Press, 1964); Andrea White, *Joseph Conrad and the Adventure Tradition* (Cambridge: Cambridge University Press, 1993), chaps. 1–3; Patrick Brantlinger, *Rule of Darkness: British Literature and Imperialism, 1830–1914* (Ithaca: Cornell University Press, 1988), chap. 6; and Tim Youngs, *Travellers in Africa: British Travelogues, 1850–1900* (Manchester: Manchester University Press, 1994).

3. Pratt, *Imperial Eyes*, p. 60.

4. Ibid., pp. 76–85.

5. Ibid., p. 85.

6. Ibid., pp. 204–5.

7. Dolf Sternberger, *Panorama of the Nineteenth Century* (Oxford: Basil Blackwell, 1977), p. 43. Interestingly, Pratt comes to a similar conclusion in pointing out the parallel between travel writing and painting (*Imperial Eyes*, p. 204f). She also suggests that the idealization of the landscape was a specifically female perspective (p. 214).

8. African-language travel writing about Europe, although extant from as early as the 1880s, has not yet been systematically studied.

9. Pratt, *Imperial Eyes*, pp. 135−36.

10. John Comaroff and Jean Comaroff, *Ethnography and the Historical Imagination* (Boulder: Westview, 1992), p. 280.

11. John Philip, *Researches in South Africa Illustrating the Civil, Moral, and Religious Condition of the Native Tribes*, vol. 2 (London, 1828), pp. 72−73.

12. Quoted in Moitsadi Thoane Moeti, "Ethiopianism: Separatist Roots of African Nationalism in South Africa" (Ph.D. dissertation, Syracuse University, 1981), p. 155.

13. Valerie Y. Mudimbe, *The Invention of Africa: Gnosis, Philosophy, and the Order of Knowledge* (Bloomington: Indiana University Press, 1988), p. 47.

14. Colin Bundy, *The Rise and Fall of the South African Peasantry* (London: Heinemann, 1979), p. 54.

15. Ibid., p. 36.

16. Stanley Trapido, "The Friends of the Natives: Merchants, Peasants and the Political and Ideological Structure of Liberalism in the Cape, 1854−1910," in *Economy and Society in Pre-Industrial South Africa*, ed. Shula Marks and Anthony Atmore (London: Longman, 1980), pp. 247−74.

17. R. H. W. Shepherd, *Bantu Literature and Life* (Lovedale: Lovedale Press, 1955), p. 73.

18. Ibid., pp. 74−75.

19. These early-nineteenth-century discourses of English missionaries to the southern Tswana are lucidly discussed in Comaroff and Comaroff, *Ethnography and the Historical Imagination*, pp. 265−95.

20. For an elaboration of the Africa-as-woman theme in imperialist ideology see Anne McClintock, *Imperial Leather: Race, Gender and Sexuality in the Colonial Conquest* (New York: Routledge, 1995), pp. 1−4, 232−57.

21. Comaroff and Comaroff, *Ethnography and the Historical Imagination*, p. 281.

22. Quoted in Rob Turrell, "Kimberley: Labour and Compounds, 1871−1888," in *Industrialisation and Social Change in South Africa: African Class Formation, Culture, and Consciousness, 1870−1930*, ed. Shula Marks and Richard Rathbone (London: Longman, 1982), p. 57.

23. *Daily Independent* (October 12, 1880).

24. Brian Willan, "An African in Kimberley: Sol T. Plaatje, 1894−1898," in Marks and Rathbone, *Industrialisation and Social Change in South Africa*, p. 239.

25. Quoted in ibid., p. 13.

26. *Diamond Fields Advertiser* (August 23, 1895).

27. Reprinted in *Outlook on a Century: South Africa 1870−1970*, ed. Francis Wilson and Dominique Perrot (Lovedale and Johannesburg: Lovedale Press and Spro-Cas, 1973), pp. 19−20.

28. Willan, "An African in Kimberley," p. 30.

29. Marks and Rathbone, *Industrialisation and Social Change in South Africa*, p. 30.

30. Ibid.

31. For the early history of publishing at Morija, see Albert S. Gérard, *Four African Literatures: Xhosa, Sotho, Zulu, Amharic* (Berkeley: University of California Press, 1971), pp. 101−8. Another early contributor to *Leselinyana* was Azariel Sekese, who wrote on Sesotho proverbs. See Leloba S. Molema, *The Image of Christianity in Sesotho Literature: Thomas Mofolo and his Contemporaries* (Hamburg: H. Buske, 1989), p. xxxi.

32. On a later occasion Semouse added another gruesome note to this somber pic-

ture of the "place of diamonds." In an article that offers detailed information on mining technology and telegraphy, Semouse reports of an accident that left more than 200 miners dead (*Leselinyana* [September 1, 1888]).

33. J. M. Coetzee, *White Writing: On the Culture of Letters in South Africa* (New Haven: Yale University Press, 1988), p. 6.

34. Daniel P. Kunene, "Written Art and Oral Tradition in Southern Africa," in *European-Language Writing in Sub-Saharan Africa*, ed. Albert Gérard (Budapest: Akademiai Kiadó, 1986), p. 1042.

35. Ibid., p. 1044. On Bunyan and early Sesotho literature, see also Daniel P. Kunene, *Thomas Mofolo and the Emergence of Written Sesotho Prose* (Johannesburg: Ravan, 1989).

36. On this point, see Gareth Stedman Jones, *Outcast London: A Study in the Relationship between Classes in Victorian Society* (Oxford: Clarendon, 1971), chaps. 13–18.

37. The entire article has been reedited by Bernth Lindfors as *A Zulu View of Victorian London* (Pasadena: California Institute of Technology, 1979).

38. Pratt, *Imperial Eyes*, p. 190.

39. Tim Couzens, "Widening Horizons of African Literature, 1870–1900," in *Literature and Society in South Africa*, ed. Landeg White and Tim Couzens (New York: Longman, 1984), p. 71.

40. McClintock, *Imperial Leather*, pp. 28–29.

41. Coetzee, *White Writing*, p. 174.

42. Ibid., p. 10.

43. Ibid., p. 177.

44. Ibid., p. 176.

45. Jones, *Outcast London*. On London and empire, see also Anthony King, *Global Cities: Post-Imperialism and the Internationalisation of London* (London: Routledge, 1990), esp. pp. 71–81.

46. Raymond Williams, *The Country and the City* (London: Chatto and Windus, 1973).

47. Ibid., p. 165.

48. Ibid., p. 180.

49. U. C. Knoepflmacher, "The Novel between City and Country," in *The Victorian City: Images and Realities*, ed. Harold J. Dyos and Michael Wolff (London: Routledge and Kegan Paul, 1973), p. 517.

50. Williams, *The Country and the City*, p. 159.

51. Henry James, *The American Scene*, introduction and notes by Leon Edel (Bloomington: Indiana University Press, 1968), p. 343.

52. G. K. Chesterton, "A Defence of Detective Stories" (1907), quoted in William B. Thesing, *The London Muse: Victorian Poetic Responses to the City* (Athens: University of Georgia Press, 1982), p. 150.

53. Fredric Jameson, *Postmodernism, Or: The Cultural Logic of Late Capitalism* (Durham, NC: Duke University Press, 1991), p. 412.

54. Quoted in Williams, *The Country and the City*, p. 215.

55. Ibid., p. 232.

56. Bang ba re: Bonang meriri ea bona e mekhutšoanyane, eka ba e kutile, matlo a bona a matšō, a mathle, ba na le linko le molomo yualeka bathō.

57. London ke motse o mogōlō hagōlō, ga ke e-s'o bone moo o fellang teng, ke thla o tlalōsa motla ke eng ke bone moo o fellang teng, ke o bontšisitse hanthle-nthle.

58. Ka kakaretso nka re, li khōlō hape li ngata hagōlō, tseo ke li bonang motseng ona, ha nka leka go li tlalōsa, nka fapana tlogo.

59. Semouse's infatuation with things British was shared by another, if somewhat more illustrious—and politically more successful—group of South African visitors only five years later: the Tswana chiefs Khama, Sebele, and Bathoen. As Neil Parson in *King Khama, Emperor Joe and the Great White Queen: Victorian Britain through African Eyes* (Chicago: University of Chicago Press, 1998), a remarkable day-to-day account of the chiefs' visit, suggests, the chiefs, like the young choristers, drew a sharp line between white settlers in South Africa and English people in England.

60. Molemo le mohau o entsoeng ke Dr. Stewart ho libini tsa Africa, ke o moholo haholo, o sé nang ho lebaloa ke batsuali le metsualle ea African Choir, hoya o sé be ka Dr. Stewart, re ka be re hasane yualeka linku tse sé nang molisa. *Leselinyana* (October 1, 1892).

61. Frantz Fanon, *The Wretched of the Earth* (New York: Grove, 1968), p. 96.

62 Raymond Williams, "Metropolitan Perceptions and the Emergence of Modernism," *The Politics of Modernism: Against the New Conformists* (London: Verso, 1989), pp. 37–48.

63. Williams, *The Country and the City*, p. 288.

## Chapter 4

1. E. Gowing Scopes, "African Music," *Ludgate Monthly* 2 (1891–92):107–12.

2. See Greg Myers, "Nineteenth-Century Popularizations of Thermodynamics and the Rhetoric of Social Prophecy," in *Energy and Entropy: Science and Culture in Victorian Britain: Essays from Victorian Studies*, ed. Patrick Brantlinger (Bloomington: Indiana University Press, 1989), pp. 307–38. For a discussion of Ludwig Boltzmann's work on entropy and its relevance for emergent modernism, see William R. Everdell, *The First Moderns: Profiles in the Origins of Twentieth-Century Thought* (Chicago: University of Chicago Press, 1997), pp. 47–62.

3. Thomas Richards, *The Imperial Archive: Knowledge and the Fantasy of Empire* (London: Verso, 1993), p. 87.

4. Ibid., p. 74.

5. Jean Baudrillard, *For a Critique of the Political Economy of the Sign* (St. Louis: Telos, 1981), p. 146.

6. Guy Debord, *The Society of the Spectacle* (New York: Zone Books, 1994), p. 12.

7. Thomas Richards, *The Commodity Culture of Victorian England: Advertising and Spectacle, 1851–1914* (Stanford: Stanford University Press, 1990), p. 16.

8. Eric J. Hobsbawm, *The Age of Capital, 1848–1875* (London: Weidenfeld and Nicolson, 1975), p. 32.

9. Walter Benjamin, *Das Passagen-Werk* (Frankfurt: Suhrkamp, 1962), p. 151.

10. A substantial amount of literature on world fairs has become available in recent years. Among the best accounts I have found are the following: Zeynep Çelik, *Displaying the Orient: Architecture of Islam at Nineteenth Century World's Fairs* (Berkeley: University of California Press, 1992); Paul Greenhalgh, *Ephemeral Vistas: The Expositions Universelles, Great Exhibitions and World's Fairs, 1851–1939* (Manchester: Manchester University Press, 1988); and Robert W. Rydell, *All the World's a Fair: Visions of Empire at American International Expositions, 1876–1916* (Chicago: University of Chicago Press, 1984).

11. Çelik, *Displaying the Orient*, p. 61.

12. Anne McClintock, "Soft-Soaping Empire: Commodity Racism and Imperial Advertising," in *Travellers' Tales: Narratives of Home and Displacement*, ed. George Robert-

son, Melinda Mash, Lisa Tickner, Jon Bird, Barry Curtis, and Tim Putnam (London: Routledge, 1994), pp. 131–54. See also Richards, *The Commodity Culture of Victorian England*, chap. 3.

13. Carol Breckenridge, "The Aesthetics and Politics of Colonial Collecting: India at World Fairs," *Comparative Studies in Society and History* 31, no. 2 (1989):195–216.

14. Eric J. Hobsbawm, *The Age of Empire, 1875–1914* (New York: Vintage, 1989), pp. 105f.

15. Ibid., p. 106. See also *Imperialism and Popular Culture*, ed. John MacKenzie (Manchester: Manchester University Press, 1982).

16. Bernth Lindfors, "The Hottentot Venus and other African Attractions in Nineteenth-Century England," *Australian Drama Studies* 1, no. 2 (1982):83–104. See also Richard D. Altick, *The Shows of London* (Cambridge: Harvard University Press, 1978), pp. 269–72.

17. Altick, *Shows of London*, pp. 279–83.

18. *Times* (London) (March 21, 1890), quoted in Annie E. Coombes, *Reinventing Africa: Museums, Material Culture and Popular Imagination in Late Victorian and Edwardian England* (New Haven: Yale University Press, 1994), p. 3. My account of the Stanley exhibit is largely based on Dr. Coombes's excellent book.

19. *The Stanley and African Catalogue of Exhibits, 1890*, p. 1, quoted in Coombes, *Reinventing Africa*, p. 81.

20. Ibid., pp. 161–86.

21. Stephan Oettermann, *Das Panorama* (Frankfurt: Syndikat, 1980), p. 9.

22. See Benjamin, *Passagen-Werk*, p. 238.

23. Michel Foucault, *Discipline and Punish: The Birth of the Prison* (New York: Pantheon, 1977), p. 217.

24. Timothy Mitchell, *Colonising Egypt* (Cambridge: Cambridge University Press, 1988), p. 13.

25. Ibid., pp. 2–5, 12.

26. Ibid., pp. 18–19.

27. Ibid., p. 13.

28. Johannes Fabian, *Time and the Other: How Anthropology Makes Its Object* (New York: Columbia University Press, 1983), p. 106. On the role of vision, more generally in Western philosophical thought and scientific imagination, see *Modernity and the Hegemony of Vision*, ed. David M. Levin (Berkeley: University of California Press, 1993). Also see Jonathan Crary, *Techniques of the Observer: On Vision and Modernity in the Nineteenth Century* (Cambridge: MIT Press, 1990).

29. Max Weber, "'Objectivity' in Social Science," in *Max Weber: Sociological Writings*, ed. Wolf Heydebrand (New York: Continuum, 1994), p. 256.

30. The full details may be gleaned from the following sources: *Imvo Zabantsundu* (January 14 and 21, 1892); *Christian Express* (February 1, March 1, August 1, and November 1, all 1892); *Cape Mercury* (March 22, 1892); and *Review of Reviews* (September 1892). Another problem that dogged the choir appears to have been caused by Paul Xiniwe having impregnated Sannie Koopman. While Xiniwe himself was expelled from the choir as a result of this affair (he and his wife returned to South Africa at the end of 1891), the mother got into even deeper waters. After giving birth to a stillborn child, she concealed the body and was consequently sentenced to one year's imprisonment. See *South Africa* (June 18, 1892).

31. *Imvo Zabantsundu* (January 14, 1892); *Cape Mercury* (March 22, 1892); interview with Kate Manye by Margaret Nixon. Thanks to Mrs. Nixon for sharing this document.

32. *Irish Times* (March 15, 1892).

33. *Christian Express* (November 2, 1891), p. 170; *Leselinyana* (December 1, 1892); *Christian Express* (March 1, 1892), p. 35.

34. Jean Baudrillard, *The Mirror of Production* (St. Louis: Telos, 1975), p. 54.

35. Mitchell, *Colonising Egypt*, p. 61.

36. John Comaroff and Jean Comaroff, *Ethnography and the Historical Imagination* (Boulder: Westview, 1992), pp. 155–80.

37. Transcript of interview with Kate Manye.

38. Jean Comaroff, "The Empire's Old Clothes: Fashioning the Colonial Subject," in *Cross-cultural Consumption: Global Markets, Local Realities*, ed. David Howes (London: Routledge, 1996), p. 35.

39. Susan Stewart, *On Longing: Narratives of Miniature, the Gigantic, the Souvenir and the Collection* (Baltimore: Johns Hopkins University Press, 1984), pp. 139–45.

40. Coombes, *Reinventing Africa*, pp. 107–8.

41. Comaroff, "Empire's Old Clothes," p. 38.

42. Margaret McCord, *The Calling of Kate Makanya* (Cape Town: David Philip, 1995).

43. Ibid., p. 42.

44. Harriet Ngubane, *Body and Mind in Zulu Medicine: An Ethnography of Health and Disease in Nyuswa-Zulu Thought and Practice* (New York: Academic Press, 1977), p. 149.

45. Clement Doke and Benedict W. Vilakazi, *Zulu-English Dictionary*, 2d ed. rev. with addendum (Johannesburg: Witwatersrand University Press, 1972); Axel-Ivar Berglund, *Zulu Thought-Patterns and Symbolism* (Bloomington: Indiana University Press, 1989), pp. 290–95.

46. On this point, see Ralph Austen, "The Moral Econonmy of Witchcraft: An Essay in Comparative History," in *Modernity and Its Malcontents: Ritual and Power in Postcolonial Africa*, ed. Jean Comaroff and John Comaroff (Chicago: University of Chicago Press, 1993), pp. 89–110.

## Chapter 5

1. For a useful treatment of this period, see Clifton C. Crais, *White Supremacy and Black Resistance in Pre-Industrial South Africa: The Making of the Colonial Order in the Eastern Cape, 1770–1865* (New York: Witwatersrand University Press, 1992).

2. Ibid., p. 100.

3. For an excellent account of these two historical figures, see Jeffrey Peires, *The House of Phalo: A History of the Xhosa People in the Days of Their Independence* (Berkeley: University of California Press, 1982), pp. 69–74.

4. Janet Hodgson, *Ntsikana's "Great Hymn": A Xhosa Expression of Christianity in the Early Nineteenth Century Eastern Cape* (Cape Town: University of Cape Town, Centre for African Studies, 1980), p. 5.

5. Peires, *The House of Phalo*, pp. 73–74.

6. Ibid., p. 74.

7. J. Brownlee, *A Few Brief Details Referring to Two Prominent Characters (Makanda and Ntsikana) Mentioned in the School Book, Compiled by the Rev. J. Bennie* (Cape Town: Grey Collection, n.d.); A. Kropf, "Ntsikana, der Erstling aus den Kaffern und ein Prophet unter seinem Volk," *Berliner Missions-Freund* (June–August and October–December 1888).

8. S. E. K. Mqhayi, *Isikumbuzo zom Polofiti uNtsikana* (Johannesburg, 1926); M. Pelem,

*Umongameli We Sikumbuzo So Mprofiti u-Ntsikana Gaba* (King William's Town, n.d. [ca. 1916]); B. Ntsikana, *The Life of Ntsikana: His Prophecies and His Famous Hymn* (Lovedale: Lovedale Press, 1902). Note also that John K. Bokwe's biography of Ntsikana published in 1914 in its subtitle calls Ntsikana "an African convert" (*Ntsikana: The Story of an African Convert* [Lovedale: Lovedale Press, 1914]).

9. Bowke, *Ntsikana*, p. 4.

10. Bengt G. Sundkler, *Bantu Prophets in South Africa* (Oxford: Oxford University Press, 1961), pp. 109, 256.

11. For the East African context, see, for instance, David M. Anderson and Douglas H. Johnson eds., *Revealing Prophets: Prophecy in Eastern African History* (London: James Currey, 1995).

12. Partha Chatterjee, *Nationalist Thought and the Colonial World: A Derivative Discourse?* (Minneapolis: University of Minnesota Press, 1986), p. 38.

13. Ibid., p. 169.

14. Ibid., p. 42.

15. Ibid., pp. 50f.

16. Nicholas B. Dirks, Introduction, *Colonialism's Culture: Anthropology, Travel and Government* (Princeton: Princeton University Press, 1994), p. 3.

17. Marcia Wright, "Maji Maji: Prophecy and Historiography," in Anderson and Johnson, p. 125.

18. Chatterjee, *Nationalist Thought and the Colonial World*, p. 51.

19. Hodgson, *Ntsikana's "Great Hymn,"* pp. 14–21.

20. Ibid., pp. 22–26. See also Jeff Opland, *Xhosa Oral Poetry: Aspects of a Black South African Tradition* (Cambridge: Cambridge University Press, 1983), p. 214.

21. Hodgson, *Ntsikana's "Great Hymn,"* p. 26.

22. John Philip, *Researches in South Africa* (London, 1828), quoted in R. H. W. Shepherd, *Bantu Literature and Life* (Lovedale: Lovedale Press, 1955), p. 164.

23. David Dargie, "The Music of Ntsikana," *South African Journal of Musicology* 2 (1982):7–28.

24. Hugh Tracey, "Ulo, tixo omkhulu," *The Sound of Africa* (TR 26, Roodepoort, 1957), side B, track 1.

25. Dargie, "The Music of Ntsikana," p. 11.

26. Ibid., p. 12.

27. See, inter alia, "Ntsikana's Vision," a poem by Isaac Wauchope, one of the first examples of literature in English written by an African author (reprinted in *The Return of the Amasi Bird: Black South African Poetry, 1891–1981*, ed. Tim Couzens and Essop Patel [Johannesburg: Ravan, 1982]); also the choral song titled "U-Ntsikana" by the well-known composer Benjamin Tyamzashe (Lovedale: Lovedale Press, 1949).

28. Jacques P. Malan, ed., *South African Music Encyclopedia*, vol. 1 (Cape Town: Oxford University Press, 1979), pp. 201f; F. Z. van der Merwe, *Suid-Afrikaanse Musiekbibliografie, 1787–1952* (Pretoria: J. L. van Schaik, 1958).

29. Malan, *South African Music Encyclopedia*, p. 201.

30. Hodgson, *Ntsikana's "Great Hymn,"* pp. 22, 71.

31. Partha Chatterjee, *The Nation and Its Fragments: Colonial and Postcolonial Histories* (Princeton: Princeton University Press, 1993), p. 14.

32. Ibid., p. 22.

33. Dirks, Introduction, p. 4.

34. Quoted in Hodgson, *Ntsikana's "Great Hymn,"* p. 68.

35. Isaac Wauchope, *The Natives and Their Missionaries* (Lovedale: Lovedale Press, 1908), p. 22.

36. Archibald C. Jordan, *Towards an African Literature: The Emergence of Literary Form in Xhosa* (Berkeley: University of California Press, 1973), pp. 50–51.

37. Quoted in Hodgson, Ntsikana's "Great Hymn," p. 77.

38. "Kaffir Poetry," *Kaffir Express* 4, no. 47 (August 1, 1874).

39. Colin Bundy, *The Rise and Fall of the South African Peasantry* (London: Heinemann, 1979), p. 137.

40. *Bradford Daily Telegraph* (September 10, 1891).

41. *South Africa* (July 4, 1891), p. 17.

42. *Musical Standard* (July 11, 1891).

43. Renato Rosaldo, *Culture and Truth: The Remaking of Social Analysis* (Boston: Beacon, 1989).

44. Rider Haggard, "A Zulu War-Dance," *Gentleman's Magazine* (July–September 1877), p. 96.

45. See also Robert J. C. Young, *Colonial Desire: Hybridity in Theory, Culture, and Race* (London: Routledge, 1995), p. 26.

46. *Musical Times* 32 (August 1, 1891):483.

## Chapter 6

1. Colin Bundy, *The Rise and Fall of the South African Peasantry* (London: Heinemann, 1979), pp. 165–66.

2. *Inkanyiso Yase Natal* (hereafter *Inkanyiso*) (November 5, 1891).

3. On Saul Msane, see Solomon T. Plaatje, "Mr. Saul Msane: Death of a Rand Native Leader," *African World* (October 25, 1919).

4. *Weekly Dispatch* (June 12, 1892).

5. Memorandum of Agreement, Ladysmith, Zulu Choir Papers, Natal Provincial Archives (December 16, 1891).

6. Letter by Holloway, Illing & Co. to the Editor, *South Africa* (October 22, 1892).

7. *Inkanyiso* (February 24, 1893).

8. *Inkanyiso* (March 17, 1892).

9. Norman Etherington, *Preachers, Peasants, and Politics in Southeast Africa, 1835–1880: African Christian Communities in Natal, Pondoland, and Zululand* (London: Royal Historical Society, 1978), p. 24.

10. The best study on Shepstone and Natal's "native" policy remains David Welsh, *The Roots of Segregation: Native Policy in Colonial Natal, 1845–1910* (Cape Town: Oxford University Press, 1971).

11. Ibid., p. 246.

12. *Natal Witness* (March 27, 1863).

13. On Edendale, see Bundy, *The Rise and Fall of the South African Peasantry*, pp. 179–80; and Etherington, *Preachers, Peasants, and Politics in Southeast Africa*, pp. 111–14.

14. On Herbert Dhlomo, see Tim Couzens, *The New African: A Study of the Life and Work of H. I. E. Dhlomo* (Johannesburg: Ravan, 1985). On Reuben Caluza, see Veit Erlmann, *African Stars: Studies in Black South African Performance* (Chicago: University of Chicago Press, 1991), pp. 112–55. On Alfred A. Kumalo, see David K. Rycroft, "Black South African Urban Music since the 1890s: Some Reminiscences of Alfred Assegai Kumalo (1879–1966)," *African Music* 7, no. 1 (1991):5–31.

15. F. Reginald Statham, *Blacks, Boers and British: A Three-Cornered Problem* (London: Macmillan, 1881), p. 182.

16. Etherington, *Preachers, Peasants, and Politics in Southeast Africa*, pp. 135–38. See also Welsh, *The Roots of Segregation*, pp. 262–68.

17. Etherington, *Preachers, Peasants, and Politics in Southeast Africa*, pp. 159, 161. See also Bengt G. Sundkler, *Bantu Prophets in South Africa* (Oxford: Oxford University Press, 1961), pp. 38–64.

18. *South Africa* (June 11 and July 2, 1892). On Colenso, see Jeff Guy, *The Heretic: A Study of the Life of John William Colenso, 1814–1883* (Johannesburg: Ravan, 1983).

19. Quoted in Hugh Tracey, *Lalela Zulu: 100 Zulu Lyrics* (Johannesburg: African Music Society, 1948), pp. 35, 97.

20. *Ilanga Lase Natal* (June 12, 1911).

21. Welsh, *Roots of Segregation*, p. 318.

22. *Inkanyiso* (March 10, 1892).

23. *Weekly Dispatch* (June 5, 1892).

24. *Inkanyiso* (May 5, 1892).

25. *South Africa* (June 4 and 11, 1892).

26. Shula Marks, *Reluctant Rebellion: The 1906–8 Disturbances in Natal* (Oxford: Clarendon, 1970), p. 58. See also Nicholas Cope, "The Zulu Petit Bourgeoisie and Zulu Nationalism in the 1920s: Origins of Inkatha," *Journal of Southern African Studies* 16, no. 3 (1990):431–51.

## Chapter 7

1. John W. Cell, *The Highest Stage of White Supremacy: The Origins of Segregation in South Africa and the American South* (Cambridge: Cambridge University Press, 1982), p. 22.

2. Thanks to Bernth Lindfors for assistance in tracking down this photograph. For the personnel of the first group, see *Imvo Zabantsundu* (February 1, 1893).

3. *Halifax Herald* (March 20, 1893); *Montreal Daily Herald* (April 1, 1893); *Toronto Daily Mail* (April 8, 1893; *Gazette* (April 12, 1893). On the choir in Ohio, see *Cleveland Gazette* (November 3 and November 10, 1894); on Charles S. Morris, see Walter L. Williams, *Black Americans and the Evangelization of Africa, 1877–1900* (Madison: University of Wisconsin Press, 1982).

4. See Reverdy C. Ransom, *The Pilgrimage of Harriet Ransom's Son* (Nashville: Sunday School Union, n.d.).

5. André Odendaal, *Vukani Bantu! The Beginnings of Black Protest Politics in South Africa to 1912* (Cape Town: David Philip, 1984), pp. 7–10. See also Les Switzer, *Power and Resistance in an African Society: The Ciskei Xhosa and the Making of South Africa* (Madison: University of Wisconsin Press, 1993), p. 151.

6. Quoted in Archibald C. Jordan, *Towards an African Literature: The Emergence of Literary Form in Xhosa* (Berkeley: University of California Press, 1973), p. 93.

7. Quoted in Albert S. Gérard, *Four African Literatures: Xhosa, Sotho, Zulu, Amharic* (Berkeley: University of California Press, 1971), p. 40.

8. Although the classic work on Ethiopianism remains Bengt Sundkler's *Bantu Prophets*, a useful, if not always reliable, historical account is J. Mutero Chirenje, *Ethiopianism and Afro-Americans in Southern Africa, 1883–1916* (Baton Rouge: Louisiana State University Press, 1987). The definitive account of the AME Church (and its early "Ethiopian" connections in South Africa) is James Campbell's *Songs of Zion: The African Methodist Episcopal*

*Church in the United States and South Africa* (New York: Oxford University Press, 1995). My summary of the early years relies on chapter 4 of Dr. Campbell's remarkable book.

9. For a full account of McAdoo's tours, see Veit Erlmann, *African Stars: Studies in Black South African Performance* (Chicago: University of Chicago Press, 1991), pp. 21–53.

10. *Cape Argus* (July 1, 1890).

11. *Imvo Zabantsundu* (October 16, 1890).

12. *South African Citizen* (December 1, 1897); *Southern Workman* (April 1882), p. 43.

13. "Likheleke tsa America," *Leselinyana* (October 1, 1890). "Uthluang! Kayen', ba na le likolo tsa bona tse kh'l' le tse nyennyane, li mathleng a bona ka nthlè go thuso ea makhooa. Ba na le baatlōli, le banna ba lekhothla, le bomagistrata, le liagent, le bobishopo, le baruti le baboleli, ka balisa ba likolo. Ba Bang ba ithutile mesebestsi ea matsogo, e yualeka bogagi, bolali etc., etc. Na tsatsi le thla chaba neōng leo ka lona batho ba Africa ba thlang o touana le Ba-America? Ba tsuele pele e sé makhoba, e le chaba tse mebusong ea tsona?"

14. Quoted in interview of Kate Manye conducted by Margaret McCord. For the Bohee Brothers, see Eileen Southern, *The Music of Black Americans: A History*, 2d ed. (New York: Norton, 1983), pp. 220, 234, 236, 300.

15. Helen Bradford, *A Taste of Freedom: The ICU in Rural South Africa 1924–1930* (New Haven: Yale University Press, 1987), pp. 214–18.

16. W. E. B. Du Bois, *The Souls of Black Folk* (New York: New American Library, 1969), p. xi.

17. Campbell, *Songs of Zion*, pp. 64, 398.

18. Ibid., p. 82. On Merriman, see Vivian Bickford-Smith, *Ethnic Pride and Racial Prejudice in Victorian Cape Town: Group Identity and Social Practice, 1875–1902* (Cambridge: Cambridge University Press, 1995), p. 138.

19. *Leselinyana* (October 1, 1890).

20. *Freeman* (October 26, 1895).

21. Campbell, *Songs of Zion*, p. 81.

22. *Freeman* (October 26, 1895).

23. Campbell, *Songs of Zion*, p. 99. On African-American notions about Africa and the role of African-American missionization, see also Williams, *Black Americans and the Evangelization of Africa, 1877–1900* (Madison, Wis.: University of Wisconsin Press, 1982).

24. See also George M. Fredrickson, *Black Liberation: A Comparative History of Black Ideologies in the United States and South Africa* (New York: Oxford University Press, 1995).

25. Paul Gilroy, *The Black Atlantic: Modernity and Double Consciousness* (Cambridge: Harvard University Press, 1993), p. 73.

26. Campbell, *Songs of Zion*, p. 132.

27. Ibid., pp. 211, 198–202.

28. For useful summaries, see Guthrie P. Ramsey, Jr., "Cosmopolitan or Provincial?: Ideology in Early Black Music Historiography, 1867–1940," *Black Music Research Journal* 16, no. 1 (1996):11–42.

29. Gilroy, *The Black Atlantic*, pp. 37–38, 44–45.

30. Ibid., pp. 73–76.

31. Ibid., pp. 36, 75f.

32. For the battle over music in the early AME Church see Southern, *The Music of Black Americans*, pp. 80–88, 127–31; and Campbell, *Songs of Zion*, pp. 41ff.

33. On respectability and African Methodists' dilemma, see also Campbell, *Songs of Zion*, p. 50.

34. Ronald Radano, "Denoting Difference: The Writing of the Slave Spirituals," *Critical Inquiry* 22, no. 3 (1996):508.

35. Ibid., p. 544.

36. Gilroy, *The Black Atlantic*, p. 91.

37. *Inkanyiso* (November 5, 1891).

38. For details on this group, see Campbell, *Songs of Zion*, pp. 252–94.

39. On Gow, see *Umteteli wa Bantu* (May 4, 1934) and *R. Langham-Carter Papers* (KABA, A 1691). For more details on this period, see Erlmann, *African Stars*, pp. 50–53. It still remains to be ascertained whether phonograph recordings of black American music had an impact, however limited, on South African musicians. Contary to Charles Hamm's assertion that such direct influence did not occur before the 1950s, a 1941 handbill by the South African Cultural Club that announces "A Grand Musical Evening" with "American Workers' and Negro Songs, from Records Just Arrived in South Africa" seems to suggest otherwise (Institute of Race Relations, ABX.410705e).

40. *Umteteli wa Bantu* (April 16, 1927).

41. Fredrickson, *Black Liberation*, pp. 91–92.

42. The best account of this period and of the strengthening transatlantic ties is Tim Couzens, "'Moralizing Leisure Time': The Transatlantic Connection and Black Johannesburg, 1918–1936," in *Industrialisation and Social Change in South Africa: African Class Formation, Culture, and Consciousness, 1870–1930*, ed. Shula Marks and Richard Rathbone (London: Longman, 1982), pp. 314–37.

43. *South African Christian Recorder* (August 15, 1925). On Booker T. Washington's influence in South Africa, see Tim Couzens, *The New African: A Study of the Life and Work of H. I. E. Dhlomo* (Johannesburg: Ravan, 1985), p. 84.

44. Quoted in Couzens, *The New African*, p. 115, n.7.

45. Campbell, *Songs of Zion*, p. 271; Wilson J. Moses, *The Golden Age of Black Nationalism, 1850–1925* (Hamden, CT: Archon, 1978).

46. *Umteteli wa Bantu* (May 4, 1929). Another article by African-American churchman H. H. Proctor discussed "The Theology of the Old American Slave Songs," *Umteteli wa Bantu* (November 6, 1926). Johnson's views are nicely echoed in the preface to a tonic sol-fa collection of spirituals that missionary Alexander Sandilands was busy compiling in the early 1940s: "[The spirituals] are a legacy to which all Africa has a right [and that] still strikes a chord in true African hearts" (*A Hundred and Twenty Negro Spirituals* [Morija, Basutoland, Morija Press, 1951]).

47. *Umteteli wa Bantu* (December 18, 1926).

48. *Umteteli wa Bantu* (April 16, 1927).

49. Gilroy, *The Black Atlantic*, pp. 124–45.

## Chapter 8

1. *South African Citizen* (August 18, 1897); Les Switzer, *Power and Resistance in an African Society: The Ciskei Xhosa and the Making of South Africa* (Madison: University of Wisconsin Press, 1993), p. 170.

2. For Charlotte Maxeke's career after 1894, see James Campbell, *Songs of Zion: The African Methodist Episcopal Church in the United States and South Africa* (New York: Oxford University Press, 1995), pp. 282–94. Another useful source is Cherryl Walker, *Women and Resistance in South Africa* (London: Onyx, 1982), pp. 36–40.

3. Margaret McCord, *The Calling of Kate Makanya* (Cape Town: David Philip, 1995).

4. Campbell, *Songs of Zion*, p. 287.


*Part II*

1. The statement is by South African African music scholar Andrew Tracey, in "A Word from the Editor," *African Music* 6, no. 4, 1987, p. 3.

2. Rob Nixon, *Homelands, Harlem and Hollywood: South African Culture and the World Beyond* (New York: Routledge, 1994), p. 165; *Newsweek* (November 17, 1986).

3. George Lipsitz, *Dangerous Crossroads: Popular Music, Postmodernism and the Poetics of Place* (London: Verso, 1994), p. 61.

4. Nixon, *Homelands*, p. 83.


*Chapter 9*

1. Eric J. Hobsbawm, *Age of Extremes: The Short Twentieth Century, 1914–1991* (London: Michael Joseph, 1994).

2. Arjun Appadurai, *Modernity at Large: Cultural Dimensions of Globalization* (Minneapolis: University of Minnesota Press, 1996), p. 3.

3. Hobsbawm, *Age of Extremes*, p. 14.

4. The point is elaborated very aptly by Dipesh Chakrabarty in "Provincializing Europe: Postcoloniality and the Critique of History," *Cultural Studies* 6, no. 3 (1992):337–57.

5. Ibid., p. 352. Chakrabarty's example is India, of course.

6. Scott Lash, "Discourse or Figure? Postmodernism as a 'Regime of Signification,'" *Theory, Culture and Society* 5 (1988):311–36.

7. Steven Connor, "The Modern Auditory I," in *Rewriting the Self: Histories from the Renaissance to the Present*, ed. Roy Porter, (London: Routledge, 1997), pp. 208–9.

8. Appadurai, *Modernity at Large*, p. 31.

9. Ibid., p. 7.

10. Zygmunt Bauman, *Modernity and Ambivalence* (Cambridge: Polity Press, 1991).

11. Michel Maffesoli, *The Contemplation of the World: Figures of Community Style* (Minneapolis: University of Minnesota Press, 1996), p. 125.

12. For a particularly suggestive anthropological elaboration, see Michael Taussig, *Mimesis and Alterity: A Particular History of the Senses* (New York: Routledge, 1993).

13. Maffesoli, *The Contemplation of the World*, p. 34.

14. Ibid., p. 10.

15. The most prominent text in this regard is perhaps Judith Butler, *Gender Trouble: Feminism and the Subversion of Identity* (New York: Routledge, 1990).


*Chapter 10*

1. *Encyclopaedia Britannica*, 11th ed. (New York, 1910), p. 737.

2. Rob Nixon, *Homelands, Harlem and Hollywood* (New York: Routledge, 1994), p. 172.

3. Renato Rosaldo, *Culture and Truth: The Remaking of Social Analysis* (Boston: Beacon, 1989).

4. Edward Said, *Culture and Imperialism* (New York: Knopf, 1993), p. 189.

5. Lieven de Cauter, "The Panoramic Ecstasy: On World Exhibitions and the Disintegration of Experience," *Theory, Culture and Society* 10 (1993):1–23.

6. Said, *Culture and Imperialism*, pp. 189f.

7. Will Straw, "Popular Music and Postmodernism in the 1980s," in *Sound and Vision: The Music Video Reader*, ed. Simon Frith, Andrew Goodwin, and Lawrence Grossberg (London: Routledge, 1993), pp. 10–11.

8. Ibid., p. 11.

9. Lawrence Grossberg, *We Gotta Get out of this Place: Popular Conservatism and Post-modern Culture* (New York: Routledge, 1992), p. 148.

10. Ibid., p. 158.

11. Charles Hamm, "Graceland Revisited," in *Putting Popular Music in Its Place* (Cambridge: Cambridge University Press, 1995), pp. 342–43.

12. Ibid., p. 343.

13. All these citations are from *Newsweek* (November 17, 1986).

14. Steven Feld, "From Schizophonia to Schismogenesis: On the Discourses and Commodification Practices of "World Music' and 'World Beat,'" in *Music Grooves*, Charles Keil and Steven Feld (Chicago: University of Chicago Press, 1994), pp. 270–72.

15. Jacques Attali, *Noise: The Political Economy of Music* (Minneapolis: University of Minnesota Press, 1985), p. 118.

16. John Shepherd and Peter Wicke, *Music and Cultural Theory* (Cambridge: Polity Press, 1997), p. 95.

17. Ibid., pp. 116–17.

18. Ibid., pp. 95–96.

19. Ibid., p. 116.

20. Gregory Bateson, *Ecology of the Mind* (Boston: Arcade, 1987), p. 413.

21. Paul Virilio, *Die Eroberung des Körpers* (Munich: Hanser, 1995), p. 62.

22. Murray Schafer, *The Tuning of the World* (New York: Knopf, 1977), p. 91.

23. Neil Lazarus, "Unsystematic Fingers at the Conditions of the Time: 'Afropop' and the Paradoxes of Imperialism," in *Recasting the World: Writing after Colonialism*, ed. Jonathan White (Baltimore: Johns Hopkins University Press, 1994), p. 142.

24. John Shepherd, "Music and Male Hegemony," in *Music and Society: The Politics of Composition, Performance and Reception*, ed. Richard Leppert and Susan McClary (Cambridge: Cambridge University Press, 1987), p. 167.

25. For a discussion of the political connotations of such black South African decodings, see Louise Meintjes, "Paul Simon's *Graceland*, South Africa, and the Mediation of Musical Meaning," *Ethnomusicology* 34, no. 1 (1990):37–73.

26. Patrick Humphries, *Paul Simon: Still Crazy after All These Years* (New York: Doubleday, 1989), p. 132.

27. Antoine Hennion, "The Production of Success: An Antimusicology of the Pop Song," in ed. Simon Frith and Andrew Goodwin, *On Record: Rock, Pop and the Written Word* (New York: Pantheon, 1990), pp. 185–206.

28. Humphries, *Paul Simon*, p. xi.

29. Ibid., p. 156.

## Chapter 11

1. Patrick Humphries. *Paul Simon: Still Crazy after All These Years* (New York: Doubleday, 1989), p. 156.

2. I have documented elsewhere in considerable detail the history of *isicathamiya* and shall therefore content myself here with an outline of its main trajectories and ac-

tors. See Veit Erlmann, *Nightsong: Performance, Power, and Practice in South Africa* (Chicago: University of Chicago Press, 1996).

3. Caesar Nldovu, "Religion, Tradition and Custom in a Zulu Male Vocal Idiom" (Ph.D. dissertation, Rhodes University, 1996), pp. 149ff.

4. See also Erlmann, *Nightsong*, pp. 218f; and Musa Xulu, "The Re-Emergence of Amahubo Song Styles and Ideas in Some Modern Zulu Musical Styles" (Ph.D. dissertation, University of Natal, 1992).

5. Hoyt Alverson, *Mind in the Heart of Darkness: Value and Self-Identity among the Tswana of Southern Africa* (New Haven: Yale University Press, 1978), p. 193.

6. David B. Coplan, "A Terrible Commitment: Balancing the Tribes in South African National Culture," in George E. Marcus, ed., *Perilous States: Conversations on Culture, Politics, and Nation* (Chicago: University of Chicago Press, 1993), p. 323.

7. For a useful assessment of this era, see Alfred William Stadler, *The Political Economy of Modern South Africa* (New York: St. Martin's Press, 1987), p. 174.

8. Dunbar Moodie, *Going for Gold: Men, Mines and Migrants* (Berkeley: University of California Press, 1994), p. 42.

9. See Colin Murray, "Migrant Labour and Changing Family Structure in the Rural Periphery of Southern Africa," *Journal of Southern African Studies* 6, no. 2 (1980):139–56.

10. See also some of the articles in Philip Mayer, *Black Villagers in an Industrial Society: Anthropological Perspectives on Labor Migration in South Africa* (Cape Town: Oxford University Press, 1980).

11. Erlmann, *Nightsong*, p. 252. See also Charles Hamm, "The Constant Companion of Man: Separate Development, Radio Bantu, and Music," in *Putting Popular Music in Its Place* (Cambridge: Cambridge University Press, 1995), pp. 230–32.

12. *Bantu Education Journal* (April 1971), p. 7.

13. Yvonne Huskisson, *The Bantu Composers of Southern Africa* (Johannesburg: South African Broadcasting Corporation, 1969).

14. Alexius Buthelezi, *Cothoza Mfana* (Pietermaritzburg: Reachout Publications, 1996).

15. Rob Nixon, *Homelands, Harlem and Hollywood: South African Culture and the World Beyond* (New York: Routledge, 1994), p. 250. For a more nuanced treatment of migrant workers and violence in Natal, see Catherine Campbell, "Learning to Kill? Masculinity, the Family and Violence in Natal," *Journal of Southern African Studies* 18, no. 3 (1992): 614–28.

16. Greytown Evening Birds, "Sanibonani Nonke MaAfrika" (Heritage HT 313, 1982).

17. James W. Fernandez, "The Argument of Images and the Experience of Returning to the Whole," in *The Anthropology of Experience*, ed. Victor W. Turner and Edward M. Bruner (Urbana: University of Illinois Press, 1986), pp. 59–187.

18. Paul Gilroy, *Small Acts: Thoughts on the Politics of Black Cultures* (London: Serpent's Tail, 1993), p. 134.

*Chapter 12*

1. Rob Nixon, *Homelands, Harlem and Hollywood: South African Culture and the World Beyond* (New York: Routledge, 1994), p. 3.

2. I am indebted to Doug Seroff for making a copy of this video available to me.

3. *Shaka Zulu* (Warner Brothers 25582, HUL40157).

4. Another film in this genre is *A Brother with Perfect Timing*, a documentary that stars Abdullah Ibrahim (New York: Rhapsody Films, 1988).

5. Alex J. Thembela and Edmund P. M. Radebe, *The Life and Works of Joseph Shabalala and the Ladysmith Black Mambazo* (Pietermaritzburg: Reach Out Publishers, 1993).

6. Nikolas Rose, "Assembling the Modern Self," in *Rewriting the Self: Histories from the Renaissance to the Present*, ed. Roy Porter (London: Routledge, 1997), pp. 224–48.

7. Thembela and Radebe, *Life and Works*, p. 17–00.

8. Ibid., pp. 18–19.

9. See Carolyn Hamilton, *Terrific Majesty: The Powers of Shaka Zulu and the Limits of Historical Invention* (Cambridge: Harvard University Press, 1998), p. 204.

10. Thembela and Radebe, *The Life and Works*, p. 22.

11. Ibid., pp. 33–37.

12. Clifford Geertz, *Local Knowledge: Further Essays in Interpretive Anthropology* (New York: Basic Books, 1983), p. 59. Among the texts that question this charge are the following: Anthony P. Cohen, *Self Consciousness: An Alternative Anthropology of Identity* (London: Routledge, 1994); and Melford Spiro, "Is the Western Conception of the Self 'Peculiar' within the Context of World Cultures?" *Ethos* 21 (1993):107–53. Within the context of Zulu conceptions of the self, see the evidence in Axel-Ivar Berglund, *Zulu Thought-Patterns and Symbolism* (Bloomington: Indiana University Press, 1989), pp. 82–88.

13. Rose, "Assembling the Modern Self," p. 226.

14. Among the more influential philosophical formulations of this notion are Foucault's "aesthetics of existence" and Richard Rorty's "aesthetic life" (*Contingency, Irony, and Solidarity* [Cambridge: Cambridge University Press, 1989]).

15. Simon Frith, *Performing Rites: On the Value of Popular Music* (Cambridge: Harvard University Press, 1996), p. 185.

16. This is another way of saying, as Simon Frith does, that capitalist control of popular music rests not on record company control of recording technology but on its recurring appropriation of fans' and musicians' ideology of art. See Simon Frith, "Art versus Technology: The Strange Case of Popular Music," *Media, Culture and Society* 8, no. 3 (1986):278.

17. Antoine Hennion, "The Production of Success," in *On Record: Rock, Pop, and the Written Word*, ed. Simon Frith and Andrew Goodwin (New York: Pantheon, 1990), pp. 185–206, 200–201.

18. *Journey of Dreams* (Warner Brothers 25753, HUL40170).

19. Ian R. Phimister and Charles van Onselen, "The Political Economy of Tribal Animosity: A Case Study of the 1929 Bulawayo Location 'Faction Fights,'" *Journal of Southern African Studies* 6, no. 1 (1979):1–43.

20. Jonathan Clegg, "Ukubuyisa Isidumbu—Bringing Back the Body: An Examination into the Ideology of Vengeance in the Msinga and Mpofana Rural Locations, 1882–1944," in *Working Papers in Southern African Studies*, vol 2, ed. Philip Bonner (Johannesburg: Ravan, 1981), pp. 164–98; Jonathan Clegg, "Towards an Understanding of African Dance: The Zulu Isishameni Style," in *Papers Presented at the Second Symposium on Ethnomusicology*, ed. Andrew Tracey (Grahamstown: International Library of African Music, 1982), p. 4.

21. Clegg, "Towards an Understanding of African Dance," p. 9.

22. Empangeni Home Tigers, *Ufakazi Yibheshu* (Mavuthela BL 22, 1974).

23. Robert Thornton, "The Colonial, the Imperial, and the Creation of the 'European' in Southern Africa," in *Occidentalism: Images of the West*, ed. James G. Carrier (New York: Oxford University Press, 1995), pp. 192–217.

24. See Zygmunt Bauman, "From Pilgrim to Tourist—or a Short History of Identity," in *Questions of Cultural Identity*, ed. Stuart Hall and Paul Du Gay (London: Sage, 1996), pp. 18–36.

25. Ibid., p. 21.

26. Michel de Certeau, *The Writing of History* (New York: Columbia University Press, 1988), p. 219.

27. Veit Erlmann, *Nightsong: Performance, Power, and Practice in South Africa* (Chicago: University of Chicago Press, 1996), pp. 191–97.

28. Rose, "Assembling the Modern Self," p. 246.

29. Timothy Mitchell, *Colonising Egypt* (Cambridge: Cambridge University Press, 1988), p. 35; Sidney W. Mintz, *Sweetness and Power: The Place of Sugar in Modern History* (New York: Viking, 1985); Gwendolyn Wright, *The Politics of Design in French Colonial Urbanism* (Chicago: University of Chicago Press, 1991).

*Chapter 13*

1. Tug Yourgrau, *The Song of Jacob Zulu* (New York: Arcade, 1993).

2. The actual trial is discussed by Fatima Meer in *The Trial of Andrew Zondo: A Sociological Insight* (Johannesburg: Skotaville, 1987).

3. Yourgrau, *The Song of Jacob Zulu*, p. xii.

4. Ibid., p. ix.

5. Richard A. Wilson, "The Sizwe Will Not Go Away: The Truth and Reconciliation Commission, Human Rights and Nation-Building in South Africa," *African Studies* 55, no. 2 (1996):7.

6. Ibid., pp. 14–18.

7. Yourgrau, *The Song of Jacob Zulu*, p. x.

8. Ibid., p. xi.

9. Brochure in Archives, Hampton University; *Hampton Student* (May 1, 1913).

10. The Curtis-Burlin recordings are housed in the Archives of Traditional Music, Indiana University (tape nos. 1546.1–8). Transcriptions of these recordings were published in Natalie Curtis, *Songs and Tales from the Dark Continent: Recorded from the Singing and the Sayings of C. Kamba Simango, Ndau Tribe, Portuguese East Africa, and Madikane Cele, Zulu Tribe, Natal, Zululand, South Africa* (New York/Boston: Schirmer, 1920). On Curtis-Burlin's activities at Hampton, see "Natalie Curtis Burlin at the Hampton Institute," *Resound: A Quarterly of the Archives of Traditional Music* 1, no. 2 (1982), pp. 1–2.

11. James W. Fernandez, "The Mission of Metaphor in Expressive Culture," in *Persuasions and Performances: The Play of Tropes in Culture* (Bloomington: Indiana University Press, 1986), p. 31.

12. Ibid., p. 38.

13. Jon Pareles, "Musical Comedy Review: Nomathemba," *New York Times* (April 22, 1996), p. C11.

14. "Nomathemba—Notes by Eric Simonson, Director," http://kennedy-center.org/stage/images/learnbar.gif.

15. See Cherryl Walker, "Gender and the Development of the Migrant Labour System c. 1850–1930: An Overview," in *Women and Gender in Southern Africa to 1945* (Cape Town: David Philip, 1990), pp. 168–96.

16. See in this regard, Catherine Campbell, "Learning to Kill? Masculinity, the Family and Violence in Natal," *Journal of Southern African Studies* 18, no. 3 (1992): 614–28.

17. See Veit Erlmann, *Nightsong: Performance, Power, and Practice in South Africa* (Chicago: University of Chicago Press, 1996), pp. 164–67.

## Chapter 14

1. Charles Hamm, *Afro-American Music, South Africa, and Apartheid* (Brooklyn: Institute for Studies in American Music, Conservatory of Music, Brooklyn College, 1988), p. 33.

2. See Tim Couzens, "Moralizing Leisure Time: The Transatlantic Connection and Black Johannesburg, 1918–1936," in *Industrialisation and Social Change in South Africa: African Class Formation, Culture, and Consciousness, 1870–1930*, ed. Shula Marks and Richard Rathbone (London: Longman, 1982), pp. 314–37; also Christopher Ballantine, *Marabi Nights: Early South African Jazz and Vaudeville* (Johannesburg: Ravan, 1993).

3 Eugene D. Genovese, *Roll, Jordan, Roll: The World the Slaves Made* (New York: Vintage, 1976), p. xvi.

4. Spike and Co., *Do It A Cappella* (Elektra 60953-2). The Ladysmith Black Mambazo album *Phansi Emgodini* was released on Gallo (Mavuthela, BL 321).

5. Michael Eric Dyson, *Reflecting Black: African American Cultural Criticism* (Minneapolis: University of Minnesota Press, 1993), p. 24.

6. Henry Louis Gates, Jr., *The Signifying Monkey: A Theory of Afro-American Literary Criticism* (New York: Oxford University Press, 1988), p. 51.

7. Matthew Brown, "Funk Music as Genre: Black Aesthetics, Apocalyptic Thinking and Urban Protest in Post-1965 African-American Pop," *Cultural Studies* 8, no. 3 (1994):484–508; David Brackett, "James Brown's 'Superbad' and the Double-Voiced Utterance," in *Interpreting Popular Music*, ed. David Brackett (Cambridge: Cambridge University Press, 1995), pp. 108–56; Ingrid Monson, "Doubleness and Jazz Improvisation: Irony, Parody, and Ethnomusicology," *Critical Inquiry* 20, no. 2 (1994):283–313; Samuel A. Floyd, Jr., "Troping the Blues: From Spirituals to the Concert Hall," in *The Power of Black Music: Interpreting Its History from Africa to the United States* (New York: Oxford University Press, 1995), pp. 212–26.

8. Gates, *Signifying Monkey*, p. 79.

9. Ibid., p. 81.

10. For good overviews of African rhythm, see Robert Kauffman, "African Rhythm: A Reassessment," *Ethnomusicology* 24 (1980):393–415.

11. Richard Middleton, "In the Groove, or Blowing Your Mind? The Pleasures of Musical Repetition," in *Popular Culture and Social Relations*, ed. Tony Bennett, Colin Mercer, and Janet Woollacott (Milton Keynes: Open University Press, 1986), pp. 159–75.

12. John M. Chernoff, *African Rhythm and African Sensibility: Aesthetics and Social Action in African Musical Idioms* (Chicago: University of Chicago Press, 1979), p. 36.

13. Ibid., p. 151. For a good overview of African performance practice and, therein, a discussion of repetition, see Margaret Thompson Drewal, "The State of Research on Performance in Africa," *African Studies Review* 34, no. 3 (1991):1–64.

14. James A. Snead, "Repetition as a Figure of Black Culture," in *Black Literature and Literary Theory*, ed. Henry Louis Gates, Jr. (London: Routledge, 1984), pp. 59–80.

15. Tricia Rose, *Black Noise: Rap Music and Black Culture in Contemporary America* (Hanover, NH: Wesleyan University Press, 1994), p. 71.

16. Eric Lott, *Love and Theft* (New York: Oxford University Press, 1995). Other examples include Robert Walser, "Rhythm, Rhyme, and Rhetoric in the Music of Public Enemy," *Ethnomusicology* 39, no. 2 (1995):193–217; and Christopher A. Waterman, "Race/

Music: Corrine Corrina, Bo Chatmon, and the Excluded Middle," in *Music and the Racial Imagination*, ed. Philip Bohlman and Ronald Radano (Chicago: University of Chicago Press, in press).

17. Lott, *Love and Theft*, p. 180.

18. Ibid., p. 182.

19. Ibid., p. 184.

20. A reissue of the original recording is available on *Mbube Roots: Zulu Choral Music from South Africa, 1930s–1960s* (Rounder 5025), track 5. The times indicated in the text and musical examples refer to this recording. For a recent rendering of Linda's song, see Easy Walkers, *Imbube* (Heritage HT 313). The following are some of the cover versions known to me: Brian Eno (ISL 36/19065, 1975); Wilder Brothers (WIN 90046X45 1955); and the Stylistics (H&L 4702, 1978).

21. David Rycroft, "Nguni Vocal Polyphony," *Journal of the International Folk Music Council* 19 (1967):90.

22. John Blacking, "Problems of Pitch, Pattern and Harmony in the Ocarina Music of the Venda," *African Music* 2, no. 2 (1969):23; David Coplan with David Rycroft, "Marabi: The Emergence of African Working-Class Music in Johannesburg," in *Discourse in Ethnomusicology II: A Tribute to Alan P. Merriam*, ed. Caroline Card et al. (Bloomington: Ethnomusicology Publications Group, Indiana University, 1981), p. 50, Gerhard Kubik, *The Kachamba Brothers' Band: A Study of Neo-Traditional Music in Malawi*. (Lusaka: Zambian Papers no. 9, Institute for African Studies, University of Zambia, 1975), p. 24.

23. Blacking, "Problems of Pitch," p. 23.

24. Middleton, "In the Groove."

25. Ralph Trewhela, *Song Safari* (Johannesburg: Limelight, 1980), p. 138.

26. Charles Keil, Participatory Discrepancies and the Power of Music, *Cultural Anthropology* 2, no. 3 (1987), pp. 275–83.

27. A parallel recording that I shall be referring to is of a public performance at Carnegie Hall in 1955 released in 1961. Its main difference from the 1952 recording is the absence of the orchestra.

28. Pete Seeger, *The Incomplete Folksinger*, ed. Jo Metcalf Schwartz (Lincoln: University of Nebraska Press, 1992), p. 576.

29. Fred Bronson, *The Billboard Book of Number One Hits: The Inside Story behind the Top of the Charts* (New York: Billboard, 1985), p. 102; Nat Shapiro and Bruce Pollock, eds., *Popular Music, 1920–1979, a Revised Cumulation* (Detroit: Gale Research, 1985), p. 2058. The recording is RCA 447-0702.

30. Reissued on Polydor 825 494-2. For a wonderfully wacky history of the Tokens, see bandleader Phil Margo's autobiography in progress in http://www.btpuppy.com.

31. I am grateful to Christopher Waterman for making some of these versions available to me.

32. Seeger, *Incomplete Folksinger*, p. 131.

33. Bronson, *Billboard Book of Number One Hits*, p. 102.

34. Louise Meintjes, "Paul Simon's *Graceland*, South Africa, and the Mediation of Musical Meaning," *Ethnomusicology* 34, no. 1 (1990):37–73.

35. Carol J. Clover, "Dancin' in the Rain," *Critical Inquiry* 24 (1995):722–47.

36. In a similar, although this time visual, way, this ambiguity is reflected in the booklet that accompanies the compact disc reissue of Kaempfert's album *Swingin' Safari*. Although the credits list Kaempfert as the composer of Mabaso's song, two photographs show Kaempfert and an unnamed young pennywhistle player.

37. *Home of the Heroes*, program brochure, n.p., n.d. Thanks to Doug Seroff for providing me with a copy of this document.

38. Paul Gilroy, *The Black Atlantic: Modernity and Double Consciousness* (Cambridge: Harvard University Press, 1993), p. 101.


## Chapter 15

1. Phillip Brian Harper, "Synesthesia, 'Crossover,' and Blacks in Popular Music," *Social Text* (Fall/Winter 1989), pp. 102, 111.

2. Ibid., p. 113.

3. Michael Eric Dyson, *Reflecting Black: African American Cultural Criticism* (Minneapolis: University of Minnesota Press, 1993), p. 58.

4. Ibid.

5. Quoted in Roger D. Abrahams, *Singing the Master: The Emergence of African-American Culture in the Plantation South* (New York: Penguin, 1992), p. 148.

6. A similar point is made in Susan Willis's brilliant book *A Primer for Daily Life* (New York: Routledge, 1991, pp. 125–29), a text which I only become aware of as this book was going into production.

7. Albert Goldman, "Analyzing the Magic," special issue of *People* (November–December 1984), quoted in Harper, "Synesthesia, 'Crossover,' and Blacks in Popular Music," p. 111.

8. Dyson, *Reflecting Black*, pp. 56–57.

9. Ibid., p. 48.

10. Susan McClary and Robert Walser, "Theorizing the Body in African-American Music," *Black Music Research Journal* 14, no. 1 (1994):82.

11. Carol J. Clover, "Dancin' in the Rain," *Critical Inquiry* 24 (1995):747.

12. Stuart Hall, "What Is This 'Black' in Black Popular Culture?" in *Black Popular Culture*, ed. Gina Dent (Seattle: Bay Press, 1992), p. 27.

13. Kobena Mercer, "Monster Metaphors: Notes on Michael Jackson's *Thriller*," in *Sound and Vision: The Music Video Reader*, ed. Simon Frith, Andrew Goodwin, and Lawrence Grossberg (London: Routledge, 1993), p. 93. The emphasis is mine.

14. See, however, Abrahams, *Singing the Master*, pp. 3–21.

15. Three of the best studies on the topic are *Sound and Vision*; E. Ann Kaplan, *Rocking around the Clock: Music Television, Postmodernism, and Consumer Culture* (London: Routledge, 1988); and Andrew Goodwin, *Dancing in the Distraction Factory: Music Television and Popular Culture* (Minneapolis: University of Minnesota Press, 1992).

16. Deborah James, "*Mmino wa setso*: Songs of Town and Country and the Experience of Migrancy by Men and Women from the Northern Transvaal" (Ph.D. thesis, University of the Witwatersrand, 1993); Carol Muller, *Rituals of Fertility and the Sacrifice of Desire: Nazarite Women's Performance in South Africa* (Chicago: University of Chicago Press, in press); Harold J. Thomas, *Ingoma Dancers and Their Response to Town: A Study of Ingoma Dance Troupes among Zulu Migrant Workers in Durban* (Durban: University of Natal, 1988); and Veit Erlmann, "'Horses in the Race Course': The Domestication of Ingoma Dancing in South Africa," *Popular Music* 8, no. 3 (1989):259–74.

17. McClary and Walser, "Theorizing the Body in African-American Music," p. 44.

18. See Roger Abrahams, "The Changing Concept of the Negro Hero," in *The Golden Log*, ed. Mody C. Boatright, Wilson M. Hudson, and Allen Maxwell (Dallas: Southern Methodist University Press, 1962), pp. 119–34; and John W. Roberts, *From Trickster to Bad-*

*man: The Black Folk Hero in Slavery and Freedom* (Philadelphia: University of Pennsylvania Press, 1989).

19. Keith Breckenridge, "Migrancy, Crime and Faction Fighting: The Role of the Isitshozi in the Development of Ethnic Organisations in the Compounds," *Journal of Southern African Studies* 16, no. 1 (1990): 55–78.

20. Paul la Hausse, "'The Cows of Nongoloza': Youth, Crime and Amalaita Gangs in Durban, 1900–1936," *Journal of Southern African Studies* 16, no. 1 (1990):79–111.

21. Clive Glaser, "The Mark of Zorro—Sexuality and Gender Relations in the Tsotsi Subculture on the Witwatersrand," *African Studies* 51, no. 1 (1992):49.

22. For a more detailed discussion of dress in *isicathamiya*, see Veit Erlmann, *Nightsong: Performance, Power, and Practice in South Africa* (Chicago: University of Chicago Press, 1996), pp. 197–203.

23. Mercer, "Monster Metaphors," p. 95.

24. Ibid., p. 105.

25. Ibid., p. 106.

26. For the discussion about music, repetition, and narrative, see Goodwin, *Dancing in the Distraction Factory*, pp. 78–85.

27. See Jackson's acknowledgment in Michael Jackson, *Moonwalk* (New York: Doubleday, 1988), p. 210.

28. Erlmann, *Nightsong*, p. 192.

29. Hugh Tracey, *African Dances of the Witwatersrand Gold Mines* (Johannesburg: African Music Society, 1952).

30. David Rycroft, "The Guitar Improvisations of Mwenda Jean Bosco," *African Music* 3, no. 1 (1962):88.

31. See, for instance, Paul Gilroy, *The Black Atlantic: Modernity and Double Consciousness* (Cambridge: Harvard University Press, 1993); and Willis, *Primer for Daily Life*, p. 132.

*Epilogue*

1. Peter Sloterdijk, *Im selben Boot: Versuch über die Hyperpolitik* (Frankfurt: Suhrkamp, 1993), pp. 11–12, 41.

2. Ibid., pp. 79–81.

3. Ibid., p. 22.

# Index

Abantu-Batho, 55
aesthetics, 5, 7, 92, 177, 187–88,
    192–98
Africa
    African representations of the
        West, 48–49, 71–72, 74–85,
        214
    and back-to-Africa movement,
        153
    as a concept and object of
        Western knowledge, 94
    European accounts of, 59–63
    and European hegemony,
        24–26
    imperial stereotypes about,
        129–32, 152–53
    its meaning to African Ameri-
        cans, 145, 151–53
    musical dialogues with the di-
        aspora, 247
    and Paul Simon, 220
    twentieth-century views of,
        181, 200
African Americans, 30, 57, 144–45,
    151–52, 155–64, 246–48
    dual sense of identity, 155
African Choir, 34, 45, 48, 55, 58,
    62–63, 70, 74, 84–86, 102,
    105, 110, 129–31, 133, 142–44,
    148, 154, 182, 216, 232, 247
    performance of Great Hymn,
        111
    reviews, 87–91, 131–39
    tours, 13–14, 144–48, 153
African National Congress, 135
African Quartette, 247
altha, 192
amadlozi, 229
amahubo, 140, 202, 204, 243
amakholwa, 134, 138–140, 142
amakhoti, 203
amalaita, 273–4
amaQaba, 120

amathongo, 242
amaZayoni, 203
AME church, 150–51, 155, 157–61
American Board of Missions, 202
apartheid, 164, 166, 169–70,
    180–81, 206, 210, 212, 217, 237
    isicathamiya as statement
        against, 199
    and the TRC, 234–35
art, 21, 25, 68, 83, 111
    distancing itself from reality,
        176
    as a machine, 222–25
    prophecy and nationalist
        thought in, 117–18
    and role of dreaming in Zulu,
        225
autobiography, 35, 39–40, 57, 70,
    216

Baartman, Saartjie (the Hotten-
    tot Venus), 94
Balmer, John, 13, 52, 62, 84,
    145–46
Basotho, 41–42, 51, 56, 77–78, 99
bhes, 192, 253–54
biography, 35–36, 38–40, 50,
    54–57, 223
Birmingham Sunlights, 264
Blyden, Edward, 151
body
    in black culture, 157–58, 247,
        272
    in black performance, 270
    in Moonwalker, 272
    as site for racialization and
        deracialization, 269
Boers, 28, 51, 79
Bohee, James and George, 150
Bokwe, John Knox, 58, 65–68, 76,
    115, 121–25, 128
Bud-M'belle, Isaiah, 149, 152
Buthelezi, Alexius, 207–8

Caluza, Reuben, 139, 247
Cape Colony, 13, 48, 51, 65, 71–72,
    155
Cape liberalism, 35, 47, 50, 56, 65
Cape Town, 63, 68, 71, 76, 148–49,
    162
capitalism, 23, 35, 61, 68, 98, 108
Cele, Madikane, Hampton cylin-
    der recordings, 247
Chief Gatsha Buthelezi, 212
Christianity, 34–35, 38, 45, 47, 50,
    56, 112, 114, 115, 136, 162–64
Clark, Lillian, 14, 99, 146
clothing, 66, 100, 102–8. See also
    dress
Colenso, Harriet, 140
colonialism, 7–8, 24–25, 40
Comaroff, Jean, 28, 40, 67, 101, 105
Comaroff, John, 28, 40, 67, 101
commodity, 18–20, 30, 89, 91, 96,
    98, 100–2
    the slave's body as, 269
    spectacle of, 86, 92–93
    the "star" as, 185
commodity fetishism, 94, 98, 100
commodity racism, 93
Coppin, Levi, 152
Creatore, Luigi, 258
Crummell, Alexander, 151

Daemaneng. See Kimberley
Dargie, David, 120, 123
Day of Reconciliation, 237
De Beers Consolidated Mines, 68
Delany, Martin, 151
Dett, Nathaniel, 247
Dhlamini, Zephaniah, 134–35
Dhlomo, Herbert and Rolfes, 139
"Diamonds on the Soles of Her
    Shoes," 170, 189, 192–93, 195,
    199, 210, 220
    analysis of, 192–98
Dickens, Charles, 17, 81, 94, 129

Dieterlen, H., 100
Dingaan's Day, 237
Dinizulu, 139, 141
*Do It A Cappella*, 247–48. *See also* Lee, Spike
*Do the Right Thing*, 248. *See also* Lee, Spike
*doshaba*, 254
dress, 108
    as a metonymic gesture, 99, 102
    stage dress, African choir, 100, 102–8, 130
    as symbolic domain, 140
Du Bois, W. E. B., 150, 159–60
Dube, Charles, 145
Dube, John, 140, 143, 240
Durban Evening Birds, 206
Dutch East India Company, 112

Edwards, Mamie, 152–53
Empangeni Home Tigers, 210, 227
empire, 5–6, 15, 23–25, 38–39, 62, 64, 69, 76, 85, 92–93, 106
    biographical fiction concerned with, 37–38
    fantasies of, 153
entropy, 36, 91
Ethiopianism, 148, 153, 155, 161
ethnicity, 6, 27
    political history in South Africa, 212–13
ethnography, 4, 7, 35
Europe, 129–30, 174, 175,
    African accounts of, 59, 62–63
    and images of Zuluness, 219
    the invention of, 8
    Josiah Semouse's notion of, 85
    in nineteenth century, 14, 17–26, 30, 38–41, 54, 59–62, 67, 79, 82, 85–86, 91, 94, 97, 101–143, 219
Evening Birds, 204, 206, 208, 252, 254. *See also* Linda, Solomon
evolution, 18, 21, 62, 96, 115

Fairfield Four, 264
faspathi, 192
fetishism, 20, 30, 91–92
figuration, 16, 83, 92, 96, 176, 249
figure, 177–78
Fingoes (Ma-Fengu), 77
Fisk Jubilee Singers, 13, 44, 148, 158
"For Unkulunkulu's Sake," 240
Four Eagle Gospel, 264

gangster, 273–74, 280
Garvey, Marcus, 56–57
gender, 4, 50, 53, 67, 89, 99, 103, 107, 171, 178, 245, 272–73
    bias in B. Shabalala's music, 220, 222
    issues in early *isicathamiya*, 201
    in *Nomathemba*, 244
    in Paul Simon's song "Diamonds . . . ," 171
    and the Western male subject, 189–90
genre, 61, 70, 73, 81
    aesthetic of, 30, 36, 61–62, 66
    as historical topos, 21
global culture, 3–4, 6, 7–8, 10, 127, 137, 157, 189
global imagination, 3–4, 6–8, 47, 92, 131, 182
    diasporic forms of, 280
    in late nineteenth century, 16, 20, 30–31, 35–45, 50–58, 61–63, 68, 85, 89, 94–99, 110–111, 114, 118, 126–127, 132, 141–45, 147–48, 157–65
    in late twentieth century, 171, 175–76, 180–81, 214, 217
    music as medium of, 157–65
    post *Graceland* manifestations of, 178, 180–81
globalization, 5, 10, 35, 281
    from 1870 to mid 1920s, 15
    of musical aesthetics, 188–89
Goodwill Zwelithini, 212
Gow, Francis Herman, 161, 247
Gqoba, Frances, 13
*Graceland*, 169–72, 185, 199, 220, 282
    album cover, 180–83
    within the anti-apartheid struggle, 180–81
    and the development of *isicathamiya*, 209–10
    Elvis's, and rock iconography, 191
    and the global imagination, 214
    in *Journey of Dreams*, 217
    as political intervention, 180–81
    in Simon biography, 190–91
    songbook, 195
    *See also* Simon, Paul
"Great Hymn," 111–13, 118–20, 123–29, 131–32, 158, 282
Gun War, 48, 51, 78

hegemony, 9, 10, 24–25, 27, 61, 98
hero, 37–38, 41–43, 51, 160, 205–6, 216
    O. McAdoo as, 160
    and Paul Simon, 184
    songwriter/musician as, 184
    South African discourses of, 205, 229
*hlabelela*, 120
*hlonipa*, 52–53, 220, 224
"Homeless," 221
"Home Sweet Home," 65, 67
Huskisson, Yvonne, 207, 208
hybridity, 7, 30, 82, 91, 131
    and *Graceland*, 169
    of *isicathamiya*, 210
hymns, 14
    and *amahubo*, 243
    disputes over, 158–61
    influence on African traditional genres, 201–2

identity, 5, 7–8, 30, 32, 35, 38–42, 50, 55–56, 59, 62–63, 68, 107–8, 144, 150, 241–44, 251
    *amahubo* and collective Zulu, 243
    body styles as the primary site of, 270
    construction of African American, 150–52
    in the "Great Hymn," 111–15
    *isicathamiya*, 205–6, 208–213
    modern black identity in America, 158–60
    modern black South African, 56–57
    pan-Zulu ethnic and cultural, 212–13
    postcolonial politics of, 233
    Victorian notions of female, 109
*ihubo*, 204
*ikhetho*, 201, 203
*ilizwe*, 212
*imbongi*, 119
Imbumba Yama Nyama, 147
imperialism, 4–5, 13, 16, 20, 23–25, 37, 50, 68
*impi*, 202, 242
*imusic*, 140
Imvo Zabantsundu, 39
*indlavini*, 273
*ingoma*, 226
Inkatha Freedom Party, 211
"Intselelo," 227

*isicathamiya*, 171–72, 189–90,
  192–93, 198–205, 206, 208,
  211, 215, 218, 220–21, 225–26,
  231–32
  and *amahubo*, 243
  bounderies of class ethnicity
    and language, 210
  choreography, 211, 276–80
  competition and conflict in
    performance, 211, 225–28
  early, 201–4, 210–13
  expression of mythic African
    past, 200–13
  history of, 199–213
  and parallels with black gospel
    music, 264–65
  parallels to Zionist ritual, 203
  poetic structure, 209–12
  social organization of choirs,
    202, 225
  song texts, 205, 211–12
*isicathulo*, 277
*isifekezeli*, 203
*isigekle*, 140, 201
*isikhambula*, 206, 232
*isikhunzi*, 203, 204
*isikhwela Jo*, 189, 206, 209
*isiphonso*. See *ufufunyane*
*isitshozi*, 273
*isiZulu*, 140, 171, 189, 190, 200
*isoka*, 219
*istep*, 204, 231, 277
*izibongo*, 41, 119, 205
*Izingoma zaseAfrican*, "The Songs
  of the African Jubilee
  Singers," 44
*izingoma zomtshado*, 201, 204

Jabavu, John T., 14, 149
Jackson, Michael, 10, 169, 172, 220,
  247, 268–80, 282
  collaboration with Ladysmith
    Black Mambazo, 270–71,
    275–80
  description of performance,
    269–80
  as media product, 275–76
  questions of identity, 268–69
Jenkins, Gordon, 258
Jonas, Albert, 13
Jonkers, Johanna, 13, 32, 45, 47,
  108–9, 154
  biographical vignette, 46–47
Jordan, Archibald C., 127
*Journey of Dreams*, 215, 218–21,
  225, 229, 232

*Jungle Fever*, 8. *See also* Lee,
  Spike

Kaempfert, Bert, 258
Katiya, Thomas, 146
Kimberley, 13–14, 44–45, 48, 52,
  55, 62–63, 68–72, 74, 76, 108,
  150, 152–53
King Star Brothers, 208
Konongo, Samuel, 13
Koopman, Sannie, 13
Kumalo, Alfred A., 139
Kumalo, Hetty, 134
Kumalo, Johannes, 135, 138
Kumalo, Joseph, 134
Kumalo, Solomon, 134

Ladysmith Black Mambazo,
  170–72, 178, 189, 199, 208,
  211, 213, 217–21, 225, 229,
  242–43, 247, 279, 282
  on *Do It A Cappella*, 248
  founding of, 208–10
  on *Graceland*, 10, 169–72,
    192–99
  "Homeless," 228
  in *Jacob Zulu*, 240–44
  with the Mint Juleps, 258
  in *Moonwalker*, 270–71, 274–75
  in *Nomathemba*, 244–45
  in "Smooth Criminal," 270–71
  sound texture, 209
  and Spike Lee, 264–65
  vocal timbre, 190
  *See also* Shabalala, Bhekizizwe
Lane, William Henry, alias Juba,
  269
"Leaning on the Everlasting
  Arm," 265
Lee, Spike, 10, 247–48, 252,
  264–65
Leitch, Barry, 219
Lenkoane, Patrick, 69, 149
Letty, Walter, 13, 62, 90
liberalism, 36–38, 47, 68, 155, 184
*lifela*, 41–42
Linda, Solomon, 204, 206
  and "Mbube," 204, 205, 252–59,
    261, 266, 275–76
"Lion Sleeps Tonight, The" 248,
  252, 262–63, 265–66, 282
*lithoko*, 41
Little Lemmy, 258
London
  Josiah Semouse comments,
    *Libini*, 76–80, 83

Ladysmith Black Mambazo in,
  228
  as metaphor of power, 228–29
  in nineteenth century, 14–16,
    32, 45, 48, 50, 54, 63–64, 72,
    74, 76, 80, 82–87, 89, 94–95,
    99–100, 108, 131, 133, 135–37,
    139, 141–142
Lovedale, 13–14, 32, 34, 37, 43, 48,
  54, 63–68, 70–72, 88

Mabandla, Neli, 13
Madonna, 169
Magaya, Edward T., 145
Mahotella Queens, 209
Makeba, Miriam, 258
*Malcolm X*, 248. *See also* Lee, Spike
Mandela, Nelson, 246
Manye, Charlotte, 13, 14, 32–33,
  44, 47, 50–51, 55, 58, 62, 99,
  106–7, 127, 129, 142, 145,
  149–50, 166, 217, 220, 240
  biographical vignette, 45–47,
    51–53
Manye, Kate, 103, 107–10
Maxeke, Marshall, 52, 145, 163
Mbaqanga, 241
*mbombing*, 206, 208–9
Mbongwe, John, 13, 150
*mbube*, 189, 204, 206, 252–53
"Mbube," 172, 204–5, 210, 276,
  282
  alleged folk origins of, 264
  analysis, 252–60
  cover versions, 252, 258–67
  as founding text of a genre,
    255–56
  Mint Juleps and Ladysmith
    Black Mambazo, 258,
    264–66
McAdoo, Orpheus, 13, 62, 134,
  147–53, 158, 160, 202, 246
Mcanyana, Gershon, and the
  Scorpions, 208
McCord, Margaret, 107–9, 166
McLellan, George, 13
Mdalidiphu, 113
media, 3, 5–6, 8, 39–40, 98, 107,
  181, 208, 275
Merriman, John X., 69, 151
Mfengu, 51, 64
Mini, Edith, 134
Mini, Lydia, 134
Mini, Stephanus, 135
Minstrel, Vaudeville and Concert
  Company, 202

minstrelsy, 135, 153, 159, 202, 222, 251, 269
Mint Juleps, 248, 258, 264–66, 282
missionaries, 14, 40, 43–44, 47, 51, 57, 63–64, 66–67, 102, 107, 112, 127, 137, 141, 162
modernity, 3–4, 6–10, 14, 17–19, 28–29, 36, 45, 54–58, 67, 72–73, 81, 86, 98, 102, 107, 116–18, 126, 129, 136, 138–39, 144, 153–54, 156, 158, 165, 173–75, 177–78, 184
   aesthetics and late, 223–25
   black constructions of, 9
   the crisis of the subject, 38
   twentieth-century concepts of, 174–78
Mokone, Reverend Mangena, 148–49, 161
Molife, Bessie, 134
Molife, Martha, 134
"Moon Is Walking, The" 270, 271, 275–79
*Moonwalker*, 172, 247, 270, 272–80. *See also* Jackson, Michael
Morie, Naphtali, 71
Morija, 43, 48, 100
Morija Training Institute, 71
Morris, Charles S., 147
Moshoeshoe, 42, 51, 56, 77
Motsieloa, Griffith, 204
Msane, Asiana, 134
Msane, Rosaline Julia Mini, 134
Msane, Saul, 134–37, 139, 141–42, 149, 166
Msikinya, Henry C., 145
Msimang, Selby, 139
Mzamo, Joseph D., 134

nationalism, 3, 49–50, 111, 116–18, 155, 161, 163
   African, 35, 48–49
   nineteenth-century black, 155
   and post apartheid South Africa, 237
Ndebele, 28–30, 77–78
Ndlambe, 114
*ndlamu*, 141
New York, 171, 221
Ngcayiya, Henry, 149, 152
Ngidi, Mbiana, 139
Ngqika, 113–14
Nguni, 9, 66, 104, 256
Nkosi Sikelel IAfrika, 236
   on *Do It A Capella*, 248
   at the end of *Jacob Zulu*, 241–43

Nkosi, West, 217, 219
*Nomathemba*, 244, 245
Ntsikana, Gaba, 58, 66, 111–12, 114–15, 118–21, 123–25, 127–29, 132, 158, 282
   biography of, 113–14
Ntsiko, Jonas, 147
Nxele, 112–15, 129
*nyanga*, 217

occidentalism, 8
orientalism, 5, 8, 116

pan-Africanism, 35, 152
panopticon, 21–22, 37, 60
panorama, 5, 14, 20–25, 29, 36, 60–61, 81, 94, 96, 111, 176
Pasha, Emin, 95
perception, 5, 21, 25, 95
Peretti, Hugo, 258
Persuasions, 248
Philip, John, 64, 120, 127
phrase shift, in African performance, 279
Plaatje, Solomon, 149, 152
power, 26–28, 37–39, 42–43, 50, 60–61, 63, 66, 99–100, 126, 156, 160–61, 163, 236, 243
   colonial, 5, 24, 26–28, 37
   gender and sexuality, 273
   global imbalances of, 4
   London as metaphor of, 228
   postcolonial struggles, 4
   pre-colonial domains of male, 189
praise-poetry, 40–41, 120
prophecy, 111, 115, 117, 118

Queen Victoria, 14, 52, 63, 94, 166, 228

race, 4, 34, 62, 85, 93, 99–100, 106–7, 138, 178
   African dance and the production of, 272–73
   *Graceland* and the politics of, 170
   mythologies of, 6
   and repetition in minstrelsy, 251
racism, 72, 74, 130, 137, 141, 228
Radasi, John Boyana, 146
Radio Bantu, 207, 208
Rhodes, Cecil, 68, 69, 70, 151
Rockapella, 248

Sakie, Magazo, 146–47
*sangoma*, 221
Sedaka, Neal, 258
Seeger, Pete, "Wimoweh," 252, 258–60
Sefokeng, 71
Sekoena, 71
self, 15, 36, 39–40, 44, 50, 55, 60, 102, 114–15, 178, 216, 223, 225, 227, 230–31, 251
   discourses of, 217
   and *Journey of Dreams*, 222
   liberalism, 184
   predicaments of the modern, 215
   Western representations of, 36, 224–25
   and world music, 181
semiotics, 92, 249
Semouse, Josiah, 32, 44, 48–50, 55, 62, 69–76, 78, 106, 142, 149, 165–66, 217, 231
   description of Cape Colony, 79
   "The Journey Back to Africa," 84
   life story, 48
   "Likheleke tsa America," 150
Sesotho, 43, 73, 76, 78
Sethlaping, 71
Setswana, 71
sexuality, and music video, 272–73
Shabalala, Bhekizizwe, 2, 169, 170–72, 215, 217–21, 225, 229
   and the aesthetics machine, 233
   biographical texts, 214–33
   collaboration with Tug Yourgrau, 238–39
   dreams as self-fashioning, 218, 229
   in *Jacob Zulu*, 240–44
   in *Journey of Dreams*, 215, 217–22
   as media product, 275
   in *Nomathemba*, 245
   in Paul Simon's "Under African Skies," 220
   relationship with the West, 215
Shaka Zulu, 51, 56–57, 202, 210, 212, 219, 224, 243–44
Shakaland, 219
signification, 6, 101–2, 176, 249, 263
signifyin(g), 249, 275
Simon, Paul, 10, 169–71, 179–81, 190, 191, 213, 215, 220–21, 224, 282
   and B. Shabalala, 190, 217

Simon, Paul (*continued*)
  as cross-cultural mediator, 186
  as cultural intermediary, 184
  "Diamonds on the Soles of
    Her Shoes," 192–98
  and liberalism, 186
  post 1970s career, 185
  vocal style, 189
  vocal timbre, 190
"Skokiaan," 258
"Smooth Criminal," 270–71,
  275–76
Social Darwinism, 21–23, 130,
  152
*Song of Jacob Zulu, The,* 234–44
Sopela, Waka, 134
soul music and Nelson Mandela,
  246
South Africa, 8, 26, 62, 161–62,
  169, 282
  the AME church in, 150–52
  interrelationships with Ameri-
    can musics, 247–48
  minstrelsy in, 202–3
  nationalism and Ethiopianism,
    148, 155
  new forms of biographical
    narrative, 50
  O. McAdoo and the Virginia
    Jubilee Singers tour, 134,
    147–50
  politics of memory and *Jacob
    Zulu,* 244
  post apartheid, 234, 237
  radio broadcasting, 207
  slavery in, 154
  struggle for democracy in, 9
South African Broadcasting Corporation, 207
South African Choir, 10, 32, 35. See
  *also* African Choir
spectacle, 5, 20–23, 86, 89, 92,
  95–100, 102, 108, 110
Stephen, John, 43, 99, 135
Stewart, James, 14, 37–38, 64–65,
  67, 84–85, 122
style, 39, 243, 177–78, 246–67
*Swingin' Safari, A,* 258
syntony, 188

Take 6, 248
Tantsi, Adelaide, 145
Tantsi, James Y., 145
technology, 17, 26, 34, 49, 64, 70,
  116, 217

Thema, R.V. Selope, 162
*thena,* 192
Thompson, Will, 152
"Thriller," 169, 272, 274. *See also*
  Jackson, Michael
Tile, Nehemiah, 148
Tiyopia, Ethiopian church, 148
Tokens, the, 252, 258–59, 264–65,
  282
  "The Lion Sleeps Tonight,"
    258–66
Tracey, Hugh, 120–21, 123–24
travel, 21, 38, 60, 62–63, 212,
  230–32
True Image, 248
Truth and Reconciliation Com-
  mission, 234, 236
Tshangana, Josiah, 134
Tshidi Barolong, 101
*tsotsi,* 274
Tswana, 40, 71
Turner, Henry, 57, 151–52
twentieth century
  artistic production in,
    183–84
  concept of modernity in,
    174–76
  decline of individualism in,
    177–78
  Euro-African cultural ecu-
    menes in, 7
  global imagination in, 171,
    175–76, 180–81, 214, 217,
  and links to the nineteenth
    century, 173–78
  postcolonialism in, 5
  South African politics in,
    212–13
  triumph of the symbolic in,
    177
*Two Worlds, One Heart,* 265

*ubuntu,* 237
*ufufunyane,* 109
*ugubhu,* 241
*ukureka,* 203
*ukusina,* 202
"Ulo Thixo Omkhulu." *See*
  "Great Hymn"
*umgangela,* 226
*umgqashiyo,* 209
*umlindelo,* 203
*umqhawe,* 160, 205, 229
*umthimba,* 201
*umuzi,* 229

United States, 8, 25, 101, 161
  the AME church in, 150–52
  Nelson Mandela tour of, 246
  tour of the African Choir in,
    1890–94, 13–14

Virginia Concert Company,
  148
Virginia Jubilee Singers, 13, 147
*vuthiwe,* 276

Washington, Booker T., 162
Wauchope, Isaac, 127
Weavers, the, 252, 258–59. *See
  also* Seeger, Pete
"Wimoweh," 258–61, 264. *See also*
  the Weavers
Winans, Marvin L., 265
witchcraft, 109, 113
world music, 3, 6, 10, 181, 185–
  90

Xhosa, 14, 41, 58, 77, 99, 114, 124
  music, 124
Xiniwe, Eleanor, 105, 106–7
Xiniwe, Paul, 13, 32–35, 44–45, 47,
  54–55, 58, 62, 70, 99, 109, 142,
  147, 165–66, 216
  autobiography, 33–34
  vignette in "African Yearly
    Register," 54
Xuma, Alfred, 50–53, 55–56, 58,
  220

Yourgrau, Tug, 235–39

Zondo, Andrew, alias Jacob Zulu,
  235, 238, 243
Zulu, 10, 14, 30, 41, 46, 56, 72, 74,
  109, 139, 142, 166, 171, 244
  ethnic absolutism, 143
  images of self, 216
  *ingoma* dancing and the body,
    272–73
  musical tradition and
    "Mbube," 256–57
  occidentalism, 228
  work ethic and concepts of
    labor, 28
Zulu Choir, 10, 14, 134–38, 140–43,
  182
  story of, 134–37
Zulu Mbiana Congregational
  Church, 139
Zwelitsha Choral Society, 124

DATE DUE